www.wadsworth.com

www.wadsworth.com is the World Wide Web site for
Thomson Wadsworth and is your direct source to dozens
of online resources.

At *www.wadsworth.com* you can find out about supple-
ments, demonstration software, and student resources. You
can also send email to many of our authors and preview
new publications and exciting new technologies.

www.wadsworth.com
Changing the way the world learns®

Guide to Criminal Law
for Florida

Guide to Criminal Law
for Florida

Third Edition

PATRICIA CASHMAN, J.D.
University of Central Florida

THOMSON

WADSWORTH

Australia • Canada • Mexico • Singapore • Spain • United Kingdom • United States

Executive Editor: Sabra Horne
Development Editor: Julie Sakaue
Assistant Editor: Jana Davis
Editorial Assistant: Elise Smith
Marketing Manager: Terra Schultz
Marketing Assistant: Annabelle Yang

Project Manager, Editorial Production: Jennifer Klos
Print Buyer: Emma Claydon
Permissions Editor: Stephanie Lee
Cover Designer: Yvo Riezebos
Cover Image: Donovan Reese/Getty Images
Text and Cover Printer: Thomson West

Printed in the United States of America
1 2 3 4 5 6 7   08 07 06 05 04

For more information about our products,
contact us at:
Thomson Learning Academic Resource Center
1-800-423-0563

For permission to use material from this text or product,
submit a request online at
http://www.thomsonrights.com.

Any additional questions about permissions
can be submitted by email to
thomsonrights@thomson.com.

Library of Congress Control Number: 2004108379

ISBN: 0-534-64415-5

Thomson Wadsworth
10 Davis Drive
Belmont, CA 94002-3098
USA

Asia
Thomson Learning
5 Shenton Way #01-01
UIC Building
Singapore 068808

Australia/New Zealand
Thomson Learning
102 Dodds Street
Southbank, Victoria 3006
Australia

Canada
Nelson
1120 Birchmount Road
Toronto, Ontario M1K 5G4
Canada

Europe/Middle East/South Africa
Thomson Learning
High Holborn House
50/51 Bedford Row
London WC1R 4LR
United Kingdom

Latin America
Thomson Learning
Seneca, 53
Colonia Polanco
11560 Mexico D.F.
Mexico

Spain/Portugal
Paraninfo
Calle/Magallanes, 25
28015 Madrid, Spain

CONTENTS

CASE INDEX

CHAPTER 1

No cases

CHAPTER 2

CHAPTER 3

CHAPTER 4

Guide to Criminal Law
for Florida

CHAPTER 1

THE NATURE AND LIMITS
OF CRIMINAL LAW

INTRODUCTION

People are fascinated by criminal law. Who didn't watch a portion of the O.J. Simpson trial? Were you there for the moment O.J. tried on the glove in front of the jury? What would have happened had it fit? Martha Stewart was on the news for months, did you follow the case? Did you cheer when she was convicted? Did you want to send her to prison? Should she have testified on her own behalf? Who didn't follow the celebrated "nanny" trial and then anxiously await the verdict? And when the judge reduced the charge to manslaughter, did you admire his courage? Or were you angered? You can't pick up a newspaper without reading about a criminal case. You can't turn on the TV without being informed of the status of an investigation. You can log onto the Internet and read the latest pleadings filed in a high profile case or the autopsy report of the latest murder victim. Criminal law is newsworthy.

To truly comprehend what occurs and why and what far reaching consequences might result, one must first learn the basics. To begin, go to the library, log on the Internet, or go to a bookstore, and get your own copy of the criminal laws of the State of Florida. Pouring over Florida Statutes is not exciting, but learning how the laws are applied and why and what happens to those who find themselves in the system as a defendant or a victim or a lawyer or a judge or in law enforcement will give you a whole new perspective on criminal law.

THE NATURE OF CRIMINAL LAW

What exactly is a crime? The easy answer is that Florida Statutes tells you what constitutes a crime. The challenge is to determine whether a particular set of facts fits the definition of a crime under the current law. The city you live in may have their own additional ordinances that citizens are to obey and abide by. There is usually a city prosecutor who charges individuals who camp in the park or beg on street corners.

CLASSIFYING CRIMES

A felony is a crime punishable by death or imprisonment in a State penitentiary. The minimum Department of Corrections sentence is a year and a day. There are five different categories of felonies in the State of Florida. The different categories subject an individual to different punishments. A third degree felony is punishable by up to five years, a second degree felony by up to fifteen years, and a first degree felony by up to forty years in the Department of Corrections. A first degree felony punishable by life means the maximum penalty is a life sentence.

The fifth category is a capital felony. There are two offenses in that category. They are a capital sexual battery and a capital murder. A capital sexual battery conviction results in a sentence of life imprisonment with a day for day twenty-five year mandatory minimum. A capital murder conviction means a sentence of life without possibility of parole or a sentence of death.

There are two classes of misdemeanors. First degree misdemeanors are punishable by up to one year in a county jail and second degree misdemeanors by up to sixty days.

PUNISHMENT

The State can enhance the penalties for certain crimes. This means that under certain circumstances harsher penalties may be imposed. A defendant must have notice of the enhancement. An individual with a prior record who is charged with a felony may qualify as a career criminal, a habitual felony offender, or a prisoner releasee reoffender. First time offenders may be facing 10/20/Life if they possess or use a firearm during certain felonies. 10/20/Life stands for 10 years, 20 years, and life in prison. It applies to cases where an individual carries or uses a firearm. If a firearm is carried, one faces 10 years in prison; if it is fired, 20 years; and if someone is seriously injured, the defendant may be sentenced to life in prison. Certain misdemeanor charges may be filed as felonies if the statutory requirements are met.

The different categories of charges subject a person to a particular maximum period of incarceration. There is also a maximum length of time an individual may be placed on probation. Florida Statutes addresses the issue of monetary fines. There is an amount a fine cannot exceed for each degree of the offense.

Certain traffic offenses may be criminal in nature. Driving under the influence of alcohol is an example. Driving with a suspended license can be a crime in some situations.

Individuals may be sentenced to a period of probation in lieu of a jail sentence or in addition to a jail sentence. Standard conditions of probation include not violating any laws, obtaining full time employment, and reporting to a probation officer once a month, among others. There also may be special conditions imposed such as obtaining a drug or alcohol evaluation or attending mental health counseling. Another condition may be for the individual to have no contact with the victim of the crime. If an individual violates any condition of his or her probation, a judge can impose a sentence for the violation.

There are diversionary programs some individuals may qualify for to "divert" them from court proceedings. A person may participate in pretrial diversion. Some jurisdictions have drug courts. Those with drug problems get counseling and their progress is monitored. Upon successful completion charges may be dropped. On the other end of the spectrum are ROC courts. These are repeat offender courts. The harshest punishments are sought for individuals in those courts.

The Legislature passed the Criminal Punishment Code. It applies to all felonies committed on or after October 1, 1998. An individual scores a certain number of points based on the crime he or she is convicted of. Points are added for victim injury. Additional points are added for someone's prior record. A score is calculated that gives the minimum sentence a judge may impose. The maximum sentence is now the statutory maximum. No longer does the judge have to justify a departure upward.

The state and the defense may agree to a departure downward from that minimum sentence. The defense may present mitigating circumstances to the court and ask that the court impose a sentence less than the minimum required by the score sheet.

Florida has a law that applies to sexually violent predators. It is known as the Jimmy Ryce Act. The Act establishes a procedure by which an individual is subject to involuntary civil commitment upon expiration of a prison sentence.

Florida recognizes common law crimes in cases where no statute exists on the subject. Florida also defines "non-criminal" violations. Only civil penalties may be imposed for non-criminal violations.

Misdemeanor cases are prosecuted in County Court. Circuit courts have jurisdiction over felony crimes. Misdemeanor convictions may be appealed to the Circuit Court; felony convictions to the District Court of Appeals. The highest court in the state is the Florida Supreme Court. The Florida Supreme Court sometimes acts as an appellate court for cases from the District Courts.

THINKING CRITICALLY

1. Spend thirty minutes in a criminal courtroom watching the proceedings. Write a brief synopsis of what you observed in that courtroom. Then express your opinion on what occurred. Be specific about the different parties involved. Who or what was effective? Were there things that happened that you didn't understand? Did you learn anything? Was it different than what you expected?

2. Were any new laws enacted this year? When does the legislature meet? Were any proposed laws not passed? Give an example of a recently proposed law. Did it pass or not?

3. Do you live in a place with local ordinances? If so, find a copy of one of the ordinances. Why do you think that ordinance was passed? Is there a city prosecutor who charges violations of the local ordinances? Who is it?

4. Give an example of a third degree felony.

5.   Is there a state prison in your county? If so, what is the name of the prison?

6.   What is the maximum fine for a third degree felony?

7.   What is the maximum period of probation that can be imposed for a first degree misdemeanor?

8.   What is 10/20/Life? Give an example of a felony that 10/20/Life applies to. Is this a good law? Why or why not?

9.   Give an example of a traffic offense other than driving under the influence of alcohol that constitutes a crime.

10.   Give an example of a special condition of probation.

11.   Give an example of a reason to depart on a sentence.

12.   Does the Criminal Punishment Code apply to misdemeanors?

13.   Give an example of a level 7 crime.

14. Give an example of a non-criminal violation.

15. How are common law offenses punished under Florida law?

16. What judicial circuit do you live in? Which District Court of Appeals hears cases from your circuit?

17. Where is the Florida Supreme Court located? Name one of the justices.

18. Which federal district are you in? Where is that court located?

19. Is crime a problem in your neighborhood? What can be done on a local level to help solve the problem?

20. Does your community have neighborhood or community policing? If so, is it effective? Does your neighborhood have bicycle cops? Are they more effective in some situations than law enforcement officers in marked vehicles? If so, give an example.

21.   What do you think about the death penalty in the State of Florida?   Should it be abolished? Why? If not, why not?

22.   Who is the State Attorney in your circuit? Name a county court judge. Name a circuit court judge. Who is the Public Defender in your circuit? Are these individuals elected or appointed?

23.   Do you see any constitutional problems with passing an act such as the Jimmy Ryce Act? Is this not a violation of *ex post facto* or double jeopardy clauses of the Constitution?

24.   What can be done to reduce crime?   Should we build more prisons?   Hire more law enforcement officers?

25.   Do we need more laws, or better enforcement of the laws we already have?

26. Do diversionary programs work? Why or why not?

ANSWER KEY

Questions 1-5, 9-18 and 20-26 Answer will vary.

6. $5,000.00

7.   one year

8.   A mandatory sentence of 10 years is imposed if a defendant carried a gun, 20 years if the gun is fired, and a life sentence is imposed if a victim is shot regardless of the injury.

18.   Tallahassee

19.   11th Circuit, Atlanta, Georgia.

CHAPTER 2

CONSTITUTIONAL LIMITS ON
CRIMINAL LAW

INTRODUCTION

Article One of the Florida Constitution is a Declaration of Rights comprised of twenty-five sections detailing the rights of the individual. These individual rights are frequently at issue in criminal proceedings.

In 1988, Florida amended a portion of the Constitution to give victims certain rights under Section 16 of the Florida Constitution. Victims of crimes or next of kin of homicide victims now have the right to be informed, to be present, and to be heard when relevant at crucial stages of the proceedings. There is a limitation, however, in that the exercise of a victim's rights may not infringe upon the defendant's exercise of his constitutional rights.

All citizens enjoy certain rights under both the Federal and Florida Constitutions. Some of these include the right to due process, privacy, free speech, and equal protection under the law. While these rights may be greater under the State Constitution, State rights cannot be less than what are guaranteed under the Federal Constitution. Many times issues arise concerning whether a law is constitutional. The court must determine if the State government has overstepped the boundaries of the Federal Constitution. The government may not violate the rights of the individual as guaranteed by the Federal Constitution even if the intention is good.

As stated above, citizens have the right to "due process." Due process consists of two components: (1) the right to notice; and (2) the right to be heard. The government gives its citizens notice by writing statutes that clearly define crimes. Where a statute is ambiguous or unclear, it fails to give proper notice. It is unconstitutional for the government to fail to give proper notice as to what constitutes a crime.

Due process also puts limits on what action law enforcement may take to make arrests. They cannot commit illegal acts to arrest citizens who are committing crimes. Law enforcement must abide by the law just as every other individual must.

EX POST FACTO LAWS

The constitution forbids the passing of any *ex post facto* laws. An *ex post facto* law is a law adopted after an act is committed making it illegal although it was legal when done, or increasing the penalty for a crime after it is committed. *Ex post facto* laws are unconstitutional because they fail to give proper notice of what constitutes a crime.

CASE

Jackson v. State, 729 So.2d 947 (Fla. 1st DCA 1998).

Defendant was convicted in the Circuit Court, Alachua County, David Reiman, Acting Circuit Court Judge, of possession of firearm by violent career criminal. Defendant appealed. The District Court of Appeal, Davis, J., held that: (1) statute making juvenile adjudications of delinquency elements of crime of possession of firearm by violent career criminal is constitutional, but (2) defendant was prejudiced by inadvertent remark by judge in front of prospective jurors alluding to the existence of multiple charges against defendant.

Reversed and remanded for new trial.

Wolf, J., concurred in part and dissented in part and filed a separate opinion.

DAVIS, Judge.

Lavon D. Jackson appeals his conviction for possession of a firearm by a violent career criminal under section 790.235, Florida Statutes (1995). Jackson asserts that his constitutional rights to due process [FN1] and equal protection [FN2] and against ex post facto laws [FN3] were violated by virtue of his conviction under this statute because the predicate offenses necessary to qualify him as a violent career criminal were juvenile adjudications of delinquency predating the effective date of section 790.235. He further asserts that the trial court erred in denying his motion to dismiss the jury venire after the prospective jurors were made aware that there were three other charges pending against him. We conclude that section 790.235 is constitutional, both facially and as applied by Jackson. We must nevertheless reverse and remand for retrial because the trial court erred in commenting in the presence of the jury as to other charges against Jackson which had been severed from the count for which he was being tried.

In the early morning of January 19, 1996, three police officers on foot patrol in Gainesville, Florida, saw Jackson sitting in the passenger seat of a car parked outside a tavern. As they looked through the windshield it appeared that Jackson was passed out or asleep. The officers knocked on the windows to get his attention, and used a flashlight to look for alcohol or drugs, to find out why he appeared to have passed out. Officer Forsberg saw what appeared to be a short-barrelled shotgun on the passenger floorboard. When Officer O'Neal opened the door, he saw what appeared to be another gun between Jackson's legs. Jackson was arrested and searched; the police found marijuana and cocaine and shotgun shells. The gun which was between Jackson's legs was a ".357."

In February 1996, the state filed a four-count information charging Jackson with one count of possession of a firearm by a convicted felon; one count of possession of a short-barrelled shotgun; one count of possession of cocaine and one count of possession of less than 20 grams of marijuana. A second amended information was later filed, changing the charge in count one to possession of a firearm by a violent career criminal

[FN4] The state alleged that the prior juvenile adjudications of delinquency which satisfied the terms of that statute were an escape for which Jackson was adjudicated delinquent on 3/13/91, an armed robbery for which Jackson was adjudicated delinquent on 7/2/91, and an aggravated assault for which Jackson was adjudicated delinquent on 7/1/91. In addition, it was stipulated that Jackson had been incarcerated in the state prison system as an adult within the five years preceding the current offense, as necessary to satisfy the remainder of the requirement for classification as a violent career criminal contained in section 775.084(1)(c), Florida Statutes (1995). [FN5] The statute under which Jackson was convicted was enacted effective October 1, 1995. See Ch. 95-182, §§ 7, 12, at 1673, 1675, Laws of Fla.

We find no merit to Jackson's challenges to the constitutionality of section 790.235. Jackson argues that section 790.235 is arbitrary and oppressive in violation of his due process rights and violates the equal protection clause because it bears no rational relationship to the purpose of the statute. Jackson asserts that the legislature's purpose is to "get tough" on juvenile crime, but that making juvenile adjudications of delinquency elements of the crime of possession of a firearm by a violent career criminal is not a rational means of achieving the state's goal. Appellant's due process and equal protection arguments are based upon the flawed premise that the legislature's only rational basis for this statute is prevention of juvenile crime. If this court can conceive of a rational basis it must uphold the statute. See *McElrath v. Burley, 70 So.2d 836, 839 (Fla. 1st DCA 1998).* The Florida Supreme Court has already cogently concluded that statutes limiting the right to possess guns by those who have demonstrated a propensity for violent crime serve a legitimate and rational purpose. See *State v. Snyder, 673 So.2d 9, 10 (Fla. 1996)* ("Section 790.23 is intended to protect the public by preventing the possession of firearms by persons who, because of their past conduct, have demonstrated their unfitness to be entrusted with such dangerous instrumentalities.").

Furthermore, we conclude that the statute does not violate the ex post facto clauses of the Florida or United States constitutions. "The ex post facto prohibition forbids the Congress and the States to enact any law 'which imposes a punishment for an act which was not punishable at the time it was committed; or imposes additional punishment to that then prescribed.' " *Weaver v. Graham, 450 U.S. 24, 28, 101 S.Ct. 960, 67 L.Ed.2d 17 (1981)* (quoting *Cummings v. Missouri, 4 Wall. 277, 325-326, 18 L.Ed. 356 (1867)).* This statute was not enacted to increase the punishment for the enumerated prior offenses, nor does it make punishable an act which was not punishable when committed. As the Florida Supreme Court indicated in *Snyder,* the purpose of laws prohibiting convicted felons from possessing firearms is to protect the public prospectively by preventing such possession by those "who, because of their past conduct, have demonstrated their unfitness to be entrusted with such dangerous instrumentalities." In section 790.235, the legislature has created a new substantive offense which does not apply retroactively to earlier offenses but operates prospectively. *Cf. State v. Ferguson, 691 So.2d 578 (Fla. 2d DCA 1997)* (holding that the minimum mandatory sentence imposed pursuant to section 790.235 was not permissive, the court stated that "section 790.235 is a substantive offense statute, not a sentencing statute"). The only punishment imposed on Jackson pursuant to this statute is for the current offense, which took place after the effective date of section 790.235. *Cf. Perkins v. State,* *583 So.2d 1103, 1105 (Fla. 1ˢᵗ DCA 1991),* approved, *616 So.2d 9 (Fla. 1993)* (rejecting ex post facto challenge to habitual violent felony offender sentencing "[b]ecause appellant's enhanced punishment is an incident of his current offense ..."). The goal of this provision was not to increase the punishment for the enumerated prior offenses, or to impose punishment for an act that was not punishable at the time it was committed, but rather, to protect the public by prohibiting the possession of firearms by persons previously convicted of, or adjudicated delinquent for, the commission of certain enumerated felonies. Jackson's act of possessing a firearm took place after the effective date of this law. Therefore, punishing him for doing so does not violate the ex post facto prohibition.

We find merit, however, to Jackson's argument that the trial court erred in denying his motions to dismiss the jury venire, and we therefore reverse and remand for a new trial.

Accordingly, we REVERSE and REMAND for a new trial.

ALLEN, J., concurs.

WOLF, J., concurs and dissents with written opinion.

WOLF, Judge, concurring in part and dissenting in part. WRITTEN OPINION OMITTED.

FN1. U.S. Const. Amend. XIV, § 1; Fla. Const. Art. I, § 9.

FN2. U.S. Const. Amend. XIV, § 1; Fla. Const. Art. I, § 2.

FN3. U.S. Const. Art. I §§ 9, 10; Fla. Const. Art. I, § 10.

FN4. Section 790.235, Fla. Stat. (1995):

(1) Any person who meets the violent career criminal criteria under s. 775.084(1)(c), regardless of whether such person is or has previously been sentenced as a violent career criminal, who owns or has in his or her care, custody, possession, or control any firearm or electric weapon or device, or carries a concealed weapon, including a tear gas gun or chemical weapon or device, commits a felony in the first degree, punishable as provided in s. 775.082, s. 775.083, or s. 775.084. A person convicted of a violation of this section shall be sentenced to a mandatory minimum of 15 years' imprisonment; however, if the person would be sentenced to a longer term of imprisonment under s. 775.084(4)(c), the person must be sentenced under that provision. A person convicted of a violation of this section is not eligible for any form of discretionary early release, other than pardon, executive clemency, or conditional medical release under s. 947.149.

(2) For purposes of this section, the previous felony convictions necessary to meet the violent career criminal criteria under s. 775.084(1)(c) may be convictions for felonies committed as an adult or adjudications of delinquency for felonies committed as a juvenile. In order to be counted as a prior felony for purposes of this section, the felony must have resulted in a conviction sentenced separately, or an adjudication of delinquency entered separately, prior to the current offense, and sentenced or adjudicated separately from any other felony that is to be counted as a prior felony.

(3) This section shall not apply to a person whose civil rights and firearm authority have been restored.

FN5. Section 775.084(1), Fla. Stat. (1995):

(c) "Violent career criminal" means a defendant for whom the court must impose imprisonment pursuant to paragraph (4)(c), if it finds that:

> 1. The defendant has previously been convicted as an adult three or more times for an offense in this state or other qualified offense that is:
> > a. Any forcible felony, as described in s. 776.08;
> > b. Aggravated stalking, as described in s. 784.048(3) and (4);
> > c. Aggravated child abuse, as described in s. 827.03;
> > d. Lewd, lascivious, or indecent conduct, as described in s. 800.04;
> > e. Escape, as described in s. 944.40; or
> > f. A felony violation of chapter 790 involving the use or possession of a firearm.
>
> 2. The defendant has been incarcerated in a state prison or a federal prison.
>
> 3. The primary felony offense for which the defendant is to be sentenced is a felony enumerated in subparagraph 1, and was committed on or after October 1, 1994, and within 5 years after the conviction of the last prior enumerated felony or within 5 years after the defendant's release, on parole or otherwise, from a prison sentence or other commitment imposed as a result of a prior conviction for an enumerated felony, whichever is later.
>
> 4. The defendant has not received a pardon for any felony or other qualified offense that is necessary for the operation of this paragraph.
>
> 5. A conviction of a felony or other qualified offense necessary to the operation of this paragraph has not been set aside in any postconviction proceeding.

1. An *ex post facto* law _____.
   a. is adopted after an act was committed making it illegal
   b. increases penalty for crime after it is committed
   c. both a and b
   d. neither a nor b

DUE PROCESS
THE VOID FOR VAGUENESS DOCTRINE

A statute may also be unconstitutional if the wording is too vague to communicate and explain what constitutes a crime. A vague statute fails to put citizens on notice of what is a crime, thereby violating the requirements of both the U.S. and Florida Constitutions.

CASE

Papachristou v. City of Jacksonville, 405 U.S. 156, 31 L.Ed. 2d 110, 92 S.Ct. 839 (1972).

Eight defendants were convicted in a Florida Municipal Court of violating City of Jacksonville vagrancy ordinance. They appealed and their convictions were affirmed by the Florida Circuit Court in a consolidated appeal and their petition for certiorari was denied by the Florida District Court of Appeals, 236 So.2d 141. Petition for certiorari was granted. The Supreme Court, Mr. Justice Douglas, held that vagrancy ordinance containing the archaic classifications of vagrancy laws is void for vagueness because it fails to give person of ordinary intelligence fair notice that his contemplated conduct is forbidden, it encourages arbitrary and erratic arrests and convictions, makes criminal those activities which by modern standards are normally innocent and places almost unfettered discretion in hands of the police.

Reversed.

Mr. Justice Powell and Mr. Justice Rehnquist took no part in consideration or decision of the case.

DOUGLAS, JUSTICE.

This case involves eight defendants who were convicted in a Florida municipal court of violating a Jacksonville, Florida, vagrancy ordinance. [FN1] Their convictions were affirmed by the Florida Circuit Court in a consolidated appeal, and their petition for certiorari was denied by the District Court of Appeal, *236 So.2d 141*, on the authority of *Johnson v. State, 202 So.2d 852*. [FN2] The case is here on a petition for certiorari, which we granted. *403 U.S. 917, 91 S.Ct. 2233, 29 L.Ed 694.* For reasons which will appear, we reverse.

At issue are five consolidated cases. Margaret Papachristou, Betty Calloway, Eugene Eddie Melton, and Leonard Johnson were all arrested early on a Sunday morning, and charged with vagrancy - "prowling by auto."

Jimmy Lee Smith and Milton Henry were charged with vagrancy - "vagabonds."

Henry Edward Heath and a codefendant were arrested for vagrancy - "loitering" and "common thief."

Thomas Owen Campbell was charged with vagrancy - "common thief."

Hugh Brown was charged with vagrancy - "disorderly loitering on street" and "disorderly conduct - resisting arrest with violence."

The facts are stipulated. Papachristou and Calloway are white females. Melton and Johnson are black males. Papachristou was enrolled in a job-training program sponsored by the State Employment Service at Florida Junior College in Jacksonville. Calloway was a typing and shorthand teacher at a state mental institution located near Jacksonville. She was the owner of the automobile in which the four defendants were arrested. Melton was a Vietnam war veteran who had been released from the Navy after nine months in a veterans' hospital. On the date of his arrest he was a part-time computer helper while attending college as a full-time student in Jacksonville. Johnson was a tow-motor operator in a grocery chain warehouse and was a lifelong resident of Jacksonville.

At the time of their arrest the four of them were riding in Calloway's car on the main thoroughfare in Jacksonville. They had left a restaurant owned by Johnson's uncle where they had eaten and were on their way to a nightclub. The arresting officers denied that the racial mixture in the car played any part in the decision to make the arrest. The arrest, they said, was made because the defendants had stopped near a used-car lot which had been broken into several times. There was, however, no evidence of any breaking and entering on the night in question.

Of these four charged with "prowling by auto" none had been previously arrested except Papachristou who had once been convicted of a municipal offense.

Jimmy Lee Smith and Milton Henry (who is not a petitioner) were arrested between 9 and 10 a.m. on a weekday in downtown Jacksonville, while waiting for a friend who was to lend them a car so they could apply for a job at a produce company. Smith was a part-time produce worker and part-time organizer for a Negro political group. He had a common-law wife and three children supported by him and his wife. He had been arrested several times but convicted only once. Smith's companion, Henry, was an 18-year-old high school student with no previous record of arrest.

This morning it was cold, and Smith had no jacket, so they went briefly into a dry cleaning shop to wait, but left when requested to do so. They thereafter walked back and forth two or three times over a two-block stretch looking for their friend. The store owners, who apparently were wary of Smith and his companion, summoned two police officers who searched the men and found neither had a weapon. But they were arrested because the officers said they had no identification and because the officers did not believe their story.

Heath and a codefendant were arrested for "loitering" and for "common thief." Both were residents of Jacksonville, Heath having lived there all his life and being employed at an automobile body shop. Heath had previously been arrested but his codefendant had no arrest record. Heath and his companion were arrested when they drove up to a residence shared by Heath's girl friend and some other girls. Some police officers were already there in the process of arresting another man. When Heath and his companion started backing out of the driveway, the officers signaled to them to stop and asked them to get out of the car, which they did. Thereupon they and the automobile were searched. Although no contraband or incriminating evidence was found, they were both arrested, Heath being charged with being a "common thief" because he was reputed to be a thief. The codefendant was charged with "loitering" because he was standing in the driveway, an act which the officers admitted was done only at their command.

Campbell was arrested as he reached his home very early one morning and was charged with "common thief." He was stopped by officers because he was traveling at a high rate of speed, yet no speeding charge was placed against him.

Brown was arrested when he was observed leaving a downtown Jacksonville hotel by a police officer seated in a cruiser. The police testified he was reputed to be a thief, narcotics pusher, and generally opprobrious character. The officer called Brown over to the car, intending at that time to arrest him unless he had a good explanation for being on the street. Brown walked over to the police cruiser, as commanded, and the officer began to search him, apparently preparatory to placing him in the car. In the process of the search he came on two small packets which were later found to contain heroin. When the officer touched the pocket where the packets were, Brown began to resist. He was charged with "disorderly loitering on street" and "disorderly conduct - resisting arrest with violence." While he was also charged with a narcotics violation, that charge was nolled.

Jacksonville's ordinance and Florida's statute were "derived from early English law," *Johnson v. State, 202 So.2d, at 854,* and employ "archaic language" in their definitions of vagrants. *Id., at 855.* The history is an often-told tale. The breakup of feudal estates in England led to labor shortages which in turn resulted in the Statutes of Laborers, [Footnote 3 omitted] designed to stabilize the labor force by prohibiting increases in wages and prohibiting the movement of workers from their home areas in search of improved conditions. Later vagrancy laws became criminal aspects of the poor laws. The series of laws passed in England on the subject became increasingly severe. [FN4] But "the theory of the Elizabethan poor laws no longer fits the facts," *Edwards v.*

California, 314 U.S. 160, 174, 62 S.Ct. 164, 167, 86 L.Ed. 119. The conditions which spawned these laws may be gone, but the archaic classifications remain.

This ordinance is void for vagueness, both in the sense that it "fails to give a person of ordinary intelligence fair notice that his contemplated conduct is forbidden by the statute," *United States v. Harriss*, 347 U.S. 612, 617, 74 S.Ct. 808, 812, 98 L.Ed. 989, and because it encourages arbitrary and erratic arrests and convictions. *Thornhill v. Alabama*, 310 U.S. 88, 60 S.Ct. 736, 84 L.Ed. 1093; *Herndon v. Lowry*, 301 U.S. 242, 57 S.Ct. 732, 81 L.Ed. 1066.

Living under a rule of law entails various suppositions, one of which is that "[all persons] are entitled to be informed as to what the State commands or forbids." *Lanzetta v. New Jersey*, 306 U.S. 451, 453, 59 S.Ct. 618, 619, 83 L.Ed. 888.

Lanzetta is one of a well-recognized group of cases insisting that the law give fair notice of the offending conduct. See *Connally v. General Construction Co.*, 269 U.S. 385, 391, 46 S.Ct. 126, 127, 70 L.Ed. 322; *Cline v. Frink Dairy Co.*, 274 U.S. 445, 47 S.Ct. 681, 71 L.Ed. 1146; *United States v. L. Cohen Grocery Co.*, 255 U.S. 81, 41 S.Ct. 298, 65 L.Ed. 516. In the field of regulatory statutes governing business activities, where the acts limited are in a narrow category, greater leeway is allowed. *Boyce Motor Lines, Inc. v. United States*, 342 U.S. 337, 72 S.Ct. 329, 96 L.Ed. 367; *United States v. National Dairy Products Corp.*, 372 U.S. 29, 83 S.Ct. 594, 9 L.Ed.2d 561; *United States v. Petrillo*, 332 U.S. 1, 67 S.Ct. 1538, 91 L.Ed. 1877.

The poor among us, the minorities, the average householder are not in business and not alerted to the regulatory schemes of vagrancy laws; and we assume they would have no understanding of their meaning and impact if they read them. Nor are they protected from being caught in the vagrancy net by the necessity of having a specific intent to commit an unlawful act. See *Screws v. United States*, 325 U.S. 91, 65 S.Ct. 1031, 89 L.Ed. 1495; *Boyce Motor Lines, Inc. v. United States*, supra.

The Jacksonville ordinance makes criminal activities which by modern standards are normally innocent. "Nightwalking" is one. Florida construes the ordinance not to make criminal one night's wandering, *Johnson v. State*, 202 So.2d, at 855, only the "habitual" wanderer or, as the ordinance describes it, "common night walkers." We know, however, from experience that sleepless people often walk at night, perhaps hopeful that sleep-inducing relaxation will result.

Luis Munoz-Marin, former Governor of Puerto Rico, commented once that "loafing" was a national virtue in his Commonwealth and that it should be encouraged. It is, however, a crime in Jacksonville.

"[P]ersons able to work but habitually living upon the earnings of their wives or minor children" - like habitually living "without visible means of support" – might implicate unemployed pillars of the community who have married rich wives.

"[P]ersons able to work but habitually living upon the earnings of their wives or minor children" may also embrace unemployed people of the labor market, by reason of a recession [Footnote omitted] or disemployed by reason of technological or so-called structural displacements."

[FN5] Persons "wandering or strolling" from place to place have been extolled by Walt Whitman and Vachel Lindsay. [FN6] The qualification "without any lawful purpose or object" may be a trap for innocent acts. Persons "neglecting all lawful business and habitually spending their time by frequenting ... places where alcoholic beverages are sold or served" would literally embrace many members of golf clubs and city clubs.

Walkers and strollers and wanderers may be going to or coming from a burglary. Loafers or loiterers may be "casing" a place for a holdup. Letting one's wife support him is an intra-family matter, and normally of no concern to the police. Yet it may, of course, be the setting of numerous crimes.

The difficulty is that these activities are historically part of the amenities of life as we have known them. They are not mentioned in the Constitution or in the Bill of Rights. These unwritten amenities have been in part responsible for giving our people the feeling of independence and self-confidence, the feeling of creativity. These amenities have dignified the right of dissent and have honored the right to be nonconformists and the right to defy submissiveness. They have encouraged lives of high spirits rather than hushed, suffocating silence.

They are embedded in Walt Whitman's writings, especially in his "Song of the Open Road." They are reflected too, in the spirit of Vachel Lindsay's "I Want to Go Wandering," and by Henry D. Thoreau. [FN7]

This aspect of the vagrancy ordinance before us is suggested by what this Court said in 1876 about a broad criminal statute enacted by Congress: "It would certainly be dangerous if the legislature could set a net large enough to catch all possible offenders, and leave it to the courts to step inside and say who could be rightfully detained, and who should be set at large." *United States v. Reese*, 92 U.S. 214, 221, 23 L.Ed. 563.

While that was a federal case, the due process implications are equally applicable to the States and to this vagrancy ordinance. Here the net cast is large, not to give the courts the power to pick and choose but to increase the arsenal of the police. In *Winters v. New York*, 333 U.S. 507, 68 S.Ct. 665, 92 L.Ed. 840, the Court struck down a New York statute that made criminal the distribution of a magazine made up principally of items of criminal deeds of bloodshed or lust so massed as to become vehicles for inciting violent and depraved crimes against the person. The infirmity the Court found was vagueness--the absence of "ascertainable standards of guilt" *(id., at 515, 68 S.Ct., at 670)* in the sensitive First Amendment area. [FN8] Mr. Justice Frankfurter dissented. But concerned as he, and many others, [FN9] had been over the vagrancy laws, he added:

19

"Only a word needs to be said regarding *Lanzetta v. New Jersey, 306 U.S. 451, 59 S.Ct. 618, 83 L.Ed. 888*. The case involved a New Jersey statute of the type that seek to control 'vagrancy.' These statutes are in a class by themselves, in view of the familiar abuses to which they are put.... Definiteness is designedly avoided so as to allow the net to be cast at large, to enable men to be caught who are vaguely undesirable in the eyes of police and prosecution, although not chargeable with any particular offense. In short, these 'vagrancy statutes' and laws against 'gangs' are not fenced in by the text of the statute or by the subject matter so as to give notice of conduct to be avoided." *Id., at 540, 68 S.Ct., at 682.*

Where the list of crimes is so all-inclusive and generalized [FN10] as the one in this ordinance, those convicted may be punished for no more than vindicating affronts to police authority:

"The common ground which brings such a motley assortment of human troubles before the magistrates in vagrancy-type proceedings is the procedural laxity which permits 'conviction' for almost any kind of conduct and the existence of the House of Correction as an easy and convenient dumping-ground for problems that appear to have no other immediate solution." Foote, Vagrancy-Type Law and Its Administration, 104 U.Pa.L.Rev.603, 631. [FN11]

Another aspect of the ordinance's vagueness appears when we focus, not on the lack of notice given a potential offender, but on the effect of the unfettered discretion it places in the hands of the Jacksonville police. Caleb Foote, an early student of this subject, has called the vagrancy-type law as offering 'punishment by analogy.' *Id., at 609.* Such crimes, though long common in Russia, [FN12] are not compatible with our constitutional system. We allow our police to make arrests only on "probable cause," [FN13] a Fourth and Fourteenth Amendment standard applicable to the States [FN14] as well as to the Federal Government. Arresting a person on suspicion, like arresting a person for investigation, is foreign to our system, even when the arrest is for past criminality. Future criminality, however, is the common justification for the presence of vagrancy statutes. See *Foote, supra, at 625.* Florida has, indeed, construed her vagrancy statute "as necessary regulations," *inter alia*, "to deter vagabondage and prevent crimes." *Johnson v. State, Fla., 202 So.2d 852; Smith v. State, Fla., 239 So.2d 250, 251.*

A direction by a legislature to the police to arrest all "suspicious" persons [Footnote 15 Omitted] would not pass constitutional muster. A vagrancy prosecution may be merely the cloak for a conviction which could not be obtained on the real but undisclosed grounds for the arrest. *People v. Moss, 309 N.Y. 429, 131 N.E.2d 717.* But as Chief Justice Hewart said in *Frederick Dean, 18 Crim.App. 133, 134 (1924):*

"It would be in the highest degree unfortunate if in any part of the country those who are responsible for setting in motion the criminal law should entertain, connive at or coquette with the idea that in a case where there is not enough evidence to charge the prisoner with an attempt to commit a crime, the prosecution may, nevertheless, on such insufficient evidence, succeed in obtaining and upholding a conviction under the Vagrancy Act, 1824."

Those generally implicated by the imprecise terms of the ordinance - poor people, nonconformists, dissenters, idlers - may be required to comport themselves according to the lifestyle deemed appropriate by the Jacksonville police and the courts. Where, as here, there are no standards governing the exercise of the discretion granted by the ordinance, the scheme permits and encourages an arbitrary and discriminatory enforcement of the law. It furnishes a convenient tool for "harsh and discriminatory enforcement by local prosecuting officials, against particular groups deemed to merit their displeasure." *Thornhill v. Alabama, 310 U.S. 88, 97-98, 60 S.Ct. 736, 742, 84 L.Ed. 1093.* It results in a regime in which the poor and the unpopular are permitted to "stand on a public sidewalk ... only at the whim of any police officer." *Shuttlesworth v. Birmingham, 382 U.S. 87, 90, 86 S.Ct. 211, 213, 15 L.Ed.2d 176.* Under this ordinance,

> "[I]f some carefree type of fellow is satisfied to work just so much, and no more, as will pay for one square meal, some wine, and a flophouse daily, but a court thinks this kind of living subhuman, the fellow can be forced to raise his sights or go to jail as a vagrant." Amsterdam, Federal Constitutional Restrictions on the Punishment of Crimes of Status, Crimes of General Obnoxiousness, Crimes of Displeasing Police Officers, and the Like, 3 Crim.L.Bull. 205, 226 (1967).

A presumption that people who might walk or loaf or loiter or stroll or frequent houses where liquor is sold, or who are supported by their wives or who look suspicious to the police are to become future criminals is too precarious for a rule of law. The implicit presumption in these generalized vagrancy standards--that crime is being nipped in the bud--is too extravagant to deserve extended treatment. Of course, vagrancy statutes are useful to the police. Of course, they are nets making easy the roundup of so-called undesirables. But the rule of law implies equality and justice in its application. Vagrancy laws of the Jacksonville type teach that the scales of justice are so tipped that even-handed administration of the law is not possible. The rule of law, evenly applied to minorities as well as majorities, to the poor as well as the rich, is the great mucilage that holds society together.

The Jacksonville ordinance cannot be squared with our constitutional standards and is plainly unconstitutional.

Reversed.

MR. Justice POWELL and MR. Justice REHNQUIST took no part in the consideration or decision in this case.

FN1. Jacksonville Ordinance Code § 26-57 provided at the time of these arrests and convictions as follows:

"Rogues and vagabonds, or dissolute persons who go about begging, common gamblers, persons who use juggling or unlawful games or plays, common drunkards, common night walkers, thieves, pilferers or pickpockets, traders in stolen property, lewd, wanton and lascivious persons, keepers of gambling places, common railers and brawlers, persons wandering or strolling around from place to place without any lawful purpose or object, habitual loafers, disorderly persons, persons neglecting all lawful business and habitually spending their time by frequenting houses of ill fame, gaming houses, or places where alcoholic beverages are sold or served, persons able to work but habitually living upon the earnings of their wives or minor children shall be deemed vagrants and, upon conviction in the Municipal Court shall be punished as provided for Class D offenses." Class D offenses at the time of these arrests and convictions were punishable by 90 days' imprisonment, $500 fine, or both. Jacksonville Ordinance Code § 1--8 (1965). The maximum punishment has since been reduced to 75 days or $450.00 § 304.101 (1971). We are advised that that downward revision was made to avoid federal right-to-counsel decisions. The Fifth Circuit case extending right to counsel in misdemeanors where a fine of $500 or 90 days' imprisonment could be imposed is *Harvey v. Mississippi, 340 F.2d 263 (1965).*

We are advised that at present the Jacksonville vagrancy ordinance is § 330.107 and identical with the earlier one except that "juggling" has been eliminated.

FN2. Florida also has a vagrancy statute, Fla. Stat. s 856.02 (1965), which reads quite closely on the Jacksonville ordinance. Jacksonville Ordinance Code s 27--43 makes the commission of any Florida misdemeanor a Class D offense against the City of Jacksonville. In 1971 Florida made minor amendments to its statute. See Laws 1971, c. 71-132. Section 856.02 was declared unconstitutionally overbroad in *Lazarus v. Faircloth, D.C., 301 F. Supp. 266.* The court said: 'All loitering, loafing, or idling on the streets and highways of a city, even though habitual, is not necessarily detrimental to the public welfare nor is it under all circumstances an interference with travel upon them. It may be and often is entirely innocuous. The statute draws no distinction between conduct that is calculated to harm and that which is essentially innocent.' *Id., at 272,* quoting *Hawaii v. Anduha,* 48 F.2d 171, 172. See also *Smith v. Florida,* 405 U.S. 172, 92 S.Ct. 848, 31 L.Ed.2d. 122.

The Florida disorderly conduct ordinance, covering 'loitering about any hotel, block, barroom, dramshop, gambling house or disorderly house, or wandering about the streets either by night or by day without any known lawful means of support, or without being able to give a satisfactory account of themselves' has also been held void for "excessive broadness and vagueness" by the Florida Supreme Court, *Headley v. Selkowitz, 171 So.2d 368, 370.*

FN4. See 3 J. Stephen, *History of the Criminal Law of England 203-206, 266-275; 4 W. Blackstone, Commentaries *169.*

Ledwith v. *Roberts, (1937) 1 K. B. 232, 271*, gives the following summary:
'The early Vagrancy Acts came into being under peculiar conditions utterly different to those of the present time. From the time of the Black Death in the middle of the 14th century till the middle of the 17th century, and indeed, although in diminishing degree, right down to the reform of the Poor Law in the first half of the 19th century, the roads of England were crowded with masterless men and their families, who had lost their former employment through a variety of causes, had no means of livelihood and had taken to a vagrant life. The main causes were the gradual decay of the feudal system under which the labouring classes had been anchored to the soil, the economic slackening of the legal compulsion to work for fixed wages, the break up of the monasteries in the reign of Henry VIII, and the consequent disappearance of the religious orders which had previously administered a kind of 'public assistance' in the form of lodging, food and alms; and, lastly, the economic changes brought about by the Enclosure Acts. Some of these people were honest labourers who had fallen upon evil days, others were the 'wild rogues,' so common in Elizabethan times and literature, who had been born to a life of idleness and had no intention of following any other. It was they and their confederates who formed themselves into the notorious 'brotherhood of beggars' which flourished in the 16th and 17th centuries. They were a definite and serious menace to the community and it was chiefly against them and their kind that the harsher provisions of the vagrancy laws of the period were directed.' And see Sherry, Vagrants, Rogues and Vagabonds - Old Concepts in Need of Revision, *48 Calif. L. Rev. 557, 560-561 (1960)*; Note, The Vagrancy Concept Reconsidered: Problems and Abuses of Status Criminality, *37 N. Y. U. L. Rev. 102 (1962)*.

FN5. In *Edwards v. California, 314 U.S. 160, 177, 62 S.Ct. 164, 168, 86 L.Ed. 119*, in referring to *City of New York v. Miln, 11 Pet. 102, 142, 9 L.Ed. 648*, decided in 1837, we said:

> 'Whatever may have been the notion then prevailing, we do not think that it will now be seriously contended that because a person is without employment and without funds he constitutes a 'moral pestilence.' Poverty and immorality are not synonymous.'

FN6. And see Reich, Police Questioning of Law Abiding Citizens, 75 Yale L. J. 1161, 1172 (1966): 'If I choose to take an evening walk to see if Andromeda has come up on schedule, I think I am entitled to look for the distant light of Almach and Mirach without finding myself staring into the blinding beam of a police flashlight.'

FN7. 'I have met with but one or two persons in the course of my life who understood the art of Walking, that is, of taking walks, --who had a genius, so to speak, for *sauntering:* which word is beautifully derived 'from idle people who roved about the country, in the Middle Ages, and asked charity, under pretence of going *a la Sainte Terre,*' to the Holy Land, till the children exclaimed, 'There goes a Sainte Terrer,' a Saunterer, a Holy-Lander. They who never go to the Holy Land in their walks, as they pretend, are indeed mere idlers and vagabonds; but they who do go there are saunterers in the good sense, such as I mean. Some, however, would derive the word from *sans terre,* without land or a home, which, therefore, in the good sense, will mean, having no particular home, but equally at home everywhere. For this is the secret of successful sauntering. He who sits still in a house all the time may be the greatest vagrant of all; but the saunterer, in the good sense, is no more vagrant than the meandering river, which is all the while sedulously seeking the shortest course to the sea. But I prefer the first, which, indeed, is the most probable derivation. For every walk is a sort of crusade, preached by some Peter the Hermit in us, to go forth and reconquer this Holy Land from the hands of the Infidels.' Excursions 251-252 (1893).

FN8. For a discussion of the void-for-vagueness doctrine in the area of fundamental rights see Note, The Void-For-Vagueness Doctrine in the Supreme Court, *109 U. Pa. L. Rev. 67, 104 et seq.*; Amsterdam, Federal Constitutional Restrictions on the Punishment of Crimes of Status, Crimes of General Obnoxiousness, Crimes of Displeasing Police Officers, and the Like, *3 Crim. L. Bull. 205, 224 et seq. (1967).*

FN9. See ***Edelman* v. *California,*** *344 U.S. 357, 362, 73 S.Ct. 293, 296, 97 L.Ed. 387* (Black, J., dissenting); ***Hicks* v. *District of Columbia,*** *383 U.S. 252, 254, 86 S.Ct. 798, 799, 15 L.Ed.2d. 744* (Douglas, J., dissenting); ***District of Columbia* v. *Hunt,*** *82 U.S. App. D.C. 159, 163 F.2d 833* (Judge Stephens writing for a majority of the Court of Appeals); Judge Rudkin for the court in ***Hawaii* v. *Anduha,*** *48 F.2d 171.* The opposing views are numerous: Ex parte ***Branch,*** *234 Mo. 466, 137 S.W. 886*; H.R.Rep. No. 1248, 77th Cong., 1st Sess., 2; Perkins, The Vagrancy Concept, *9 Hastings, L.J. 237 (1958)*; ***People v. Craig,*** *152 Cal. 42, 91 P. 997.*

FN10. President Roosevelt, in vetoing a vagrancy law for the District of Columbia, said:

> 'The bill contains many provisions that constitute an improvement over existing law. Unfortunately, however, there are two provisions in the bill that appear objectionable. 'Section 1 of the bill contains a number of clauses defining a 'vagrant.' Clause 6 of this section would include within that category 'any able-bodied person who lives in idleness upon the wages, earnings, or property of any person having no legal obligation to support him.' This definition is so broadly and loosely drawn that in many cases it would make a vagrant of an adult daughter or son of a well-to-do family who, though amply provided for and not guilty of any improper or unlawful conduct, has no occupation and is dependent upon parental support.

'Under clause 9 of said section 'any person leading an idle life . . . and not giving a good account of himself' would incur guilt and liability to punishment unless he could prove, as required by section 2, that he has lawful means of support realized from a lawful occupation or source. What constitutes 'leading an idle life' and 'not giving a good account of oneself' is not indicated by the statute but is left to the determination in the first place of a police officer and eventually of a judge of the police court, subject to further review in proper cases. While this phraseology may be suitable for general purposes as a definition of a vagrant, it does not conform with accepted standards of legislative practice as a definition of a criminal offense. I am not willing to agree that a person without lawful means of support, temporarily or otherwise, should be subject to the risk of arrest and punishment under provisions as indefinite and uncertain in their meaning and application as those employed in this clause. 'It would hardly be a satisfactory answer to say that the sound judgment and decisions of the police and prosecuting officers must be trusted to invoke the law only in proper cases. The law itself should be so drawn as not to make it applicable to cases which obviously should not be comprised within its terms.' H. R. Doc. No. 392, 77th Cong, 1st Sess.

FN11. Thus, 'prowling by auto,' which formed the basis for the vagrancy arrests and convictions of four of the petitioners herein, is not even listed in the ordinance as a crime. But see *Hanks* v. *State,* 195 So.2d 49, 51, in which the Florida District Court of Appeal construed 'wandering or strolling from place to place' as including travel by automobile.

FN12. J. Hazard, The Soviet Legal System 133 (1962):
'The 1922 code was a step in the direction of precision in definition of crime, but it was not a complete departure from the concept of punishment in accordance with the dictates of the social consciousness of the judge. Laying hold of an old tsarist code provision that had been in effect from 1864 to 1903 known by the term 'analogy,' the Soviet draftsmen inserted an article permitting a judge to consider the social danger of an individual even when he had committed no act defined as a crime in the specialized part of the code. He was to be guided by analogizing the dangerous act to some act defined as crime, but at the outset the analogies were not always apparent, as when a husband was executed for the sadistic murder of a wife, followed by dissection of her torso and shipment in a trunk to a remote railway station, the court arguing that the crime was analogous to banditry. At the time of this decision the code permitted the death penalty for banditry but not for murder without political motives or very serious social consequences.'

'On the traditionally important subject of criminal law, Algeria is rejecting the flexibility introduced in the Soviet criminal code by the 'analogy' principle, as have the East-Central European and black African states.' Hazard, The Residue of Marxist Influence in Algeria, *9 Colum. J. of Transnat'l L. 194, 224 (1970).*

FN13. *Johnson v. United States, 333 U.S. 10, 15–17, 68 S.Ct. 367, 369–371, 92 L.Ed. 436.*

FN14. *Whiteley v. Warden, 401 U.S. 560, 91 S.Ct. 1031, 28 L.Ed.2d. 306.*

REVIEW

1. The amount of discretion given to law enforcement is _____.
   a. always unlimited
   b. sometimes unlimited
   c. limited by the federal and state constitutions
   d. limited only by the federal constitution

2. A statute found to be void for vagueness _____.
   a. fails to give notice of what conduct is forbidden
   b. may be enforced by law enforcement
   c. makes innocent conduct a crime
   d. both a and c

3. An ordinance that is all-inclusive and generalized is _____.
   a. constitutional
   b. always unconstitutional
   c. sometimes unconstitutional
   d. sometimes constitutional

CASE

State v. Williams, 623 So.2d 462 (Fla. 1993).

Defendant was convicted before the Circuit Court, Broward County, William P. Dimitrouleas, J., of purchasing a controlled substance within 1000 feet of a secondary school, and he appealed. The District Court of Appeal, 593 So.2d 1064, reversed and remanded. State filed motion for certification which was granted. The Supreme Court, Harding, J., held that illegal manufacture of crack cocaine by law enforcement officials for use in reverse-sting operation within 1,000 feet of school constituted governmental misconduct which violated due process clause of the Florida Constitution.

Decision of District Court of Appeal approved.

McDonald, J., dissented.

HARDING, Justice.

We have for review ***Williams v. State***, *593 So.2d 1064 (Fla. 4ᵗʰ DCA 1992)*, in which the Fourth District Court of Appeal certified the following question as one of great public importance:

> DOES THE SOURCE OF ILLEGAL DRUGS USED BY LAW ENFORCEMENT PERSONNEL TO CONDUCT REVERSE STINGS CONSTITUTIONALLY SHIELD THOSE WHO BECOME ILLICITLY INVOLVED WITH SUCH DRUGS FROM CRIMINAL LIABILITY?

Id. at 1064. We accept jurisdiction pursuant to article V, Section 3(b)(4) of the Florida Constitution, and rephrase the question as follows:

> Whether the manufacture of crack cocaine by law enforcement officials for use in a reverse-sting operation constitutes governmental misconduct which violates the due process clause of the Florida Constitution?

We answer the rephrased question in the affirmative and thus approve the decision of the district court below. We hold that the illegal manufacture of crack cocaine by law enforcement officials for use in a reverse-sting operation within 1000 feet of a school constitutes governmental misconduct which violates the due process clause of the Florida Constitution. Thus, we find that the defendant's conviction for purchasing the crack cocaine must be reversed.

On February 15, 1990, the police arrested Leon Williams (Williams) for allegedly purchasing crack cocaine within 1000 feet of a school. Williams filed a motion to dismiss the charges because of alleged police misconduct that violated his due process rights. The State and Williams entered the following stipulation of facts relevant to a hearing on Williams' motion to dismiss the charges: [FN1]

> 1. On April 21, 1988, [Detective] Mary Guess, of the Broward Sheriff's Office (B.S.O.), discovered 991.2 grams of cocaine in a Greyhound bus station locker, under case number BS88-4-10524.
>
> 2. [Detective] Guess turned this abandoned cocaine in to the B.S.O. Crime Lab where it was signed in by Sal Anzelone, an employee of the Broward Sheriff's Office.
>
> 3. The cocaine, which was in powder form, was placed into destroy case 4604X, it being the intention of B.S.O. at that time to destroy that cocaine as no arrests were made as a result of its discovery, there was no case pending regarding that cocaine, no medicinal use was contemplated for said cocaine, and no order by any court had been entered requiring or permitting any other use of said cocaine.
>
> 4. The normal procedure of the destruction of seized narcotic contraband would have been for aforementioned B.S.O. employee Sal Anzelone to sign the cocaine out of the lab, transport it to a local incinerator and have it burned there.

5. A decision was made by the B.S.O. Crime Lab technician to retain the cocaine for use in B.S.O. reverse sting operations.

6. Sometime prior to February 14, 1989, John Pennie, B.S.O. Crime Lab Supervisor, and Randy Hilliard decided it was necessary to convert the powder cocaine to "crack" cocaine. They cleared this procedure through the proper B.S.O. chain of command, and was approved by Sheriff Nick Navarro.

7. On February 14, 1989, B.S.O. chemist Randy Hilliard began cooking up "crack" cocaine in the B.S.O. lab...

8. Following the conversion procedure, B.S.O. chemist, Randy Hilliard cut the "crack" cocaine into small pieces, places [sic] the pieces into individual plastic ziplock bags, and heat-sealed the bags.

9. The individually packaged "crack" rocks were then distributed to B.S.O. deputies for reverse sting operations, by B.S.O. employee, Sal Anzelone.

10. These "crack" rocks were used in the reverse sting operation which resulted in the Defendant's arrest and prosecution in the above-styled case.

11. Powder form cocaine and "crack" form cocaine are separate and distinct chemical structures. Powder form cocaine is represented chemically as C sub17 H sub21 NO sub4 HC sub1. "Crack" cocaine is represented chemically as C sub17 H sub21 NO sub4.

12. B.S.O. Chemist, Randy Hilliard is not a "pharmacist" as defined in Chapter 893.02(14), Florida Statutes (1989).

13. B.S.O. Chemist, Randy Hilliard is not a "practitioner" as defined in Chapter 893.02(16), Florida Statutes (1989).

In denying Williams' motion to dismiss, the trial court found that the Broward County Sheriff's Office manufactured crack cocaine for "a bonafide [sic] and legitimate law enforcement purpose" and that the Sheriff's Office acted pursuant to Section 893.13(5)(b)(5), Florida Statutes (1989), and *State v. Bass, 451 So.2d 986 (Fla. 2d DCA 1984)*. Williams proceeded to trial and the jury convicted him of purchasing a controlled substance within 1000 feet of a secondary school. Section 893.13(1)(e), Fla.Stat. (1989).

On appeal, the district court reversed Williams' conviction, citing its decision in *Kelly v. State, 593 So.2d 1060 (Fla. 4th DCA), review denied, 599 So.2d 1280 (Fla. 1992)*. In *Kelly*, the district court stated:

We have reconsidered the issue of the police manufacture or reconstitution of powdered cocaine into "crack" rocks, and we find that the practice is illegal. We hold that the use by the police of such reconstituted "crack" infringed on the appellant's right to due process of law. In other words, the police agencies cannot themselves do an illegal act, albeit their intended goal may be legal and desirable.

Id. at 1061. Consequently, the district court in **Kelly** reversed the defendant's conviction. Following the district court's reversal in the instant case, the State filed a motion for certification which the district court granted. We accepted jurisdiction to answer the certified question.

In *State v. Glosson*, 462 So.2d 1082 (Fla. 1985), this Court developed its own due process analysis based on article I, section 9 of the Florida Constitution. [FN2] In Glosson, the State and an informant entered a contingent-fee agreement in which the informant would receive ten percent of all civil forfeitures resulting from criminal prosecutions in which the informant provided testimony and cooperation. *Id. at 1083.* As this Court stated:

> We can imagine few situations with more potential for abuse of a defendant's due process right. The informant here had an enormous financial incentive not only to make criminal cases, but also to color his testimony or even commit perjury in pursuit of the contingent fee. The due process rights of all citizens require us to forbid criminal prosecutions based upon the testimony of vital state witnesses who have what amounts to a financial stake in criminal convictions.

> Accordingly, we hold that a trial court may properly dismiss criminal charges for constitutional due process violations in cases where an informant stands to gain a contingent fee conditioned on cooperation and testimony in the criminal prosecution when that testimony is critical to a successful prosecution.

Id. at 1085. In deciding **Glosson**, this Court rejected the federal court's narrow application of the federal due process defense. [FN3] *Id.* This Court also cited opinions from two other states for the proposition that the courts could use the due process defense to overturn criminal convictions as a check against outrageous police conduct. *State v. Hohensee, 650 S.W.2d 268 (Mo.Ct.App.1982)* (reversing a predisposed defendant's conviction for burglary because the police violated state due process rights in sponsoring and operating a burglary in which the defendant acted as a lookout); *People v. Isaacson, 44 N.Y.2d 511, 406 N.Y.S.2d 714, 378 N.E.2d 78 (N.Y. 1978)* (reversing a predisposed defendant's conviction for drug sales because police misconduct and trickery violated state due process rights). This Court also agreed with the courts in **Hohensee** and **Isaacson** that "governmental misconduct which violates the constitutional due process right of a defendant, regardless of that defendant's predisposition, requires the dismissal of criminal charges." *Glosson, 462 So.2d at 1085.*

Due process of law is a summarized constitutional guarantee of respect for personal rights which are "so rooted in the traditions and conscience of our people as to be ranked as fundamental." *Snyder v. Massachusetts, 291 U.S. 97, 105, 54 S.Ct. 330, 78 L.Ed. 674 (1934).* Due process of law imposes upon a court the responsibility to conduct "an exercise of judgment upon the whole course of the proceedings in order to ascertain whether they offend those canons of decency and fairness which express the notions of justice." *Malinski v. New York*, 325 U.S. 401, 416-417, 65 S.Ct. 781, 788-89, 89 L.Ed. 1029 (1945). Defining the limits of due process is difficult because " 'due process,' unlike some legal rules, is not a technical conception with a fixed content unrelated to time, place and circumstances." *Joint Anti-Facist Refugee Comm. V. McGrath*, 341 U.S. 123, 162, 71 S.Ct. 624, 643, 95 L.Ed. 817 (1951) (Frankfurter, J., concurring). Rather, due process is a general principle of law that prohibits the government from obtaining convictions "brought about by methods that offend 'a sense of justice.' " *Rochin v. California*, 342 U.S. 165, 173, 72 S.Ct. 205, 210, 96 L.Ed. 183 (1952).

This Court is also aware of the difficulties that law enforcement officials face in detecting and stopping narcotic trafficking in our state. As Justice Powell stated in *Hampton v. United States*, 425 U.S. 484, 96 S.Ct. 1646, 48 L.Ed.2d 113 (1976):

> One cannot easily exaggerate the problems confronted by law enforcement authorities in dealing effectively with an expanding narcotics traffic, which is one of the major contributing causes of escalating crime in our cities. Enforcement officials therefore must be allowed flexibility adequate to counter effectively such criminal activity.

Id., 425 U.S. at 495-96 n. 7, 96 S.Ct. at 1653 n. 7 (Powell, J., concurring in the judgment) (citations omitted). Undercover tactics and limited participation in drug rings are often the only methods law enforcement officials have to gather evidence of drug-related offenses. Law enforcement tactics such as reverse-sting operations can hardly be said to violate fundamental fairness or be shocking to the universal sense of justice. See *State v. Burch*, 545 So.2d 279 (Fla. 4th DCA 1989) (holding that reverse sting operations involving undercover police officers selling controlled substances within 100 feet of a school is not outrageous conduct as a matter of law), *approved, 558 So.2d 1 (Fla. 1990)*; see also *State v. Brider*, 386 So.2d 818 (Fla. 2d DCA) (holding that furnishing of a controlled substance by government agents in a reverse-sting operation did not constitute outrageous conduct to invoke due process considerations), *review denied, 392 So.2d 1372 (Fla. 1980)*. While we must not tie law enforcement's hands in combating crime, there are instances where law enforcement's conduct cannot be countenanced and the courts will not permit the government to invoke the judicial process to obtain a conviction. See, e.g., *Glosson; Hohensee; Isaacson*. As Justice Frankfurter recognized in *Rochin*, "[t]he Due Process Clause places upon this Court the duty of exercising a judgment, within the narrow confines of judicial power in reviewing State convictions, upon interests of society pushing in opposite directions." *Rochin*, 342 U.S. at 171, 72 S.Ct. At 209.

Applying these principles to the facts of the instant case, we find that the law enforcement's conduct here was so outrageous as to violate Florida's due process clause.

Section 893.02(12)(a), Florida Statutes (1989), defines "manufacture" as:

the production, preparation, propagation, compounding, cultivating, growing, conversion, or processing of a controlled substance either directly or indirectly, by extraction from substances of natural origin, or independently by means of chemical synthesis, or by a combination of extraction and chemical synthesis, and includes any packaging of the substance or labeling or relabeling of its container...

The factual stipulation in the instant case shows that the chemist for the Broward County Sheriff's Office took the seized powdered cocaine and converted it into crack cocaine pursuant to the Sheriff's approval. The stipulation also shows the procedure which the chemist used in making the crack cocaine. [FN4] The chemists's conversion of the powdered cocaine into crack cocaine clearly meets the definition of manufacture under the statute.

Section 893.13, Florida Statutes (1989), which prohibits the sale, purchase, manufacture, delivery, or possession of a controlled substance contains two exclusions for law enforcement officials. Section 893.13(5)(b)5 excludes the " actual or constructive possession of controlled substances" by "[o]fficers or employees of state, federal, of local governments acting in their official capacity," and section 893.13(5)(c) excludes the "delivery of controlled substances by a law enforcement officer for bona fide law enforcement purposes in the course of an active criminal investigation." Section 893.13, however, does not contain a provision allowing law enforcement officials to manufacture a controlled substance. Therefore, we find that the Broward County Sheriff's Office acted illegally in manufacturing the crack cocaine it used in the reverse-sting operation which led to Williams' arrest.

The State argues that the police do not need specific statutory authority to manufacture crack cocaine for use in reverse-sting operations. The State cites **Bass**, *451 So.2d 986,* for support of its proposition. In **Bass**, state law enforcement officers delivered marijuana, obtained from federal agents, to the defendants as part of a reverse-sting operation. *Id. at 987.* The trial court dismissed the charges of trafficking in marijuana because it concluded that the state law enforcement officers lacked statutory authority to deliver the marijuana. The Second District Court of Appeal reversed the trial court's dismissal and held that law enforcement officials did not need a specific statutory authority to engage in reverse-sting deliveries of controlled substances. *Id. at 988.* The district court noted that the Legislature had provided law enforcement officials with immunity from civil or criminal liability for lawfully enforcing controlled substance laws. *Id.* Moreover, the district court recognized that it had held in **Brider**, *386 So.2d 818,* that delivery of a controlled substance by government agents in a reverse-sting operation did not constitute entrapment as a matter of law. *Id.*

We find that **Bass** is distinguishable from the instant case. The delivery of a controlled substances in a reverse sting operation is worlds apart from the manufacture of a dangerous controlled substance. Thus, unlike **Bass,** the facts in the instant case show that the law enforcement officers' conduct in illegally manufacturing crack cocaine is so outrageous that it violates the due process clause.

Another disturbing fact in the instant case is the nature of the controlled substance manufactured by the Broward County Sheriff's Office. It is undisputed that crack cocaine is highly addictive and has caused death. The State argues that the Broward County Sheriff's Office manufactured its own crack cocaine, rather than use confiscated crack cocaine, because of fears that the confiscated crack cocaine might be tainted with foreign substances. The State urges that the manufacture of crack cocaine is safer than the use of confiscated crack cocaine in a reverse-sting operation. We find that the record does not support the State's argument. The chemist who manufactured the crack cocaine for the Broward County Sheriff's Office testified that the had not found any detrimental foreign substances in the over 20,000 seized crack cocaine rocks he had examined for the sheriff's office. Further it is incredible that law enforcement's manufacture of an inherently dangerous controlled substance, like crack cocaine, can ever be for the public safety.

Further, we are alarmed that a significant portion of the crack cocaine manufactured for use in reverse-sting operations was lost. As the district court in *Kelly* stated:

> Even more disturbing is the fact that some of the "crack," which is made in batches of 1200 or more rocks, escapes into the community where the reverse sting operations are conducted. The police simply cannot account for all of the rocks which are made for the purpose of the reverse stings.

593 So.2d at 1062. In this case, the State conceded at oral argument that some of the crack cocaine was lost during the reverse-sting operations. This fact is particularly outrageous considering that the police conducted the reverse-sting operation within one thousand feet of a high school. This lack of strict inventory control over the crack cocaine resulted in an undetermined amount of the dangerous drug escaping into the community. We find that this is n anomalous consequence inasmuch as the Sheriff is responsible for protecting the community.

Finally, the State argues that even if the Broward County Sheriff's Office illegally manufactured crack cocaine, Williams' conviction should stand. At oral argument, the State conceded that it did not condone the Sheriff's practice of manufacturing crack cocaine for reverse-sting operations. However, the State argues that this conduct can be deterred by prosecuting those law enforcement officers involved in the manufacture of crack cocaine, rather than overturning Williams' conviction. We find this argument without merit, especially in light of the State's concession that no law enforcement officials have been charged with illegally manufacturing crack cocaine. Moreover, the protection of due process rights requires that the courts refuse to invoke the judicial process to obtain a conviction where the facts of the case show that the methods used by law enforcement officials cannot be countenanced with a sense of justice and fairness. The illegal manufacture of crack cocaine by law enforcement officials violates this Court's sense of justice and fairness. As Justice Brandeis pointed out in *Olmstead v. United States*, 277 U.S. 438, 485, 48 S.Ct. 564, 575, 72 L.Ed. 944 (1928) (Brandeis, J., dissenting):

32

Decency, security, and liberty alike demand that government officials shall be subjected to the same rules of conduct that are commands to the citizen. In a government of laws, existence of the government will be imperiled if it fails to observe the law scrupulously. Our government is the potent, the omnipresent teacher. For good or for ill, it teaches the whole people by its example. Crime is contagious. If the government becomes a lawbreaker, it breeds contempt for law; it invites every man to become a law unto himself; it invites anarchy. To declare that in the administration of the criminal law the end justifies the means - to declare that the government may commit crimes in order to secure the conviction of a private criminal - would bring terrible retribution. Against that pernicious doctrine this court should resolutely set its face.

Thus, the only appropriate remedy to deter this outrageous law enforcement conduct is to bar the defendant's prosecution.

Accordingly, we approve the decision of the district court below.

It is so ordered.

BARKETT, C.J., and OVERTON, SHAW, GRIMES and KOGAN, JJ., concur.
McDONALD, J., dissents.

FN1. The stipulation contains written notations indicating that the policies and procedures of the Broward Sheriff's Office in paragraphs 3, 4, and 5 are unknown. However, the stipulation is clear that the manufacture of the crack cocaine was pursuant to proper procedures and was approved by Sheriff Nick Navarro.

FN2. Article I, section 9 of the Florida Constitution reads in pertinent part:
Due Process. --No person shall be deprived of life, liberty or property without due process of law. ...

FN3. In *State v. Glosson, 462 So.2d 1082 (Fla. 1985)*, this Court noted that the federal courts have been reluctant to allow the federal due process defense. Indeed, as pointed out by *Glosson*, "a recent federal circuit court stated that nothing short of 'the infliction of pain or physical or psychological coercion' will establish the due process defense." *Id. at 1084* (quoting *United States v. Kelly, 707 F.2d 1460, 1477 (D.C.Cir.), cert. denied, 464 U.S. 908, 104 S.Ct. 264, 78 L.Ed.2d 247 (1983)*).

FN4. The specific procedure used to make the crack cocaine has been deleted from the stipulation quoted in this opinion.

REVIEW

1. In sting operations, law enforcement officers may use drugs illegally manufactured by law enforcement agencies _____.
    a. never
    b. always
    c. only in cocaine cases
    d. only in reverse sting operations

2. If a person's due process rights are violated, on appeal their conviction will be _____.
    a. always upheld
    b. sometimes upheld
    c. sometimes reversed
    d. always reversed

3. Law enforcement agencies may do illegal acts _____.
    a. if their goal is legal
    b. if their goal is desirable
    c. both a and b
    d. neither a nor b

CASE

State v. O.C., 748 So.2d 945 (Fla. 1999).

Juvenile was adjudicated delinquent in the Circuit Court, Orange County, Bob Wattles, J., on finding that juvenile was guilty of attempted aggravated battery and misdemeanor battery. Juvenile appealed and the District Court of Appeal, Cobb, J., 722 So.2d 839, declared statute enhancing penalties based on defendant's membership in criminal street gang unconstitutional. The state appealed. The Supreme Court, Pariente, J., held that statute enhancing degree of crime based on membership in a gang punished mere association and violated a defendant's substantive due process rights.

Decision of District Court of Appeal Affirmed.

PARIENTE, JUSTICE.

We have on appeal the Fifth District's decision in *O.C. v. State, 722 So.2d 839 (Fla. 5th DCA 1998),* declaring section 874.04, Florida Statutes (Supp. 1996), unconstitutional. We have jurisdiction. See art. V §3(b)(1), Fla. Const.

O.C., a juvenile, was charged by an amended delinquency petition with attempted aggravated battery to cause great bodily harm, a third-degree felony, and battery, a misdemeanor. The Fifth District's opinion details the evidence presented at the adjudicatory hearing:

The victim testified that on January 29, 1997, he was getting off a bus at his stop. According to the victim, O.C. "grabbed me and threw me ... towards Kenny. And then he [Kenny] hit me in the face with his fist." The victim continued that "they [O.C. and Kenny] picked me up and threw me through the fence. They just took my arms and threw me." The fence was wooden and the victim's head went through it. The victim further testified that "then they just started kicking" him "on my head, my whole body." The attack lasted about five or ten minutes and then they left. According to the victim, another youth, Everett, who was present and watching, "screamed that this is a message for your brother or something." Pictures showing the injuries sustained by the victim were introduced into evidence. He suffered no broken bones but could barely open his right eye.

The victim stated on cross examination that Kenny and O.C. "did about the same amount" of kicking and beating on him. The victim reiterated that O.C. started the incident by grabbing him and throwing him towards Kenny. An eyewitness confirmed the victim's account of the incident.

At the close of the evidence, O.C. moved for a judgment of acquittal arguing the evidence was insufficient to establish an attempted aggravated battery, that at most O.C. committed a simple battery. The juvenile court denied the motion and found O.C. guilty of attempted aggravated battery and misdemeanor battery.

O.C. 722 So.2d at 840-41 (alteration in original).

Subsequent to the finding of guilty, the State moved to have O.C. declared a gang member for penalty enhancement purposes pursuant to section 874.04. O.C. opposed the State's motion, asserting that section 874.04 is unconstitutional "because it omits an intent requirement, violates free speech and freedom of association and imputes guilt by association." *O.C., 722 So.2d at 840.*

The trial court deferred ruling on O.C.'s constitutional challenge and heard the State's motion for "gang enhancement." *Id. at 840.* During the hearing,

[a] sheriff's deputy involved in gang surveillance testified that O.C. is a member of an Orlando gang known as Universal Mafia Crew (UMC). Additional members were identified. The deputy testified that O.C. told him while on the street that she was a member of UMC and in fact was the leader.

Another deputy sheriff who specializes in gangs testified that UMC has a hierarchy consisting of a godfather, godmother, bosses and foot soldiers. O.C. was the godmother. The gang had colors, met monthly and was implicated in other crimes. Several members of the gang had been arrested on felony charges including armed burglary, aggravated battery with a knife, possession of a short barrel shotgun and grand theft auto. At least three of the arrests had occurred within the past year.

Id at 841. After the hearing, the trial court denied O.C.'s constitutional challenge to section 874.04, found O.C. to be a criminal street gang member, and stated that O.C.'s third-degree felony and misdemeanor would be enhanced upward by one degree to second- and third-degree felonies pursuant to the provisions of section 874.04. The court then sentenced O.C. based on the enhanced felony. See *O.C., 722 So.2d at 841.*

On appeal to the Fifth District, O.C. challenged the constitutionality of the statute. In considering this challenge, the Fifth District framed the inquiry as whether the Legislature, "in accordance with due process principles, see *State v. Saiez, 489 So.2d 1125 (Fla. 1986),* [can] constitutionally enhance criminal penalties based on a criminal's simple association with others who may be criminals?" *O.C., 722 So.2d at 841-42.* The court concluded that such an enhancement punishes "mere association," and is unconstitutional on its face. *Id. at 842.* We agree with the Fifth District's conclusion that the statute is unconstitutional as a violation of substantive due process.

Chapter 874, the Criminal Street Gang Prevention Act of 1996, provides for enhancement of criminal penalties for a defendant who is a member of a "criminal street gang":

> 874.04 Criminal street gang activity; enhanced penalties. – Upon a finding by the court at sentencing that the defendant is a member of a criminal street gang, [FN1] the penalty for any felony or misdemeanor, or any delinquent act or violation of law which would be a felony or misdemeanor if committed by an adult, may be enhanced if the offender was a member of a criminal street gang at the time of the commission of such offense. Each of the findings required as a basis for such sentence shall be found by a preponderance of the evidence. The enhancement will be as follows:
>
> > (2)(a) A felony of the third degree may be punished as if it were a felony of the second degree.
> > (b) A felony of the second degree may be punished as if it were a felony of the first degree.
> > (c) A felony of the first degree may be punished as if it were a life felony.

§874.04 (emphasis supplied). A "criminal street gang" is broadly defined in section 874.03 as

> a formal or informal ongoing organization, association, or group that has as one of its primary activities the commission of criminal or delinquent acts, and that consists of three or more persons who have a common name or common identifying signs, colors, or symbols and have two or more members who, individually or collectively, engage in or have engaged in a pattern of criminal street gang activity. [FN2]

§874.03(1).

The Fourteenth Amendment to the United States Constitution, and article I section 9 of the Florida Constitution, protect a citizen's right to "due process of law." [FN3] In delineating the scope of a citizen's substantive due process protections, this Court explained in *Saiez*:

> The due process clauses of our federal and state constitutions do not prevent the legitimate interference with individual rights under the police power, but do place limits on such interference.
> ... [T]he guarantee of due process requires that the means selected [by the Legislature to achieve its legitimate police-power objectives] shall have a reasonable and substantial relation to the object sought to be attained and shall not be unreasonable, arbitrary or capricious.

489 So.2d at 1127-28 (emphasis supplied). *Saiez* further quotes with approval then-Judge Grimes' observation in *State v. Walker, 444 So.2d 1137, 1140 (Fla. 2d DCA),* aff'd, *461 So.2d 108 (Fla. 1984)*, that the statute at issue in Walker was unconstitutional because, " 'without evidence of criminal behavior, the prohibition of this conduct lacks any rational relation to the legislative purpose' and 'criminalizes activity that is otherwise inherently innocent.' " *Saiez, 489 So.2d at 1129.*

In *Saiez*, we found section 817.63, which prohibited the possession of machinery designed to reproduce credit cards, to be unconstitutional because it violated substantive due process. *Id. at 1127.* While we agreed with the State that the curtailment of credit card fraud was a legitimate goal within the scope of the state's police power, we found that the statute did not bear a "rational relationship" to this proper goal because "it fail[ed] to require proof of the intent essential to any crime such as showing that the equipment was possessed with an intent to put it to unlawful use. Instead the law penalize[d] the mere possession of equipment which in itself is wholly innocent...." *Id. at 1128* (emphasis supplied) (quoting *Delmonico v. State, 155 So.2d 368, 369-70 (Fla. 1963)*, which held unconstitutional a statute prohibiting the mere possession of otherwise legal spearfishing equipment.)

More recently, in *Wyche v. State, 619 So.2d 231, 237-38 (Fla. 1993)*, this Court invalidated a Tampa ordinance making it illegal to loiter in a manner manifesting the purpose of procuring sex for hire. Under the ordinance, a person who was a "known prostitute" could be convicted for beckoning to motor vehicle operators to stop. See *id. at 235.* The Court found that not only was the statute vague and overbroad, but it also violated a citizen's substantive due process rights because it " ' unjustifiably transgress[ed] the fundamental restrictions on the power of government to intrude upon individual rights and liberties' " by "punish[ing] entirely innocent activities" such as hailing a cab or signaling to a friend in an automobile. *Id. at 237* (quoting *Walker, 444 So.2d at 1138*).

Applying the reasoning of these cases, we conclude that section 874.04 violates a defendant's substantive due process rights because the statute subjects the defendant to conviction for a higher degree crime than originally charged, resulting in an increased penalty range, based only upon a defendant's "simple association" with others, who may or may not be criminals. *O.C., 722 So.2d at 842.* As explained by the Fifth District:

> The statute does not require any relationship between the criminal act, here attempted aggravated battery, and gang membership. Under the statute, the defendant's punishment is enhanced for the substantive offense plus gang membership without the need for any nexus between the particular criminal act and such membership.
>
> ....
>
> ... [Thus,] [t]his enhancement statute increases criminal penalties based on non-criminal acts. In effect, the increased punishment is based on association with other people, who may or may not have committed unrelated criminal acts
>
> *Id.*

For example, without a required nexus between the crime and the enhancement, an individual charged with a nonviolent crime, such as shoplifting, could be subject to the enhanced penalty range for a higher degree crime simply because the State establishes that the defendant is a gang member. The enhancement provided for by statute is extremely significant in that each crime is enhanced by one degree [FN4] so that a felony of the third degree is punished as if it were a penalty of the second degree, a felony of the second degree punished as if it were a felony of the first degree, and a felony of the first degree punished as if it were a life felony. See § 874.04(2)(a)-(c). [FN5] In this case, O.C. was sentenced based on a second-degree felony, although the crime with which she was originally charged, attempted aggravated battery to cause great bodily harm, is a third-degree felony. [FN6]

In reaching the conclusion that section 874.04 is unconstitutional, the Fifth District distinguished *People v. Gardeley, 14 Cal.4th 605, 59 Cal.Rptr.2d 356, 927 P.2d 713 (1996), cert. denied, 522 U.S. 854, 118 S.Ct. 148, 139 L.Ed.2d 94 (1997),* a decision from the California Supreme Court rejecting constitutional challenges to California's version of a gang enhancement statute. See *O.C., 722 So.2d at 842.* The California statute, unlike the statute in this case, provided that the defendant's sentence could be enhanced if the defendant committed the crime "for the benefit of, at the direction of, or in association with any criminal street gang, with the specific intent to promote, further, or assist in any criminal conduct by gang members." *Gardeley, 927 P.2d at 720.* The California Supreme Court concluded that this statute "fully comport[ed] with due process" because it did not impose criminal penalties for "mere gang membership," but only when the criminal conduct at issue was committed for the gang's benefit and with the specific intent to assist in criminal conduct by gang members. *Id. at 725.*

Unlike the statute in *Gardeley*, section 874.04 punishes mere association by providing for an enhancement of the degree of a crime based on membership in a criminal gang, even where the membership had no connection with the crime for which the defendant had been found guilty. We conclude that because the statute punishes gang membership without requiring any nexus between the criminal activity and gang membership, it lacks a rational relationship to the legislative goal of reducing gang violence or activity and thus fails to have a "reasonable and substantial relation" to a permissible legislative objective. *Saiez, 489 So.2d at 1128.*

Because we agree that section 874.04 is unconstitutional as a violation of substantive due process, we find it unnecessary to reach O.C.'s challenge to the statute based on First Amendment grounds. Accordingly, we affirm the decision of the Fifth District for the reasons stated in this opinion.

It is so ordered.

HARDING, C.J., and SHAW, WELLS, ANSTEAD, LEWIS and QUINCE, JJ., concur.

FN1. Section 874.03(2), Florida Statute (Supp. 1996), defines "[c]riminal street gang member," and lists eight criteria for classifying a defendant as a "gang member" as follows:

(2) "Criminal Street Gang Member" is a person who is a member of a criminal street gang as defined in subsection (1) and who meets two or more of the following criteria:

(a) Admits to criminal street gang membership.

(b) Is identified as a criminal street gang member by a parent or guardian.

(c) Is identified as a criminal street gang member by a documented reliable informant.

(d) Resides in or frequents a particular criminal street gang's area and adopts their style of dress, their use of hand signs, or their tattoos, and associates with known criminal street gang members.

(e) Is identified as a criminal street gang member by an informant of previously untested reliability and such identification is corroborated by independent information.

(f) Has been arrested more than once in the company of identified criminal street gang members for offenses which are consistent with usual criminal street gang activity.

(g) Is identified as a criminal street gang member by physical evidence such as photographs or other documentation.

(h) Has been stopped in the company of known criminal street gang members four or more times. §874.03(2)(a)-(h).

FN2. According to subsection 874.03(3), a "pattern of criminal street gang activity means":

> [T]he commission or attempted commission of, or solicitation or conspiracy to commit, two or more felony or three or more misdemeanor offenses, or one felony and two misdemeanor offenses, or the comparable number of delinquent acts or violations of law which would be felonies or misdemeanors if committed by an adult, in separate occasions within a 3-year period.

FN3. The Fourteenth Amendment of the United States Constitution provides in pertinent part that no State shall "deprive any person of life, liberty or property without due process of law." Article I, section 9 of the Florida Constitution similarly provides that "[n]o person shall be deprived of life, liberty or property without due process of law." The constitutional protection provided by the due process clauses encompasses both procedural and substantive due process. See, e.g., *Department of Law Enforcement v. Real Property, 588 So.2d 957, 960 (Fla. 1991)*.

FN4. Life felonies are punishable by a term of imprisonment for life if the life felony occurred after July 1, 1995. See § 775.82(3)(a) 3, Fla. Stat. (1995). First-degree felonies are punishable by a maximum term of imprisonment not to exceed 30 years, unless the offense is one that specifically provides for a life term. See § 775.082(3)(b). Second degree felonies are punishable by a maximum term of imprisonment not to exceed fifteen years, see section 775.082(3)(c), and third-degree felonies are punishable by a maximum term of imprisonment not to exceed five years. See § 775.082(3)(d).

FN5. Misdemeanors are also subject to enhancement by one degree so that a misdemeanor of the first degree may be punished as a felony of the third degree, see § 874.04(1)(b), thus raising additional concerns about the jurisdiction of the county and circuit courts in this circumstance. Further, the enhancement occurs at sentencing by the court, upon a finding by "the preponderance of the evidence" rather than as an element of a crime that must be proven beyond a reasonable doubt. We do not address these additional concerns at this time because of our decision that the statute is facially unconstitutional.

FN6. Though the trial court noted that the misdemeanor battery would be enhanced to a third degree felony, it only sentenced O.C. on the conviction for attempted aggravated battery to cause great bodily harm, enhanced from a third- to a second-degree felony. This was "because there was only a single incident and victim and only one charge could be pursued." *O.C. v. State, 722 So.2d 839, 841 (Fla. 5th DCA 1998)*.

REVIEW

1. Membership in a street gang is _____.
   a. a criminal offense
   b. not a criminal offense because it is based on a mere association
   c. acceptable to use to enhance punishment
   d. not a violation of due process

2. Gang enhancement is unconstitutional because _____.
   a. it is a violation of due process
   b. makes mere association a crime
   c. both a and b
   d. neither a nor b

3. The due process clause is found _____.
   a. in only the federal constitution
   b. in both the federal and the state constitution
   c. in neither the federal or the state constitution
   d. in only the state constitution

EQUAL PROTECTION OF THE LAWS

The constitution guarantees all persons equal protection under the law. It speaks to male and female alike, and it prohibits the use of race, religion, national origin, and/or physical disabilities to deprive any person of his or her rights. However, being deprived of a right is not the same thing as being treated unequally, and at times it may be constitutionally permissible to treat persons differently. For example, we do not allow those underage to drink alcohol, and we protect children by punishing defendants more harshly in some cases where the victim is a young child.

CASE

D.P. v. State, 705 So.2d 593 (Fla. 3d DCA 1997).

Juvenile was adjudicated delinquent, by the Circuit Court, Dade County, Thomas K. Peterson, J., Juvenile appealed. The District Court of Appeal, Cope, J., held that statute prohibiting person under age of 18 from possessing jumbo markers or spray paint on public property, unless accompanied by supervising adult, and from possessing items on private property, without consent of owner, did not violate federal or state constitutional due process rights of juvenile.

Affirmed.

Green, J., dissented and filed opinion.

Before COPE, GREEN and SORONDO, JJ.

COPE, Judge.

Dade County passed a comprehensive anti-graffiti ordinance, which forbids the sale to minors of spray paint cans and broad-tipped markers ("jumbo markers"). The ordinance provides that minors can possess spray paint or jumbo markers on public property only if accompanied by a responsible adult. On private property, the minor must have the consent of the property owner, but need not be accompanied by an adult. It is a misdemeanor for a minor to possess spray paint or a jumbo marker without the required supervision or consent.

D.P. challenges the facial constitutionality of the provisions of the anti-graffiti ordinance that restrict minors' possession of spray paint or jumbo markers. We conclude that the ordinance is constitutional and affirm the adjudication of delinquency.

In 1994, Dade County enacted a comprehensive anti-graffiti ordinance. Dade County Ord. No. 94-199, codified as Metropolitan Dade County Code §§ 21-30.01. The ordinance prohibits the making of graffiti and establishes the responsibility of property owners to remove graffiti promptly. Metropolitan Dade County Code §§ 21-30.01(c),(d).

The ordinance prohibits the sale of spray paint or broad-tipped markers to minors. See id. §§ 21-30.01(f)(1). A broad-tipped marker is an indelible felt tip marker having a writing surface of one-half inch or greater. See id. §§ 21-30.01(a)(1). This is a so-called jumbo marker. The ordinance does not prohibit the possession of ordinary sized felt tip markers.

Sellers of spray paint and jumbo markers are required to keep them in a place not accessible to the public, such as a locked display case. See id. §§ 21-30.01(f)(2)(III). Alternatively, the goods must be stored within sight of a work station which is continuously occupied while the store is open. See id. The rationale evidently is that graffiti artists frequently obtain spray paint and jumbo markers by shoplifting. See *Sherwin-Williams Co. v. City and County of San Francisco, 857 F. Supp. 1355, 1361-62 (N.D. Cal. 1994).*

The ordinance makes it a misdemeanor to possess spray paint or jumbo markers with intent to make graffiti. See id. §§ 21-30.01(e)(1). That portion of the ordinance applies to all persons, be they adult or minor. See id.

The ordinance then sets forth special provisions pertaining to minors. Subdivision (e)(2) of the ordinance addresses possession of spray paint and jumbo markers by minors on public property, while subdivision (e)(3) addresses possession on private property:

(e) Possession of Spray Paint and Markers

* * *

(2)   Possession of spray paint and markers by minors on public property prohibited. No person under the age of eighteen (18) shall have in his or her possession any aerosol container or spray paint or broad-tipped indelible marker while on any public property, highway, street, alley or way except in the company of a supervising adult.

(3)   Possession of spray paint and markers by minors on private property prohibited without consent of owner. No person under the age of eighteen (18) shall have in his or her possession any aerosol container of spray paint or broad-tipped indelible marker while on any private property unless the owner, agent, or manager, or person in possession of the property knows of the minor's possession of the aerosol container or marker and has consented to the minor's possession while on his or her property.

Id. §§ 21-30.01(e)(2)-(3).

A petition for delinquency was filed against D.P., alleging violations of subdivisions (e)(2) and (3). D.P. entered a plea of no contest, reserving the right to appeal the trial court order holding the ordinance constitutional.

II.

D.P. argues that the ordinance violates the due process clauses of the state and federal constitutions because the ordinance imposes a criminal penalty for a minor's possession of spray paint or jumbo markers without the State being required to show that the minor had any criminal intent. D.P. reasons that spray paint and jumbo markers are ordinary household items that have legitimate uses. D.P. urges that it is impermissible for the County to criminalize simple possession of ordinary household objects.

D.P. suggests that in its attack on graffiti, the County has two viable alternatives. First, the County can impose a criminal penalty for possession of spray paint or jumbo markers with intent to make graffiti. The anti-graffiti ordinance already does this. See id. §§ 21-30.01(e).

Alternatively, D.P. states that the County could constitutionally place a total ban on possession and sale of spray paint and jumbo markers by anyone, adult or minor. This is an approach that was taken in the City of Chicago and was held constitutional. See *National Paint & Coatings Association v. City of Chicago, 45 F.3d 1124, 1126 (7th Cir. 1995)*. D.P. reasons that if spray paint and jumbo markers cannot legally be purchased or possessed by anyone, then there would be no such thing as innocent possession of spray paint or jumbo markers. It would follow, therefore, that a criminal penalty could be imposed for possession of the forbidden objects. D.P. reasons, however, that so long as spray paint and jumbo markers are available in households in Dade County (because spray paint and jumbo markers can be lawfully purchased by adults), it follows that the

County cannot impose a criminal penalty on minors for possession of the same household objects.

A.

D.P. relies on a line of Florida cases that has struck down statutes and ordinances that have imposed a criminal penalty for ordinary innocent conduct.

In *State v. Saiez, 489 So.2d 1125 (Fla. 1986)*, the court struck down a statute which imposed a criminal penalty for the possession of credit card embossing machines, regardless of whether the machines were being used legitimately. See *id. at 1126.* The court explained that "the guarantee of due process requires that the means selected shall have a reasonable and substantial relation to the object sought to be attained and shall not be unreasonable, arbitrary, or capricious." *Id. at 1128* (citations omitted). The court concluded that " 'without evidence of criminal behavior, the prohibition of this conduct lacks any rational relation to the legislative purpose' and 'criminalizes activity that is otherwise inherently innocent.' " *Id. at 1129* (citations omitted). The court added the caveat that "there are instances where the public interest may require the regulation or prohibition of innocent acts in order to reach or secure enforcement of law against evil acts," *id. at 1129 n.3* (citation omitted), but concluded that the public interest did not so require in this case. See *id.*

Other examples relied on by D.P. include *Robinson v. State, 393 So.2d 1076, 1077 (Fla. 1980)* (invalidating statute prohibiting wearing of mask or hood because "this law is susceptible of application to entirely innocent activities . . .so as to create prohibitions that completely lack any rational basis"); *Foster v. State, 286 So.2d 549, 551 (Fla. 1973)* (prohibiting punishment of possession of a simple screwdriver as being a burglary tool, without any showing of criminal intent); *Delmonico v. State, 155 So.2d 368, 369-71 (Fla. 1963)* (invalidating statute prohibiting possession of spear fishing equipment in fishing preserve when possession was permitted on each side of the preserve and boats often needed to traverse the preserve to reach waters where spear fishing was legal; "When there exist other methods by which violations can be detected, halted and penalized, then the confiscation of equipment or outlawing its possession goes beyond the bounds of 'such reasonable interferences with the liberty of action of individuals as [is] really necessary to preserve and protect' the public interest."); *State v. Walker, 444 So.2d 1137, 1138-41 (Fla. 2d DCA 1984)* (invalidating statute which required prescription drugs to be kept in the container in which originally delivered because the statute "criminalizes activity that is otherwise inherently innocent. We do not believe that taking a lawfully prescribed medication from its original container and placing it in a different container, whether for convenience, dosage, or for some other personal reason, is criminal behavior."); see also *Wyche v. State, 619 So.2d 231, 233-37 (Fla. 1993)* (invalidating ordinance which prohibited "known prostitute" from engaging passers-by in conversation or stopping or attempting to stop motor vehicles by hailing, waiving, or gesturing, because ordinance did not require proof of unlawful intent and could be used to punish entirely innocent activities).

On the other hand, the court has also said that "[a]cts innocent and innocuous in themselves may . . . be prohibited, if this is practically made necessary to be done, in order to secure efficient enforcement of valid police regulations covering the same general field." *L. Maxcy, Inc. v. Mayo, 103 Fla. 552, 572-73, 139 So. 121, 129-30 (1932)* (citations omitted).

> Such inclusion must be reasonably required for the accomplishment of the legislative intent with respect to the ultimate object. It cannot be relied on to sustain a measure of prohibition so loosely or broadly drawn as to bring within its scope matters which are not properly subject to police regulations or prohibitions.

Id. at 573, 139 So. at 130 (citations omitted). In that case, the court upheld a statute which imposed a criminal penalty for use of arsenic spray on citrus trees, even though such sprays were harmless when used in small quantities and harmful only if used excessively. *Id. at 573-77, 139 So. at 130-31.* Given the magnitude of the hazard to the citrus crop, and the practical difficulty in monitoring the amount of arsenic spray being used by individual growers, the court upheld a blanket ban (and criminal penalty) for arsenic spray. *See id.*

B.

In our view, the anti-graffiti ordinance passes constitutional muster.

In the first place, this ordinance does not place an outright ban on possession of spray paint or jumbo markers by minors. The ordinance allows a minor to possess these items on public property, so long as the minor is accompanied by a responsible adult. See Metropolitan Dade County Code §§ 21-30.01(e)(2). Possession is allowed on private property so long as the minor has the consent of the owner. Rather than imposing an outright ban, the ordinance simply requires that possession be with supervision.

Furthermore, the cases relied on by D.P. involve situations in which a statute or ordinance made it a crime for defendant to possess certain property (a credit card embossing machine, a mask, a screwdriver, spear fishing equipment) even though it was legal for the defendant to purchase the same property. In the present case, it is unlawful for a minor to purchase spray paint or jumbo markers at all, and lawful to possess only if the minor is under supervision.

D.P. concedes that the County could constitutionally pass an ordinance that totally banned all spray paint and jumbo markers. Under this approach, which was taken in Chicago, no one (adult or minor) could buy or possess spray paint or jumbo markers anywhere in Dade County. See *National Paint & Coatings Association v. City of Chicago, 45 F.3d at 1126.* If a total ban is permissible, then surely it is permissible to take the less extreme measure of prohibiting sales to minors and allowing possession only with supervision. [FN1]

D.P. suggests that it is impermissible to treat minors differently than adults. That suggestion is clearly incorrect. There are many activities that are legal for adults but prohibited to minors: drinking, and driving under legal age, being the most obvious examples. Some supervisory requirements apply to minors that do not apply to adults, such as compulsory school attendance and the curfew ordinance. See *Metropolitan Dade County v. Pred, 665 So.2d 252, 253-54 (Fla. 3d DCA 1995), review denied, 676 So.2d 413 (Fla. 1996)* (curfew ordinance).

In the trial court order holding the ordinance to be constitutional, the Judge Petersen said:

> Having considered the cases and authorities cited by the Juvenile, this Court finds that the analysis under the due process and equal protection provisions of the Florida Constitution do not differ in a manner that changes the result of this case from the analysis under . . . the United States Constitution. Indeed, the cases cited by the Juvenile referred interchangeably to Florida and Federal due process and equal protection provisions. See *State v. Saiez, 489 So.2d 1125 (Fla. 1986).*
>
> No fundamental right is implicated in the possession of spray paint and jumbo markers. See *National Paint & Coating Association v. City of Chicago, 45 F.3d 1124 (1995)* ("One could scan the most wild-eyed radical's list of candidates for the status of fundamental rights without encountering spray paint."), *cert. denied, 115 S.Ct. 2579 (1995).* Nor is youth a suspect classification. *White Egret Condominium, Inc. v. Franklin, 379 So.2d 346, 351 (Fla. 1979)* ("The law is now clear that restriction of individual rights on the basis of age need not pass the strict scrutiny test, and therefore age is not a suspect class."); *Metropolitan Dade County v. Pred, 665 So.2d 252 (Fla. 3d DCA 1995)[, review denied, 676 So.2d 413 (Fla. 1996)].* ("[U]nder both the Florida and United States Constitution, children, due to their special nature and vulnerabilities, do not enjoy the same quantum or quality of rights as adults.").
>
> The Court's review is therefore limited to the rational basis test. The rational basis test does not turn on whether this Court agrees or disagrees with the legislation at issue, and this Court will not attempt to impose on a duly-elected legislative body his reservations about the wisdom of the subject ordinance. Instead, the rational basis test focuses narrowly on whether a legislative body could rationally believe that the legislation could achieve a legitimate government end. The end of controlling the blight of graffiti is obviously legitimate and the Juvenile does not challenge this fact.
>
> In addition, a legislative body could rationally conclude that the subject prohibition of possession by minors of spray paint and jumbo markers without supervision on public property or permission of the private-property owner would serve to control and limit incidences of graffiti. Indeed, the prohibition at issue is less restrictive than the prohibitions on spray paint and jumbo markers upheld in *National Paint*. The Court notes that juveniles can avoid the restrictions at issue

by using markers less than one-half inch in [writing surface] or markers that contain water-soluble ink.

For the above reasons, the Court finds that the challenged graffiti ordinance does not offend the due process or equal protection provisions of either the Florida or Federal Constitutions. Accordingly, the Juvenile's Motion to Dismiss is denied.

We concur with the trial court's ruling that the statute is constitutional.

Affirmed.

SORONDO, J., concurs.

GREEN, J. (dissenting)

Respectfully, I believe that sections 21-30.01(e)(2) and (3) of the Dade County Graffiti Ordinance are facially unconstitutional in that they are violative of the due process clause of both the state and federal constitutions.

I.

Section 21-30.01(e)(2) of the graffiti ordinance criminalizes a minor's mere possession of spray paint and broad-tipped markers on public property, highways, and streets, except when in the company of a supervising adult. Metropolitan Dade County, Code §§ 21-30.01(e)(2) (1994). Section 21-30.01(e)(3) of the ordinance criminalizes a minor's mere possession of spray paint and markers on private property without the consent and knowledge of the property owner. Neither of these subsections require a showing by the state of the minor's intent to make graffiti while he or she is in possession of the spray paint or markers. [FN2] Any minor who is found to be in violation of these sections is subject to a mandatory fine of $250.00 for a first offense, $500.00 for a second offense, and $1000.00 for each subsequent offense, and/or imprisonment in the county jail for a term not to exceed 60 days. See id. at §§ 21-30.01(e)(4). In the case of a minor, the parents or legal guardian are responsible for the payment of all fines, and their failure to do so will result in the filing of a lien against their property. See id.

Thus, a minor is subject to criminal penalties under the challenged subsections when traveling between two points where his or her possession of spray paint and jumbo markers is permissible. For example, the minor science student or school pep squad member who is given spray paint or markers by a teacher to complete a school project at home is subject to being fined and/or jailed under the graffiti ordinance if the student is stopped by a police officer en route home without being accompanied by an adult. Further, a minor who may be spotted by an officer in the minor's own yard spray painting a go-cart or model airplane is subject to having his or her actions criminalized under the ordinance if his or her parents are unaware of this activity or have not consented to the same. [FN3] Aside from the absurdity of these results under the ordinance, the ordinance violates the substantive due process rights of these minors in that it criminalizes the mere possession of inherently innocent items without requiring the state to show any intent to violate the county's anti-graffiti ordinance. As such, in accordance with a long line of established cases from our supreme court, these subsections of the anti-graffiti ordinance are an unconstitutional exercise of the county's police power.

II.

Initially, it should be noted that although the federal constitution contains no express substantive due process provision, the United States Supreme Court stated in *Bowers v. Hardwick, 478 So.2d 186 (1986)*, that:

> [D]espite the language of the Due Process Clauses of the Fifth and Fourteenth Amendments, which appears to focus only on the processes by which life, liberty, or property is taken, the cases are legion in which those Clauses have been interpreted to have substantive content, subsuming rights that to a great extent are immune from federal or state regulation or proscription.

Id. at 191. Since the due process provision of Florida's constitution is patterned after the due process provision of the federal constitution, see *Cash v. Culver, 122 So.2d 179, 182 (Fla. 1960)*; see generally *State v. Saiez, 489 So.2d 1125, 1127 (Fla. 1986)*, the Florida Constitution similarly provides an individual with substantive due process rights. Specifically, with regard to criminal statutes, substantive due process places limitations on the manner and extent to which an individual's conduct may be deemed criminal. See 1 Wayne R. LaFave & Austin W. Scott, Jr., *Substantive Criminal Law* §§ 2.12, at 208 (1986).

To withstand scrutiny under substantive due process, a statutory prohibition must be rationally related to a legitimate governmental objective or purpose. See *Lite v. State, 617 So.2d 1058, 1059 (Fla. 1993)*; *Saiez, 489 So.2d at 1128*; see also *L. Maxcy, Inc. v. Mayo, 139 So. 121, 130, 103 Fla. 552, 553 (1931)*. On the other hand, however, if the statutory provision infringes upon a fundamental constitutional right, the statute is subject to strict scrutiny, which is to say that it must be necessary to promote a compelling governmental interest. See *In re Forfeiture of 1969 Piper Navajo, 592 So.2d 233, 236 (Fla. 1992)*. Clearly, it cannot be realistically asserted (and D.P. does not so assert) that there is a fundamental right to the possession of spray paint or jumbo markers. Thus, the constitutional analysis and review of sections 21-30.01(e)(2) and (e)(3) must necessarily be confined to the rational basis test. [FN4]

Under the rational basis test, a statutory prohibition comports with due process if it bears a real and substantial relationship to the public's health, safety or morals, and is not unreasonable, arbitrary or capricious. [FN5] See *Saiez, 489 So.2d at 1127*; *In re Forfeiture of 1969 Piper Navajo, 592 So.2d at 236*; *L. Maxcy, Inc., 139 So. at 129, 103 Fla. at 570-71*; see also *City of St. Petersburg v. Calbeck, 114 So.2d 316, 319-20 (Fla. 2d DCA 1959)*.

I do not believe that it can be realistically maintained, as the state attempts to do on this appeal, that sections 21-30.01(e)(2) and (e)(3) of the graffiti ordinance were enacted for the protection of the public's health, safety, welfare or morals. They were clearly enacted solely for the protection of property within the county. Moreover, the act of criminalizing the possession of spray paint and/or jumbo markers by all unsupervised minors, regardless of their intent, is wholly unreasonable, arbitrary, and capricious and is not reasonably related to the county's legitimate objective in protecting property from graffiti. See *State v. Walker, 444 So.2d 1137, 1140 (Fla. 2d DCA), aff'd, 461 So.2d 108 (Fla. 1984)* (where then Judge Grimes succinctly stated: "Without evidence of criminal behavior, the prohibition of this conduct lacks any rational relation to the legislative purpose []" and "criminalizes activity that is otherwise inherently innocent."). For these reasons, I see no legal or logical reason why the subject subsections of the graffiti ordinance do not squarely fall within that same line of supreme court decisions which have consistently struck down laws which seek to criminalize inherently "innocent activity" without evidence of criminal intent. See *Wyche v. State, 619 So.2d 231, 235-37 (Fla. 1993)* (ordinance prohibiting a "known prostitute" from engaging in routine activities such as stopping automobiles and engaging passers-by in conversation violated substantive due process); *Saiez, 489 So.2d at 1127-29* (statute which criminalized mere possession of credit card embossing machine without regard to intent of possessor violated due process); *Robinson v. State, 393 So.2d 1076, 1077 (Fla. 1980)* (statute making the wearing of a mask in public a crime struck down where statute was "susceptible of application to entirely innocent activities" and was "susceptible of being applied so as to create prohibitions that completely lack any rational basis"); *Foster v. State, 286 So.2d 549, 551 (Fla. 1973)* ("It would be an unconstitutional act - in excess of the State's police power - to criminalize the simple possession of a screwdriver, just as much as it would be to criminalize the possession of such items as ladies' hat pins, automobile tire iron kits, et cetera, without first requiring that they first be *used* as burglary tools."); *Delmonico v. State, 155 So.2d 368, 368-70 (Fla. 1963)* (statute which criminalized the possession of spearfishing equipment violated due process because "the law penalizes the mere possession of equipment which in itself is wholly innocent and virtually indispensable to the enjoyment of the presently lawful and unrestricted right of appellants in common with the public at large to engage in spearfishing in waters on all sides of the area covered by the statute"); see also *In re T.C., 573 So.2d 121, 123 (Fla. 4th DCA 1991)* (where court construed statute prohibiting planting of a hoax-bomb to include element of intent which therefore precluded statute from being constitutionally infirm under "innocent acts doctrine"); *Walker, 444 So.2d at 1140* (without evidence of criminal behavior, statute prohibiting removal of lawfully dispensed controlled substance from its original container lacked any rational relation to the legislative purpose of controlling drug distribution). But *cf. L. Maxcy, Inc., 139 So. at 129-31, 103 Fla. at 572-77* (upholding law prohibiting use of arsenic spray on citrus fruit where such practice is of "general and predominantly evil tendency, so that it is impossible to distinguish the evil from the innocent in it except as to degree").

The majority first attempts to distinguish this long line of cases on the grounds that they all placed an outright ban on possession of the prohibited object or activity, and the challenged graffiti subsections permit a minor's possession of spray paint and/or jumbo markers under certain delineated circumstances. *Majority op. at 8.* [FN6] With all due respect, I do not believe that such a distinction exists, or if it does exist, is of any meaningful significance to this constitutional analysis. First of all, virtually all of the statutes in the "innocent acts" line of cases similarly did not place an outright ban on the proscribed items. See, e.g., *Saiez, 489 So.2d at 1126* (possession of credit card embossing machine prohibited only when credit card issuer has not consented to the preparation of the cards); *Robinson, 393 So.2d at 1076* (wearing of mask, hood or other device to conceal any portion of face, prohibited only within the public property of any municipality or county of the state); *Delmonico, 155 So.2d at 369, n.3* (use or possession of spear fishing equipment prohibited only on the surface of and under the waters in the area in Monroe County set forth in statute).

Further, I note that courts of other jurisdictions have similarly struck down laws that have prohibited the use or possession of items that have some lawful and unlawful uses, as being violative of substantive due process, if the prohibition is "too sweeping in encompassing activity which is wholly innocent." See LaFave & Scott, supra, at §§ 2.12(c). In *People v. Munoz,* for example, a criminal statute was enacted which prohibited anyone under 21 years of age, in a public place, from being in possession of any knife or sharp pointed or edged instrument which could be used for cutting or puncturing. [FN7] See *172 N.E.2d at 537.* A minor would not be in violation of this law:

> [I]f his possession of such knife or instrument is then necessary for his employment, trade or occupation, or if such possession is for use while he is engaged in or is proceeding to or returning from a place of hunting, trapping or fishing, and wherever required, is also carrying a currently valid license Issued to him under the provisions of section one hundred eighty of the conservation law, or if such person is a duly enrolled member of the Boy Scouts of America or a similar organization or society and such possession is necessary to participate in the activities of such organization or society, or if the said knife or instrument is carried under circumstances that tend to establish that its possession is for a lawful purpose, not however to include self-defense or amusement.

Id. The court found that although this statute was "designed to meet a limited, though serious evil," the statute was nevertheless an invalid exercise of police power because there was no reasonable relation between the evil and the means chosen. See *id. at 537, 540.* The court pointed out that the statute could apply to penknives, knitting needles, etc., which are "so far from being ordinarily for criminal purposes, that merely carrying them on the person cannot be regarded as a criminal or quasi-criminal offense." *Id. at 540.*

In *People v. Bunis, 172 N.E.2d 273 (N.Y. 1961),* the Court of Appeals of New York struck down a statute which prohibited the sale of coverless books and magazines, regardless of the circumstances. It observed that what was "wrongful [was] not the sale of coverless magazines, but rather their sale by a vendor who takes part in a scheme to defraud a magazine publisher." *Id. at 274.* Insightfully, the court also stated that:

[B]y denominating as criminal all sales, section 436-d necessarily tends to prevent corrupt sales. But, even were we to suppose that it had power to prohibit such corrupt sales, it is unreasonable and beyond the legitimate exercise of the police power for the Legislature to interdict all sales, permissible and illicit alike, in order to prevent those which are illicit. The Legislature may not validly make it a crime to do something which is innocent in itself merely because it is sometimes done improperly, sometimes attended by improper motives or done as part of an illegal scheme.

Id.

Similarly, the Louisiana Supreme Court in *State v. Birdsell,104 So.2d 148 (1958)*, addressed a statute which prohibited the possession of a hypodermic syringe and needles without regard to the intent of the possessor. The high court found the statute unconstitutional as an unreasonable and thus an improper exercise of police power in violation of the due process clause of the federal constitution:

Thus, we are concerned here with an object that is not inherently dangerous, noxious or harmful. Rather, the article in question, as is well recognized, is widely used for numerous beneficial and helpful purposes. True, it may be employed in the illegal administering of narcotics with deleterious results; however, so may numerous other generally advantageous appliances be used for ulterior motives. For example, the blow torch is frequently resorted to by burglars in the opening or [sic] iron safes. Yet, certainly it would not be reasonable for the Legislature (as a means of suppressing safe robberies) to denounce as a crime the possessing of a blow torch without, at the same time, permitting an accused possessor to show (in his defense) that his possession was for a lawful purpose.

Id. at 153-54.

III.

We are likewise confronted in this case with two inherently innocuous items (i.e, spray paint and jumbo markers) that are widely utilized both privately and commercially by minors and adults alike for a variety of innocent purposes as well as to make graffiti. It is true, as a general proposition, that the "[r]egulation of items that have some lawful as well as unlawful uses is not an irrational means of discouraging [criminal behavior]." *Village of Hoffman Estates v. Flipside, Hoffman Estates, Inc., 455 U.S. 489,497, n.9 (1982).* Although the regulation of such items is not per se irrational, the legislature still has constitutional constraints when enacting a blanket or conditional prohibition on the possession or use of such items. See *Saiez,* 489 So.2d at 1128-29; *Munoz,* 172 N.E.2d at 540; see also *People v. Nangapareet,* 210 N.Y.S.2d 446, 448 (Erie County Ct. 1960) ("[T]he judiciary must be ever alert to insure that [police] power not be exercised in an arbitrary and unreasonable fashion."). Our state supreme court has said that any prohibition against the possession of objects having a common and widespread lawful use

51

must be "reasonably 'required as incidental to the accomplishment of the primary purpose of the Act.' " *Delmonico, 155 So.2d at 370* (quoting *Caldwell v. Mann, 26 So.2d 788, 790 (Fla. 1946)*); see also *Saiez, 489 So.2d at 1128.* To be sure, sections 21-30.01(e)(2) and (e)(3) will simplify the state's burden of enforcing the graffiti ordinance against minors, who are deemed to be the primary makers of graffiti. [FN8] "Expediency, however, is not the test . . . ." *Delmonico, 155 So.2d at 370*; see also *Saiez, 489 So.2d at 1129.* I therefore cannot agree that the county can constitutionally criminalize all possession of spray paint and jumbo markers by unsupervised minors on public property, regardless of the circumstances, in the hopes of ensnaring the actual graffiti artists. Thus, based upon the "innocent acts doctrine" espoused in the *Saiez* line of cases, I do not believe that sections 21-30.01(e)(2) and (e)(3) of the graffiti ordinance can pass constitutional muster.

IV.

The challenged subsections of the graffiti ordinance are virtually indistinguishable from the statutes and ordinances repeatedly struck down under the "innocent acts doctrine" with one exception; the challenged subsections under the graffiti ordinance pertain solely to minors. For this reason, I believe that the central issue in this case is whether minors possess diminished substantive due process rights when it comes to statutes or ordinances that seek to criminalize the possession of inherently innocent items which can be used in criminal endeavors. Neither our state nor the federal supreme court appears to have squarely addressed this issue, but I do not believe that existing law supports the notion that the substantive due process rights of minors are not co-equal to those of adults under the "innocent acts doctrine." To begin with, all of the statutes, ordinances, etc., which were struck down as unconstitutional by our state supreme court under the *Saiez* line of cases were applicable to adults and minors alike. Thus, it could scarcely be argued that in the aftermath of these decisions, state and local legislative bodies could constitutionally reenact any such laws to pertain solely to minors.

The only decisions which I have located which have construed the substantive due process rights of minors under the "innocent acts doctrine" [FN9] are *In re T.C., 573 So.2d 121 (Fla. 4th DCA 1991)* and *People v. Munoz, 172 N.E.2d 535 (N.Y. 1961).* The holdings in both of these decisions recognize, albeit implicitly, that a minor's substantive due process rights are co-extensive with those of adults. [FN10] As stated earlier, the court in *Munoz* was reviewing a statute which prohibited minors under the age of twenty-one from carrying a knife or sharp object on public property. See *id. at 536.* The legislative findings indicated that the purpose of the statute was to prevent "youth crime and gangsterism." *Id.* The highest appellate court in the state of New York, nevertheless, struck this statute as unconstitutional, but signaled that this statute may have been salvaged with a scienter requirement:

If the draftsman of this local law had included carrying the article with criminal intent, there would have been less difficulty in sustaining it as subdivision 11 of section 722 of the Penal Law, Consol. Laws, c.40, was sustained in *People v.*

Pieri, *269 N.Y. 315, 199 N.E. 495* on the basis of performing the acts forbidden while harboring an evil intent.

Id. at 538. Ultimately, the ***Munoz*** court recognized that the only purpose of the challenged statute was to "enable [the] prosecution of those whom the police believe to be bad boys or girls," and that did not warrant conviction of a criminal or quasi-criminal offense. See *id. at 539.*

In the case of ***In re T.C.***, the Fourth District was confronted with a constitutional challenge to section 790.165 (1), Florida Statutes, which made it a felony for any person to manufacture, possess, sell or deliver a hoax bomb or to mail or send a hoax bomb to another person. See *573 So.2d at 122.* T.C., a juvenile, was arrested for violating this statute after a police officer discovered, in T.C.'s automobile, a three inch long brass pipe with one brass cap and one plastic cap. See *id.* The police officers testified that although the pipe was common in the construction trade, based upon their experience, they thought it might be a pipe bomb. See *id.* When they determined that it was not, T.C. was arrested for possession of a hoax bomb. See *id.*

T.C. argued on appeal, among other things, that this statute did not contain an element of intent, and thus was unconstitutional as violative of due process. The Fourth District reviewed the legislative history of this statute and determined that what the legislature had proscribed was the misrepresentation of a harmless device as a destructive device. See *id. at 123.* The court then reasoned that since misrepresentation requires knowledge and intent, the statute must be construed to necessarily include an element of intent. See *id.* Because the trial court had not read the statute to include an intent requirement, the case was remanded for a new trial. See *id. at 124.*

It is significant, however, that the Fourth District explicitly recognized in this juvenile proceeding that it was the element of intent that precluded the statute from otherwise being constitutionally infirm. Otherwise, reasoned the court, the statute would be susceptible of application to entirely innocent activities. See *573 So.2d at 123.* Citing to the ***Saiez*** line of cases, the court stated that "[t]he criminalization of inherently innocent objects or activity which interferes [sic] with the legitimate personal and property rights of individuals without evidence of criminal behavior has repeatedly been condemned as violative of due process and unconstitutional." *Id. at 124.*

Unlike the challenged statute in T.C., a scienter requirement cannot be read into sections 21-30.01(e)(2)-(3) because it affirmatively appears that it was the county's intention for them to be strict liability offenses as a supplemental law enforcement tool where minors are concerned. As was pointed out earlier, there is already a provision in the graffiti ordinance which makes it unlawful for both adults and minors to be in possession of spray paint and jumbo markers with the intent to commit graffiti. See Metropolitan Dade County Code §§ 21-30.01(e)(1). It is clear to me that the challenged subsections of the ordinance, under which D.P. was charged and adjudicated delinquent, were added as "catch-all provisions" to prosecute unsupervised minors under those circumstances where the state has no direct or circumstantial evidence of the minor's intent to make graffiti.

The majority points out that it is not constitutionally impermissible to treat minors differently from adults. *Majority op. at 9.* While that is certainly true, it is true only in some delineated areas. Our United States Supreme Court has recognized as a general proposition, that "[a] child, merely on account of his [or her] minority, is not beyond the protection of the Constitution." ***Bellotti v. Baird,*** *443 U.S. 622, 633 (1979)*; see also ***In re Gault,*** *387 U.S. 1, 13 (1967)* ("[W]hatever may be their precise impact, neither the Fourteenth Amendment nor the Bill of Rights is for adults alone."). For example, in criminal juvenile proceedings, juveniles are afforded the constitutional safeguards of proof beyond a reasonable doubt, notice of the charges, right to counsel, rights of confrontation and examination and the privilege against self-incrimination. See ***In re Winship,*** *397 U.S. 358, 368 (1970).* Notwithstanding these general principles, the constitutional rights of minors are still not co-equal with those of adults. The ***Bellotti*** court cited three reasons for not equating the constitutional rights of children with those of adults, namely, "the peculiar vulnerability of children; their inability to make critical decisions in an informed, mature manner; and the importance of the parental role in child rearing." *443 U.S. at 634.* The central rationale for finding diminished constitutional rights of minors, in limited circumstances, appears to be for the personal protection of the child or the personal protection of others from the acts of minors. For example, in ***T.M. v. State,*** *689 So.2d 443 (Fla. 3d DCA 1997)*, we found section 790.22(9)(a), Florida Statutes, which mandates the imposition of a five day detention period on any juvenile who commits any offense involving the use or possession of a firearm, to be constitutional notwithstanding the fact that an adult who similarly commits any such offense is not subject to the same mandatory incarceration period. See *id. at 444, 446*; §§ 790.22(9)(a), Fla. Stat. (1995). The statute in ***T.M.,*** unlike the graffiti subsections in this case, was attempting to regulate a minor's possession and/or use of an inherently dangerous item. See ***T.M.,*** *689 So.2d at 445-46.* In ***Metropolitan Dade County v. Pred,*** *665 So.2d 252, 253 (Fla. 3d DCA 1995), review denied, 676 So.2d 413 (Fla. 1996)*, we similarly upheld the power of the county to impose a curfew for minors, for the personal well-being of minors. Likewise, the laws which prohibit minors from drinking and driving under the legal age limit are constitutionally permissible because they are for the purpose of protecting minors from inherently dangerous activities.

Thus, although the constitutional rights of minors are not co-equal with those of adults under certain circumstances, I must conclude that those factors which generally tend to support a reduction of the rights of minors are simply not present in this case. The purpose of the challenged subsections of the graffiti ordinance is wholly unrelated to the personal protection of minors or others. The county's sole aim is to protect property from graffiti artists. While that is certainly a legitimate and laudable objective, I do not believe that it can be pursued by the county at the expense and deprivation of fundamental due process rights which both adults and minors share. Because I conclude that minors do not have diminished substantive due process rights under the "innocent acts" doctrine, the challenged subsections of this ordinance are no different than the statutes which have been repeatedly struck down by our supreme court under the "innocent acts" doctrine. For that reason, I believe that the challenged subsections of the graffiti ordinance must suffer the same fate.

FN1.   The trial court noted that based on anecdotal evidence, the graffiti problem appeared to be concentrated in the fifteen-, sixteen-, and possibly seventeen-year-old age group.   See also ***Sherwin-Williams Co. v. City & County of San Francisco***, *857 F. Supp. at 1360* (suggesting age range from twelve to twenty).

FN2.   The majority correctly points out that section 21-30.01(e)(1) makes it a misdemeanor for adults and juveniles alike to be in possession of spray paint and jumbo markers with the intent to make graffiti.   Majority op. at 3.   D.P., however, was neither charged or adjudicated delinquent under this subsection.

FN3.   The irony here is that the parents of this minor will be fined for their child's innocuous activity on their own private property and will have a lien placed against their property if they fail to satisfy the fine.

FN4.   Since no fundamental right is implicated in this case, the majority's reasoning that sections 21-30.01(e)(2) and (3) are constitutional because the county could constitutionally ban the possession of spray paint and jumbo markers respectfully misses the mark.

FN5.   Thus, within this context, the rational basis test does not simply focus "narrowly on whether a legislative body could rationally believe that the legislation could achieve a legitimate government end," as found by the learned trial court below.   See *Majority op. at 11*.   As one court put it: "It is for the courts to determine, not how the police power should be exercised, but whether there is reasonable relation between the statute or ordinance and the object sought to be attained." ***People v. Munoz,*** *172 N.E.2d 535, 539 (N.Y. 1961).*

FN6.   The majority similarly distinguishes the challenged graffiti subsections on the grounds that the prohibited items (i.e., jumbo markers and spray paint) may not be lawfully sold to minors and in the "innocent acts" line of cases, the items could be lawfully sold but unlawfully possessed.   See *Majority op. at 8.*   I am not certain that I understand the significance of this distinction and the majority does not elucidate on the same.   Nevertheless, while the sale of spray paint and markers to minors may be illegal under the ordinance, the gratuitous receipt of such items by minors from others (e.g., teacher, parent, peer, etc.) is not.   The fact that the sale of such items is prohibited still does not eliminate or negate the wide range of innocent uses of such items received gratuitously.

FN7.   This law was enacted based upon legislative findings that minors in possession of such knives or instruments in public places had resulted in the commission of many crimes and contributed to gangsterism and juvenile delinquency.   See ***Munoz,*** *172 N.E.2d at 537.*   It was further deemed that unless the possession of such items by minors were banned, there was an increased danger of public violence. See *id.*

FN8. Indeed, the state candidly concedes in its brief that the absence of a scienter requirement is a necessary law enforcement tool. According to the state, unless the graffiti artist is caught in the act, the ordinance is difficult to enforce.

FN9. This does not include those cases in which the law was enacted for the protection of the minor's welfare, i.e., curfew laws.

FN10. LaFave and Scott discuss the innocent acts doctrine in their treatise on substantive criminal law. See *supra,* at §§ 212(c). In discussing the constitutionality of these laws, they make no distinction at all between those laws directed at all persons (i.e., in **Bunis,** *172 N.E.2d 273,* and **Birdsell,** *104 So.2d 148),* and those directed at minors (i.e., in **Munoz,** *172 N.E.2d 535*), in terms of the quantum of the defendant's due process rights.

REVIEW

1. It is a violation of equal protection to treat persons differently based on _____.
   a. race
   b. gender
   c. religion
   d. all of the above

2. Persons may be treated differently with out violating the equal protection clause if it is _____.
   a. to protect children
   b. to punish more harshly if the victim is a child
   c. both a and b
   d. neither a nor b

FREE SPEECH AND EXPRESSIVE CONDUCT

The right to free speech is not unlimited. People may be restricted from making public certain information (such as names of victims) due to a stronger public policy interest of the government. For example, victims of sexual offenses have a right to privacy, and that right outweighs a person's right to free speech. The government's interest is to encourage the reporting of such crimes and to protect the safety of these victims. Even so, this does not allow the government to make criminal all situations where the name of a victim is published.

Some intimate relationships are also protected under the law. Nonetheless, "consenting adults" may not always be always constitutionally protected when engaging in certain behaviors even though both are adult and both consent.

CASE

State v. Globe Communications Corporation, *648 So.2d 110 (Fla. 1994).*

Newspaper publisher was charged with violating Florida statute mandating criminal sanctions for identifying sex offense victim in instrument of mass communication, claiming that statute was unconstitutional. Motion was granted by the County Court, Palm Beach County, Robert V. Parker, J., and state appealed. The District Court of Appeal, 622 So.2d 1066, affirmed, and State appealed. The Supreme Court, Kogan, J., held that Florida statute mandating criminal sanctions for identifying sex offense victim in instrument of mass communication is facially unconstitutional under free speech and free press provisions of United States and Florida Constitutions.

Affirmed.

KOGAN, Justice.

The State appeals ***State v. Globe Communications Corp.,*** *622 So.2d 1066 (Fla. 4th DCA 1993)*, in which the Fourth District Court of Appeal declared section 794.03, Florida Statutes, which mandates criminal sanctions for identifying a victim of a sexual offense in any instrument of mass communication, facially unconstitutional under both the United States and Florida Constitutions. [FN1] We affirm.

Globe Communications Corporation (Globe) was charged with two counts of printing, publishing, or causing to be printed or published in an instrument of mass communication the name, photograph, or other identifying facts or information of the victim of a sexual offense, in violation of section 794.03, Florida Statutes (1989). That section provides:

> No person shall print, publish, or broadcast, or cause or allow to be printed, published, or broadcast, in any instrument of mass communication the name, address, or other identifying fact or information of the victim of any sexual offense within this chapter. An offense under this section shall constitute a misdemeanor of the second degree, punishable as provided in § 775.082, § 775.083, or § 775.084.

The charges resulted from the Globe's identification of the Palm Beach woman William Kennedy Smith allegedly raped in 1991. In its April 23, 1991 issue and again in its April 30, 1991 issue the Globe published the alleged victim's name and other identifying information, contrary to section 794.03. The Globe had lawfully learned of the alleged victim's identify through standard investigative techniques. Prior to the Globe's identification of the woman, at least four British newspapers had published articles identifying her as Smith's alleged victim.

The Globe filed a motion to dismiss the information arguing that section 794.03 violates the free speech and press provisions of both the First Amendment to the United

States Constitution and article I, section 4 of the Florida Constitution. The Globe maintained that the statute is unconstitutional both on its face and as applied in this case. The trial court accepted both arguments and dismissed the information.

On appeal to the district court, the State conceded that the record supported the ruling that section 794.03 is unconstitutional as applied to Globe. Thus, the only issue before the district court was the facial constitutionality of the statute. *622 So.2d at 1067.* Noting its general agreement with the trial court's opinion, which it quoted in full, the district court affirmed.

Both the trial and district courts relied extensively on the United States Supreme Court's decision in *Florida Star v. B.J.F.*, *491 U.S. 524, 109 S.Ct. 2603, 105 L.Ed.2d 443 (1989)*. In *Florida Star*, a rape victim brought a civil suit against the Florida Star, a weekly newspaper, for publishing her name in violation of section 794.03, Florida Statutes (1987). The newspaper had obtained the victim's name from a publicly released police report. The Supreme Court held that The Florida Star could not be subjected to civil liability under section 794.03 for publishing truthful information that had been lawfully obtained. In reaching this conclusion, the Court looked to the principles articulated in *Smith v. Daily Mail Publishing Co.*, *443 U.S. 97, 99 S.Ct. 2667, 61 L.Ed.2d 399 (1979)*, for analyzing a state's attempts to punish truthful publication.

Under the Daily Mail standard, "if a newspaper lawfully obtains truthful information about a matter of public significance then state officials may not constitutionally punish publication of the information, absent a need to further a state interest of the highest order." *Daily Mail, 443 U.S. at 103, 99 S.Ct. at 2671.* Applying this standard, The Florida Star could not be held civilly liable under section 794.03, Florida Statutes (1987), unless the statute was narrowly tailored to further a state interest of the highest order. The Supreme Court concluded that the same interests relied on by the State in this case--the privacy of victims of sexual offenses; the physical safety of victims; and encouraging victims to report sexual offenses--were not sufficiently furthered by the automatic imposition of civil sanctions under the statute to establish a "need" within the meaning of *Daily Mail* for such extreme measures. *491 U.S. at 537, 109 S.Ct. at 2611.*

We agree with Judge Anstead, writing for the majority below, that the "essence" of the holding in *Florida Star* is that a state may not automatically impose liability for the publication of lawfully obtained truthful information about a matter of public concern. Before liability can be imposed, the state must provide for a "discrete determination of whether the prohibition on publication is justified under the particular circumstances presented." *622 So.2d at 1077.* As explained by the Supreme Court, a major problem with imposition of liability for publication under Florida's statute:

is the broad sweep of the negligence per se standard applied under the civil cause of action implied from § 794.03... [C]ivil actions based on § 794.03 required no case-by-case findings that the disclosure of a fact about a person's private life was one that a reasonable person would find highly offensive. On the contrary, under the per se theory of negligence adopted by the courts below, liability follows automatically from publication. This is so regardless of whether the identity of the victim is already known throughout the community; whether the victim has voluntarily called public attention to the offense; or whether the identity of the victim has otherwise become a reasonable subject of public concern--because, perhaps, questions have arisen whether the victim fabricated an assault by a particular person. Nor is there a scienter requirement of any kind under § 794.03, engendering the perverse result that truthful publications challenged pursuant to this cause of action are less protected by the First Amendment that even the least protected defamatory falsehoods: those involving purely private figures, where liability is evaluated under a standard, usually applied by a jury, of ordinary negligence. We have previously noted the impermissibility of categorical prohibitions upon media access where important First Amendment interests are at stake. More individualized adjudication is no less indispensable where the State, seeking to safeguard the anonymity of crime victims, sets its face against publication of their names.

491 U.S. at 539, 109 S.Ct. at 2612 (citations omitted).

Another deficiency recognized by the Supreme Court is the "facial underinclusiveness" of section 794.03, which raises "serious doubts" about whether the statute is serving the significant interests urged by the State in support of affirmance. *491 U.S. at 540, 109 S.Ct. at 2612.* As explained by the Court:

[s]ection 794.03 prohibits the publication of identifying information only if this information appears in an "instrument of mass communication," a term the statute does not define. Section 794.03 does not prohibit the spread by other means of the identities of victims of sexual offenses. An individual who maliciously spreads word of the identity of a rape victim is thus not covered, despite the fact that the communication of such information to persons who live near, or work with, the victim may have consequences as devastating as the exposure of her name to large numbers of strangers.

When a State attempts the extraordinary measure of punishing truthful publication in the name of privacy, it must demonstrate its commitment to advancing this interest by applying its prohibition evenhandedly, to the smalltime disseminator as well as the media giant. Where important First Amendment interests are at stake, the mass scope of disclosure is not an acceptable surrogate for injury. A ban on disclosures effected by "instrument[s] of mass communication" simply cannot be defended on the ground that partial prohibitions may effect partial relief. Without more careful and inclusive precautions against alternative forms of dissemination, we cannot conclude that Florida's selective ban on publication by the mass media satisfactorily accomplishes its stated purpose.

491 U.S. at 540-41, 109 S.Ct. at 2612-13 (citations omitted).

We agree with the trial court and district court below that the "broad sweep" and "underinclusiveness" of section 794.03 are even more troublesome when the statute is used to mandate criminal sanctions. In an attempt to avoid the obvious conclusion that these facial defects render the statute invalid under both the First Amendment and article I, section 4 of the Florida Constitution, the State asks us to effectively rewrite Section 794.03. The state asks us to read various affirmative defenses into the statute and to adopt appropriate jury instructions to narrow the sweep of the statute. As to the underinclusiveness problem, the State asks us to construe the term "instrument of mass communication" to include both media giants and non-media individuals who broadcast the victim's identity through non-media instruments, such as megaphones, fliers, and facsimile machines.

The State is correct that whenever possible we will construe a statute so as not to conflict with the constitution. *Firestone v. News-Press Publishing Co., 538 So.2d 457, 459 (Fla.1989)*. We will resolve all doubts as to the validity of the statute in favor of its constitutionality, provided that is consistent with the Florida and federal constitutions and with legislative intent. *State v. Stalder, 630 So.2d 1072, 1076 (Fla. 1994); State v. Elder, 382 So.2d 687, 690 (Fla.1980)*. Unlike Florida's Hate Crime Statute, [FN2] which we were able to uphold against First Amendment challenge in *State v. Stalder* by giving the statute a narrowing construction, extensive rewriting and broadening of the statute's scope would be required to rehabilitate section 794.03. Rewriting would be necessary because numerous affirmative defenses, which are entirely absent from the statute, would have to be added and defined by the Court. And, as noted by Judge Anstead, "[t]here is no indication the legislature intended any 'ifs, ands, or buts' to be read into the statute's unambiguous language" *622 So.2d at 1080*. Similarly, we cannot say that expanding the scope of the statute to include publications by non-media individuals would be consistent with legislative intent. Although we decline to rewrite section 794.03 to correct the defects outlined in *Florida Star*, we do not rule out the possibility that the legislature could fashion a statute that would pass constitutional muster.

Accordingly, we affirm the district court's decision holding section 794.03 facially invalid under the free speech and free press provisions of both the United States and Florida Constitution.

It is so ordered.

GRIMES, C.J., and SHAW, HARDING and WELLS, JJ., concur.

OVERTON, J., concurs in result only.

FN1. We have mandatory jurisdiction pursuant to article V, section 3(b)(1) of the Florida Constitution.

FN2. Section 775.085, Florida Statutes (1989).

REVIEW

1. The right to free speech applies to _____.
   a. individuals
   b. the press
   c. both a and b
   d. neither a nor b

2. A statute that is found to violate the right to free speech is _____.
   a. always unconstitutional
   b. never unconstitutional
   c. sometimes constitutional
   d. sometimes unconstitutional

CASE

Shapiro v. State, *696 So.2d 1321 (Fla. 4th DCA 1997).*

Defendant, a licensed psychologist, was convicted in the Circuit Court, Broward County, James I. Cohn, J., of sexual misconduct by a psychotherapist, and he appealed. The District Court of Appeal, Stone, C.J., held that: (1) evidence was sufficient to support conviction; (2) similar fact evidence regarding prior act of sexual misconduct by defendant was admissible; (3) statute prohibiting sexual misconduct by psychotherapist was not unconstitutionally overbroad; (4) statute was not unconstitutionally vague; (5) defendant's conviction did not violate his right to privacy under Florida Constitution; (6) conviction did not violate defendant's substantive due process rights; and (7) statute did not violate equal protection.

Affirmed.

Warner, J., filed specially concurring opinion.

STONE, Chief Judge.

The judgment and sentence are affirmed.

Appellant, a licensed psychologist, was convicted of sexual misconduct by a psychotherapist under section 491.0112, Florida Statutes.

Appellant was charged under subsection two of the statute, which prohibits sexual misconduct "by means of a therapeutic deception" which is defined to mean "a representation to the client that sexual contact by the psychotherapist is consistent with or part of the treatment of the client." § 491.0112(4)(b). The record reveals ample evidence from which the jury could find Appellant guilty of making such a representation.

Initially, we find no error in denying Appellant's motion for judgment of acquittal as the evidence demonstrates, prima facie, that Appellant used therapeutic deception to convince the female victim to engage in prohibited sexual conduct. *See **Lynch v. State**, 293 So.2d 44, 45 (Fla. 1974).* Appellant counseled the victim-patient for low self-esteem in an effort to help her avoid gaining weight. In the course of the counseling, Appellant raised issues involving the victim's sexuality. He told the victim that he wanted to prepare her for future sexual relationship, and suggested that her self-esteem would be improved by masturbation. During a subsequent session, Appellant asked the victim to masturbate in front of him, so he could "help" her; she complied. Appellant then digitally penetrated the victim. He told her that he did this so that she would feel good about herself, and that he only wanted what was best for her. He also warned her that "it has to stay between you and I because you cannot tell anyone, since I can get in trouble." On one occasion, Appellant tried to kiss the victim, and on another, he lowered his pants to demonstrate that she had "excited him." Appellant told the victim that when she lost weight, his "gift" to her would be that he would have sex with her.

The victim reported these actions to the police and allowed them to wire her and videotape a meeting at a restaurant. The police recorded Appellant tell the victim that he did not think what happened would be hurtful, since she was "obviously not with someone at the moment, needful, at the moment. You got me needful." Appellant also essentially admitted that he used his offer to have sex with the victim as an incentive for her to reach her goal weight. Later in the conversation, the victim states "But I came there to build my self-esteem but then I trusted you" – to which Appellant replied, "that's what I was trying to do.... The point is that one of the reasons I was doing that to help build--"

The state called a former patient who was treated by Appellant for stress 20 years earlier. She testified that during their first session Appellant went out of his way to make her feel good about herself. Appellant had asked the witness about her sexual history, representing to her, as he had to the victim in this case, that he was also a sex therapist. During the second visit, he continued to question her about her sex life. Then, he slid his hand up her skirt and inserted his finger into the witness' vagina, telling her that this would make her "feel good." She did not return.

We find no abuse of discretion in the court's admission of the prior act testimony. Section 90.404(2)(a), Florida Statutes (1991), provides:

Similar fact evidence of other crimes, wrongs, or acts is admissible when relevant to prove a material fact in issue, such as proof of motive, opportunity, intent, preparation, plan, knowledge, identity, or absence of mistake or accident, but is inadmissible when the evidence is relevant solely to prove bad character or propensity.

See also ***Williams v. State**, 110 So.2d 654 (Fla. 1959).*

Here, the witness' testimony reveals Appellant's common scheme, plan, or design to sexually exploit his patients while purporting to help them improve self-esteem and feel good about themselves. Similar fact evidence of collateral crimes may be admitted as relevant even if it is not uniquely similar. E.g., *Finney v. State, 660 So.2d 674 (Fla. 1995)*; *Bryan V. State, 533 So.2d 744 (Fla. 1988)*. See also *Gould v. State, 558 So.2d 481 (Fla. 2d DCA 1990), rev'd on other grounds, 577 So.2d 1302 (Fla. 1991)*; *State v. Ayala, 604 So.2d 1275 (Fla. 4th DCA 1992)*. In both instances the victims were married but separated from their husbands. Neither victim sought sexual counseling from Appellant, but rather he initiated their conversations about sex. Both victims were complimented and then digitally penetrated by Appellant in the office during a therapy session. See *Woodfin v. State, 553 So.2d 1355 (Fla. 4th DCA 1989)*; *Rossi v. State, 416 So.2d 1166 (Fla. 4th DCA 1982)*; *Townsend v. State, 420 So.2d 615 (Fla. 4th DCA 1982)*; *Anderson v. State, 549 So.2d 807 (Fla. 5th DCA 1989)*. See also *Ayala*. We thus find this other incident of alleged sexual misconduct sufficiently similar to be admissible as Williams rule evidence.

Appellant also raises several constitutional issues. As to these, we first note the general presumption of validity in favor of legislative acts, and the need to resolve doubt in favor of the constitutionality of statutes. *Carter v. Sparkman, 335 So.2d 802, 805 (Fla. 1976); Sarasota County v. Barg, 302 So.2d 737 (Fla. 1974); Scarborough v. Newsome, 150 Fla. 220, 7 So.2d 321 (1942)*. We reject Appellant's assertion that Florida Statute § 491.0112 (1993) is facially unconstitutional . Appellant alleges that: (1) the statute is overbroad in its potential application to speech and conduct in violation of the First Amendment, (2) the law is void for vagueness because the terms "psychotherapist" and "client" are defined too broadly, (3) subsection one of the statute, not at issue in this prosecution, violates Florida's constitutional right to privacy by prohibiting sex by consenting adults, and (4) that the statute violates equal protection by creating a distinct class of otherwise competent adults to receive heightened protection. We have considered and reject each of these and find the statute facially constitutional.

Appellant first alleges that the statute is overbroad. A statute is overbroad when it restricts speech or conduct that is protected under the First Amendment. *State v. Greco, 479 So.2d 786 (Fla. 2d DCA 1985)*. The Florida Supreme Court has recognized that, "the overbreadth doctrine that must be used sparingly, especially where the statute in question is primarily meant to regulate conduct and not merely pure speech." *Schmitt v. State, 590 So.2d 404, 412 (Fla. 1991); Wilkerson v. State, 401 So.2d 1110 (Fla. 1981)*. See also *Broadrick v. Oklahoma, 413 U.S. 601, 615, 93 S.Ct. 2908, 2917-18, 37 L.Ed.2d 830 (1973)*.

The Supreme Court of Colorado recently held a similar statute constitutional, and found that it was not unconstitutionally overbroad. See *Ferguson v. People, 824 P.2d 803 (Colo. 1992) (en banc)*. In *Ferguson*, the court upheld the constitutionality of a Colorado statute prohibiting the knowing infliction of sexual penetration by a psychotherapist on a client. The court found that the overbreadth doctrine did not apply because there is no fundamental constitutional right for psychotherapists to engage in sexual relations with their patients. The court reasoned that:

> Notwithstanding the elevated constitutional status accorded to certain privacy and associational interests, the Supreme Court had emphasized that there is no open-

ended immunity for consenting adults to engage in any and all types of sexual behavior. On the contrary, the court has emphasized that its fundamental-right jurisprudence does not stand for the proposition "that any kind of private sexual conduct between consenting adults is constitutionally insulated from state proscription." *Bowers v. Hardwick*, 478 U.S. 186, 191, 106 S.Ct. 2841, 2844, 92 L.Ed.2d 140 (1986). Thus, while certain private activities and intimate relationships may qualify for the elevated status of fundamental constitutional rights, it has never been the law that consenting adults, solely by virtue of their adulthood and consent, have a constitutionally protected privacy or associational right to engage in any type of sexual behavior of their choice under any circumstance.

Ferguson, 824 P.2d at 808.

However, Florida's statute differs from Colorado's statute in one critical respect: Colorado's statute prohibits sexual activity only when there is an ongoing professional relationship. Florida's statute prohibits a sexual relationship between a psychotherapist and patient even after the professional relationship is terminated, where "the professional relationship is terminated primarily for the purpose of engaging in sexual contact." § 491.0112(1). Appellant argues that the statute is overbroad since it does not allow anyone to pursue a romantic relationship no matter how brief the professional relationship or how sincere the feelings.

This aspect of the challenge is patently inapplicable to the charge against Appellant since his alleged sexual misconduct occurred while the professional relationship was ongoing. However, Appellant argues that he has standing to question the facial validity of a statute as a whole, since the statute would deter or threaten others not before the court from engaging in constitutionally protected speech or expression. See *ATS Melbourne, Inc. v. City of Melbourne*, 475 So.2d 1257 (Fla. 5th DCA 1985); *Wyche v. State*, 619 So.2d 231 (Fla. 1993). The overbreadth doctrine has been recognized as allowing persons who are themselves unharmed by the defect in a statute to nevertheless challenge the statute on the ground that it may be applied unconstitutionally to others. E.g., *Dimmitt v. City of Clearwater*, 985 F.2d 1565, 1571 (11th Cir.1993) (under overbreadth doctrine, car dealer, who displayed a government flag, had standing to attack ordinance on the ground that it places greater restrictions upon flags which do not represent a government body, even though dealer violated ordinance because of number, and not the type of flags displayed). See also, *Board of Trustees of State Univ. of N.Y. v. Fox*, 492 U.S. 469, 109 S.Ct. 3028, 106 L.Ed.2d 388 (1989).

It is established that the First Amendment protects certain fundamental intimate relationship rights. *State v. Conforti*, 688 So.2d 350 (Fla. 4th DCA 1997). See also *Roberts v. U.S.*, 468 U.S. 609, 104 S.Ct. 3244, 82 L.Ed.2d 462 (1984); *McCabe v. Sharrett*, 12 F.3d 1558, 1563 (11th Cir. 1994). However, we need not determine whether Appellant has standing to challenge subsection one of the statute because we find that the statute clearly is not overbroad. The Supreme Court has recognized that the overbreadth doctrine is "strong medicine" and must be used only in the most compelling circumstances. *New York v. Ferber*, *458 U.S. 747, 768, 102 S.Ct. 3348, 3360-61, 73 L.Ed.2d 1113 (1982)*. "Particularly where conduct and not merely speech is involved...the overbreadth of a statute must not only be real, but substantial as well, judged in relation to the statute's plainly legitimate sweep." *Broadrick v. Oklahoma*, *413 U.S. 601, 615, 93 S.Ct. 2908, 2918, 37 L.Ed.2d 830 (1973)*. "Thus, even if there are marginal applications in which a statute would infringe on First Amendment values, facial invalidation is inappropriate if the remainder of the statute...covers a whole range of easily identifiable and constitutionally proscribable conduct." *Parker v. Levy*, *417 U.S. 733, 760, 94 S.Ct. 2547, 2563, 41 L.Ed.2d 439 (1974)*, quoting, *United States Civil Serv. Comm'n v. National Ass'n of Letter Carriers*, *413 U.S. 548, 580-81, 93 S.Ct. 2880, 2898, 37 L.Ed.2d 796 (1973)*. The courts "have never held that a statute should be held invalid on its face merely because it is possible to conceive of a single impermissible application." *Broadrick*, *413 U.S. at 630, 93 S.Ct. at 2925* (Brennan, J., dissenting). In the instant case, the statute's legitimate reach clearly dwarfs its arguably impermissible application. We thus reject Appellant's overbreadth challenge because the overbreadth involved is not substantial when weighed against "legitimate state interests in maintaining comprehensive controls over harmful, constitutionally unprotected conduct." *Pallas v. State*, *636 So.2d 1358, 1363 (Fla. 3d DCA 1994), approved, 654 So.2d 127 (Fla. 1995)*. See *Young v. American Mini Theatres, Inc.*, *427 U.S. 50, 96 S.Ct. 2440, 49 L.Ed.2d 310 (1976)* (a statute's deterrent effect on legitimate expression must be both real and substantial).

We briefly address Appellant's assertion that the definitions of "psychotherapist" and "client" are unconstitutionally vague. The standard for testing vagueness under Florida law is whether the statute gives a person of ordinary intelligence fair notice of what constitutes forbidden conduct. *Brown v. State*, *629 So.2d 841, 842 (Fla. 1994)*. However, a party who engages in conduct that is clearly proscribed cannot complain of the vagueness of the law as applied to the conduct of others. *Plante v. Department of Bus. And Prof'l Regulation*, *685 So.2d 886 (Fla. 4th DCA 1996)*. See also *Wilkerson*. Here, Appellant's sexual misconduct was clearly proscribed and the evidence reflects that Appellant knew his activities were prohibited.

Appellant also asserts a right to protection under the Florida Constitution's right to privacy provision. Art. 1, § 23, Fla. Const. The privacy provision in Florida's Constitution embraces more privacy interests and extends more protection than does the Federal Constitution. *In re T.W.*, *551 So.2d 1186 (Fla. 1989)*. Because privacy rights are fundamental, once the provision is implicated, it is evaluated under the compelling state interest standard. *City of N. Miami v. Kurtz*, *653 So.2d 1025 (Fla. 1995)*. Under this standard, the state has the burden of demonstrating that the challenged regulation serves a compelling state interest and accomplishes its goal by the least intrusive means. *Winfield v. Division of Pari-Mutuel Wagering*, *477 So.2d 544 (Fla. 1985)*. We conclude that in this case there is patently a compelling state interest supporting the statute.

Furthermore, before a right to privacy attaches, a reasonable expectation of privacy must exist. *State v. Long*, *544 So.2d 219 (Fla. 2d DCA), approved, 570 So.2d 257 (Fla. 1990)*. We find that Appellant had no reasonable expectation of privacy in the challenged conduct. We recognize that the Florida Supreme Court has previously held that one has a reasonable expectation of privacy in carnal intercourse. See *B.B. v. State, 659 So.2d 256, 259 (Fla. 1995); Shevin v. Byron, Harless, Schaffer, Reid and Assocs., Inc., 379 So.2d 633, 636 (Fla. 1980)*. However, there is no legitimate reasonable expectation of privacy in using therapeutic deception to promote and engage in sexual activities with a patient. Thus, as applied, Appellant's right to privacy was not violated because he had no expectation of privacy in using therapeutic deception.

Neither have Appellant's substantive due process rights been violated. There clearly is no fundamental due process right for a therapist to use therapeutic deception to engage a client in sexual activities. In the absence of a fundamental constitutional right, the rational-basis standard of review is appropriate. *Ferguson*. Clearly the state may enact laws to protect particularly vulnerable members of society from sexual exploitation. *Jones v. State, 640 So.2d 1084, 1086 (Fla. 1994)* (upholding Florida's statutory rape laws). Clients seeking psychological advice are frequently in a particularly vulnerable state and may develop a dependency relationship with their therapist. *Ferguson at 810*. The state has a legitimate interest in protecting psychotherapy clients from sexual exploitation and in maintaining the integrity of this important public health service.

The statute is also not invalid for denying equal protection of law. In the absence of a suspect classification or invasion of fundamental interest, the constitution merely requires classifications to be rationally related to a legitimate state interest. *Haves v. City of Miami, 52 F.3d 918 (11th Cir. 1995)*. Because therapists are not a suspect class, and there is no fundamental right to use therapeutic deception to engage in sexual activities with clients, the rational basis standard of review is applicable to the classifications made in the instant case. In *Ferguson*, the Colorado Supreme Court concluded that prohibiting therapists from engaging in sexual misconduct with their patients did not violate equal protection, reasoning:

> The special character of psychotherapeutic treatment, involving as it frequently does a person who is in a vulnerable emotional state and likely to develop an extreme dependency relationship with the therapist, provides a reasonable basis in fact for the legislative decision to limit the scope of the statutory scheme to the psychotherapeutic relationship. This limitation is reflective of a legislative judgment that there presently exists a more urgent need to address the problem of sexual exploitation in the psychotherapist-client relationship than in other health-care professional relationships.

Id. at 811.

We also affirm as to all other issues raised by Appellant. Therefore, the judgment and sentence are affirmed.

SHAHOOD, J., concurs.

WARNER, J., concurs specially with opinion.

WARNER, J., concurring specially.

I concur in the affirmance of the conviction and the majority's resolution of the issues regarding the motion for judgment of acquittal and Williams rule evidence, and the constitutional arguments regarding the section of the statute under which appellant was charged and convicted. While I do not disagree with the overbreadth analysis of section one of the statute, I would not reach this issue as appellant has no standing to assert it. See *Broadrick v. Oklahoma, 413 U.S. 601, 613-15, 93 S.Ct. 2908, 2916-18, 37 L.Ed.2d 830 (1973); New York v. Ferber, 458 U.S. 747, 766-75, 102 S.Ct. 3348, 3359-63, 73 L.Ed.2d 1113 (1982); Sandstrom v. Leader, 370 So.2d 3 (Fla. 1979); State v. Summers, 651 So.2d 191 (Fla. 2d DCA 1995); Pallas v. State, 636 So.2d 1358 (Fla. 3d DCA 1994),* approved, *654 So.2d 127 (Fla. 1995).*

REVIEW

1. Having a sexual relationship with your therapist is _____.
   a. a crime
   b. not a crime if consented to
   c. both a and b
   d. neither a nor b

2. A statute found to be overbroad restricts _____.
   a. speech under the First Amendment
   b. conduct under the First Amendment
   c. both a and b
   d. neither a nor b

THE RIGHT TO PRIVACY

The right to privacy of an individual must be weighed against the State's interest in protecting its citizens. This issue often arises in the context of underage citizens where the government's interest in protecting children may outweigh certain rights to privacy. For example, minors are to be protected from sexually exploitation.

CASE

Jones v. State, 640 So.2d 1084 (Fla. 1994).

Defendants were convicted in the Circuit Court, Lake and Orange Counties, Jerry T. Lockett, J., and Helio Gomez, Senior Judge, of statutory rape. Defendants appealed. The District Court of Appeal , Harris, J., 619 So.2d 418, affirmed in part, reversed in part, and remanded and certified question as of great public importance. Review was granted. The Supreme Court, McDonald, Senior Justice, held that statutory rape provision is constitutional.

Decision approved.

Kogan, J., concurred and filed opinion.

McDONALD, Senior Justice.

We review ***Jones v. State****, 619 So.2d 418 (Fla. 5th DCA 1993)*, which upheld the constitutionality of section 800.04, Florida Statutes (1991). The district court certified the issue to this court as a question of great public importance. *Id. at 422.* We have jurisdiction pursuant to article V, section 3(b)(4) of the Florida Constitution. We approve the decision of the district court.

In case number 81,970, Quarry Jones, age eighteen, was charged and convicted of violating section 800.04, Florida Statutes (1991). Section 800.04 provides that any person who:

(1) Handles, fondles or makes an assault upon any child under the age of 16 years in a lewd, lascivious, or indecent manner;

(2) Commits actual or simulated sexual intercourse, deviate sexual intercourse, sexual bestiality, masturbation, sadomasochistic abuse, actual lewd exhibition of the genitals, or any act or conduct which simulates that sexual battery is being or will be committed upon any child under the age of 16 years or forces or entices the child to commit any such act;

(3) Commits an act defined as sexual battery under § 794.011(1)(h) upon any child under the age of 16 years; or

(4) Knowingly commits any lewd or lascivious act in the presence of any child under the age of 16 years, without committing the crime of sexual battery, commits a felony of the second degree, punishable as provided in § 775.082, § 775.083, or § 775.084. Neither the victim's lack of chastity nor the victim's consent is a defense to the crime proscribed by this section.

At trial Jones was denied the opportunity to raise consent as a defense. The court sentenced him to four and one-half years' imprisonment, to be followed by six months probation. The district court affirmed the conviction.

In case number 81,992, Rodriguez, age nineteen, and Williams, age twenty, were also charged with violating section 800.04. The parties stipulated at trial that the girls with whom the defendants had sexual intercourse were fourteen years of age and consented to having intercourse. Neither girl desired to prosecute and the charges were instituted by the sister in ***Rodriguez*** and by the mother in ***Williams.*** The trial court held section 800.04 unconstitutional as applied and the district court reversed. The district court certified the issue to this Court as one of great public importance.

We first address the merits of the State's argument that the petitioners do not have standing to assert the claimed privacy rights of the girls with whom they had sexual intercourse. In *Stall v. State*, 570 So.2d 257 (Fla.1990), cert. denied, 501 U.S. 1250, 111 S.Ct. 2888, 115 L.Ed.2d 1054 (1991), we held that the sellers of obscene materials had vicarious standing to raise the privacy rights of their customers. The petitioners in the instant case, like the sellers in *Stall*, stand to lose from the outcome of this case and yet they have no other effective avenue for preserving their rights. *State v. Saiez*, 489 So.2d 1125 (Fla.1986). Therefore, the petitioners have standing to attack the constitutionality of the statute under which they were prosecuted. See.,e.g., *Eisenstadt v. Baird*, 405 U.S. 438, 92 S.Ct. 1029, 31 L.Ed.2d 349 (1972); *Griswold v. Connecticut*, 381 U.S. 479, 85 S.Ct. 1678, 14 L.Ed.2d 510 (1965).

As evidenced by the number and breadth of the statutes concerning minors and sexual exploitation, the Florida Legislature has established an unquestionably strong policy interest in protecting minors from harmful sexual conduct. [FN1] As we stated in *Schmitt v. State*, 590 So.2d 404 (Fla.1991), cert. denied, 503 U.S. 964, 112 S.Ct. 1572, 118 L.Ed.2d 216 (1992), "any type of sexual conduct involving a child constitutes an intrusion upon the rights of that child, whether or not the child consents ...[S]ociety has a compelling interest in intervening to stop such misconduct." *Id. at 410-11*. In *Schmitt* the issue involved the constitutionality of a statute making it unlawful to possess material depicting sexual conduct by children. The issue in the instant case involves the constitutionality of a statute making it unlawful to have sexual intercourse with a child under the age of sixteen. In both of these cases, the State intervened in an effort to protect the health, safety, and welfare of children who are inevitably vulnerable to the sexual misconduct of others.

The district court stated that it would seem "disingenuous" to rely on *Schmitt* for the conclusion that "anytime a minor is seduced, sexual exploitation has occurred." *619 So.2d at 420 n.2*. We are of the opinion that sexual activity with a child opens the door to sexual exploitation, physical harm, and sometimes psychological damage, regardless of the child's maturity or lack of chastity. Therefore, in the instant case, it is appropriate to consider the child protection policies discussed in *Schmitt*. The petitioners argue that the statute is unconstitutional as applied because the girls in this case have not been harmed; they wanted to have the personal relationships they entered into with these men; and, they do not want the "protections" advanced by the State. However, neither the level of intimacy nor the degree of harm are relevant when an adult and a child under the age of sixteen engage in sexual intercourse. The statutory protection offered by section 800.04 assures that, to the extent the law can prevent such activity, minors will not be sexually harmed. "[S]exual exploitation of children is a particularly pernicious level that sometimes may be concealed behind the zone of privacy that normally shields the home. The state unquestionably has a very compelling interest in preventing such conduct." *590 So.2d at 410*.

The State has the prerogative to safeguard its citizens, particularly children, from potential harm when such harm outweighs the interests of the individual. *Griffin v. State, 396 So.2d 152 (Fla.1981).*

Despite its intimate character, sexual conduct is highly regulated activity. At any given point, the picture that emerges of the complex web of legal regulation is impressionistic, and some features are difficult to discern. The law of sex, however, can operate as a value generating force when those who create or who are governed by it perceive in the law an underlying vision of appropriate sexual conduct.

Martha Chamallas, *Consent, Equality, and the Legal Control of Sexual Conduct,* 61 S.Cal.L.Rev. 777 (1988). The legislature enacted section 800.04 based on a "morally neutral judgment" that sexual intercourse with a child under the age of sixteen, with or without consent, is potentially harmful to the child. *Stall, 570 So.2d at 261* (quoting *Paris Adult Theater I v. Slaton, 413 U.S. 49, 69, 93 S.Ct. 2628, 37 L.Ed.2d 446 (1973)).* Although the right to be let alone protects adults from government intrusion into matters relating to marriage, [FN2] contraception, [FN3] and abortion, [FN4] the State "may exercise control over the sexual conduct of children beyond the scope of its authority to control adults." *Anderson v. State, 562 P.2d 351, 358 (Alaska 1977)* (upheld statute prohibiting fellatio with a child under sixteen years of age, regardless of consent).

The petitioners contend that section 800.04 should be struck down given our decision in *In re T.W., 551 So.2d 1186 (Fla.1989),* in which we held that the right to privacy encompasses a minor's right to terminate a pregnancy. Under the statute at issue in *T.W.,* a minor was permitted to consent without parental approval to any medical procedure involving her pregnancy or her existing child, except abortion. We recognized in *T.W.,* for example, that a minor could be authorized to order life support discontinued for a comatose child. *Id. at 1195* (citing *In re Guardianship of Barry, 445 So.2d 365 (Fla.2d DCA 1984)).* Thus, the rationale for declaring a right of privacy in *T.W.* was based on the fact that a minor possessed a right of privacy with respect to other types of medical and surgical procedures. *T.W.* did not transform a minor into an adult for all purposes.

The rights of privacy that have been granted to minors do not vitiate the legislature's efforts and authority to protect minors from conduct of others. We agree with Judge Sharp and the legislature that Florida has an obligation and a compelling interest in protecting children from "sexual activity and exploitation before their minds and bodies have sufficiently matured to make it appropriate, safe and healthy for them." *619 So.2d at 424* (Sharp, J. concurring specially). Accordingly, we approve the decision of the district court upholding the constitutionality of section 800.04, Florida Statutes (1991), affirming the conviction in *Jones,* and remanding *Rodriguez* and *Williams* for appropriate action.

It is so ordered.

GRIMES, C.J. and OVERTON, SHAW and HARDING, JJ., concur.

KOGAN, J., concurs with an opinion.

KOGAN, Justice, concurring.

The case before us involves an issue so distinct from *In re T.W., 551 So.2d 1186 (Fla. 1989)*, that I am somewhat surprised this question ever became so confounded. I have considerable difficulty understanding how the privacy interests discussed in *T.W.* could be extended to the present facts. As I noted in *Schmitt v. State, 590 So.2d 404, 418-19 n. 17 (Fla. 1991)* (Kogan, J., concurring in part, dissenting in part), *cert. denied, 503 U.S. 964, 112 S.Ct. 1572, 118 L.Ed.2d 216 (1992)*, the issue before the Court in *T.W.* was the constitutionality of the state taking actions that tended to force some adolescents to continue pregnancies without also affording them an adequate level of judicial review. In effect, such action required some adolescents to face the "enormous personal, medical, familial, psychological, and financial concerns and risks that will fundamentally change an adolescent's entire life" without due process. [FN5] *Id.*

This conclusion was especially compelling in light of the fact that the state in *T.W.* had been very inconsistent: It still permitted adolescents to consent to or withhold consent for medical procedures even though the inevitable result was termination of a pregnancy, provided the procedure was not what commonly is described as an "abortion." *T.W., 551 So.2d at 1198-99* (Ehrlich, C.J., concurring specially). Such a surprising degree of self-contradiction revealed the state's scheme to be not only uncompelling, but very nearly irrational. The state in effect had allowed adolescents to obtain much the same result by less controversial methods while greatly restricting access to another more politically unpopular procedure.

If anything, the present case presents the reverse side of the issue posed by *T.W.* What is most at stake here is legalizing the sexual exploitation of children and young adolescents, [FN6] because that is one result that must inevitably follow if the statute is stricken in its application or otherwise. As the fragmented district court below seems to have concluded, the right of privacy in no sense authorizes such behavior. I also have reached essentially the same conclusion in an earlier opinion on a highly similar question of law:

> [T]he state's intervention in this setting is designed to prevent harmful physical and psychological effects of which the child may be wholly unaware. The state's interest in preventing such harm thus clearly outweighs whatever "right" children may have in consenting to this type of exploitation.

Schmitt, 590 So.2d at 418-19 n. 17 (Fla. 1991) (Kogan, J., concurring in part, dissenting in part).

In sum, the opinion in *T.W.* held that a young adolescent cannot be required to confront the wide-ranging risks of a pregnancy absent sufficient due process and consistency in the law. By the exact same rationale, the state in the present case can prevent children and young adolescents from being exposed to the wide-ranging risks associated with sexual exploitation and premature sexual activity. State actions that may force an already-pregnant minor to confront the risks of a pregnancy are quite a distinct issue from state actions that tend to enforce celibacy among the very young, thereby avoiding the risks inherent in premature sex--including unwanted or dangerous pregnancies.

In both cases, the sole question is achieving what is best for young people in light of the state's reasons for and consistency in imposing the restrictions it has chosen. Florida clearly has not been inconsistent in preventing sexual exploitation of unemancipated minors under the age of sixteen. Indeed, the vast array of child abuse, neglect, and exploitation statutes, as well as the strict criminal penalties for child pornography, show consistency of high magnitude. This Court has upheld statutory schemes that revealed a good deal more inconsistency than this one.

I am deeply troubled that an uncritical acceptance of the notion of youths "consenting" to sexual activity will merely create a convenient smoke screen for a predatory exploitation of children and young adolescents. This problem is not slight. Some studies, for example, indicate that 5 to 9 percent of males and 8 to 28 percent of females in the general population report that they were sexually exploited as youths. Gordon C. Nagayama Hall, et al., Sexual Aggression Against Children: A Conceptual Perspective of Etiology, *19 Crim.Just. & Behav. 8, 8-9 (1992)* (citing David Finkelhor, Child Sexual Abuse: New Theory & Research (1984)). Medical science already has compiled an impressive body of evidence showing just how staggering the cost of this exploitation is to each and every one of us.

For example, some researchers have documented the way in which childhood or early adolescent sexual exploitation can cripple a person throughout adult life, sometimes even resulting in psychiatric disorders of the gravest character. Lenore Terr, Too Scared to Cry: Psychic Trauma in Childhood (1990). Other studies have documented the link between exploitation of girls and those same girls being lured into a life of prostitution. Report of the Florida Supreme Court Gender Bias Study Commission, *42 Fla.L.Rev. 803, 894-905 (1990).*

Still other studies have concluded that exploitation of youths contributes to juvenile delinquency or other more serious criminal or violent activity, even many years after the fact. Mic Hunter, 1 The Sexually Abused Male 107-08 (1990); David Tingle, et al., Childhood & Adolescent Characteristics of Pedophiles & Rapists, *9 Int'l J.L. & Psychiatry 103, 115-16 (1986)*; Brandt V. Steele, et al., A Psychiatric Study of Parents Who Abuse Infants & Small Children, in *The Battered Child 103, 111* (Ray E. Helfer, et al., eds., 1968); David M. Greenberg, et al., A Comparison of Sexual Victimization in the Childhoods of Pedophiles and Hebephiles, *38 J. Forensic Sci. 432, 432 & 435 (1993).*

I. Can Children & Young Adolescents "Consent" to Sex?

Given the grave risks at stake here, I think this Court must look very very carefully at the notion of children and young adolescents "consenting" to sex. And I think any careful examination of this question reveals it to be a slippery slope of the worst magnitude. If *T.W.* is read as abrogating Florida law on the age of consent apart from the facts of that case then countless other legal problems immediately arise. Such a loose reading of *T.W.* potentially would mean that children of a young age could enter into contracts even if they lack the experience or means to do so; could marry at a very young age without parental or judicial consent; could purchase and consume tobacco and alcoholic beverages; could attend adult movies and purchase pornography; and much else. Nothing in *T.W.* supports these troubling scenarios.

Moreover, even those who sincerely argue that *T.W.* authorizes minors to consent to sex surely must concede that some minimum age exists at which a minor simply is incapable of consenting. I cannot believe, for example, that any responsible adult seriously thinks a six-year-old legally could consent to sex. Children of that age always lack the experience and mental capacity to understand the harm that may flow from decisions of this type. They may unwittingly "consent" to something that can ruin their lives, jeopardize their health, or cause emotional scars that will never leave them. I think most concerned adults and experts in the field would agree that this lack of prudent foresight continues in youths well into the teen years.

Moreover, well established law makes it necessarily irrelevant whether the underage persons in this or any other case had sufficient "maturity" to consent to sex. If the legislature or this Court created a "maturity exception" to the present statute, I think the statute then would be subject to a serious challenge on grounds of constitutional vagueness. Maturity is a concept about which even experts strongly disagree, and conceptions of maturity differ widely in the general population.

The difficulty of defining "maturity," for example, has been noted in the context of teens seeking judicially approved abortions. Katherine M. Waters, Judicial Consent to Abort: Assessing a Minor's Maturity, *54 Geo.Wash.L.Rev. 90, 109-17 (1985).* The difficulty is magnified a thousandfold in the present context: Here, the courts would be required to deal not only with the actual "maturity" of the minor as gauged by a judge, but also with the defendant's perception of the youngster's maturity and the degree to which the statute reasonably has put the defendant on notice that the specific sexual act was illegal. Determining "maturity" in this setting can only be an insurmountable problem: At each level of the analysis it involves subjective impressions and poorly definable terminology--difficulties greatly enhanced by the constitutional rigors imposed on criminal laws.

A maturity exception thus would enfeeble the statute. A defendant could argue that the statute provides insufficient notice of the proscribed conduct, thereby rendering it facially void for vagueness. See **State v. Ferrari,** 398 So.2d 804, 807 (Fla. 1981) (statute is unconstitutionally vague if persons of reasonable intelligence must guess what conduct is proscribed). A court then could be constitutionally required to accept that argument under federal or Florida law and strike the entire statute. In that way, a maturity exception could result in all minors--even those of very tender age--receiving no protection whatsoever from the statute.

I therefore think the legislature is both reasonable and prudent in creating a bright-line cut-off at a specific age. There most probably is no better way of eliminating the vagueness problem.

In other words, the legislature has acted pursuant to its authority to protect children and young adolescents when it set the age of consent for present purposes at sixteen. The legislature, I believe, can choose any age within a range that bears a clear relationship to the objectives the legislature is advancing. Some reasonable age of consent must be established because of the obvious vulnerabilities of most youngsters and the impossibility of legally defining "maturity" for allegedly precocious teens in this context. Because an age of consent is necessary, there is no good reason why the legislature cannot set it at sixteen for present purposes, which clearly is reasonable in light of the available psychological and medical literature.

Furthermore, the concept that children and young adolescents can "consent" to sexual activity is highly problematic on a purely psychological level: It ultimately rests on the mistaken assumption that children and young adolescents think the same way adults do and thus can make a meaningful choice in sexual matters. Because of this assumption, some adults erroneously conclude that a young person who did not actively resist or who seemed to have agreed to sex has consented--a notion that uncritically accepts the same general excuses many molesters offer for their misconduct. In this way the victim is given the blame. A widely-cited psychological study strongly indicates how wrongheaded these notions are.

In 1983, Dr. Roland C. Summitt [FN7] described how young people of either gender can be entrapped in continuing sexual exploitation that may seem to be consensual from an adult perspective, but that is not actually so when the psychological differences of children and young adolescents are taken into account. Youngsters suffering exploitation, Summitt said, commonly fail to disclose the sexual activity for a variety of reasons, including fear of the abuser and shame. These children or adolescents typically are overwhelmed by helplessness and thus may effectively be coerced into accommodating the abuser's sexual demands, partly because they may believe they must do whatever an adult tells them. Sexually exploited youths often fail to make any disclosure of their victimization for long periods of time, which erroneously leads some adults to believe that the children or adolescents "consented": In actuality, they commonly are afraid, have been threatened, lack the vocabulary to even describe what has happened, or are simply too ashamed to tell anyone. Children or young adolescents also may be directly or inadvertently pressured into retracting claims of sexual exploitation they have made, leading some adults to believe the youngsters are unreliable. Roland C. Summitt, The Child Sexual Abuse Accommodation Syndrome, 7 Child Abuse & Neglect 177 (1983).

In other words, what may appear to an adult to be consent or accommodation actually can be the desperate reaction of a young person who genuinely feels trapped, intimidated, and helpless. [FN8]

Another expert has noted an analogous though slightly different problem peculiar to sexual exploitation of young males. In this context, too, scientific study indicates that any focus on "consent" misses the point:

In many cases, the duration and nature of sexual encounters between a male child and his perpetrator bear the external trappings of consensual contact. Like a veil, the notion of consent conceals the underlying coercion and manipulation experienced by the victim. Loss of control, or being overpowered, a familiar theme of girls and women who have been sexually abused, may be emotionally inaccessible or inapplicable to male victims. The dynamic of vulnerability lies outside the emotional vocabulary of many "normal" males.

Mic Hunter, supra, at 77. In many cases, the boys may view themselves as somehow being "guilty" for what has happened: They cannot concede that they were victims who had lost control of a disturbing situation-- something many boys view as unmasculine. Id. at 79. For this reason, there may be serious under-reporting of abuse directed at young males. Id. at 91.

In light of the foregoing, I cannot see how the state's interest in preventing sexual exploitation early in life is anything less than compelling. This is not a case about anyone imposing a particular view of morality on others; rather, it is a case about what psychological science, sound policy, and constitutional law show to be essential for the protection of our young people. Beyond any question, the statute at issue here is a valid exercise of the state's powers.

II. The "Precedent" of *T.W.*

On another relevant point, I must express some surprise at the rather widespread practice in Florida of referring to a "majority opinion" in *T.W.* In actuality there was no "majority opinion" at all. The views of the Justices in *T.W.* were divided into five separate opinions, none of which garnered the four votes necessary to constitute a precedential "opinion" under the Florida Constitution. Art. V, §§ 3(a), Fla. Const.; *Santos v. State, 629 So.2d 838 (Fla. 1994)*.

Rather, the "decision" [FN9] of *T.W.* may be fairly described as three general holdings on which a majority agreed, albeit in piecemeal form in five separate opinions: (a) All seven justices agreed that adult women have a right to terminate a pregnancy during the earlier stages, as described in *Roe v. Wade, 410 U.S. 113, 93 S.Ct. 705, 35 L.Ed.2d 147 (1973)*; (b) at least six justices agreed that Florida's parental consent statute [FN10] read in its literal sense was unconstitutional, though two of the six felt that the deficiencies properly could be corrected through a judicial narrowing construction; and (c) at least four Justices--and possibly all seven--agreed that minors do not share the same

75

degree of privacy rights adults possess. *T.W., 551 So.2d at 1186-1205* (separate opinions). Beyond these three points, there was no "majority" view.

The last of the three holdings of *T.W.* has gone unnoticed by a considerable number of persons, apparently because it was contained chiefly in the four separate opinions appended to the plurality. For example, in his "specially concurring" opinion [FN11] Justice Ehrlich wrote:

> I recognize that in cases involving minors, the state has an additional interest in protecting the immature minor and the integrity of the family. *Id., at 1198* (Ehrlich, C.J., concurring specially).

In this vein, Justice Ehrlich felt that it would be possible for the state to impose at least some restrictions on abortions for minors that would be impermissible for adults. *Id. at 1199-1201.* Similar views were reiterated by Justice Overton, with Justice Grimes concurring:

> [A] minor has the disability of nonage, including the inability to contract.... Our right of privacy provision ... did not absolutely remove a minor's disability of nonage ... and those parts of the majority opinion in which I have concurred did not, in my view, so hold.

Id. at 1201 (Overton, J., concurring in part, dissenting in part). Likewise, Justice Grimes stated:

> [T]he constitutional rights of children may not be equated with those of adults....

Id. at 1202 (Grimes, J., concurring in part, dissenting in part). [FN12] Finally, Justice McDonald noted:

> [T]he judiciary does not have the power to extend the capacity to consent by a minor beyond that granted by the legislature.

Id. at 1205 (McDonald, J., dissenting).

In sum, at least four members of the Court agreed that minors do not have privacy rights equal to those of an adult, though there was no four-vote agreement on the actual extent of the minors' rights. I personally do not view this general conclusion as inconsistent with the plurality, which largely left the issue unaddressed. However, the plurality did note that "a minor's rights are not absolute. [FN13] *In re T.W., 551 So.2d 1186, 1193 (Fla. 1989)* (plurality opinion).

There is language in the opinions below that perhaps may suggest to an uncareful reader that *T.W.* gave minors the same right of consent that adults possess in sexual matters. Any persons who make that assumption should engage in a more precise reading of the three separate opinions below and of the five separate opinions in *T.W.*

The views of Justices Ehrlich, Overton, Grimes, and McDonald plainly show that *T.W.* has never supported the proposition that all minors have the same degree of privacy rights as adults. *T.W.* certainly and emphatically does not mean that all minors can consent to sex as though they were adults.

III. Conclusions

There is no other reasonable conclusion: This statute comports with every requirement imposed by the Constitution, is justified by the weightiest of reasons, and shows not one fragment of inconsistency with other related Florida laws. The actual "decision" in *T.W.* is not on point with this case either legally or factually, and never has been. I therefore concur with the majority.

> FN1. See, e.g., §§ 794.011, Fla. Stat. (1993) (making it a felony of varying degrees to commit a sexual battery on a minor); id., §§ 847.013 (prohibiting the sale or loan of videotapes depicting sexual conduct to minors); id., §§ 847.0133 (prohibiting the distribution of obscene materials to minors); id., §§ 847.0145 (prohibiting the sale or custodial transfer of minors with knowledge that they may be involved in portraying or engaging in sexually explicit conduct).

> FN2. *Loving v. Virginia, 388 U.S. 1, 87 S.Ct. 1817, 18 L.Ed.2d 1010 (1967).*

> FN3. *Eisenstadt v. Baird, 405 U.S. 438, 92 S.Ct. 1029, 31 L.Ed.2d 349 (1972).*

> FN4. *Roe v. Wade, 410 U.S. 113, 93 S.Ct. 705, 35 L.Ed.2d 147 (1973).*

> FN5. It deserves emphasizing that *T.W.* did not directly or indirectly address the propriety of teens engaging in sexual activities. The *T.W.* Court was concerned solely with the distinct question of what happens once a young girl already is pregnant. Some have argued that recognizing a minor's right to an abortion, however limited that right may be, necessarily means there is a corresponding right for minors to engage in "consensual" sex. Such an argument is no different than saying that, because minors have a right to consent to alcohol- and drug-abuse treatment, §§ 397.601, Fla. Stat. (1991), they also must have a right to consume alcohol and ingest drugs in the first instance. This is an insupportable brand of logic. Absent sound reasons to the contrary, we do not deny substance-abusing children the treatment available to adults merely because of the youthful folly of becoming addicted. Nor do we thereby condone the folly itself. Likewise, sex in early adolescence is a dangerous folly that the state clearly does not condone; but once a girl is pregnant, very different issues and dangers of a completely different magnitude arise. *T.W.*, in sum, does not create a right for young adolescents to "consent" to sex.

> FN6. I recognize that some of the parties attempt to distinguish "consensual" sex with minors from "exploitation." For reasons more fully developed in Part I. below, I must respectfully disagree. The relevant psychological literature strongly

indicates this is a distinction without a difference in the case of children. Moreover, the question of "consent" is bound up with the problem of a minor's "maturity," which also is highly problematic in the present context for reasons noted below in Part I.

FN7. When his study of this subject was issued, Dr. Summitt was clinical assistant professor of psychiatry at the Harbor-UCLA Medical Center in Torrance, California.

FN8. I recognize that child sexual abuse accommodation syndrome has been controversial in other states when used to help prove child sexual exploitation in a criminal context. E.g., *State v. Foret, 628 So.2d 1116 (La. 1993)*. However, the controversy stems in part from the unusually severe burden of proof the state must shoulder in a prosecution or from the strict procedural rules of a criminal trial, which may differ from Florida's. Dr. Summitt's study is widely respected on a psychological and sociological level. It thus has strong value for present purposes, where I am attempting to identify the broader societal impact of childhood sexual exploitation.

FN9. We have noted elsewhere that a "decision" is the result or results approved by at least four members of the Court in a case. An "opinion," which is the analysis supporting a decision, can constitute precedent only to the extent at least four Justices have concurred in it. *Santos v. State, 629 So.2d 838 (Fla. 1994)*. It thus is possible for a case to result in a "decision" even if there is no "majority opinion," as happened in *T.W.*

FN10. The statute required parental consent before a minor could obtain an abortion, subject to some exceptions. See §§ 390.001(4), Fla. Stat. (Supp. 1988).

FN11. By customary practice of the Court, a "specially concurring" or "concurring specially" opinion is one in which a Justice elaborates on or explains some aspect of the plurality or majority opinion to which it is attached. A specially concurring opinion also sometimes may express reservations about some aspect of the plurality or majority's analysis, as Justice Ehrlich did. When this happens with a plurality opinion, there obviously is no fourth vote and thus no binding "decision" or "opinion" with respect to any portion of the plurality about which the specially concurring opinion has stated a reservation. However, a specially concurring opinion typically agrees with the result and general thrust of the plurality or majority, as Justice Ehrlich's did.

FN12. Justice Grimes at one point did state his belief that a majority of the Court "has said that the state's interest in regulating abortions is no different with respect to minors than it is with adults." *In re T.W., 551 So.2d 1186, 1203 (Fla. 1989)*. That is true if the particular facts of *T.W.* are taken into account, especially the inconsistency in the relevant statutes that helped sway Justice

Ehrlich. However, it remains clear that at least four members of the Court agreed that the privacy rights of children and adults are not coequal in every situation.

FN13. Some have noted that *T.W.*'s plurality recognized that minors possess constitutional rights. This certainly is true. But many seem to have overlooked that the plurality did not say whether the rights were as broad as those of adults or what the scope actually was. I agree that constitutional rights of minors are not nugatory. Rather, they are subject to the degree of diminishment necessary to provide children the protection required by their diminished ability to make considered and meaningful choices in light of the state's interests and the law's consistency. This is peculiarly true for the right of privacy, which by its very nature protects the right of choice in matters of personal life. That right necessarily must be diminished to the extent that a considered and meaningful choice is not possible, which certainly is the case with children becoming involved in sexual activity.

REVIEW

1. Statutory rape _____.
    a. is a crime
    b. is not a crime
    c. is not a crime if the victim consents
    d. both a and c

2. The age of consent in Florida is _____.
    a. 15
    b. 16
    c. 18
    d. 14

3. Statutory rape includes _____.
    a. fondling
    b. sexual intercourse
    c. both a and b
    d. only acts that are not consented to

CRUEL AND UNUSUAL PUNISHMENT

Section 17 of the Florida Constitution prohibited cruel or unusual punishments prior to a revision made in 1998. The U.S. Constitution prohibits cruel and unusual punishments. Prior to the revision, section 17 of the Florida Constitution offered more protection than the U.S. Constitution for citizens to be free from certain punishments. The Florida Constitution also specifically addresses methods of execution. Lethal injection is now an alternative to death in the electric chair.

CASE

Brennan v. State, 754 So.2d 1 (Fla. 1999)

Defendant was convicted in the Circuit Court, Lee County, William J. Nelson, J,. of first-degree murder and was sentenced to death. Defendant appealed. The Supreme Court held that: (1) medical examiner who had not performed victim's autopsy could testify as to the victim's cause of death; (2) defendant's silence in the case of co-defendant's statements amounted to an admission by acquiescence; and (3) death penalty is cruel and unusual punishment under the age of 17.

Conviction affirmed; death penalty vacated and reduced to life imprisonment.

Anstead, J., filed a specially concurring opinion in which Kogan, Senior Justice joined.

Harding, C.J., filed and opinion concurring in part and dissenting in part in which Wells, J., and Overton, Senior Justice, joined.

Wells, J., filed an opinion concurring in part and dissenting in part.

PER CURIAM

We have on appeal the judgment and sentence of the trial court imposing the death penalty upon Keith Brennan, who was sixteen years old at the time of the crime. We have jurisdiction pursuant to article V, section 3(b)(1) of the Florida Constitution. For the reasons expressed below, we affirm the conviction and sentences imposed upon Brennan, with the exception that the death penalty is vacated and his sentence reduced to life imprisonment without the possibility of parole. We affirmed the conviction and death sentence for Brennan's codefendant, Joshua Nelson. *See Nelson v. State, 748 So.2d 237 (Fla. 1999).*

I. FACTS

The evidence presented at trial, viewed in the light most favorable to the State, established the following facts. Brennan, age sixteen, and Nelson, age eighteen, wanted to leave Cape Coral and travel to Fort Lauderdale. The two devised a plan to steal Tommy Owens' car. On March 10, 1995, Brennan and Nelson lured Owens out of his car and Nelson hits Owens with a baseball bat. After a number of hits, Owens eventually fell to the ground. Brennan attempted to slice Owens' throat with a box cutter. Brennan and Nelson also continued to strike Owens an number of times with the bat. The two eventually dragged Owens' body to nearby bushes where Owens later died.

Brennan and Nelson picked up Tina and Misty Porth, and the four left Cape Coral in Owens' car. After stopping in Daytona Beach, the four proceeded to leave the state, eventually ending up in New Jersey. At different times during the trip, Brennan and

Nelson informed Tina and Misty that they had murdered Owens. Tina and Misty both testified at trial.

Brennan and Nelson were apprehended in New Jersey. Brennan was charged with first-degree premeditated murder, first-degree felony murder, and robbery with a deadly weapon. Brennan gave a taped confession of his account of the murder, in which he admitted his involvement in the murder but denied that there had been any prior plan to kill Owens. The taped confession was played to the jury. Brennan was found guilty on all three counts.

At the time of the crime, Brennan was a sophomore in high school. He had no significant history of prior criminal activity, and his juvenile records only showed prior crimes against property. His codefendant was eighteen. Professionals who tested Brennan and his family members described him as a follower.

During the penalty phase, Brennan presented evidence that he was two years of age when his mother committed suicide. Prior to her death, his mother was confined to a mental institution and suffered from severe mental depression. When Brennan was approximately eight years of age, he was sexually abused by an older brother for a period of six months. He was small in stature, suffered from a speech impediment, and was often "picked on" by others. In 1993, he received inpatient treatment for drugs and alcohol addiction. Brennan had been using LSD the night before the homicide.

After hearing all the evidence, the jury recommended death by a vote of eight to four. The trial judge found four aggravators: (1) the capital felony was committed in the course of a robbery; (2) the capital felony was especially heinous, atrocious, or cruel (HAC); (3) the capital felony was committed in a cold, calculated, and premeditated manner without any pretense of legal or moral justification (CCR); [FN1] and (4) the capital felony was committed for the purpose of avoiding arrest. The judge also considered six statutory mitigators and twenty-five nonstatutory mitigators. The statutory mitigator of age (sixteen) was given great weight and the statutory mitigator of no significant criminal history was given moderate weight. The judge concluded that Brennan had failed to establish the statutory mitigators of (1) extreme emotional disturbance, (2) accomplice with minor participation, (3) acting under the domination of another person, and (4) limited capacity to appreciate the criminality of his conduct. The trial judge weighed each of the nonstatutory mitigators that were established. [FN2]

(FN1. and FN2. omitted)

While giving significant weight to Brennan's young age and moderate weight to his lack of significant criminal history, the trial court concluded that Brennan had "nonetheless wielded a baseball bat and a box cutter to murder another young man." In the end, the trial court followed the jury's recommendation and imposed the death penalty for the first-degree murder charge. The trial judge sentenced Brennan to 160 months imprisonment on the robbery charge. Brennan now appeals, raising fourteen guilt and penalty phase issues.

Although Brennan raises nine penalty phase issues, [FN3] one penalty phase issue is dispositive. For the reasons that follow, we conclude that the imposition of the death sentence on Brennan, for a crime committed when he was sixteen years of age, constitutes cruel or unusual punishment in violation of article I, section 17 of the Florida Constitution. [FN4] In reaching this conclusion we are guided by our decision in *Allen v. State,* 636 So.2d 494 (Fla. 1994).

(FN3. omitted)

FN4. In its motion for rehearing the State contends for the first time in this appeal that this Court must construe article I, section 17 consistent with the amendment to that section approved on November 3, 1998. That amendment changes the language of the constitutional prohibition from "cruel or unusual" to "cruel and unusual," mandates that this prohibition "shall be construed in conformity with the United States Supreme Court" precedent and provides that the section applies retroactively. Motions for rehearing may only be used to apprise a court of "the points of law or fact that the court has overlooked or misapprehended." Fla.R.App.P. 9.330(a). This argument is an entirely new issue neither raised nor briefed on appeal. See *Polyglycoat Corp. v. Hirsch Distributors Inc.,* 442 so.2d 958, 960 (Fla.4th DCA 1983). Further, this Court is presently considering the validity of this amendment in *Armstrong v. Harris,* No. 95,223 (Fla. certificate filed March 31, 1999), which was orally argued before the Court on September 2, 1999. Lastly, we have serious questions whether an amendment, which would adversely affect the substantive law in effect at the time of the original crime, could be applied retroactively without violating the United States Constitution's prohibition against ex post facto laws. *See, e.g. Gwong v. Singletary,* 683 So.2d 109, 112 (Fla. 1996); *State v. Lavazzoli,* 424 So.2d 321, 323 (Fla.1983).

In Allen, this Court found the death penalty to be unconstitutional under article I, section 17 of the Florida Constitution if imposed upon one who was under the age of sixteen at the time of the crime. Our reasoning in that case was straightforward:

[M]ore than half a century has elapsed since Florida last executed one who was less than sixteen years of age at the time of committing an offense. In the intervening years, only two death penalties have been imposed on such persons, and both these later were overturned.

There may be a variety of reasons for this scarcity of death penalties imposed on persons less than sixteen years of age. There may be public sentiment against death penalties in these cases, or prosecutors may simply be convinced that juries would not recommended death or the judge would not impose it. *We need not conduct a straw poll on this questions, in any event. Whatever the reasons, the relevant fact we must confront is that death almost never is imposed on defendants of Allen's age.*

In sum, the death penalty is either cruel or unusual if imposed upon one who was under the age of sixteen when committing the crime; and death thus is prohibited by article I, section 17 of the Florida Constitution. *Tillman v. State, 591 So.2d 167, 169 n.2 (Fla.1991). We cannot countenance a rule that would result in some young juveniles being executed while the vast majority of others are not, even where the crimes are similar.* Art. I, Sec. 17, Fla. Const.

636 So.2d at 497 (emphasis supplied) (footnotes omitted).

We further rejected the State's argument that the execution of young juveniles was no different than the execution of women because both seldom happen:

Nothing in the Constitution prohibits any court from taking notice of the peculiar condition and historical treatment of the very young. The law itself for centuries has recognized that children are not as responsible for their acts as are adults -- a conclusion also supported by the scarcity of death penalties imposed on the very young in this country.

Id. at 497 n.6.

In reaching our decision in *Allen*, we relied on article I, section 17 of the Florida Constitution, and not on either the Eighth Amendment of the United States Constitution or the United States Supreme Court's decision in *Thompson v. Oklahoma, 487 U.S. 815, 838, 108 S.Ct. 2687, 101 L.Ed.2d 702 (1988),* which held that execution of a defendant who was fifteen at the time of the crime was prohibited by the Eighth Amendment of the United States Constitution. [FN5]

(FN5. omitted)

Brennan asserts that our reasoning in *Allen* compels the same result here. We agree. In this case, the defendant presented the trial court with unrefuted data that at least since 1972, more than a quarter of a century ago, no individual under the age of seventeen at the time of the crime has been executed in Florida. In fact, our research reveals that the last reported case where the death penalty was imposed and carried out on a sixteen-year-old defendant was *Clay v. State, 143 Fla. 204, 196 So.2d 462 (1940),* over fifty-five years ago. Since 1972, the death penalty has been imposed on only four [FN6] defendants, other than Brennan, who were sixteen at the time of the crime. For each of the three defendants whose appeals have already been decided, the death penalty sentence was vacated.

Although not binding on our state constitutional analysis we are mindful that in the plurality opinion of *Stanford v. Kentucky, 492 U.S. 361, 380, 109 S.Ct. 2969, 106 L.Ed.2d 306 (1989),* five members of the United States Supreme Court held that it was not per se cruel and unusual punishment under the Eighth Amendment to impose the death penalty on an individual sixteen or seventeen years of age at the time of the crime. [FN9] Thus, the Court refused to categorically declare eighteen as the minimum age under the United State Constitution for execution to be a constitutional sentence. [FN10] *See id. at 380, 109 S.Ct. 2969.*

(FN9. and FN10. omitted)

However, there is an important aspect of the **Stanford** opinion that further supports our determination that the imposition of the death penalty in this case would be unconstitutional under both the Florida and United States Constitutions. The plurality in **Stanford** conclude that the constitutionality of capital punishment statutes depends not on the general state laws defining ages of legal disability, but on the "individualized consideration" given to the defendant's circumstances. *Id. at 375, 109 S.Ct. 2969.* [FN1] In order for the death penalty to have been constitutionally imposed on a defendant, the Court concluded that one of the "individualized mitigating factors that sentencers must be permitted to consider is the defendant's age." *Id.* The majority then observed that "the *determinations required by juvenile transfer statutes* to certify a juvenile for trial as an adult *ensure individualized consideration of the maturity and moral responsibility* of 16- and 17-year-old offenders before they are even held to stand trial as adults." *Id.* (emphasis supplied). The Kentucky and Missouri statutes under consideration of sixteen- and seventeen-year-old juvenile defendants before determining whether they should be transferred from juvenile court to stand trial as adults. *492 U.S. at 375-76 n.6, 109 S.CT. 2969.* The Kentucky statute additionally specified a minimum age for the death penalty at sixteen. *See id.*

(FN11. omitted)

Unlike the state statutes cited with approval in **Stanford,** the Florida statute neither sets a minimum age for the death penalty nor sets forth criteria to "ensure individualized consideration of the maturity and moral responsibility," *id. at 376, 109 S.Ct. 2969,* of those under eighteen before the child can be tried as an adult and sentenced to death. Section 985.225(1)(a), Florida Statutes (1997), provides that a child *of any age* may be indicted for a capital crime and, when indicated, "must be tried and handled in every respect as an adult ... on the offense punishable by death or by life imprisonment." Section 985.22593) further provides that "[i]f the child is found to have committed the offense punishable by death or by life imprisonment, the child shall be sentenced as an adult."

The Legislature's failure to impose a minimum age, the legislative mandate that a child of any age indicted for a capital crime shall be subject to the death penalty, and the failure to set up a system through our juvenile transfer statutes that "ensure[s] individualized consideration of the maturity and moral responsibility" render our statutory scheme suspect under the federal constitution and the reasoning of **Stanford** as is applies to sixteen-year-old offenders. *492 U.S. at 375, 109 S.Ct 2969.* This also distinguishes our statutory scheme form the Virginia Supreme Court. *See Jackson v. Commonwealth, 255 Va. 625, 499 S.E.2d 538 (1998), cert denied, 525 U.S. 1067, 119 S.Ct. 796, 142 L.Ed.2d 658 (1999).* The Virginia statute authorized transfer of juveniles over fourteen, provided for transfer hearings and "address[ed] the prosecution and punishment of juveniles in as much detail as the Kentucky and Missouri statutes" in *Stanford. Jackson*, *499 S.E.2d at 552.*

If given literal effect, our statutory scheme would unconstitutionally authorize the imposition of the death penalty on a child of any age. However, it is uncontroverted that imposing the death penalty n a defendant who was fifteen or younger at the time of the crime is unconstitutional. *See Allen, 636 So.2d at 497*; *Thompson, 487 U.S. at 838, 108 S.Ct. 2687.* While we have great respect for the legislative voice, it is the obligation of this Court to decide the question of whether a punishment proscribed by the legislature is unconstitutionally cruel or unusual by applying constitutional, not legislative, standards.

*****

Finally, In Florida, we have repeatedly stated that the ultimate punishment of death is reserved for the most aggravated and indefensible of crimes committed by the most culpable of offenders. *See, e.g., Urbin V. State, 714 So2d 411, 416 (Fla.1998); State v. Dixon, 283 so.2d 1, 8 (Fla.1973).* In addition, this Court is constitutionally required to perform a proportionality analysis:

> Our proportionality review requires us to "consider the totality of circumstances in a case, and to compare it with other capital cases. It is not a comparison between the number of aggravating and mitigating circumstances." *Porter v. State, 564 So.2d 1060, 1064 (Fla.1990), cert denied, 498 U.S. 1110, 111 S.Ct. 1024, 112 L.Ed.2d 1106 (1991).* In reaching this decision, we are also mindful that "[d]eath is a unique punishment in its finality and in its total rejection of the possibility of rehabilitation." *State v. Dixon, 283 So.2d 1, 7 (Fla.1973), cert denied, 416 U.S. 943, 94 S.Ct. 1950, 40 L.Ed.2d 295 (1974).* Consequently, its application is reserved only for those cases where the most aggravating and least mitigating circumstances exist. *Id.; Kramer v. State, 619 So.2d 274, 278 (Fla.1993)*

Terry v. State, 619 So.2d 274, 278 (Fla.1996). Thus, as the State acknowledges, this proportionality review requires us to compare similar defendants, facts and sentences. *See Tillman v. State, 591 So.2d 167, 169 (Fla.1991).* The difficulty in conducting a proper proportionality analysis in this case, because the death penalty has not been upheld for any other defendant who was sixteen years old at the time of the crime, highlights the inherent problems in upholding the death penalty under these circumstances.

The State urges that we should find that the impositions of the death sentence constitutional and also proportional because we have upheld the death penalty in other cases involving similar circumstances, citing to cases such as *Sliney v. State, 699 So.2d 662 (Fla.1997), cert denied, 522 U.S. 1129, 118 S.Ct. 1079, 140 L.Ed.2d 137 (1998); Walls v. State, 641 So.2d 381 (Fla.1997),* and *Hayes v. State, 581 So.2d 121 (Fla.1991).* However, the very case that the State points to as involving similar circumstances involve adults, not sixteen-year-old juveniles. The only common thread is the brutal and senseless nature of the murders.

These Cases demonstrate the dilemma posed by Allen: that death is almost never imposed on defendants who are Brennan's age and when the death sentence has been imposed, the death sentence had been subsequently vacated. There is no doubt that the murder in this case is a deplorable crime and one for which the defendant should spend the rest of his life in prison. However, we cannot impose the death penalty on this defendant who was sixteen at the time of the crime, consistent with our case law and our Constitution. *See Allen, 636 S0.2d at 497.*

Accordingly, the death sentence is vacated and reduced to life imprisonment without a possibility of parole.

It is so ordered.

REVIEW

1. The death penalty is cruel and unusual punishment if imposed upon a defendant under the age of _____.
        a. 21
        b. 19
        c. 18
        d. 17

THINKING CRITICALLY

1.   Read the Florida Constitution.

2.   Is there a corresponding prohibition against ex post facto laws in the Florida Constitution? What section can it be found in?

3.   Why do you think the Constitution was amended to address victim's rights? Would you have voted for it? Why or why not? What potential problems do you see?

4.   Find another amendment or addition to Florida's constitution. Which is it, an amendment or an addition? When did it occur? How? Why do you think the change was made?

5.   Do you agree with the *Jackson* opinion? Was his punishment more severe as a result of the new statute? How did the court get around that fact?

6. Why do you think the police stopped the individuals in *Papachristou*? What year did this case occur?

7. From where do our vagrancy laws originate? Why?

8. Do you agree with the holding in *Warren?*

9. Would it change the holding in *Williams* if the undercover officers used the cocaine in the form it was in? Should the result be different?

10. Does it violate due process to use confidential informants to set up drug transactions?

11. How far should law enforcement be allowed to go to make cases against drug dealers?

12. Find a case that was appealed on the basis of the constitutionality of a statute or the constitutionality of some action. Brief the case. Give the citation, a synopsis of the facts, the issue and the court's holding. Why do you think the court held as it did? Do you agree with the holding? Why or why not?

13. Should gang members be punished more severely? What requirements must be met to enhance a penalty without violating the Constitution? Is there a constitutional way by which gang related crime can be punished more harshly? If so, how?

14. What is the state's compelling interest to restrict a minor's right to privacy in the *Jones* case? How is the case distinguished from a minor's right to have the choice to have an abortion without parental knowledge or consent?

15. Can you differentiate between the right to engage in sexual activity and the right to vote? To drink? To drive?

16. What do you think of the arguments made in the dissent in **D.P.**? Should the punishment be a fine? If the minor doesn't pay the fine, is it constitutional to put a lien on the property owned by the parents if they fail to pay the fine?

17. Can you think of any circumstances where liability should be imposed for publishing the names of victims of crimes? Does the **Globe Communications Corporation** case say it's ever appropriate to publish names?

18. What makes a statute overbroad such that it would violate the First Amendment?

19. What standard did the court use in deciding the **Shapiro** case? Why did the equal protection argument fail? What other arguments did the defendant make?

20.   How did the Eighth Amendment to the U.S. Constitution and Section 17 of the Florida Constitution previously differ? Why do you think Florida's Constitution was broader? What is the purpose of Section 17 applying retroactively? What changed in Section 17? Do you agree with the changes? What is the process by which changes are made to the Florida Constitution?

CHAPTER 2 ANSWER KEY

REVIEW QUESTIONS

Jackson v. State
1. c

Papachristou v. City of Jacksonville
1. c
2. d
3. b

State v. Williams
1. a
2. d
3. d

State v. O.C.
1. b
2. c
3. b

D.P. v. State
1. d
2. c

State v. Globe Communications Corporation
1. c
2. a

Shapiro v. State
1. a
2. c

Jones v. State
1. a
2. b
3. c

Brennan v. State
1. d

CHAPTER 3

THE GENERAL PRINCIPLES
OF CRIMINAL LIABILITY:
THE REQUIREMENT OF ACTION

WORDS AS ACTS

Section 843 of Florida Statutes addresses the different crimes that result in the obstruction of justice.

Read the following statutem that defines the crime of resisting an officer without violence.

843.02   Resisting officer without violence to his or her person – Whoever shall resist, obstruct, or oppose any officer as defined in s. 943.10(1), (2), (3), (6), (7), (8), or (9); member of the Parole Commission or any administrative aide or supervisor employed by the commission; county probation officer; parole and probation supervisor; personnel or representative of the Department of Law Enforcement; or other person legally authorized to execute process in the execution of legal process or in the lawful execution of any legal duty without offering or doing violence to the person of the officer, shall be guilty of a misdemeanor of the first degree, punishable as provided in s. 775.082 or s. 775.083.

Many times law enforcement officers ask individuals for their name. Under certain circumstances, it can be a crime to give a false name. However, it is only a crime if the officer is executing a legal duty and the act of giving a false name obstructs that duty. The courts must review the officer's actions as well as the defendant's. If the false information is recanted prior to it interfering with the performance of the officer's duty, giving the false name is not a crime.

CASE

A.P. v. State, 760 So.2d 1010 (Fla. 3d DCA 2000).

An appeal from the Circuit Court for Dade County, Lester Langer, Judge.

Before SCHWARTZ, C.J., and FLETCHER and SORONDO, JJ.

PER CURIAM.

While being investigated as a possible runaway, the juvenile respondent gave a false last name to the interrogating police officer, thus requiring further inquiry to ascertain her identity. We conclude that these facts justify the finding that she was guilty of resisting an officer without violence, notwithstanding that she told the officer her correct name after he had already discovered it. § 843.02, Fla. Stat. (1999); *In re J.H., 559 So.2d 702 (Fla. 4th DCA 1990).*

Affirmed.

CASE

Fripp v. State, 766 So.2d 252 (Fla. 4th DCA 2000).

Defendant was convicted in the Circuit Court, Palm Beach County, Richard L. Oftedal, J., of possession of cocaine and obstructing an officer without violence, and he appealed. The District Court of Appeal, Gross, J., held: (1) defendant waived right to appellate review of issue regarding admission of cocaine evidence; (2) officer, who arrested defendant for operating motor vehicle without valid driver's license, had authority to arrest defendant on driver's license charge, even though it was later determined that defendant actually did have valid license; and (3) defendant who gave false information to officer attempting to investigate traffic infraction could be convicted of resisting arrest without violence.

Affirmed.

GROSS, Judge.

Dewayne Fripp appeals his convictions of possession of cocaine and obstructing an officer without violence. See §§ 893.13(6)(a), 843.02, Fla. Stat. (1997). We affirm, finding that appellant failed to preserve the issue raised by his motion to suppress and that his conduct amounted to a violation of section 843.02.

Officer Russell Lichter of the West Palm Beach Police Department stopped Fripp a little before midnight on April 18, 1998 for running a stop sign. Fripp told the officer that his name was "John Fripp." The officer ran a computer search and found no record of a driver's license listed under that name. When Lichter asked him for his driver's license, Fripp said that he had no license, insurance, or registration. Suspecting Fripp of lying, the officer asked him for his true name and if he had a license. The defendant "continued to stick with [the name] John Fripp." The defendant appeared nervous and "fidgety." The officer saw Fripp place a cigarette pack on the top of the car's visor.

The officer arrested the defendant for operating a motor vehicle without a valid driver's license, a misdemeanor contrary to section 322.03(1), Florida Statutes (1997). A search of the car incident to arrest revealed a small amount of cocaine in the cigarette pack the defendant had put on top of the visor.

While being booked at the police station, the defendant identified himself by his actual name, Dewayne Fripp, and said that he had a driver's license. A computer check verified that a valid license had been issued to Fripp under that name.

The trial court denied a motion to suppress the cocaine and found the defendant guilty of both charges after a bench trial.

Addressing the merits, we reject Fripp's contention that the officer did not have the authority to arrest him on the driver's license charge. A violation of section 322.03(1) is a second degree misdemeanor. See § 322.39, Fla. Stat. (1999). A law enforcement officer may arrest a person without a warrant when the person has committed a misdemeanor "in the presence of the officer." §901.15(1), Fla. Stat. (1999); see *State v. Carmody, 553 So.2d 1366 (Fla. 5th DCA 1989)*. At the time of the arrest, the officer had probable cause to believe that the defendant had violated section 322.03(1).

Fripp also argues that the evidence at trial was "insufficient to prove obstruction" under section 843.02. To support a conviction under this statute, the state must prove that (1) a law enforcement officer was engaged in the lawful execution of a legal duty; and (2) the defendant's action constituted an obstruction of that legal duty. See *S.G.K. v. State, 657 So.2d 1246, 1247 (Fla. 1st DCA 1995)*.

Fripp concedes that he gave a false name to the officer and did not correct that falsehood until he arrived at the booking desk after his arrest, but argues that such conduct did not amount to an "obstruction" under the statute. Fripp relies upon *C.T. v. State, 481 So.2d 9 (Fla. 1st DCA 1985)*, but this case is distinguishable.

In *C.T.*, the defendant was stopped for riding a bicycle without a headlight. He gave a false name to the officer. After partially filling out the citation form, the officer ran the false name through the police computer to check for outstanding warrants. "Immediately thereafter, and while still at the scene of the initial stop, the appellant admitted his falsehood and gave the officer his true legal name." *Id. at 10*. The first district reversed the defendant's conviction because, even though the false name had been "officially recorded" on the citation, "it was undisputed that the juvenile promptly and voluntarily recanted the false information and thus did not interfere with the officer's performance of his duties other than by causing a relatively insignificant loss of time." *Id.*

Similarly, in *Burdess v. State, 724 So.2d 604 (Fla. 5th DCA 1998)*, while a police officer was conducting a theft investigation, the defendant gave the officer a false name. When a passerby recognized the defendant, she admitted her true name to the officer and gave her correct date of birth. The officer testified that no more than three minutes had elapsed between the time he first approached her and the time he learned her correct name, but he arrested her for resisting an officer without violence, pursuant to section 843.02. The fifth district reversed the conviction, observing that

> [t]here was no testimony that the officer was impeded in any way by the giving of the original false information. No reports were prepared based on it, nor was any action taken in reliance on it. The information was corrected before it did any harm, and appellant was not being legally detained.

Id. at 604 (citations omitted).

Unlike the defendants in **Burdess** and **C.T.**, Fripp twice gave a false name at the scene of the stop and did not correct the falsehood until he was at the booking desk after he was arrested and transported to the police station. This case is controlled by **In the Interest of J.H.,** *559 So.2d 702 (Fla. 4ᵗʰ DCA 1990)*, where this court affirmed a defendant's conviction under section 843.02 for giving a false name after he had been pulled over for a traffic infraction; this court found it significant that the defendant "was already under arrest for the theft of the motor scooter before confessing to his true identity." *Id. at 703.* As the fifth district observed in **State v. Townsend,** *585 So.2d 495, 496 (Fla. 5ᵗʰ DCA 1991)*, "the policy reason for excusing false testimony in order to induce witnesses to change their statement and tell the truth ... is no longer applicable after an arrest has occurred." (Citation omitted).

AFFIRMED.

STEVENSON and SHAHOOD, JJ., concur.

REVIEW

1. It is not a crime to give a false name to a law enforcement officer _____.
    a. if stopped for a traffic violation
    b. if the defendant immediately gives his or her true and correct name
    c. both a and b
    d. neither a nor b

2. It is a crime to give a false name when _____.
    a. arrested
    b. stopped for a traffic violation
    c. both a and b
    d. neither a nor b

OBSTRUCTION

It is a crime to act as a lookout and interfere with an arrest for a crime that that already been committed. To simply announce an undercover officer is an officer prior to commission of a crime is mere speech and not a crime. In a area where prostitutes work a citizen may yell "He's a cop." Similarly if an officer goes to a neighborhood to buy drugs an individual may yell "He's a cop" before any illegal activity occurs and not be guilty of obstructing justice.

CASE

J.V. v. State, 763 So.2d 511 (Fla. 1ˢᵗ DCA 2000).

Defendant was convicted in Nineteenth Judicial Circuit, St. Lucie County, Burton Connor, J., of obstructing an officer in the lawful execution of a legal duty. On appeal, the District Court of Appeal, Klein, J., held that defendant's conduct consisted only of speech, which was not a crime.

Reversed.

Polen, J., dissented with opinion.

KLEIN, Judge.

The issue in this case is whether a person who identifies an undercover officer as an officer, and thus frustrates the officer's attempt to purchase drugs from a suspected drug seller, is guilty of obstructing a police officer in the lawful performance of a legal duty. We hold that the conduct, which consisted only of speech, is not a crime.

Detective Silverman of the St. Lucie County Sheriff's Office, who was operating undercover, was attempting to purchase drugs from a suspect. The suspect was speaking to the officer while the officer was sitting in his vehicle. Before any illegal activity had occurred, appellant, who had been sitting in another vehicle, got out and yelled to the suspect "don't sell anything to that man, that's Silverman, he's a cop." The suspect then lost interest in the transaction, but appellant was charged under section 843.02 Florida Statutes (1997) with obstructing an officer "in the lawful execution of any legal duty," and convicted.

Jay v. State, 731 So.2d 774 (Fla. 4ᵗʰ DCA 1999) is on all fours. In *Jay* an undercover officer was attempting to solicit two females to engage in prostitution. While the officer was speaking with the females, and prior to any illegal conduct occurring, Jay told the females "don't get in the car, he's a cop." The females then walked away and were not arrested. We held that Jay's conduct did not violate section 843.02 and reversed his conviction.

Porter v. State, 582 So.2d 41 (Fla. 4ᵗʰ DCA 1991), on which the appellee and the dissent rely, is distinguishable in two important respects. [FN1] First, in *Porter*, the police had already observed criminal activity and were in the process of making arrests. Second, the defendant in *Porter* was a "lookout" who was interfering with arrests. In contrast, in the present case, no criminal activity had occurred, and there is no evidence that the appellant was a lookout.

In *S.D. v. State, 627 So.2d 1261, 1262 (Fla. 3d DCA 1993)*, officers were posing as drug dealers in order to arrest prospective drug purchasers. S.D., who was standing on the same side of the street as the operation, was waving at people walking towards him and the officers, causing them to turn around and leave. He refused to stop after an officer threatened him with arrest, and he was charged with obstructing an officer in the exercise of a lawful duty. The third district reversed his conviction, holding that S.D.'s verbal protest of police authority was protected free speech. The court relied on *City of Houston, Texas v. Hill*, 482 U.S. 451, 107 S.Ct. 2502, 2510, 96 L.Ed.2d 398 (1987) ("The freedom of individuals verbally to oppose or challenge police action without thereby risking arrest is one of the principle characteristics by which we distinguish a free nation from a police state.").

In *D.G. v. State*, 661 So.2d 75, 76 (Fla. 2d DCA 1995), the defendant was found by the trial court to have violated section 843.02, because he was yelling and encouraging his mother not to allow the police to search their house. The second district reversed, and Judge Altenbernd, writing for the panel, summarized the law:

> These cases, and other Florida cases, seem to support the following general proposition: If a police officer is not engaged in executing process on a person, is not legally detaining that person, or has not asked the person for assistance with an ongoing emergency that presents a serious threat of imminent harm to person or property, the person's words alone can rarely, if ever, rise to the level of an obstruction. Thus, obstructive conduct rather than offensive words are normally required to support a conviction under this statute. Such obstructive conduct was not established in this case.

> Reversed.

> HAZOURI, J., concurs.

> POLEN, J., dissents with opinion.

> POLEN, J., dissenting.

I would affirm J.V.'s conviction, as I believe this case is controlled by *Porter v. State*, 582 So.2d 41 (Fla. 4th DCA 1991), not those relied upon in the majority opinion. For one thing, Judge Altenbernd's reference in *D.G.* as to the three circumstances when a violation of section 843.02 can be committed by the use of words alone would not allow for the situation where an undercover officer was in the middle of a sting transaction, but the money for drugs exchange had not yet been made. In such a situation, I would hold a third party who then yells "He's a cop!" could be found guilty of obstruction. [FN2] That is somewhat closer to the facts in the present case, where the suspected drug seller had directed Detective Silverman to drive his car to a spot that faced a car in which J.V. was sitting. While we do not know whether J.V.'s role was as a "lookout," like Porter, the actions of the suspected seller indicated some likelihood that he was about to sell Silverman illegal drugs. I would hold that Silverman was performing a legal duty, and J.V.'s warning interfered with or obstructed that performance. I therefore, respectfully, dissent.

FN1. The dissent also relies on a California case which does support the view that this type of conduct should be criminalized; however, if we were to follow that decision it would require us to recede from *Jay*, which is on all fours. The dissent does not address *Jay*.

FN2. See *People v. Robles,* 48 Cal.App.4th Supp. 1, 56 Cal.Rptr.2d 369 (Dep't Super. Ct. 1996).

REVIEW

1. Identifying an officer as a member of law enforcement is a crime _____.
   a. always
   b. if the defendant is interfering with the execution of a search warrant
   c. if the defendant is acting as a lookout for a crime
   d. both b and c

POSSESSION

To be in constructive possession, the State must prove a defendant had control over the item and knew the item was in his or her presence. The courts may have this issue arise when drugs are found in a car occupied by multiple parties or in a house where more than one person lives. Statements made by the defendant may be used to show knowledge and/or control. Additionally, the location of the drugs may be taken into account. A person can be in constructive possession of not only drugs, but also drug paraphernalia, weapons, and other contraband. Paraphernalia can include razor blades, soda cans, or rolling papers.

In constructive possession cases, a defendant is entitled to a special jury instruction. The instructions that may apply are:

Mere proximity to a thing is not sufficient to establish control over that thing when the thing is not in a place over which the person has control.

Constructive possession means the thing is in a place over which the person has control, or in which the person has concealed it.

If a thing is in a place over which the person does not have control, in order to establish constructive possession the State must prove the person's (1) control over the thing, and (2) knowledge that the thing was within the person's presence.

Possession may be joint, that is, two or more persons may jointly have possession of an article, exercising control over it. In that case, each of those persons is considered to be in possession of that article.

If a person has exclusive possession of a thing, knowledge of its presence may be inferred or assumed.

Dubose testified that on December 16, 1988, an acquaintance invited him to an apartment located in Pensacola. He had only been in one of the bedrooms of the apartment for two or three minutes when narcotics investigators entered and arrested the nine people inside. At the time of his arrest, Dubose was standing within arm's reach of a coffee table, upon which lay a piece of crack cocaine, two razor blades, and a crushed beer can, which was used, according to Officer Shelby to smoke crack. Dubose was also within arm's reach of a rolled cigarette containing marijuana and cocaine, which was lying on a pile of clothes inside an open closet. Another crushed beer can was found on the floor of the room, and a case of rolling papers was found on Dubose.

Officer Shelby testified that when he advised Dubose he was under arrest for possession of cocaine and marijuana, Dubose exclaimed that the drugs were not his, but that he had just gone to the apartment to smoke. Later, at the station, Dubose informed Shelby that a woman had invited him and a friend to the apartment to smoke crack and that he would not pass up such an opportunity. Finally, Shelby reported that Dubose said he intended to sell the rolling papers. Dubose admitted during his testimony at trial that he uses cocaine and marijuana and stated that his purpose in going to the apartment might have been to smoke such drugs, but he denied that he had in fact gone to the apartment for such purpose. He said that he had not seen the crack on the coffee table, but that he had seen the crushed beer cans and knew what they were used for. When asked whether he knew that a marijuana/cocaine cigarette was in the closet, Dubose merely said, "When I came in, I didn't have time to search. I mean, I walked in the door and I was waiting."

To establish constructive possession of contraband, the state must show that the defendant 1) had the ability to exercise control over the contraband, 2) knew of the presence of the contraband, and 3) knew of its illicit nature. *Brown v. State*, 428 So.2d 250, 252 (Fla.), cert. denied, 463 U.S. 1209, 103 S.Ct. 3541, 77 L.Ed.2d 1391 (1983); *Wade v. State*, 558 So.2d 107, 107 (Fla. 1st DCA 1990); *Frank v. State*, 199 So.2d 117, 120-21 (Fla. 1st DCA 1967). In order for the state to prove a defendant's constructive possession of contraband by circumstantial evidence, as here, the evidence must be inconsistent with the defendant's theory of innocence. *State v. Law.* 559 So.2d 187 (Fla. 1989). We conclude that the state established its case only as to the cocaine and marijuana charges.

It is well established that if a defendant's status is that of a visitor to a dwelling, as was Dubose, rather than that of an owner or occupant, the state must show more than the defendant's mere proximity to contraband in order to prove constructive possession. *Wade*, 558 So.2d at 107; *Herrera v. State*, 532 So.2d 54, 58 (Fla.3d DCA 1988); *Agee v. State*, 522 So.2d 1044, 1046 (Fla.2d DCA 1988). The elements of constructive possession may be shown by a defendant's incriminating statements or conduct. *Frank*, 199 So.2d at 120; *Herrera*, 532 So.2d at 59; *Taylor v. State*, 319 So.2d 114, 116 (Fla.2d DCA 1975). In the case at bar, the jury was justified in concluding that Dubose's proximity to the drugs, coupled with the incriminating statements he made to Officer Shelby, established that Dubose knew the drugs were present, that he knew they were illicit, and that, based upon his statement that he intended to smoke both the cocaine and the marijuana, he could have exercised control over the drugs.

On the other hand, we cannot agree that the evidence was legally sufficient to support appellant's conviction for possession of drug paraphernalia. There was no competent, substantial evidence presented that Dubose was in constructive possession of two of the items listed as drug paraphernalia: razor blades and crushed beer cans. That they were seen near Dubose and the crack cocaine that Dubose intended to smoke was not competent evidence that he constructively possessed them. Although the evidence was consistent with defendant's guilt, it was not inconsistent with his innocense on this count. *D.K.W. v. State*, 298 So.2d 885, 886 (Fla. 1st DCA 1981) (defendant's proximity to marijuana cigarettes, reference to a "roach" found near him, were not inconsistent with defendant's innocence on charge of possession of marijuana). Unlike the charges relating to possession of cocaine and cannabis in the case at bar, the state introduced no other evidence, such as incriminating statements, that Dubose intended to use the razor blades or the cans to smoke the crack cocaine.

The state also failed to prove that the rolling papers found on Dubose constituted illegal drug paraphernalia under Section 893.145, Florida Statutes (1981). (FN1) The state argues that the evidence establishing that Dubose intended to use the papers to smoke marijuana was that the officers found loose marijuana on individuals other than Dubose; that Officer Shelby searched for and found no cigarette tobacco in the apartment; and that Dubose told Shelby he had gone to the apartment to smoke drugs. However, this evidence was not inconsistent with defendant's theory of innocence that he intended to sell the individual packages of rolling papers to others. In the absence of evidence disclosing that Dubose actually used or intended to use the papers for smoking cocaine or marijuana, the state was required to prove "not only ... that the [papers] could be so used, but also that by reason of some peculiar characteristic of design the [papers] could be recognized as being intended only for such use." *Williams v. State*, 529 So.2d 345, 347-48 (Fla. 1st DCA 1988) (state did not prove that triple-beam scale was drug paraphernalia). The state presented no evidence on this point.

Dubose's convictions for possession of cocaine and marijuana are affirmed; his conviction for possession of drug paraphernalia is reversed, and the case is remanded with directions that appellant be discharged as to the later conviction.

WENTWORTH and BARFIELD, JJ., concur.

FN1. Section 893.145(12) defines drug paraphernalia to include "[o]bjects used, intended for use, or designed for use in ingesting, inhaling, or otherwise introducing cannabis, cocaine, hashish, or hashish oil into the human body or..." A list of thirteen categories of such objects follows, none of which includes rolling papers.

REVIEW

1. To be convicted of constructive possession of drugs found in a house, one may be _____.
   a. the owner
   b. a visitor
   c. a renter
   d. all of the above

2. To be convicted of constructive possession, the State must prove the defendant _____.
   a. had control over the contraband
   b. knew of the presence of the contraband
   c. knew of its illicit nature
   d. all of the above

CASE

Isaac v. State, 730 So.2d 757 (Fla. 2d DCA 1999).

Defendant was convicted in the Circuit Court, Pinellas County, R. Timothy Peters, J., of possession of cocaine. Defendant appealed. The District Court of Appeal, Northcutt, J., held that evidence was insufficient to support conviction.

Reversed with direction.

NORTHCUTT, Judge.

Willie Isaac challenges his conviction and sentence for possession of cocaine. We agree with his argument that the evidence of his guilt was insufficient.

Clearwater Police Department Officers Donnelly and Stonelake were responding to another call when they happened upon Isaac and another man, standing no more than a foot apart, passing an object between them. From the officers' vantage point, they could not discern the nature of the object. When the men noticed that they were being observed, one of them dropped a plastic baggie to the ground, and the two began walking away. The officers did not see which man dropped the baggie. Based on his experience, Officer Stonelake identified the substance in the baggie as crack cocaine. He remained to secure the contraband while Officer Donnelly gave chase and apprehended Isaac. A search incident to arrest revealed no money or other contraband on Isaac's person.

At trial, the State proved the foregoing facts. Isaac's attorney moved for a judgment of acquittal, arguing that the State had not shown that Isaac constructively possessed the cocaine. The trial court denied the motion, and thereafter the jury found Isaac guilty of possession of cocaine.

Because the State could not establish that Isaac had actual possession of the baggie, it was obliged to prove that he possessed it constructively. See *Lewis v. State, 570 So.2d 346, 348 (Fla. 2d DCA 1990)*. To do so, the State was required to show that Isaac had dominion and control over the cocaine, was aware of its presence, and knew of its illicit nature. See *Green v. State, 667 So.2d 208, 211 (Fla. 2d DCA 1995)*; see also *E.A.M. v. State, 684 So.2d 283, 284 (Fla. 2d DCA 1996)*.

Mere proximity to contraband is not enough to establish dominion and control. See *State v. Snyder, 635 So.2d 1057, 1058 (Fla. 2d DCA 1994)*. Rather, to prove dominion and control the evidence must establish the defendant's conscious and substantial possession, as distinguished from mere involuntary or superficial possession, of the contraband. See *Chicone v. State, 684 So.2d 736, 738 (Fla. 1996)*.

Whether a defendant had dominion and control over contraband is generally a fact issue for the jury, but a judgment of acquittal is proper when there is no evidence from which dominion or control can be inferred. See *Campbell v. State, 577 So.2d 932, 935 (Fla. 1991)*. In *State v. Law, 559 So.2d 187 (Fla. 1989)*, the supreme court described the trial court's task when considering a motion for judgment of acquittal in a circumstantial evidence case:

> [I]t is for the court to determine, as a threshold matter, whether the state has been able to produce competent, substantial evidence to contradict the defendant's story. If the state fails in this initial burden, then it is the court's duty to grant a judgment of acquittal to the defendant as to the charged offense.... Otherwise, there would be no function or role for the courts in reviewing circumstantial evidence, as was stated so well in *Davis v. State,436 So.2d [196 (Fla. 4th DCA 1983)], 200*: "If we were to follow the state's logic, a trial judge could never ... grant a motion for judgment of acquittal pursuant to Florida Rule of Criminal Procedure 3.380 when the evidence [is] circumstantial. Instead, every case would have to go to the jury."

559 So.2d at 189 (quoting *Fowler v. State, 492 So.2d 1344, 1347 (Fla. 1st DCA 1986))*. "Where the only proof of guilt is circumstantial, no matter how strongly the evidence may suggest guilt, a conviction cannot be sustained unless the evidence is inconsistent with any reasonable hypothesis of innocence." *559 So.2d at 188*.

Here, the State did not meet its burden of excluding every reasonable hypothesis of innocence. To be sure, the circumstances suggested that one or both men possessed the cocaine. At the same time, however, those circumstances did not exclude the reasonable hypotheses that the men found the baggie at that spot and were simply examining it when the policemen happened by, or that the other fellow brought the cocaine there and was showing it to Isaac. Therefore, we reverse Isaac's conviction and direct the circuit court to discharge him.

PATTERSON, A.C.J., and SALCINES, J., Concur.

REVIEW

1. Mere proximity to contraband establishes _____.
   a. dominion
   b. control
   c. neither a nor b
   d. both a and b

2. To convict a defendant of constructive possession, the state must _____.
   a. exclude every reasonable hypothesis of innocence
   b. exclude most reasonable hypotheses of innocence
   c. exclude some reasonable hypotheses of innocence
   d. none of the above

CASE

T.W. V. Florida, *666 So.2d 1001 (Fla. 5th DCA 1996).*

Defendant was found guilty of possessing controlled substances, in the Circuit Court, St. Johns County, Richard G. Weinberg, J. Defendant appealed. The District Court of Appeal held that state failed to make necessary showing that defendant knew that there was cocaine rolled up in dollar bill inserted between transmission hump and passenger seat of automobile.

Reversed.

PER CURIAM.

T.W. appeals her judgment of guilty of possession of a controlled substance. She contends that there was insufficient evidence to show she had constructive possession of the controlled substance. We agree and reverse.

According to the answer brief, the hearing was recorded on audiotape but could not be transcribed because it was unintelligible. Unfortunately, this is a common occurrence and is disturbing in this age of technology. The court and the attorneys therefore entered a "Stipulated Reconstruction of the Record" that provides: during a legal traffic stop, the driver/owner of the car was found to have money and marijuana. The driver also dropped a small packet of cocaine near the car. T.W., the passenger, was found to have $900 in her pants and marijuana in her purse. (The trial court later suppressed the controlled substance found in her purse.) After an extensive search a deputy found a folded-up dollar bill which had cocaine residue on it. The bill was found in the space between the transmission hump and the side of the passenger seat of the auto in which T.W. had been riding. T.W. was found guilty of possession of this residue although no evidence existed indicating that it was hers or that she had knowledge of its presence.

Because the dollar bill was accessible to both occupants of the car, this case must be analyzed as a constructive possession case. **S.B. v. State**, *657 So.2d 1252 (Fla. 2d DCA 1995)*. To prove constructive possession, the state must prove three elements: (1) the accused's dominion and control over the contraband, (2) the accused's knowledge that the contraband is within his or her presence; and (3) the accused's knowledge of the illicit nature of the contraband. *Id.* Knowledge of the contraband's presence in a constructive possession case cannot be inferred from the accused's presence but must be established by independent proof. **In Interest of E.H.**, *579 So.2d 364, 365 (Fla. 4th DCA 1991)*.

In the instant case, independent proof of T.W.'s knowledge of the presence of the cocaine residue was not established; therefore, the court's finding that T.W. was guilty of possession of a controlled substance must be reversed.

REVERSED.

PETERSON, C.J., W. SHARP and GRIFFIN, JJ., concur.

REVIEW

1. Knowledge of presence of contraband _____.
   - a. is presumed
   - b. is inferred
   - c. must be proven
   - d. none of the above

CASE

Hamilton v. State, *732 So.2d 493 (Fla. 2d DCA 1999).*

Defendant was convicted in the Circuit Court, Pinellas County, Nelly N. Khouzam, J., for possession of cocaine and sale of cocaine. He appealed. The District Court of Appeal held that evidence was insufficient to support convictions.

Reversed and remanded.

PER CURIAM.

Bart Hamilton challenges his judgment and sentences for possession of cocaine and sale of cocaine. He argues that there was insufficient evidence upon which to base the convictions. We agree, and reverse the convictions and remand to the trial court with instructions to discharge Hamilton.

Detective Reed of the Pinellas County Sheriff's Department testified that he arranged to purchase sixty dollars' worth of cocaine through a confidential informant. The informant contacted the seller, Terry Frasier, and arranged to meet him in a supermarket parking lot. Frasier pulled into the parking lot in a pickup truck with Hamilton in the front passenger seat. The informant parked his car on the passenger side of Frasier's pickup truck so that the driver's door of the car was next to the passenger door of the pickup. Detective Reed was sitting in the front passenger seat of the informant's car. The informant rolled down his window and asked Frasier if he had the "stuff." Frasier responded affirmatively and handed Hamilton a clear plastic baggie containing rock cocaine which Hamilton passed on to the informant. The informant then handed Hamilton sixty dollars in cash which Hamilton immediately passed on to Frasier. Neither Frasier, the informant, nor Detective Reed spoke to Hamilton. Hamilton said nothing during the entire transaction, and there had never been any mention of his name prior to the transaction taking place. When the uniformed officers stopped Frasier's pickup truck several blocks from the supermarket parking lot, Frasier fled while Hamilton remained seated in the passenger seat. Hamilton was convicted after jury trial. He received a sentence of seven years' imprisonment as a habitual offender on the sale-of-cocaine conviction and a concurrent five years in prison on the conviction for possession of cocaine. Hamilton was not sentenced as a habitual offender on the possession count.

We conclude that the mere fact that Hamilton passed the cocaine from one party to another party, where he was sitting between the two, did not establish that he had dominion and control over the cocaine and, therefore, did not support a conviction for possession of cocaine. *Campbell v. State, 577 So.2d 932 (Fla. 1991)*, held that dominion and control is not established where a "defendant takes temporary possession of contraband, in the presence of the owner, for the sole purpose of verification or testing, and there is no other evidence from which dominion or control could be inferred." *Id. at 935*. In the instant case, Hamilton's "possession" of the cocaine was of an even more temporary and incidental nature than was the defendant's in *Campbell*, and there was no evidence from which to infer that Hamilton was otherwise involved in the transaction. In fact, it would appear that Hamilton only handled the cocaine because the informant pulled up on the passenger side of the pickup truck rather than the driver's side. We note that in 1992 the legislature added subsection (16) to the definitions outlined in section 893.02. That subsection states: " 'Possession' includes temporary possession for the purpose of verification or testing, irrespective of dominion and control." However, this statutory exception to *Campbell* does not apply in the instant case, and the common law definition of possession still controls.

A defendant may commit the offense of sale of cocaine without ever being in possession of that cocaine. See *State v. McCloud, 577 So.2d 939 (Fla. 1991)*. Here, however, the evidence supporting Hamilton's conviction for sale of cocaine was based solely on his incidental and temporary possession of that cocaine. We conclude that, under the peculiar facts of this case, there was insufficient evidence to support the conviction for sale of cocaine. Accordingly, we reverse Hamilton's convictions and remand to the trial court with instructions to discharge him.

PATTERSON, A.C.J., and SALCINES, J., and DANAHY, PAUL W., Senior Judge, Concur.

REVIEW

> 1. Temporary possession of contraband is enough to convict if _____.
>   a. for the purpose of verification
>   b. for the purpose of testing
>   c. both a and b
>   d. neither a nor b

CASE

Hill v. State, 736 So.2d 133 (Fla. 1ˢᵗ DCA 1999).

Defendant was convicted in the Circuit Court, Escambia County, Nickolas Geeker, J., of possession of cocaine, and he appealed. The District Court of Appeal, Allen, J., held that there was insufficient evidence to establish that defendant constructively possessed the cocaine.

Reversed and remanded.

ALLEN, Judge.

The appellant challenges his conviction for possession of cocaine. Because the evidence at trial was insufficient to prove his constructive possession of the cocaine, we reverse the conviction.

The appellant was accompanied by one front-seat passenger as he drove an automobile. After the automobile was lawfully stopped and searched by police officers who found cocaine inside a bag just barely underneath the front seat on the driver's side, the appellant was charged with possession of cocaine. The prosecution theory at trial was that the cocaine had been within the appellant's constructive possession because it was only partially concealed underneath the seat and was directly beneath where the appellant had been sitting while driving the automobile.

The appellant argued in his motion for judgment of acquittal at trial and also argues on appeal that the prosecution did not present sufficient evidence for the jury to find his constructive possession of the cocaine. To establish the appellant's constructive possession of the cocaine, the prosecution was required to present legally sufficient evidence that the appellant had (1) dominion and control over the cocaine; (2) knowledge that the contraband was within his presence; and (3) knowledge of the illicit nature of the substance. See, e.g., *Harris v. State, 647 So.2d 206 (Fla. 1ˢᵗ DCA 1994).*

Although the appellee acknowledges that mere proximity to contraband when a defendant is not in exclusive possession of the area is insufficient to demonstrate the necessary dominion and control and is not evidence inconsistent with innocence, see

109

Moffatt v. State, 583 So.2d 779 (Fla. 1ˢᵗ DCA 1991), the appellee nonetheless asserts that the evidence was sufficient in the present case. We disagree.

In *Skelton v. State, 609 So.2d 716 (Fla. 2d DCA 1992)*, the court reversed a drug conviction under circumstances very similar to those in the present case. In *Skelton*, drugs were found partially concealed under the passenger seat of the automobile in which Skelton was the passenger. Similarly, in *Cordero v. State, 589 So.2d 407 (Fla. 5ᵗʰ DCA 1991)*, the court found insufficient evidence of constructive possession by the passenger of a vehicle in which cocaine was found underneath the passenger seat between the seat and transmission tunnel. The court explained:

> While appellant, sitting in the passenger seat, might have seen the bag if he looked for it or reached under the seat for it, this does not support a finding that appellant had knowledge of the presence of that cocaine or at any time controlled it. No fingerprints were found on the cocaine bag. While the state notes that the cocaine bag was located near where appellant's feet would have been, we find this argument merely illustrates that the state has failed to demonstrate "circumstances other than the mere location of the substance" from which the jury might lawfully infer appellant's knowledge of the presence of cocaine.

Id. at 409 (citation omitted).

In addition to the appellant's proximity to the bag containing the cocaine, the only additional fact the appellee can cite to demonstrate the appellant's requisite knowledge is that the appellant was nervous when he exited the automobile. But the appellant's nervousness does not provide a legally sufficient nexus between the appellant and the cocaine because his nervousness could be attributed to the fact that he had been stopped for speeding. See *Green v. State, 667 So.2d 208 (Fla. 2d DCA 1995)*.

Because the state failed to present sufficient evidence of constructive possession, the trial court erred in denying the appellant's motion for judgment of acquittal. We accordingly reverse the conviction and remand this case with directions that the appellant be discharged.

LAWRENCE and BENTON, JJ., CONCUR.

REVIEW

1. Possession can be proved by _____.
    a. mere proximity
    b. nervousness
    c. both a and b
    d. neither a nor b

THINKING CRITICALLY

1. Was A.P. guilty of a crime? What if A.P. wasn't a runaway? Is your answer the same? Do you agree with the court's analysis in *Fripp*? Why or why not?

2. Sam works as a lookout for a couple of drug dealers. When Sam sees a law enforcement officer coming, it is his job to yell "Five Oh". "Five Oh" is the street name for a cop. It comes from the TV show Hawaii Five O. Has Sam committed the crime of resisting an officer without violence? Compare the facts in *J.V.*.

3. Were either or both of the defendants in possession of drugs in *E.A.M.* and *Dubose*?

4. Do you agree with the court's holdings?

5.   What do you think about the *Isaac* case?

6.   Should it make a difference that T.W. was in possession of a large amount of cash? If cocaine had also been found in T.W.'s purse, would the result in the case have been different? Should it be?

7.   Why do you think the court reversed Hamilton's conviction? Did he not "possess" the cocaine? What additional facts would the State need to prove in order to convict Hamilton?

8.   What additional facts would the State need to prove to convict in *Hill*? Would fingerprints on the bag be enough? Should it be?

9.   A car is stopped for a traffic violation. Law enforcement conducts a consensual search of the vehicle. A grocery bag is found in the trunk. It contains clothing and a small container. In the container, marijuana is found. Susie admits the bag is hers and some of the clothing. She denies owning the container. Is Susie in constructive possession of the marijuana? No prints of Susie's are found on the container. What effect will this have on the case? What if there was a strong smell of marijuana in the car at the time it was pulled over?

10.   A passenger in the automobile is found to have cocaine and marijuana in her purse. There are three other individuals in the vehicle. The passenger claims someone else must have put the drugs in her purse. The purse was at her feet. Can she be convicted of possession? What additional facts would be important to know?

11.   While visiting at a friend's house, Henry goes in a bedroom to use the telephone. In the bedroom closet there is cocaine. Is Henry guilty of possession? What other facts do you need to know? What if the cocaine was in plain view on the night stand where the phone was?

12.   Joan keeps her drugs hidden in her bathroom in her parents' home. Can her parents be found guilty of possession? If so, what would the State need to prove?

13. Scott is found to be in possession of a small amount of methamphetamine that is in his pocket. In the master bedroom of the house that he shares with his wife, a large quantity of methamphetamine is found. Other people live in the house and have access to the master bedroom. Is Scott guilty of possession of the large quantity found in the bedroom? What additional information do you want to have?

14. Abigail lives in an apartment. Her boyfriend Dale lives with her but his name is not on the lease. Some of his belongings are in a closet where drugs are found. The drugs are in fact his. Can Abigail be convicted of possession? Can Dale be convicted without his name being on the lease?

15. Audrey is stopped for a traffic violation. She pulls over and an unknown male exits the vehicle and takes off running. The police find a marijuana cigarette in plain view in the ashtray. Is Audrey guilty of possession? How can the state prove she knew of the illicit nature of the contraband? What if the marijuana cigarette is still hot?

CHAPTER 3 ANSWER KEY

REVIEW QUESTIONS

Fripp v. State
    1. b
    2. c

J.V. v. State
    1. d

Dubose v. State
    1. d
    2. d

Isaac v. State
    1. c
    2. a

T.W. V. Florida
    1. c

Hamilton v. State
    1. c

Hill v. State
    1. d

CHAPTER 4

THE GENERAL PRINCIPLES
OF CRIMINAL LIABILITY

INTENT

There are two types of intentional crimes under Florida law: (1) general intent crimes; and (2) specific intent crimes. A general intent statute prohibits a specific voluntary act or something substantially certain to result from the act. A person's subjective intent to cause a particular result does not matter. The law presumes the person intended what resulted from the act, and an individual need only intend to do the act. This requirement distinguishes general intent crimes from accidental non-criminal behavior or strict liability crimes.

Specific intent statutes prohibit acts accompanied by some intent other than intent to do the act itself or cause the natural and necessary consequences of the act. There is an additional subjective intent involved in a specific intent crime.

Whether a crime is one requiring specific intent or general intent can be a critical issue, and it may affect which affirmative defenses may be asserted by a defendant.

CASE

Bauer v. State, 609 So.2d 608 (Fla. 4th DCA 1992).

City cash management coordinator was convicted in the Circuit Court, Palm Beach County, Marvin U. Mounts, Jr., J., for official misconduct. Defendant appealed. The District Court of Appeal held that: (1) state presented adequate evidence as to general intent, and (2) state presented sufficient circumstantial evidence of defendant's specific intent to benefit himself required for offense of official misconduct.

Affirmed.

Warner, J., dissented on remand and filed opinion.

PER CURIAM.

Appellant claims that his conviction for official misconduct should be overturned because the state failed to prove a violation of § 839.25(1), Florida Statutes (1989). We disagree and affirm.

This case involved a financial transaction called a reverse repurchase agreement. In this type of transaction, an investor purchases a security, which in turn is used as collateral for a loan to buy that security. Thus, it involves a simultaneous purchase and

116

loan. If the value of the security increases, then money is made on the difference between the loan and the increased value of the security, but when the value of the security drops the collateral is worth less. More money is then required to support the loan through a margin call. These types of transactions are handled by "secondary" brokers for investors. The advantage of these transactions is a very attractive rate of return. However, the investment is very speculative.

After working for about ten years for the First National Bank of Palm Beach, appellant started working as the cash management coordinator of the City of West Palm Beach. In his job, the managed the City's cash investment portfolio worth over $70,000,000. When he was in training for his position with the City, appellant discussed reverse repurchase agreements with one of his superiors who told him that they were not a good idea. Furthermore, appellant was not authorized on behalf of the City to borrow money nor to invest through secondary brokers.

Despite the warnings, in 1987 appellant Bauer arranged with a secondary broker to buy into a reverse repurchase with the City's funds. It appears from the record that the first purchase was a telephone transaction with the broker, authorizing the purchase of the security. Bauer recorded absolutely nothing on the books regarding the transaction. Unfortunately, when the stock market crashed later that year, the secondary broker made numerous margin calls, demanding security to back up the transaction. Bauer made twelve payments from the City account which he controlled totaling about $600,000 between January and May 1987. Rather than properly recording these as losses in the accounting journal entries, he improperly recorded these in an asset account entitled "investment-repurchase." He made twelve such journal entries. To avoid future margin calls, appellant then authorized the bank to wire a $1,000,000 treasury bond owned by the City. Appellant claims that he thought this was to serve only as collateral; however, the broker sold the bond for approximately $816,000 and returned to the City its other $600,000 payments made on previous margin calls. At that point, appellant made a thirteenth journal entry, describing it as a redemption of repurchase, which in essence zeroed out the asset account built up by the prior twelve entries. Between May and June there were additional losses. On June 29, 1987, the broker returned to the City the remainder of the proceeds from the sale of the treasury bond which amounted to only $24,000. Thus the City lost nearly $1,000,000 on appellant's dealings.

After appellant's activities were discovered during an external audit, he was arrested for thirteen counts of official misconduct arising from the thirteen journal entries. At trial, the state's position was that appellant deliberately made the improper journal entries to cover up his prohibited activities and thereby retain his job. Appellant defended on the theory that any journal entries were simply the result of honest mistakes. Appellant's sole issue on appeal is that the trial court erred in denying his motion for judgment of acquittal.

The statute under which appellant was charged reads:

(1) "Official misconduct" means the commission of the following acts by a public servant, with corrupt intent to obtain a benefit for himself or another or to cause unlawful harm to another.

(b) knowingly falsifying ... any official record or official document.

(c) "Corrupt" means done with knowledge that act is wrongful and with improper motives.

Sec. 839.25(1), Fla..Stat. (1989). In *Linehan v. State, 442 So.2d 244 (Fla. 2d DCA 1983), modified on other grounds, 476 So.2d 1262 (Fla. 1985),* Judge Lehan distinguished between general intent crimes and specific intent crimes. He stated:

A "general intent" statute is one that prohibits either a specific voluntary act or something that is substantially certain to result from the act (e.g., damage to a building is the natural result of the act of setting a building afire). A person's subjective intent to cause the particular result is irrelevant to general intent crimes because the law ascribes to him a presumption that he intended such a result...Thus, in general intent statutes words such as "willfully" or "intentionally," without more, indicate only that the person must have intended to do the act and serve to distinguish that conduct from accidental (noncriminal) behavior or strict liability crimes...

Specific intent statutes, on the other hand, prohibit an act when accompanied by some intent other than the intent to do the act itself or the intent (or presumed intent) to cause the natural and necessary consequences of the act...Accordingly, a crime encompassing a requirement of a subjective intent to accomplish a statutorily prohibited result may be a specific intent crime...Thus, to be a "specific intent" crime, a criminal statute which contains words of mental condition like "willfully" or "intentionally" should include language encompassing a subjective intent, for example, intent to cause a result in addition to that which is substantially certain to result from a statutorily prohibited act.

Id. 442 So.2d at 247-48. As it applies to the statute here in question, the statute contains a general intent of knowing the act is unlawful but also requires a specific intent that it be done with the intent to cause a benefit to himself or harm to another. Thus, the focus of our inquiry is whether or not the various elements of intent were proved.

The trial judge in this case heard voluminous evidence regarding these transactions. There was ample evidence that appellant was told not to invest in reverse purchase options and not to deal with secondary brokers. Further, it was clear that by statute only the city commission could authorize a loan transaction. While appellant claims that the journal entries were merely honest mistakes, the net effect of the entries was to show an ever increasing asset account when in fact the exact opposite was occurring. The account was then zeroed out by the last journal entry which would have suggested a break-even situation, rather than the substantial loss that really occurred. While accounting for reverse-repurchase agreements is complicated, an accounting expert testified that the journal entries were incorrect and misleading. Furthermore, when the discrepancies were discovered, appellant was requested to produce backup documentation for the journal entries which he never did. The trial court found that the acts were done with knowledge that they were wrongful and unlawful. He further found that, contrary to these being innocent mistakes by a poorly trained bookkeeper, "considerable skill was employed to mask or cover the unlawful conduct. This is proved there and enhances the culpability of the defendant." In fact what the court found was that the acts were knowingly done and that "he had to know the serious financial injury he worked." In other words, the defendant intentionally performed the prohibited act whose natural consequences (the losses) may reasonably be expected to follow. Thus, the state presented adequate evidence as to general intent.

With regard to specific intent, it was the state's burden to prove that the appellant acted with the intent to benefit himself or another or with the intent to cause harm to another. While the trial court found that the acts of defendant caused affirmative harm to the City, harm in fact is not the test for a finding of specific intent. The commission of the act itself does not give rise to a specific intent to commit the act. Furthermore, there is simply no evidence in the record here revealing that the appellant intended to harm the City. Thus, the state failed to prove the specific intent to cause harm.

However, the state can still satisfy its burden if it proved Bauer's specific intent to benefit himself. There was no direct evidence of this here. *Cf. Barr v. State, 507 So.2d 175 (Fla. 3d DCA 1987)* (conviction for official misconduct upheld where direct evidence was presented that police officer falsified official reports in an attempt to avoid reprimand for failure to follow police procedures). However, the state can also prove specific intent by circumstantial evidence. *Rebjebian v. State, 44 So.2d 81, 82-83 (Fla. 1949); Smith v. State, 87 Fla. 502, 100 So. 738 (Fla. 1924)*. Where the state attempts to prove its case by circumstantial evidence, the state can survive a motion for judgment of acquittal simply by presenting "competent evidence from which the jury could infer guilty to the exclusion of all other inferences." See *State v. Law, 559 So.2d 187 (Fla. 1989)*. As applied here, the state only needed to present competent evidence from which the fact-finder could infer this specific intent to the exclusion of the appellant's "honest mistake" theory. The state satisfied its burden here. For a period exceeding one year, the appellant never told anyone about the reverse repurchase or that the City's million dollar bond had been sold. When the appellant's supervisor confronted him with an approximate million dollar loss and asked him for backup documentation, appellant repeatedly responded that he was going to get it from the broker. However, he never did this, and when his supervisor called the broker, she found out that the broker had gone out of business. Then, when confronted by the city attorney and city manager with the million dollar loss, he told them that he knew the money was gone but that he had not taken in and knew that they would find it. It was only at that point when he was told that there was going to be an official investigation that he resigned. From the above, the fact-finder could have logically inferred that appellant's conduct in concealing the losses which were accruing in the reverse repurchase transaction was intended to avoid punishment, whether it be in the form of a reprimand, lawsuit, criminal charges, termination or the like. Avoidance of punishment is a benefit for purposes of official misconduct. See *Barr, 507 So.2d at 177.* Furthermore, this evidence which suggests a deliberate and prolonged cover-up would be inconsistent with simply an honest mistake. Thus, we conclude that the state presented sufficient circumstantial evidence of appellant's specific intent to benefit himself to survive the motion for judgment of acquittal.

We note a possible conflict between our finding on the evidence of a benefit and the trial court's finding that the state "makes no claim that the defendant benefitted from these transactions." While the state did comment in closing that the issue in this case was *harm* to the city rather than *benefit* to the defendant, a look beyond these labels reveals that the state really did argue benefit. In its closing argument, the state raised *Barr*, which only addressed the issue of benefit, and argued that the defendant had acted because he "couldn't afford to lose his job." By doing so, we conclude that the State did raise the benefit issue, albeit somewhat unartfully. We therefore reject the trial court's finding to the contrary as unsupported by the record. See *Beaty v. Miller, 480 So.2d 196 (Fla. 1st DCA 1985).* Finally, although we disagree with the trial court's reasoning, we affirm the trial court's order as "right for the wrong reason." See *Owens v. State, 354 So.2d 118 (Fla. 3d DCA 1978).*

GLICKSTEIN, C.J., and LETTS and WARNER, JJ., concur.

ON MOTION FOR REHEARING

PER CURIAM.

We deny the appellant's motion for rehearing.

GLICKSTEIN, C.J., and LETTS, J., concur.

WARNER, J., dissents with opinion.

WARNER, Judge, dissenting.

The appellant has moved for rehearing claiming that our original opinion violates the double jeopardy clause of the Constitution by finding sufficient evidence of benefit to appellant to sustain his conviction where the trial court found none. While the claim may raise double jeopardy questions, the bottom line amounts to a contention that we impermissibly reweighed the facts and decided a fact contrary to the finding of the trial court. Having spent considerable time reviewing the record, I am compelled to agree. Therefore, I would now reverse.

Our original opinion attempts to reconcile our conclusion that the evidence would support a finding of benefit with the trial court's finding that the state "makes no claim that the defendant benefitted from these transactions." We maintained that the trial court overlooked the claim of benefit made by the state and thus did not decide the issue. Upon further review of the record, I conclude that our interpretation is wrong. Not only did the state argue benefit but the record reveals that the issue of benefit was thoroughly briefed. Appellant submitted proposed findings of fact which included a finding that the state had attempted to prove a "benefit" (which was also referred to as improper motive), either (1) to obtain stimulation from engaging in speculative activity or (2) to cover up and hide activity to keep his job. The proposed findings refuted both of these claims.

To counter appellant's presentation, the state submitted findings that appellant benefitted from preparing misleading journal entries by covering up his wrongdoing to keep his job; fed defendant's passion for the excitement generated by these speculative investments; kept a $200,000 account outside control of the city; and generated substantial fees to brokers who dealt exclusively with him. The appellant and state each filed objections to the other's proposed findings.

The trial court's order used neither set of findings, but instead the court prepared its own judgment. (The trial court mentioned all of the memorandums filed in the Final Judgment.) Our original opinion interpreted the court's opinion as overlooking the claims the state made. Given my subsequent review of what the trial court had before it, I can hardly say that the trial court was unaware of the claims of benefit to defendant that the state made.

Thus, it appears to me that we erroneously interpreted the trial judge's order in our initial opinion. I now conclude that the trial court found that the defendant did not benefit from these transactions. Given that finding of fact, which is supported by the record (all of the state's evidence of benefit being entirely circumstantial), an essential element of the charge was not proved. The trial court should have granted the motion for judgment of acquittal.

I would reverse the conviction and sentence of appellant and remand for the entry of a judgment of acquittal.

REVIEW

1. Statutes may contain _____.
   a. only a requirement of a general intent
   b. only a requirement of specific intent
   c. both a and b
   d. neither a nor b

2. The specific intent to cause harm is proven by _____.
   a. a showing that harm occurred
   b. a showing the defendant intended to cause harm
   c. both a and b
   d. neither a nor b

CASE

Proko v. State, 566 So.2d 918 (Fla. 5th DCA 1990).

Defendant was convicted in the Circuit Court, Brevard County, John Antoon, II, J., of false imprisonment and solicitation to commit lewdness or prostitution, and he appealed. The District Court of Appeal, McNeal, R.T., Associate Judge, held that: (1) victim's testimony supported conclusion that defendant used some amount of force to restrain her which was sufficient to meet requirements for conviction of false imprisonment, and (2) State was not required to allege or prove specific intent or purpose in order to establish offense of false imprisonment.

Affirmed.

McNEAL, R.T., Associate Judge.

Appellant, Michael Proko, appeals his conviction of false imprisonment and solicitation to commit lewdness or prostitution. Two of appellant's arguments merit discussion. Appellant argues that the trial court erred in denying a motion for judgment of acquittal on false imprisonment because the evidence did not establish a prima facie case of forcible restraint and because the state failed to allege or prove intent. The state contends that the conflicting evidence on the issue of forcible restraint created a factual question for the jury to resolve. They also contend that they are not required to allege or prove specific intent or purpose to establish the crime of false imprisonment. We find that the evidence of forcible restraint was sufficient to present a jury question on that issue and that the state was not required to allege or prove that the unlawful restraint was committed with specific intent.

Appellant was convicted of violating section 787.02(1)(a), Florida Statutes (1989), which provides as follows:

> The term "false imprisonment" means forcibly, by threat, or secretly confining, abducting, imprisoning, or restraining another person without lawful authority and against his will with any purpose other than those referred to in § 787.01 [the kidnapping statute].

The state filed an information that tracked the language of this statute. Appellant never moved to dismiss the information. At trial, the state presented evidence that appellant solicited sexual favors from the 15 year old victim in return for money, and after she refused, appellant grabbed the victim's arm and pulled it toward the window of his truck. When the victim tried to "jerk" her arm away, he "jerked" it back. Finally, with what she described as a "big old jerk", she "jerked" away from him. In response to the question, "what you described, was it kind of like a tug-of-war," the victim responded, "Yes." She then demonstrated this jerking motion for the jury. On cross-examination, appellant's defense attorney was able to minimize the tugging by getting the victim to admit that she was able to remove her hand when she wanted to. On redirect, the victim explained that she was able to remove her hand only after a struggle.

A motion for judgment of acquittal admits not only the facts in evidence, but every reasonable inference from the evidence favorable to the state. The court should not grant the motion unless, when viewed in the light most favorable to the state, the evidence does not establish a prima facie case of guilt. *Lynch v. State*, 293 So.2d 44 (Fla. 1974); *Herman v. State*, 472 So.2d 770 (Fla. 5th DCA 1985), rev. denied, 482 So.2d 348 (Fla. 1986). If there is sufficient evidence from which the jury could conclude that appellant unlawfully and forcibly restrained the victim against her will, the motion must be denied.

Appellant argues that the restraint must be substantial to be unlawful but cites no authority in support of that proposition. Unlike some states, the Florida statute does not require that the force or the restraint be substantial. *Compare* N.J.S.A. 2C:13-3 which requires substantial interference with the victim's liberty. To establish false imprisonment the state must prove three elements beyond a reasonable doubt: (1) defendant forcibly restrained the victim against her will; (2) defendant had no lawful authority; and (3) defendant acted for any purpose other than the purposes set forth in the kidnapping statute. Fla.Std. Jury Instr. (Crim.) From the evidence introduced in this case the jury could conclude that appellant detained the victim against her will in order to prolong his contact for the purpose of soliciting sexual favors. Because she had to use some force to remove her hand form his grasp, the jury could conclude that the defendant used some amount of force to restrain her. That is sufficient to establish forcible restraint. **Cf. *McCloud v. State***, 335 So.2d 257 (Fla. 1976); *S.W. v. State*, 513 So.2d 1088 (Fla. 3d DCA 1987); *Santiago v. State*, 497 So.2d 975 (Fla. 4th DCA 1986) (when a thief uses any degree of force to obtain possession of the property, the taking is a robbery).

The essence of false imprisonment is the act of depriving the victim of personal liberty or freedom of movement for any length of time. In this case, the victim was briefly deprived of her ability to leave. For this reason, there was sufficient evidence to submit the case to the jury. See *State v. Horton*, 442 So.2d 408 (Fla. 2d DCA 1983) (disputed facts on whether restraint or confinement occurred should have been presented to the jury); *Jane v. State*, 362 So.2d 1005 (Fla. 4th DCA 1978) (holding victim in a bear hug was sufficient evidence of false imprisonment).

On the issue of intent, there are conflicting interpretations of § 787.02(1)(a), Florida Statutes (1989). The Fourth District Court of Appeal in *Rauso v. State*, 425 So.2d 618, 620 (Fla. 4th DCA 1983), stated in dicta that "an intent (other than § 787.01(a) motives) must be alleged in the accusatory pleading and proven at trial beyond a reasonable doubt in order to convict a person of false imprisonment." The Second District Court of Appeal in *State v. Graham*, 468 So.2d 270 (Fla. 2d DCA 1985), rev. denied, 475 So.2d 694 (Fla. 1985), and *State v. Brown*, 466 So.2d 1223 (Fla. 2d DCA 1985), rev. denied, 475 So.2d 693 (Fla. 1985), held that the false imprisonment statute is a general intent statute, and, therefore, it is not necessary to allege a specific intent or purpose. Although they did not comment directly on this issue, the Florida Supreme Court found that the false imprisonment statute required only general intent and held that it was a necessarily lesser included offense of kidnapping, which requires a specific intent. *State v. Sanborn, 533 So.2d 1169, 1170 (Fla. 1988)*. Specific intent crimes require some special mental element over and above the mental state required for the criminal act itself. *State v. Medlin, 273 So.2d 394, 396 (Fla. 1973); State v. Oxx, 417 So.2d 287, 289 (Fla. 5ᵗʰ DCA 1982)*. Because the false imprisonment statute is a general intent statute, we hold it is not necessary for the state to allege or prove a specific intent or purpose to establish the offense of false imprisonment.

The judgments and sentences are AFFIRMED.

HARRIS and PETERSON, JJ., concur.

REVIEW

1. False imprisonment is an example of _____.
   a. a specific intent crime
   b. a general intent crime
   c. both a and b
   d. neither a nor b

2. Kidnapping is an example of _____.
   a. a specific intent crime
   b. a general intent crime
   c. both a and b
   d. neither a nor b

CASE

Archer v. State, 613 So.2d 446 (Fla. 1993).

Defendant was convicted of first-degree murder and sentenced to death by the Circuit Court, Escambia County, Lacey Collier, J., and he appealed. The Supreme Court held that: (1) defendant waived argument for acquittal that murder actually committed was independent of agreed-upon plan by not raising claim at trial, and (2) error in instructing jury on application of heinous, atrocious, or cruel aggravator to defendant was not harmless.

Conviction affirmed and sentence vacated.

PER CURIAM.

Robin Lee Archer appeals his conviction of first-degree murder and his sentence of death. We have jurisdiction. Art. V, §§ 3(b)(1), Fla. Const. Although we affirm

124

Archer's conviction, we vacate his sentence and remand for resentencing. [Footnote 1 omitted]

According to the testimony presented at trial, Archer was fired from his job at an auto parts store in March 1990. The following January he convinced his cousin, seventeen-year-old Pat Bonifay, to kill the clerk he apparently blamed for his having been fired. Bonifay testified that Archer told him to rob the store to hide the motive for the killing and to wear a ski mask and gloves and also told him the location of the store's cash box and emergency exit. Bonifay borrowed a handgun from a friend who gave the gun to Archer to give to Bonifay.

Bonifay talked two friends into helping him, and the trio went to the parts store on Friday night, January 24, 1991. Bonifay could not go through with the murder, however, and they left the store. The next day Archer got after Bonifay for not killing the clerk, and the trio went back to the store that night. Bonifay shot the clerk and he and one of his friends crawled into the store through the night parts window. After opening the cash boxes, Bonifay shot the clerk in the head twice as he lay on the floor begging for his life. Archer later refused to pay Bonifay because he killed the wrong clerk.

Bonifay confessed to several people, one of whom informed the authorities, resulting in the arrest of Archer, Bonifay, and Bonifay's two friends. The defendants were tried separately, and Archer's jury convicted him of first-degree murder. The judge agreed with the jury's recommendation and sentenced him to death. [FN2]

As his first point on appeal, Archer argues that his motion for judgment of acquittal should have been granted because the victim's murder was independent of the agreed-upon plan to kill a different clerk. For an issue to be preserved for appeal, however, it "must be presented to the lower court and the specific legal argument or ground to be argued on appeal must be part of that presentation if it is to be considered preserved." *Tillman v. State, 471 So.2d 32, 35 (Fla. 1985).* Archer did not make the instant argument in the trial court, and, therefore, this issue has not been preserved for appellate review.

Even if the issue had been preserved, we would find that it had no merit. As this Court has previously stated:

The law, as well as reason, prevents [a defendant] from taking advantage of his own wrong doing, or excusing himself when this unlawful act, if committed by [a defendant], strikes down an unintended victim. The original malice as a matter of law is transferred from the one against whom it was entertained to the person who actually suffered the consequences of the unlawful act.

*Coston v. State, 139 Fla. 250, 253-54, 190 So. 520, 522 (1939); **Provenzano v. State**, 497 So.2d 1177 (Fla. 1986), cert. denied, 481 U.S. 1024, 107 S.Ct. 1912, 95 L.Ed.2d 518 (1987); **Parker v. State**, 458 So.2d 750 (Fla. 1984), cert. denied, 470 U.S. 1088, 105 S.Ct. 1855, 85 L.Ed.2d 152 (1985).* Bonifay testified that he knew neither of the clerks and that he did not know that he killed the wrong one until Archer told him. Archer created the situation, and the victim's death was a natural and foreseeable result of Archer's actions. Bonifay's killing the victim was not an independent act for which Archer can deny responsibility. Compare **Bryant v. State**, *412 So.2d 347 (Fla. 1982)* (victim's death was outside the common design of the original felonious collaboration). Therefore, the evidence is sufficient to support Archer's conviction of first-degree murder.

At the penalty-phase charge conference Archer argued that the jury should not be instructed on the heinous, atrocious, or cruel aggravator because that aggravator could not be applied vicariously to him. In **Omelus v. State**, *584 So.2d 563 (Fla. 1991)*, we held that a defendant who arranges for a killing but who is not present and who does not know how the murder will be accomplished cannot be subjected vicariously to the heinous, atrocious, or cruel aggravator. Here, Archer knew that Bonifay would use a handgun to kill the victim; he did not know, however, that the victim would be shot four times or that he would die begging for his life. Witnesses testified to the manner of the victim's death, and the prosecutor argued the applicability of this aggravator. On the facts of this case we are unable to say that the error in instructing on and finding this aggravator is harmless. Therefore, we vacate Archer's death sentence and direct the trial court to empanel a jury and conduct a new sentencing proceeding. [FN3]

It is so ordered.

BARKETT, C.J., and OVERTON, McDONALD, SHAW, GRIMES, KOGAN and HARDING, JJ., concur.

FN2. Bonifay's jury also convicted him of first-degree murder, and his appeal of that conviction and his resultant death sentence is pending before this Court. **Bonifay v. State,** *no. 78,724.*

FN3. Due to this holding, we do not address the other issues raised on appeal.

REVIEW

1. It is not an independent act if _____.
   a. the result is natural
   b. the result is foreseeable
   c. both a and b
   d. neither a nor b

CASE

In the Interest of J.G., a child., *655 So.2d 1284 (Fla. 4th DCA 1995).*

Juvenile moved for judgment of acquittal on charge of criminal mischief. The Circuit Court, Broward County, Melanie May, J., denied motion. Juvenile appealed.

The District Court of Appeal, Stevenson, J., held that motion for judgment of acquittal should have been granted, since doctrine of transferred intent was inapplicable.

Reversed.

STEVENSON, JUDGE.

J.G., a juvenile, challenges the trial court's denial of his motion for judgment of acquittal on the charge of criminal mischief. Because the doctrine of transferred intent was improperly applied to the facts of this case, we reverse.

At trial, it was established that J.G. intended to strike the victim with his closed fist but instead struck the victim's automobile, shattering the rear window. After closing arguments, the trial judge stated, "there's no doubt in my mind he hit that window, but I don't think that's what he meant to hit." The trial judge asked both defense counsel and the prosecutor to do some additional legal research to determine "if you intend to strike a person and hit an object and cause damage . . . whether that will qualify for criminal mischief". At a subsequent hearing, neither counsel produced any additional authority on the trial court's point of inquiry. Finding that the doctrine of "transferred intent" applied, the trial court found J.G. guilty of criminal mischief. We reverse.

The doctrine of transferred intent was recently addressed in *D.J. v. State, 651 So.2d 1255 (Fla. 1st DCA 1995)*. There, a high school student was adjudicated delinquent after being found guilty of attempted battery on a school employee and affray. The defendant was involved in a schoolyard fistfight with another student when he mistakenly struck an assistant principal who was attempting to stop the fight. In reversing the finding of guilt on the attempted battery of a school employee charge, the court stated:

> We agree with the appellant that the doctrine of transferred intent will not sustain the finding of guilt. As we held in *Mordica v. State, 618 So.2d 301 (Fla. 1st DCA 1993)*, the doctrine only operates to transfer the defendant's intent as to the intended victim to the unintended victim. Thus, only the appellant's intent to strike his opponent - a student - could be transferred, and there could be no intent to strike a school employee.

Id. at 1256.

Similarly, in the instant case, only J.G.'s intent to strike his intended victim - a person - could be transferred. The offense of criminal mischief requires that the actor possess the specific intent to damage the property of another. [FN1] The intent to damage the property of another does not arise by operation of law where the actor's true intention is to cause harm to the person of another. The doctrine of transferred intent could only operate to transfer J.G.'s intent to commit an offensive touching, (i.e., a battery), and since there is no such charge possible against an inanimate object, the doctrine is simply not applicable in the present case.

Accordingly, because the criminal mischief statute requires that the offender act against the property of another willfully and with malice, we hold that the trial court erred in denying J.G.'s motion for judgment of acquittal.

Reversed.

WARNER and POLEN, JJ., concur.

> [FN1] Section 806.13(1)(a), Florida Statutes (1993) provides in part that:
> A person commits the offense of criminal mischief if he willfully and maliciously injures or damages by any means any real or personal property belonging to another . . .

REVIEW

1. The doctrine of transferred intent _____.
   a. transfers the defendant's intent from the intended victim to the unintended victim
   b. transfers intent to damage property to intent to damage a person
   c. both a and b
   d. neither a nor b

CULPABLE NEGLIGENCE

Every person has a duty to act reasonably toward others. Culpable negligence is more than a failure to use ordinary care for others. In order for negligence to be culpable, it must be gross and flagrant, showing a reckless disregard for human life or for the safety of persons exposed to its dangerous effects. For example, shooting a gun into a crowd of people without shooting at any one person in particular may constitute culpable negligence.

CASE

State v. Sherouse, 536 So.2d 1194 (Fla. 5th DCA 1989).

Appeal from the Circuit Court for Orange County; Michael F. Cycmanick, Judge.

PER CURIAM.

AFFIRMED.

DAUKSCH and DANIEL, JJ., concur.

COBB, J., concurs specially with opinion.

COBB, Judge, concurring specially

The appellee, Elizabeth Kay Sherouse, was charged with two counts of attempted manslaughter in violation of § 782.07 and 777.04, Florida Statutes (1987). She had tested positive for the AIDS virus, H.I.V., and had been informed that the virus was deadly and could be transmitted through sexual intercourse. The state alleged that she disregarded these warnings and offered or agreed to engage in sexual intercourse for money with two male individuals on two separate occasions. She did not inform the male individuals that she had the AIDS virus or that it could be transferred through sexual intercourse.

The trial court granted Sherouse's 3.190(c)(4) motion to dismiss on the basis that there was no crime of attempted involuntary (culpable negligence) manslaughter, and although Sherouse acted in a culpably negligent fashion, there was no evidence that her conduct evidenced an intent to kill.

Florida recognizes the existence of the criminal offense of attempted voluntary manslaughter, but not the offense of attempted involuntary (culpable negligence) manslaughter. *Taylor v. State, 444 So.2d 931 (Fla. 1983).* See also *Murray v. State, 491 So.2d 1120 (Fla. 1986); Tillman v. State, 471 So.2d 32 (Fla. 1985);* and *Brown v. State, 455 So.2d 382 (Fla. 1984).* In these cases the Florida Supreme Court held that culpable negligence is not sufficient to maintain an attempted manslaughter charge and there must be the requisite criminal intent to support the charge of attempted manslaughter.

The state reads these cases to mean that the intent to commit an unlawful act supports the attempted manslaughter charge. The state argues that Sherouse's intent to commit the unlawful act of prostitution while carrying the AIDS virus provides the inference of an intent to kill; therefore, only the intent to commit the precipitating act, and not the intent to commit homicide, must be demonstrated. Sherouse, on the other hand, contends that voluntary manslaughter is a specific intent crime and relies on the Florida Supreme Court cases cited above.

The trial court, after considering the Florida Supreme Court cases cited above, relied on our language in *Barton v. State, 507 So.2d 638, 641 (Fla. 5th DCA 1987), rev'd on other grounds, State v. Barton, 523 So.2d 152 (Fla. 1988),* wherein we interpreted *Taylor*:

> *Taylor v. State, 444 So.2d 931 (Fla. 1983),* held that an intent to kill is a prerequisite for conviction of assault with intent to commit manslaughter pursuant to *Williams v. State, 41 Fla. 295, 26 So. 184 (1899).* Adopting the *Williams* rationale, *Taylor* held that the crime of attempted manslaughter exists in situations where, if death resulted from an act of the defendant, the defendant would be guilty of voluntary (i.e., intentional) manslaughter at common law. Voluntary manslaughter at common law (as to which there can be an attempt) has been statutorily enacted in Florida as "the killing of a human being by the act (or) procurement ... of another, without lawful justification." Section 782.07, Fla.Stat.

(1985). The words "act" and "procurement" obviously refer to acts evidencing an intent to kill, as required at common law for voluntary manslaughter.

Taylor, in its discussion of voluntary manslaughter, repeatedly refers to the requisite of an intention to kill, not simply the intention to commit an unlawful act that results in homicide. In discussing the older case of *Williams v. State, 41 Fla. 295, 26 So. 184 (1899)*, the *Taylor* opinion states: "The (Williams) Court made it clear, however, that for a conviction of assault with intent to commit manslaughter to be valid, there must be proof that the defendant *did intend to kill.*" (Emphasis added). *Taylor at 933.* In discussing the facts of *Taylor*, Justice Boyd wrote: "[I]t is clear that appellant intentionally fired the shotgun at Clayton. This is sufficient proof that he *intended to kill him. Kelly v. State, 78 Fla. 636, 83 So.506 (1919)."* (Emphasis added). *Taylor at 934.*

Therefore, consistent with our interpretation in Barton, an essential element of the crime of voluntary manslaughter is an intent to kill, although that intent lacks sufficient deliberation to elevate the homicide to first degree murder. See *Williams, 41 Fla. At 299-300, 26 So. at 186.*

For the foregoing reasons, I concur with an affirmance of the trial court's dismissal. It is ironic, however, that a charge of the greater crime of attempted second degree murder arguably could have been sustained since second degree murder does not require any specific intent to kill another person. See § 782.04(2), Fla.Stat. (1987).

REVIEW

        1. Manslaughter is _____.
            a. a specific intent crime
            b. a general intent crime
            c. both a and b
            d. neither a nor b

COMMENT

Can a person commit the offense of driving under the influence without actually driving? Should it be a crime to "sleep it off" in your car? Is it a crime? Read the following case.

CASE

Griffin v. State, 457 So.2d 1070 (Fla. 2d DCA 1984).

Petitioner sought writ of certiorari to review a judgment of the Circuit Court, Pinellas County, Philip A. Federico, J., affirming County Court's conviction and sentencing of petitioner for being in actual, physical control of a motor vehicle while under the influence of alcohol. The District Court of Appeal held that: (1) the trial court correctly instructed jury on definition of "actual, physical control"; (2) petitioner was in actual, physical control of the car; and (3) petitioner's sentence, which in part revoked his driver's license for six months, was correct.

No error and petition denied.

PER CURIAM.

Petitioner seeks a writ of certiorari to review the circuit court's affirmance of the county court's conviction and sentencing of petitioner for being in actual, physical control of a motor vehicle while under the influence of alcohol, a violation of §316.193(1)(a), Florida Statutes (1982). The county court revoked petitioner's driver's license for six months pursuant to § 322.28, Florida Statutes (1982). We deny the petition.

The evidence established that at approximately 2:30 a.m., a police officer found petitioner in the driver's seat of a car which was stationary in a traffic lane facing in a direction opposite to that in which traffic was to flow. The engine was stopped, the key was in the ignition, the lights were on, and the footbrake apparently was depressed by petitioner's foot, as indicated by the illumination of the rear brake light on the car. Petitioner was, or appeared to be, asleep. The brake light went off when the petitioner got out of the car after the arresting officer shook him to awaken him. Petitioner does not take issue with the sufficiency of the evidence on the basis of which the jury found him to be under the influence of alcohol. The issues presented to us principally involve the definitions of "in actual, physical control" under § 316.193(1)(a), whether petitioner was in actual, physical control of the car, and, if so, whether his license was properly revoked under § 322.28.

We do not find merit in petitioner's argument that the trial court incorrectly instructed the jury on the definition of "actual, physical control." The instruction was the same as that found in *Florida Standard Jury Instructions in Misdemeanor Cases (1981 ed.)* which were approved by the Florida Supreme Court as guidance for trial courts. *In re Florida Standard Jury Instructions in Criminal Cases, 431 So.2d 594 (Fla. 1981).*

We do not find merit in petitioner's arguments concerning error in the failure of the county court to declare a mistrial.

Also, we find no error in the denial of petitioner's motions for judgment of acquittal and for a new trial. We disagree with petitioner's argument that he was not in actual physical control of the car. Apparently the brake light, which was illuminated when the officer approached the car, went off when petitioner got out of the car. That is circumstantial evidence that petitioner was, in fact, exercising control over the vehicle. Furthermore, even without the evidence as to the brake light, there was circumstantial evidence that petitioner had operated the vehicle on the public street. See *State v. Eckert, 186 Neb. 134, 181 N.W.2d 264, 268 (1970).* In addition, the reasoning of the factually similar case of *Hughes v. State, 535 P.2d 1023 (Okla.Crim.App. 1975),* is persuasive. In *Hughes,* defendant was found sitting in the driver's seat of an automobile which was

131

parked at a ninety-degree angle in the road. Although the engine was not running, the key was in the ignition. The Oklahoma Appellate Court used a definition of "actual physical control" as encompassing control which "meant the 'ability to keep from starting,' ... 'to exercise directing influence over,' and 'the authority to manage'." *Id. at 1024.* This is similar to the foregoing *Florida Standard Jury Instruction* saying that "[d]efendant must have had the capability and power to dominate, direct or regulate the vehicle, regardless of whether or not he is exercising that capability or power at the time of the alleged offense." The following statement of the Oklahoma court reflects our conclusions:

> We believe that an intoxicated person seated behind the steering wheel of a motor vehicle is a threat to the safety and welfare of the public. The danger is less than where an intoxicated person is actually driving the vehicle, but it does exist. The defendant when arrested may have been exercising no conscious violation with regard to the vehicle, still there is a legitimate inference to be drawn that he placed himself behind the wheel of the vehicle and could have at any time started the automobile and driven away. He therefore had "actual physical control" of the vehicle within the meaning of the statute.

Id.

We believe the intent of the Florida legislature was similar to that which the *Hughes* court attributed to the Oklahoma legislature, to wit:

> that the legislature, in making it a crime to be in "actual physical control of a motor vehicle while under the influence of intoxicating liquor," intended to enable the drunken driver to be apprehended before he strikes.

Id.

Petitioner argues that affirmance of his conviction might discourage inebriated drivers from pulling over to "sleep it off." We, of course, agree that such conduct should be encouraged. However, petitioner was found in his car in the middle of the road, and, as the Minnesota Supreme Court said in *State v. Juncewski*, 308 N.W.2d 316, 320 (Minn. 1981) (quoting *State v. Ghylin*, 250 N.W.2d 252 (N.D. 1977)), "the real purpose of the statute is to deter individuals who have been drinking intoxicating liquor from getting into their vehicles, except as passengers." See *State v. Schuler*, 243 N.W.2d 367 (N.D. 1976).

Finally, we conclude that petitioner's sentence which in part revoked petitioner's driver's license for six months was correct. Section 322.28 provides that revocation of a driver's license is a penalty for the offense of driving a motor vehicle while under the influence of alcoholic beverages. Section 316.193 defines that offense as including being in the actual physical control of a motor vehicle while under the influence of alcoholic beverages when affected to the extent that one's normal faculties are impaired.

We find no error, certainly no error constituting a miscarriage of justice, and therefore deny the petition. See **Combs v. State**, *436 So.2d 93 (Fla. 1983)*.

BOARDMAN, A.C.J., and DANAHY and LEHAN, JJ., concur.

REVIEW

1. To be convicted of driving under the influence, the state must prove _____.
    a. the defendant was exercising control over the vehicle
    b. the motor was on
    c. the car was moving
    d. all of the above

NEGLIGENCE

As stated above, every person has a duty to act reasonably toward each other. An unintentional breach of that duty is negligence. While simple negligence alone is not a criminal act, but it can be used to enhance what is already a crime. Read the following case.

CASE

State v. Smith, *638 So.2d 509 (Fla. 1994).*

Defendant was charged with driving with suspended license causing death or injury. The Circuit Court, Pasco County, Stanley R. Mills, J., dismissed, and state appealed. The District Court of Appeal, 624 So.2d 355, affirmed, and state appealed. The Supreme Court , Overton, J., held that statute making it a felony to drive with suspended license causing death or serious injury did not unconstitutionally criminalize simple negligence.

Reversed and remanded.

Kogan, J., concurred in result only with opinion, in which Shaw, J., concurred.

OVERTON, Justice.

We have on appeal **State v. Smith**, *624 So.2d 355 (Fla.2d DCA 1993)*, in which the district court declared § 322.34(3), Florida Statutes (1991), to be unconstitutional because it found that an act of simple negligence in operating a motor vehicle could not be combined with the crime of driving a motor vehicle under a canceled, suspended, or revoked license to create a new criminal offense. We have jurisdiction. Art. V, Sec. 3(b)(1), Fla.Const. For the reasons expressed, we find the statute to be constitutional and reverse the decision of the district court.

In this case, the appellee, Robert N. Smith, was charged with driving with a suspended license causing death or injury under § 322.34(3), [FN1] which provides:

Any person whose driver's license has been canceled, suspended, or revoked pursuant to § 316.655, § 322.26(8), § 322.27(2), or § 322.28(2) or (5) and who operates a motor vehicle while his driver's license is canceled, suspended or revoked and who by careless or negligent operation thereof causes death of or serious bodily injury to another human being, is guilty of a felony of the third degree, punishable as provided in § 775.082 or § 775.083.

Smith moved to dismiss the charge on the basis that § 322.34(3) unconstitutionally criminalizes mere negligence. The trial court granted the motion to dismiss and the State appealed.

On appeal, the Second District Court of Appeal affirmed. The district court noted that driving with a suspended or revoked license is normally a misdemeanor. Under the statute at issue, however, the district court determined that simple negligence is used to enhance the crime of driving with a suspended or revoked license to a felony. In reviewing whether the statute was constitutional, the district court first determined that simple negligence, standing by itself, cannot constitute a criminal act. The district court then looked to the question of whether the non-criminal act of simple negligence could be combined with the criminal act of driving with a canceled, suspended, or revoked license to create a new and distinct criminal offense. Finding no causal connection between the criminal and non-criminal acts, the district court held that simple negligence could not be used to enhance a criminal act from a misdemeanor to a felony.

As the district court correctly noted, on several occasions this Court has found statutes criminalizing simple negligence to be unconstitutional. See, e.g., *State v. Hamilton, 388 So.2d 561 (Fla. 1980); State v. Winters, 346 So.2d 991 (Fla. 1977)*. This does not mean, however, that simple negligence can never be used to enhance the penalty for a willful criminal act. For example, under section 316.193, Florida Statutes (1993), the act of driving under the influence (DUI), when combined with an act of simple negligence, is elevated to the crime of DUI manslaughter. See *Magaw v. State, 537 So.2d 564 (Fla. 1989)*. The district court distinguished the DUI manslaughter statute by stating that driving under the influence is, in and of itself, a reckless act, whereas driving with a suspended, canceled, or revoked driver's license is not. We disagree.

Only when a driver's license has been suspended, canceled, or revoked due to some wrongdoing on the part of the driver can a person be charged under section 322.34(3). For instance, only persons who have had their driver's licenses suspended, canceled, or revoked pursuant to sections 316.655 (suspension due to conviction of traffic offenses), 322.26(8) (suspension by a court due to conviction of serious traffic offense), 322.27(2) (suspension by the Department of Highway Safety and Motor Vehicles due to conviction of serious traffic offense), 322.28(2) (suspension for driving under the influence), or 322.28(5) (suspension due to conviction of manslaughter or vehicular homicide), are subject to prosecution under the statute at issue. Consequently, when a person is charged under the statute, a determination already has been made that the person is no longer fit to be driving on Florida's highways. As such, knowingly driving with a suspended, canceled, or revoked driver's license, as defined under the statute at issue, is indeed a willful act in clear violation of the law.

We also disagree with the district court's conclusion that the statute is unconstitutional because "[n]o causal connection exists between driving with a canceled, suspended or revoked license and an accident involving death or serious injury." *624 So.2d at 358*. As we stated in *Magaw*:

> [Under the DUI manslaughter statute,] *the state is not required to prove that the operator's drinking caused the accident.* The statute requires only that the operation of the vehicle...caused the accident. Therefore, *any deviation or lack of care on the part of a driver under the influence* to which the ... accident can be attributed will suffice.

537 So.2d at 567 (emphasis added). Under either the DUI manslaughter statute or the statute at issue, it is not the simple negligence of the driver that is the criminal conduct being punished; it is the *willful* act of choosing to drive a vehicle under the influence or to drive a vehicle with a suspended, canceled, or revoked license that is the criminal conduct being punished. In both instances, the legislature has simply made a policy decision that anyone who engages in the prohibited criminal conduct and who, while engaging in that prohibited criminal conduct, negligently injures another, is guilty of a more severe crime than if the prohibited conduct had not resulted in injury to another. Similarly, one who negligently kills another while engaged in the commission of certain enumerated felonies is guilty of felony murder. See § 782.04(1)(a)(2), Fla.Stat. (1993). Although the homicide may have been unintentionally committed through negligence, it is the willful act of committing the underlying felony that criminalizes the simple negligence supporting the conviction for felony murder. Consistent with that rationale, we hold that section 322.34(3) does not unconstitutionally criminalize simple negligence.

Accordingly, we find § 322.34(3), Florida Statutes (1991), to be constitutional, reverse the decision of the district court, and remand this cause for further proceedings.

It is so ordered.

GRIMES, C.J., HARDING, J., and McDONALD, Senior Justice, concur.

KOGAN, J., concurs in result only with an opinion, in which SHAW, J., concurs.

KOGAN, Justice, concurring in result only.

Criminalizing a negligent act poses serious questions of constitutional law and public policy that deserve very careful consideration. The United States Supreme Court has detailed many of these questions in *Morissette v. United States, 342 U.S. 246, 72*

135

S.Ct. 240, 96 L.Ed. 288 (1951), where Mr. Justice Jackson outlined the history of American criminal law's development from its English antecedents. As *Morissette* notes, there has been a slow drift away from the early English requirement that every crime must arise from a "vicious will" [FN2] or else there is no crime at all.

Today, some crimes can exist in the complete absence of even the slightest degree of intent, the most notable for present purposes being certain traffic regulations. These types of "strict liability" or "reduced intent" crimes generally are thought to be on their firmest footing when they involve relatively minor penalties and regulate those aspects of modern life arising from technological advances unknown to the common law. The question that generally is still unsettled in the law today is how far a legislative body can go in dispensing with scienter [FN3] or diminishing it below what the common law required.

This drift toward reduced scienter has met with criticism, some of it justified. The Pennsylvania Superior Court, for example, extended *Morissette* [FN4] to strike down a statute creating a maximum sentence of five years if a driver (a) violated a traffic regulation, and thereby (b) caused the death of another person. The Pennsylvania defendant had been tried under the statute for a form of "homicide" because he made an improper turn in his car and accidentally struck a motorcyclist he did not see, resulting in the motorcyclist's death. *Commonwealth v. Heck, 341 Pa. Super. 183, 491 A.2d 212 (1985), affirmed, 517 Pa. 192, 535 A.2d 575 (1987).* This statute obviously is both analogous to and less severe than the one at hand, so it deserves some scrutiny. [FN5]

In examining public policy and constitutional issues, the Pennsylvania Superior Court noted that the foundations of American criminal law rest on the belief that it is the criminal act combined with the culpable mind that deserves to be labeled as "infamous." See *id. 491 A.2d at 220.* Or as Oliver Wendell Holmes, Jr., once remarked, "even a dog distinguishes between being stumbled over and being kicked." O.W. Holmes, Jr., The Common Law 3 (1881). Severely criminalizing an unintentional act is contrary to the genius of Anglo-American law, which attaches the greater blameworthiness to the crime that rests on guilty intent, not mere carelessness. [FN6] Criminal statutes that reduce or eliminate traditional scienter therefore should receive greater scrutiny, though they certainly should not be stricken for want of scienter alone.

In this vein, the Pennsylvania Superior Court concluded that a "reduced intent" crime can violate due process in light of the following factors: (a) it imposes a penalty that is not light, but severe; (b) the conviction "gravely besmirches" the reputation of the offender; (c) the crime is one falling within the parameters of the traditional hierarchy of common law felonies, which is to say, those crimes regarded as "infamous." *Heck, 491 A.2d at 222.* The Pennsylvania court therefore concluded that the particular vehicular homicide statute at issue in *Heck* ran afoul of the distinction because it (a) imposed a maximum five-year penalty, which is "severe,"; (b) gravely besmirched the character of the offender because he faced lengthy imprisonment; and (c) was a modified version of the common law crime of manslaughter, an "infamous" offense. See *id.*

Clearly, all the same criteria exist in the instant case. For present purposes, the only relevant distinction between *Heck* and the case at hand is that the penalty is more severe here. Otherwise, both the Pennsylvania and Florida statutes create a type of vehicular homicide predicated solely on a negligent act associated with a violation of traffic regulations.

I think it also important to consider how cases of this type may implicate precedent dealing with impermissible burden-shifting. The United States Supreme Court repeatedly has noted that a state may not create a presumption that an element of the crime exists as a matter of law and fact. In *Sandstrom v. Montana, 442 U.S. 510, 99 S.Ct. 2450, 61 L.Ed.2d 39 (1979),* for example, the Court confronted the case of a person accused of "deliberate homicide." Although the statute obviously included a scienter element ("deliberateness"), the jury nonetheless was instructed that "the law presumes that a person intends the ordinary consequences of his voluntary acts." *Id. at 513, 99 S.Ct. at 2453.*

The *Sandstrom* Court made the following observations in finding the instruction and hence the conviction unconstitutional:

> The instruction announced to David Sandstrom's jury may well have [invaded the fact finding function]. Upon finding proof of one element of the crime (causing death), and of facts insufficient to establish the [intent element], Sandstrom's jurors could reasonably have concluded that they were directed to find against defendant on the element of intent.

Id. at 523, 99 S.Ct. at 2459. **Accord *Francis v. Franklin,** 471 U.S. 307, 105 S.Ct. 1965, 85 L.Ed.2d 344 (1985).*

It is true that *Sandstrom* is distinguishable from what we are facing today: The *Sandstrom* Court confronted a State scheme that was self-contradictory, effectively resulting in a complete lack of a scienter requirement in the jury's eyes though the statute purported to require an intent element. Here we are dealing with a statute that does not create an illusory intent element, but creates one that apparently has been reduced to the level of simple negligence.

Nevertheless, the federal burden-shifting cases to my mind pose a distinct problem when the state tries to create "reduced intent" statutes. These federal cases reasonably can be read as saying that the state may not reduce the intent element below a minimum level for certain serious offenses. After all, the difference between creating an illusory intent element and forthrightly abandoning it altogether is really only semantic.

Moreover, I think this Court also must keep in mind that, by affirming a statute criminalizing and severely punishing negligence, we open the door for more such statutes in the future notwithstanding the traditions of American law embodied in the concept of due process. Art. I, §§ 9, Fla. Const. Any person or group that may be vulnerable to a charge of negligence or malpractice has something to fear from such a holding. It means that even simple acts of negligence could be converted into serious crimes.

The *Heck* case illustrates the problem: There, a driver improperly made a turn, struck a motorcyclist he did not see, and then was prosecuted for a homicide with up to five year's imprisonment. To my mind, this constitutes a draconian result that is cruel or unusual and a violation of due process within the meaning of the Florida Constitution. *Id.* I would not equate the actual offense in *Heck* with the one here, but the statutes viewed by themselves are little different from each other.

Nevertheless, the problems I have outlined easily and constitutionally can be avoided by the adoption of a simple narrowing construction. See *State v. Stalder, 630 So.2d 1072 (Fla. 1994).* Because the present crime imposes an infamous penalty, [FN7] I would find that it cannot constitutionally be applied in the absence of *at least* criminal or "culpable" negligence, as opposed to simple negligence. *Accord State v. Ritchie, 590 So.2d 1139 (La. 1991).* This means the negligence must be gross and flagrant in character, evincing a reckless disregard of human life or the safety of others. [FN8] *Preston v. State, 56 So.2d 543 (Fla. 1952).* I believe this is necessary to make the statute conform to the requirements of Article I, section 9 of the Florida Constitution.

Turning to the facts at hand, I think it obvious beyond any doubt that the conduct of Smith met the standards for criminal negligence in connection with driving with a revoked license. Specifically, he was legally intoxicated, as shown by his contemporaneous conviction for DUI manslaughter. Choosing to drive while legally drunk is itself an act of reckless disregard of the life or safety of others. Coupled with the fact of the revoked license, this recklessness showed that Smith committed a criminal act that falls within the statute even after it is narrowly construed. Accordingly, I concur with the result reached here.

SHAW, J., concurs.

FN1. Smith was also charged with DUI manslaughter under section 782.07, Florida Statutes (1991). That charge is not at issue in this appeal.

FN2. *Morissette v. United States, 342 U.S. 246, 251, 72 S.Ct. 240, 244, 96 L.Ed. 288 (1951)* (quoting *4 Blackstone's Commentaries 21).*

FN3. "Scienter," of course, refers to the intent element of a crime. The common law generally required at least reckless disregard for others, while certain common law crimes required the higher level of "general" or "specific" intent.

FN4. *Morissette* involved the Court's attempt to deal with a federal statute that had omitted any statement about a criminal scienter element, not a statute like that one at hand, which seems to place the "scienter" element as ordinary negligence.

FN5. The majority above stresses that driving with a revoked license is itself a violation of the law. While this is true, it does not eliminate the real problem here, just as it did not in the Pennsylvania case quoted above. The act of driving with a revoked licensed, like the act of committing a traffic violation in Pennsylvania, is far and away a minor matter compared to homicide. (By contrast, DUI is itself a serious matter because of the serious risk it poses to the others.) Both here and in the Pennsylvania case, the statute does much more than just criminalize a traffic violation: It creates a form of homicide with an "intent" element apparently consisting of simple negligence. The majority argues that the penalty for this new crime is simply a matter of "policy," and that the underlying offense remains the traffic violation. That approach reads the severe penalty here as though it had no constitutional dimension at all and ignores the disproportionate penalties at stake.

FN6. It is worth noting that negligent or careless acts still could result in a lawsuit to partially compensate victims for their losses. These lawsuits often can include a claim for punitive damages.

FN7. At common law, all felonies were considered "infamous," a fact that finds some reflection in Florida's constitutional provision defining a felony as any crime punishable by death or imprisonment in the state penitentiary. Art. X, §§ 10, Fla. Const.

FN8. Obviously, there are some types of acts that constitute at least recklessness per se. These may include driving under the influence, or improper handling of ultrahazardous substances such as radioactive materials, poisons, or explosives, among others.

REVIEW

1. Negligence _____.
    a. can enhance a crime
    b. is a crime in and of itself
    c. both a and b
    d. neither a nor b

CAUSATION

Certain statutes require proof that a person's criminal actions were the actual cause of the harm suffered. In some cases, a person's actions may be consistent with one element of a criminal statute, but some intervening factor actually causes the harm to the victim. Where causation is an element of the crime, a person may not be held criminal liable if some intervening factor results in the final harm.

CASE

Velazquez v. State, 561 So.2d 347 (Fla. 3d DCA 1990).

Defendant was convicted in the Circuit Court, Dade County, Thomas M. Carney, J., of vehicular homicide, and he appealed denial of pretrial motion to dismiss. The District Court of Appeal, Hubbart, J., held that: (1) defendant operated motor vehicle in reckless manner, likely to cause death or great bodily harm to another, by participating in drag race, and (2) even though defendant behaved recklessly, driver of other vehicle acted under own volition in turning around after race was apparently over and speeding through guardrail to, in effect, kill himself, and, thus, vehicular homicide statute did not apply.

Reversed and remanded.

HUBBART, Judge.

This is an appeal by the defendant Isaac Alejandro Velazquez from a final judgment of conviction and sentence for vehicular homicide which was entered below upon a nolo contendere plea. The defendant, upon entry of such plea, specifically reserved for appeal the denial of his pretrial motion to dismiss the information herein under Fla.R.Crim.P. 3.190(c)(4). The sole issue presented for review is whether a defendant driver of a motor vehicle who participates in a reckless and illegal "drag race" on a public road may be properly convicted of vehicular homicide [§ 782.071, Fla.Stat. (1987)] for the death of one of the co-participant drivers suffered in the course of the "drag race" – when the sole basis for imposing liability is the defendant's participation in said race. We hold that the defendant may not be held criminally liable under the above statute in such case because the co-participant driver, in effect, killed himself by his voluntary and reckless driving in the subject "drag race" and thus the defendant's actions in engaging in the said race was not a proximate cause of the co-participant's death.

I

The defendant Velazquez was charged by information with the crime of vehicular homicide. Specifically, the information alleged that on April 23, 1988, the defendant

"did lawfully and feloniously operate a motor vehicle in a reckless manner, to wit: Participated in a DRAG RACE, RAN A STOP SIGN and EXCEEDED the SPEED LIMIT with his VEHICLE, and thereby cause the death of ADALBERTO ALVAREZ, in violation of 782.071 Florida Statutes."

The defendant filed a motion to dismiss this information under Fla.R.Crim.P. 3.190(c)(4) on the ground that the undisputed material facts in the case demonstrated that the state did not, as a matter of law, have a prima facie case of vehicular homicide against the defendant. The defendant set forth in the motion to dismiss certain facts which he swore to be true in open court at the hearing on the subject motion. [Footnote omitted]

The state filed a traverse in which it altered one non-material fact stated in the motion to dismiss and added an additional set of facts based on sworn depositions taken in the case. Accepting the sworn facts stated in the motion to dismiss, as supplemented and altered by the traverse, the material undisputed facts in the case are as follows.

On April 23, 1988, at approximately 2:30 a.m., the defendant Velazquez met the deceased Adalberto Alvarez at a Hardee's restaurant in Hialeah, Florida. The two had never previously met, but in the course of their conversation agreed to race each other in a "drag race" with their respective automobiles. They, accordingly, left the restaurant and proceeded to set up a quarter-mile "drag race" course on a nearby public road which ran perpendicular to a canal alongside the Palmetto Expressway in Hialeah; a guardrail and a visible stop sign [Footnote omitted] stood between the end of this road and the canal. The two men began their "drag race" at the end of this road and proceeded away from the canal in a westerly direction for one-quarter mile. Upon completing the course without incident, the deceased Alvarez suddenly turned his automobile 180 degrees around and proceeded east toward the starting line and the canal; the defendant Velazquez did the same and followed behind Alvarez. Alvarez proceeded in the lead and attained an estimated speed of 123 m.p.h.; he was not wearing a seat belt and subsequent investigation revealed that he had a blood alcohol level between .11 and .12. The defendant Velazquez, who had not been drinking, trailed Alvarez the entire distance back to the starting line and attained an estimated speed of 98 m.p.h. As both drivers approached the end of the road, they applied their brakes, but neither could stop. Alvarez, who was about a car length ahead of the defendant Velazquez, crashed through the guardrail first and was propelled over the entire canal, landing on its far bank; he was thrown from his car upon impact, was pinned under his vehicle when it landed on him, and died instantly from the resulting injuries. The defendant also crashed through the guardrail, but landed in the canal where he was able to escape from his vehicle and swim to safety uninjured.

Based on these facts, the trial court denied the motion to dismiss, finding that it was a question of fact for the jury as to whether the defendant's participation in the "drag race" was a sufficient legal cause of the deceased's death so as to support a conviction for vehicular homicide. The defendant subsequently entered a plea of nolo contendere and reserved for appeal the denial of his motion to dismiss; the trial court then placed the defendant on four years probation. This appeal follows.

II

The vehicular homicide statute, under which the defendant was charged and convicted, provides as follows:

" 'Vehicular homicide' is the killing of a human being by the operation of a motor vehicle by another in a reckless manner likely to cause the death of, or great bodily harm to, another. Vehicular homicide is a felony of the third degree, punishable as provided in § 775.082, § 775.083, or § 775.084."

Section 782.071(1), Florida Statutes (1987). There are two statutory elements to vehicular homicide: (1) the defendant must operate a motor vehicle in a reckless manner likely to cause the death of, or great bodily harm to, another, and (2) this reckless operation of a motor vehicle must be the proximate cause of the death of a human being. *Byrd v. State*, 531 So.2d 1004, 1006 (Fla. 5th DCA 1988); *M.C.J. v. State*, 444 So.2d 1001, 1004-05 (Fla. 1st DCA), rev. denied, 451 So.2d 849 (Fla. 1984); *J.A.C. v. State*, 374 So.2d 606, 607 (Fla. 3d DCA 1979), rev. denied, 383 So.2d 1203 (Fla. 1980); compare Fla.Std. Jury Instr. (Crim.) 72 (1989) (vehicular homicide).

Contrary to the defendant's argument, we have no trouble in concluding that the first element of this offense is clearly established on this record. Plainly, the defendant operated a motor vehicle in a reckless manner, likely to cause death or great bodily harm to another, in that (a) he participated in a highly dangerous "drag race" with the deceased on a public road in which both lanes were used as a speedway, and (b) he drove his vehicle at the excessive speed of 98 m.p.h. during the "drag race." Without question, the defendant's motor vehicle operation endangered the lives of all persons in the vicinity of the "drag race," namely, people in other motor vehicles and nearby pedestrians. See *McCreary v. State*, 371 So.2d 1024 (Fla. 1979).

The second element of this offense, however, has given us considerable pause, as no doubt it did the trial court, because no endangered third party in the vicinity of the "drag race" was killed in this case; moreover, it is here that the parties to this appeal marshal their primary authorities and argument. It is therefore necessary that we consult the Florida law on this subject, and survey as well the relevant law thereon throughout the country. Nonetheless, we approach this subject with a certain degree of caution, mindful that the problems raised by the element of "proximate cause" in cases of this nature "present enormous difficulty (especially in homicide [cases]) because of the obscurity of that concept," an obscurity which has resulted in the announcement of "varying and sometimes inconsistent rules in the numerous areas in which the problem has arisen." *Model Penal Code and Commentaries* Sec. 2.03 comment 1, at 255-56 (1985).

A

At the outset, it seems clear that the proximate cause element of vehicular homicide in Florida embraces, at the very least, a causation-in-fact test; that is, the defendant's reckless operation of a motor vehicle must be a cause-in-fact of the death of a human being. In this respect, vehicular homicide is no different than any other criminal offense in which the occurrence of a specified result, caused by a defendant's conduct, is an essential element of the offense - such as murder, [§ 782.04, Fla.Stat. (1989)], manslaughter [§ 782.07, Fla.Stat. (1989)], aggravated battery [§ 784.045, Fla.Stat. (1989)], and arson [§ 806.01, Fla.Stat. (1989)]. Clearly there can be no criminal liability for such result-type offenses unless it can be shown that the defendant's conduct was a cause-in-fact of the prohibited result, whether the result be the death of a human being, personal injury to another, or injury to another's property. To be sure, this cause-in-fact showing is insufficient in itself to establish the aforesaid "proximate cause" element in a vehicular homicide case, but it is clearly a sine qua non ingredient thereof. 1 W. LaFave

& A. Scott, *Substantive Criminal Law* § 3.12(a),(b), at 390-96 (1986); *Model Penal Code and Commentaries* § 2.03 explanatory note, at 254 (1985).

Courts throughout the country have uniformly followed the traditional "but for" test in determining whether the defendant's conduct was a cause-in-fact of a prohibited consequence in result-type offenses such as vehicular homicide. Under this test, a defendant's conduct is a cause-in-fact of the prohibited result if the said result would *not* have occurred "but for" the defendant's conduct; stated differently, the defendant's conduct is a cause-in-fact of a particular result if the result would *not* have happened in the absence of the defendant's conduct. Thus, a defendant's reckless operation of a motor vehicle is a cause-in-fact of the death of a human being under Florida's vehicular homicide statute [Section 782.071(1), Fla.Stat. (1987)] if the subject death would *not* have occurred "but for" the defendant's reckless driving or would *not* have happened in the absence of such driving. 1 W. LaFave & A. Scott, *Substantive Criminal Law* § 3.12(b), at 393-94 (1986); *Model Penal Code and Commentaries* § 2.03 and comment 2, at 257-58 (1985); *compare* **Stahl v. Metropolitan Dade County**, *438 So.2d 14, 17-18 (Fla. 3d DCA 1983)*.

In relatively rare cases, however, the "but for" test for causation-in-fact fails and has been abandoned in favor of the "substantial factor" test. This anomaly occurs when two defendants, acting independently and not in concert with one another, commit two separate acts, each of which alone is sufficient to bring about the prohibited result – as when two defendants concurrently inflict mortal wounds upon a human being, each of which is sufficient to cause death. In such case, each defendant's action was not a "but for" cause of death because the deceased would have died even in the absence of each defendant's conduct – although obviously not in the absence of both defendants' conduct considered together. In these rare cases, the courts have followed a "substantial factor" test, namely, the defendant's conduct is a cause-in-fact of a prohibited result if the subject conduct was a "substantial factor" in bringing about the said result. Thus, each defendant's conduct in independently and concurrently inflicting mortal wounds on a deceased clearly constitutes a "substantial factor" in bringing about the deceased's death, and, consequently, is a cause-in-fact of the deceased's death. 1 W.LaFave & A. Scott, *Substantive Criminal Law*, § 3.12(b), at 394-95 (1986); *compare* **Stahl v. Metropolitan Dade County**, *438 So.2d 14, 18 (Fla. 3d DCA 1983)*.

B

The "proximate cause" element of vehicular homicide in Florida embraces more, however, than the aforesaid "but for" causation-in-fact test as modified by the "substantial factor" exception. Even where a defendant's conduct is a cause-in-fact of a prohibited result, as where a defendant's reckless operation of a motor vehicle is a cause-in-fact of the death of a human being, Florida and other courts throughout the country have for good reason declined to impose criminal liability (1) where the prohibited result of the defendant's conduct is beyond the scope of any fair assessment of the danger created by the defendant's conduct, or (b) where it would otherwise be unjust, based on fairness and policy considerations, to hold the defendant criminally responsible for the prohibited result. *See* 1 W. LaFave & A. Scott, *Substantive Criminal Law* § 3.12(c)-(h), at 396-421 (1986), and cases collected; *compare* **M.C.J. v. State**, *444 So.2d 1001, 1004-05 (Fla. 1ˢᵗ DCA), rev. denied, 451 So.2d 849 (Fla. 1984);* **Stahl v. Metropolitan Dade County**, *438 So.2d 14, 19 (Fla. 3d DCA 1983).*

In deaths resulting from illegal "drag racing" on a public road, as here, it has been held in Florida that the driver of one of the racing vehicles was properly convicted of manslaughter when the driver of another vehicle in the race collided head on with a non-participant motor vehicles which was lawfully using the subject highway, killing the driver of same. **Jacobs v. State**, *184 So.2d 711 (Fla. 1ˢᵗ DCA 1966).* The court reasoned that the defendant, by participating in the "drag race," was aiding and abetting each of the other participant drivers in the race in committing reckless driving – so that when one of the participants committed a manslaughter in the course of the race against a third party, the defendant was also guilty of manslaughter. In reaching this result, the court relied on the following rules of law stated by Wharton and Clark & Marshall:

> " ' * * * If each of two persons jointly engage in the commission of acts which amount to criminal negligence, and as a result of which *a third person is killed*, each may be found guilty of manslaughter even though it may be impossible to say whose act actually caused the death.'

> . . . .

> 'There may be principals in the second degree and accessories before the fact to involuntary manslaughter. Thus, *if two men drive separate vehicles at a furious and dangerous speed along the highway, each inciting and abetting the other, and one of them drives the other and kills a person, the one thus causing the death is guilty of manslaughter as principal in the first degree, and the other is guilty as principal in the second degree. * * * ' "*

Jacobs v. State, *184 So.2d at 716 (quoting 1 Wharton, Criminal Law and Procedure § 290 (Anderson 1957) and Clark & Marshall, Crimes, 3d ed. § 164) (emphasis added).*

Where, however, a participant passenger in such an illegal "drag race," accidently grabs the steering wheel of a vehicle involved in the race, instead of the gear shift he was assigned to operate, causing the vehicle to go out of control, crash, and kill the passenger – this court has held that the defendant driver of the subject motor vehicle was improperly convicted of vehicular homicide. **J.A.C. v. State**, *374 So.2d 606 (Fla. 3d DCA 1979), rev. denied, 383 so.2d 1203 (Fla. 1980).* The court reasoned that the passenger's reckless act of grabbing the steering wheel was an independent intervening act which superseded the respondent's wrongful conduct in participating in the "drag race." *Id. at 607.* Although, obviously, the respondent's participation in the subject race was *a* "but for" cause-in-fact of the passenger's death and such death was plainly within the scope of the danger created by the defendant's conduct in participating in the race - this court nonetheless implicitly concluded that it would be unjust to hold the defendant criminally responsible for the passenger's death because the passenger, in effect, killed himself by his own reckless conduct.

The result reached in *J.A.C.* is in accord with the weight of better-reasoned decisions on this subject throughout the country. These courts have uniformly concluded that a driver-participant in an illegal "drag race" on a public road cannot be held criminally responsible for the death of another driver participant when (a) the deceased, in effect, kills himself by his own reckless driving during the race, and (b) the sole basis for attaching criminal liability for his death is the defendant's participation in the "drag race." [Footnote omitted] The policy reasons for reaching this result are best expressed in *State v. Petersen, 17 Or.App. 478, 495, 522 P.2d 912, 920 (1974) (Schwab, C.J., dissenting)* (dissent adopted by the Oregon Supreme Court in *State v. Petersen, 270 Or. 166, 526 P.2d 1008 (1974))*:

"[T]he question is whether defendant's reckless conduct 'caused' the death of the victim. The problem here is not 'causation in fact,' it is 'legal causation.' In unusual cases like this one, whether certain conduct is deemed to be the legal cause of a certain result is ultimately a policy question. The question of legal causation thus blends into the question of whether we are willing to hold a defendant responsible for a prohibited result. Or, stated differently, the issue is not causation, it is responsibility. In my opinion, policy considerations are against imposing responsibility for the death of a participant in a race on the surviving racer when his sole contribution to the death is the participation in the activity mutually agreed upon.

. . . .

It is not unheard of for people to engage in hazardous vacations and avocations. It could be said, for example, that professional racetrack drivers earn their living by consciously disregarding a substantial risk that death will occur on the racetrack. Yet, it would probably strike most people as strange if the surviving drivers were prosecuted for manslaughter following a fatal racetrack accident...

. . . .

My point is that people frequently join together in reckless conduct. As long as all participants do so knowingly and voluntarily, I see no point in holding the survivor(s) guilty of manslaughter if the reckless conduct results in death..."

522 P.2d at 920-21 (citations and footnote omitted). LaFave and Scott also summarize the legal basis for these decisions:

"It is submitted that the true reason for the holding [in these cases] is the court's feeling ... that A should not, in all justice, be held for the death of B who was an equally willing and foolhardy participant in the bad conduct which caused his death."

1 W. LaFave and A. Scott, *Substantive Criminal Law* § 3.12, at 418 (1986).

III

Turning now to the instant case, it is clear that the defendant's reckless operation of a motor vehicle in participating in the "drag race" with the deceased was, technically speaking, *a* cause-in-fact of the deceased's death under the "but for" test. But for the defendant's participation in the subject race, the deceased would not have recklessly raced his vehicle at all and thus would not have been killed. However, under the authority of *J.A.C.* and the better reasoned decisions throughout the country, the defendant's participation in the subject "drag race" was not a proximate cause of the deceased's death because, simply put, the deceased, in effect, killed himself by his own volitional reckless driving – and, consequently, it would be unjust to hold the defendant criminally responsible for this death.

The undisputed facts in this case demonstrate that the "drag race" was, in effect, over when the defendant and the deceased had completed the agreed-upon one-quarter mile course and had crossed the finish line. Unexpectedly, however, the deceased suddenly whirled his vehicle around and headed back toward the starting line and the canal which ran perpendicular to the road on which he was traveling; although the defendant then followed, it is plain that it was the deceased's sole decision to return to the starting line, as apparently this had not previously been agreed upon. At any rate, the deceased, who had consumed a considerable amount of alcohol and was wearing no seat belt, attained an estimated speed of 123 m.p.h. on his return trip; applied the brakes as he approached the end of the road but was unable to stop; crashed through a protective guard rail; and incredibly vaulted the entire canal, landing on the far bank. He was thrown from his vehicle upon impact, was pinned under the vehicle when it landed on him, and died instantly from the resulting injuries. Although the defendant was about one-car length in back of the deceased during the deceased's fatal return to the staring line, the defendant at no time struck the deceased's vehicle and did not physically propel it in any way across the canal. Clearly, the deceased was on a near-suicide mission when, on his own hook, he returned to the starting line of the race after the race was apparently over, attaining a murderous speed of 123 m.p.h., vaulted a canal, and killed himself. This being so, it would be unjust to hold the defendant criminally responsible for the deceased's unexpected and near-suicidal conduct.

We agree that if the deceased had collided with an oncoming motorist who happened to be in the vicinity lawfully using the subject road resulting in the said motorist's death, the defendant would be criminally liable for this death on an aiding-and-abetting theory; clearly, the deceased would be guilty of vehicular homicide in killing the oncoming motorist, and the defendant, in participating in the illegal "drag race," would be aiding and abetting the deceased in the latter's reckless driving and ultimate negligent homicide. *Jacobs v. State, 184 So.2d 711 (Fla. 1ˢᵗ DCA 1966).* In such a case, however, the oncoming motorist could in no way be said to be responsible for his own death and, consequently, no policy or fairness reason would exist for finding no proximate cause. Clearly, this cannot be said in the instant case.

The state nonetheless relies on cases from other jurisdictions which have reached a contrary result to the one we reach herein. [Footnote omitted] We have reviewed these cases, but are not persuaded by their reasoning because we think they lead to an unjust result. In our judgment, it is simply unfair, unjust, and just plain wrong to say that the defendant in the instant case is criminally responsible for the death of the deceased when it is undisputed that the deceased, in effect, killed himself. No one forced this young man to participate in the subject "drag race"; no one forced him to whirl around and proceed back toward the canal after the race was apparently over; no one forced him to travel 123 m.p.h., vault a canal, and kill himself upon impact. He did all these things himself and was, accordingly, the major cause of his own death. We are constrained by law to construe criminal statutes strictly in favor of the accused, § 775.021(1), Fla. Stat. (1989), and, given this salutary principle of statutory construction, we are unwilling to construe our vehicular homicide statute to impose criminal liability on the defendant under the circumstances of this case.

The final judgment of conviction and sentence under review is reversed, and the cause is remanded to the trial court with directions to grant the defendant's motion to dismiss.

Reversed and remanded.

REVIEW

1. To prove vehicular homicide, the state must show _____.
   a. reckless operation of a motor vehicle
   b. the reckless operation must be the proximate cause of the death
   c. both a and b
   d. neither a nor b

THINKING CRITICALLY

1.   Give an example of a general intent crime.

2.   Give an example of a specific intent crime.

3.   Should the State be required to have more than just circumstantial evidence of specific intent? Why or why not?

4.   Is there a difference between harm to the city and benefit to the defendant in *Bauer*? If so, what is it? Was this case fairly decided on the facts presented? Might the holding result in injustice as applied to a different case? Give an example.

5.   Should false imprisonment be a general intent crime? Why or why not?

6.   Based on the facts in the *Proko* case, was it fair the defendant was convicted of false imprisonment? Why or why not?

7.   In the *Archer* case would the result have been different if Bonifay went to the wrong convenience store? Do you agree with the doctrine of transferred intent?

8.   Compare *Archer* and *J.G.* Can you reconcile the two cases? Why or why not? Did the state charge the case improperly? What would you have done as the prosecutor?

9.   Did Ms. Sherouse intend to commit a crime? Do you agree with the court's dismissal of the charges? If a male with whom she had intercourse died of AIDs, should Ms. Sherouse be convicted of homicide?

10.   Do you think Ms. Sherouse should have been charged with attempted second degree murder? Why or why not?

11.   A vehicle is stuck in a ditch with someone in the driver's seat when the police arrive. The keys are in the ignition but the car is not running. Is that person "driving?" The tires appear to have been spun in an attempt to move the car. Does that change your answer?

12.   What about the case where a vehicle is mechanically inoperable? Do you need to know if there is evidence of the vehicle being driven prior to its becoming disabled? Does the person in the vehicle need to be aware that the vehicle is inoperable?

13.   Do you agree with the Florida Supreme Court in *Smith*? Why or why not? Would the results have been different if someone had not died in the accident? Should they be?

14.   Who causes a death in a drag race? Can an individual be the cause of their own death? Should all participants be held responsible? What if someone offers money to an individual to participate in a drag race? Can that individual be held criminally responsible if a death results?

15.   Do you agree with the holding in *Velazquez*? Why or why not?

16.   The State must prove a causal connection between an intoxicated driver's operation of a motor vehicle and a victim's death in order to convict a driver of DUI manslaughter. Give an example of how the State might be able to prove the causal connection. Do you agree with this concept? Why or why not?

CHAPTER 4 ANSWER KEY

REVIEW QUESTIONS

Bauer v. State
    1. c
    2. b

Proko v. State
    1. b
    2. a

Archer v. State
    1. c

In the Interest of J.G., a child
    1. a

State v. Sherouse
    1. a

Griffin v. State
    1. a

State v. Smith
    1. a

Velazquez v. State
    1. c

CHAPTER 5

PARTIES TO CRIME
AND VICARIOUS LIABILITY

The Florida legislature abolished all distinctions between principals in the first and second degrees and accessories before the fact. All principals are now equally culpable. The legislature decided the distinctions no longer served a useful purpose.

Where a person helps another commit or attempt to commit a crime, that person becomes a principal in the first degree. A principal is treated as if he or she has done all the things the other person did, and a principal need not be present when the crime is committed or attempted. To establish that a defendant is a principal, the State must prove two things: (1) the defendant had a conscious intent that the criminal act be done; and (2) the defendant did or said something which was intended to and did incite, cause, encourage, assist or advise the other person to actually commit or attempt to commit the crime.

Mere knowledge an offense is being committed is not the same as participation with criminal intent. Mere presence at a scene, even if the individual drove the defendant to and from the crime scene is insufficient to establish participation.

On the other hand, a person becomes a principal if he or she pays or promises payment for the commission of the crime. However, the State still needs to prove intent that the criminal act be done on the part of the defendant. It must be shown payment was made or promised for the commission of the crime. And, of course, the crime must be committed or attempted.

AIDING AND ABETTING

In order to convict a person of being an aider-abettor it is not necessary to show that the primary perpetrator was convicted of the same crime, nor is it even necessary to show that he was convicted at all. The State meets its burden of proof if at the trial of the aider-abettor it is established only that a crime was committed.

CASE

Potts v. State, 430 So.2d 900 (Fla. 1982).

Defendant was convicted of burglary of a structure where an assault was committed, and he appealed. The District Court of Appeal, 403 So.2d 443, affirmed, and defendant petitioned for review on ground of express and direct conflict. The Supreme Court, Ehrlich, J., held that: (1) aider-abettor statute makes an aider or abettor, principals of first or second degree, and accessories before the fact equally responsible for entire transaction, and all are principals in first degree; (2) at trial of aider or abettor, accessory or principal, it is only necessary to show that, pursuant to aider-abettor statute, there was an attempt to commit a crime or that a crime was committed during the transaction, and it is not necessary to show that principal perpetrator was convicted of same crime, nor is it even necessary to show that he was convicted at all; and (3) under aider-abettor statute, if any of the perpetrators are tried in separate trials, the judgments and sentences, even though inconsistent, are independent of one another and stand or fall on their own merits.

Affirmed.

Alderman, C.J., filed specially concurring opinion in which Boyd, J., concurred.

EHRLICH, Justice.

This cause is before the Court on petition for review of a district court of appeal decision on the ground of express and direct conflict. We have jurisdiction. [FN1] At issue is whether or not an aider or abettor to the substantive crime may be convicted of a greater crime that his confederate/principal. The decision under review, **Potts v. State**, *403 So.2d 443 (Fla. 2d DCA 1981)*, conflicts with **Turner v. State**, *369 So.2d 670 (Fla. 1st DCA 1979)*. We affirm **Potts** and disapprove **Turner**.

Petitioner and one Lawrence Scott Ramirez participated in the burglary of a Clearwater car dealer. Ramirez actually conducted the burglary during which he placed his hand on an employee, guided him to a restroom, and instructed him to remain there. Petitioner's participation in the crime consisted of driving Ramirez to the scene, waiting nearby until summoned by Ramirez, then driving the get-away vehicle.

Both were charged with burglary under sections 810.02 and 777.011, Florida Statutes (1977). Ramirez was tried separately, found guilty of simple burglary, and received a maximum sentence of five years. Petitioner was tried and found guilty of burglary of a structure wherein an assault was committed and received a sentence of thirty years.

The Second District Court of Appeal rejected petitioner's contention that he could not be convicted of being a principal in the first degree to the crime of aiding and abetting a burglary with assault when the principal perpetrator was only convicted of simple burglary. The judgment and sentence were set aside and remanded for a new trial on other grounds, but Potts nevertheless sought review in this Court on that issue only. Petitioner makes two arguments to which we will respond.

Potts was charged under the aider-abettor statute which makes all participants in a crime principals in the first degree. Section 777.011, Fla.Stat. (1977). The correct interpretation of that statute, he argues, is the one given by the first district in its opinion in **Turner**.

The history of culpability of the aider-abettor is an intricate and involved one. See Annot., 9 A.L.R. 4th 972 (1981). The courts have waivered on the issue. At common law jurists went to great lengths to classify and define the degree of culpability of each of the actors in the crime and four categories arose. These were: a) principals in the first degree, who actually committed the offense; b) principals in the second degree, who were actually or constructively at the scene of the crime and aided or abetted in its commission; c) accessories before the fact, who aided or abetted the crime but were not present at its commission; and d) accessories after the fact, who rendered assistance after the crime was committed.

Because at early common law all felonies were punishable by death, judges found it particularly hard to apply this harsh penalty to the aider or abettor who was an accessory before the fact. W.LaFave & A.Scott, *Criminal Law* 449 (1972). Consequently, procedural rules developed that tended to shield the accessories from prosecution in certain instances. Among these rules was the one that an accessory could not be convicted without the prior conviction of the principal offender. Therefore, the principal's disappearance, death or acquittal automatically served to release the accessory, and the pardon or reversal of a conviction of the principal operated in the same fashion. Indeed, '[a]n accessory follows, like a shadow, his principal." 1 J.Bishop, Criminal Law Section 666 (8th Ed. 1892).

As the law developed and punishment for felony convictions became less harsh the necessity for this equitable procedural bar became a nullity. Statutes in England and the United States were enacted to overcome these judge-made rules and permit the trial and conviction of accessories before the fact independent of their principals. Florida ventured into the legislative arena as early as 1868 [FN2] to pass legislation defining the accessory before the fact and the aider-abettor, and providing for punishment independent of the conviction of the principal. [FN3]

Despite the legislature's efforts the courts continued to draw the line between the principal in the second degree and the accessory before the fact. *Montague v. State, 17 Fla. 662 (1880).* Another distinction began to develop as to whether or not the accessory was charged under the statute or at common law. *Flynn v. State, 86 Fla. 467, 98 So. 76 (1923).* And though the courts were willing to place the principal in the first degree and the principal in the second degree in the same shoes, the accessory before the fact was treated quite differently. *Neumann v. State*b, *116 Fla. 98, 156 So. 237 (1934); see also State v. Peel, 111 So.2d 728 (Fla. 2d DCA 1959).*

In an apparent effort to clear up this growing problem of distinguishing between the accessories and principals, the legislature passed Ch. 57-310, Laws of Florida, in 1957. [FN4] This declared that principals in the first and second degree and accessories before the fact were treated equally and all were made principals in the first degree.

This statute was interpreted by *Blackburn v. State, 314 So.2d 634 (Fla. 4th DCA 1975), cert. denied, 334 So.2d 603 (Fla.), cert. denied, 429 U.S. 864, 97 S.Ct. 170, 50*

L.Ed.2d 142 (1976). The age-old argument about whether or not the aider or abettor could be convicted while the principal was acquitted was dealt with by the ***Blackburn*** court as follows:

> Some of the cases cited by appellant appear to require a conviction of the original offender as a predicate to conviction of an aider and abettor. However, this is no longer the law. Those cases were limited to prosecution of accessories before the fact. The enactment of Section 776.011 of the Florida Statutes eliminated this requirement, under the peculiar circumstances where it existed.

314 So.3d at 638. That statute remained intact until 1974 when as part of a major revision of the criminal code the language was changed. [FN5] The following underscored language was added:

> 77 7.011 Principal in first degree. – Whoever commits any criminal offense against the state, whether felony or misdemeanor, or aids, abets, counsels, hires, or otherwise procures such offense to be committed, *and such offense is committed or is attempted to be committed,* is a principal in the first degree and may be charged, convicted, and punished as such, whether he is or is not actually or constructively present at the commission of such offense.

It is this amending language that is the crux of the holding in ***Turner***, and the cornerstone of petitioner's argument. Petitioner asserts that by adding this language the legislature intended to change the statute and add a new element to the crime. He further argues that in order for the aider-abettor to be convicted of a particular crime, the primary perpetrator also has to be convicted of the same crime. In this case, the argument continues, since the primary perpetrator, Ramirez, was acquitted of burglary with assault and only convicted of simple burglary, the crime of burglary with an assault was not in fact committed and therefore, under the statute as amended, the petitioner himself cannot be convicted of any crime greater than simple burglary. In conclusion, petitioner's argument is that we should once again adopt the common law rule.

We disagree. First, after a due and diligent search we are unable to track down the illusory legislative intent relied upon by the petitioner. We are thus compelled to conclude that the reasons for the change were simply technical and designed to make the statute compatible with other sections of that chapter. [FN6] Therefore, we interpret that statute to mean that it is sufficient at the trial of the aider-abettor only to show that a crime was committed. In order to convict the aider-abettor it is not necessary to show that the principal perpetrator was convicted of the same crime, nor is it even necessary to show that he was convicted at all.

We now address petitioner's second argument which is harder to reject because it is based on a policy. He asks that we adopt either a collateral estoppel rationale or "consistency of judgments approach." We realize that both are doctrines logically developed and based on the appearance of equity and justice. We reject them, however, for several reasons.

We find illuminating the U.S. Supreme Court's opinion in **Standefer v. United States**, *447 U.S. 10, 100 S.Ct. 1999, 64 L.Ed.2d 689 (1980)*. We are aware that that decision does not prevent a state from adopting a contrary position, but we feel that the reasoning is sound and compelling. That court refused to adopt the doctrine of non-mutual collateral estoppel in criminal cases because acquittals can result from many factors other than guilt or innocence, the procedural elements pertaining to one defendant can be totally different than those applying to another, and there is no procedure for retrying a defendant once acquitted even though the verdict might be clearly erroneous.

Finally, we are loath to adopt a rule requiring consistency of judgements even though at first blush it appears that we have forgotten the mandate that "justice must satisfy the appearance of justice." **Offutt v. United States**, *348 U.S. 11, 14, 75 S.Ct.11, 13, 99 L.Ed.11 (1954)*. To adopt the consistency of judgment doctrine, however, is to trade one doctrine for another. This we refuse to do because what we gain is less than what we give up. To do so, in essence, is to invade the province of the jury which we decline to do.

The jury is the trier of fact and in weighing the evidence it decides if the requisite elements of a crime exist. To tell it what it must find in the trial of an aider or abettor is to take this function out of the hands of the jury. See **Jent v. State**, *408 So.2d 1024 (Fla.1981), cert. denied, 457 U.S. 1111, 102 S.Ct. 2916, 73 L.Ed.2d 1322 (1982); **Alvord v. State**, 322 So.2d 533 (Fla.1975), cert. denied, 428 U.S. 923, 96 S.Ct. 3234, 49 L.Ed.2d 1226 (1976)*. In its ultimate wisdom it has been given the power to "temper...justice with mercy." [FN7] If such be warranted, it can reduce the charge. This obviously was the result in Ramirez's trial. This is commonly known as jury pardon, and because that is one of the powers of this body of peers we will not disturb it. See, e.g., **State v. Abreau**, *363 So.2d 1063 (Fla. 1978); **Lightfoot v. State**, 331 So.2d 388 (Fla. 2d DCA 1976), cert. denied, 344 So.2d 326 (Fla. 1977)*.

We therefore hold that 1) this statute makes an aider or abettor, principals of the first or second degree, and accessories before the fact equally responsible for the entire transaction, and all are principals in the first degree; 2) the language added to the statute means that at the trial of the aider or abettor, accessory or principal, it is only necessary to show that there was an attempt to commit a crime or that a crime was committed during the transaction; and 3) if any of the perpetrators are tried in separate trials the judgments and sentences, even though inconsistent, are independent of one another and stand or fall on their own merits.

The decision of the district court is affirmed.

It is so ordered.

ADKINS, BOYD, OVERTON and McDONALD, JJ., concur.

ALDERMAN, C.J., concurs specially with an opinion, with which BOYD, J., concurs.

ALDERMAN, Chief Justice, concurring specially.

The majority concludes that the apparently inconsistent verdict in the trial of the codefendant, Ramirez, was the result of a "jury pardon" and that the petitioner in this case cannot benefit from the failure of the jury in Ramirez's case to do its duty. I agree. I concur specially, however, to once again restate my disapproval of the concept which has come to be known as jury pardon.

Recently in my dissent to this Court's refusal to amend Florida Rule of Criminal Procedure 3.390(a) at the present time because it did not deem the matter to be an emergency matter necessitating consideration outside the regular four-year cycle, I expressed my concern with the concept of jury pardon and said:

> The deplorable phenomenon referred to by the Conference of Circuit Judges is the exercise by a jury of its power to return a verdict contrary to the evidence. In criminal cases, this abuse of power is irremediable because once the jury has wrongfully acquitted a defendant, its abuse of power may not be corrected on appeal. Just as there are individuals who disregard the law, there may also be juries that disregard the law. A jury that returns a verdict contrary to the evidence based on feelings of prejudice, bias, or sympathy is an "outlaw" jury, and its verdict will be a miscarriage of justice.

The Florida Bar, In re Amendment to Rules of Criminal Procedure – 3.390(a), 416 So.2d 1126, 1126-27 (Fla.1982).

BOYD, J., concurs.

FN1. Art. V, Section 3(b)(3), Fla. Const.

FN2. Ch. 1637(11), Laws of Fla. (1868).

FN3. This law remained intact throughout the various codifications and finally ended up as sections 776.01 and 776.02, Florida Statutes (1941).

FN4. Section 776.011, Fla. Stat. (1957).

FN5. Comm. Substitute for H.B. 2179, Florida Criminal Code, Ch. 74-383, Laws of Fla.

FN6. The district court said in a footnote:

Because the amendment was enacted as part of the revision of the entire criminal code, it is difficult to glean the legislative intent. It may be that the words were added to extend the scope of the statute to attempted crimes or, alternatively, to differentiate from criminal solicitation which was first made a statutory crime in the same legislation. Ch. 74-383, Laws of Fla.
403 So.2d at 445 n. 2.

FN7. J. Milton, Paradise Lost, in 32 Great Books of the Western World 276 (1952).

REVIEW

1. In order to convict an aider/abettor, it is necessary for the state to show _____.
   a. the principal perpetrator was convicted of the same crime
   b. the principal perpetrator was convicted of any crime
   c. the principal perpetrator was convicted of a more serious crime
   d. the crime was committed

2. An aider/abettor is _____.
   a. less responsible than a principal
   b. more responsible than an accessory
   c. less responsible than an accessory
   d. equally responsible

PRINCIPAL TO BATTERY

In certain cases where a person participates in activity which could result in the battery of another person (i.e. throwing rocks, spitting, etc.), he can be convicted as a principal of the crime even if the victim cannot identify specifically which of the participants battered him. It is sufficient for the State to establish that the victim was in fact battered, and that the defendant committed some act which may have in fact caused the battery.

CASE

R.M. v. State, 664 So. 2d 42 (Fla. 4th DCA 1995).

Defendant was convicted in the Circuit Court, Broward County, Melanie May, J., of battery. Defendant appealed. The District Court of Appeal, Klein, J., held that: (1) evidence was sufficient to support conviction, but (2) defendant did not waive right to counsel.

Reversed for new trial.

KLEIN, Judge.

R.M. was one of three youths who threw tiles at the victim in this battery case; however, the victim was only struck by one of the tiles, and there was no evidence that R.M. threw that tile. We find that there was sufficient evidence to convict R.M. of battery as an aider and abettor, but reverse for a new trial because he did not waive his right to counsel when he agreed to be represented by a law student who was a certified legal intern.

R.M. and two other youths entered the arcade at the Coral Ridge Mall, and the manager, who had previously banned R.M. from the arcade, reached for the telephone and pretended to call the police in an effort to scare R.M. off. The manager observed all three youths then make a throwing gesture, after which he was struck in the eye by a piece of tile. Three tiles were found at the scene; however, the manager was unable to identify which of the three youths threw the one tile which struck him.

R.M. argues that, in the absence of proof that he touched or caused bodily harm to the manager, he could not have been convicted of battery under section 784.03, Florida Statutes (1993), citing *L.S. v. State, 391 So.2d 329 (Fla. 3rd DCA 1980)*. In *L.S.* the defendant was one of two youths who could have pushed the victim from behind; however, there was no evidence that the appellant was the youth who actually did the pushing, and the court reversed a conviction for battery, concluding that the mere presence of the defendant with another youth was insufficient to support a battery conviction.

The state responds that R.M. could have been convicted as an aider and abettor under section 777.011, Florida Statutes (1993), which provides:

> Principal in the first degree. – Whoever commits any criminal offense against the state, whether felony or misdemeanor, or aides, abets, counsels, hires, or otherwise procures such offense to be committed, and such offense is committed or is attempted to be committed, is a principal in the first degree and may be charged, convicted, and punished as such, whether he is or is not actually or constructively present at the commission of each offense.

In order to be convicted as an aider and abettor, the evidence must show that the defendant "(1) assisted the actual perpetrator by doing or saying something that causes, encourages or assists or incites the perpetrator to actually commit the crime; and (2) intended to participate in the crime." *Rouse v. State, 538 So.2d 1111, 1112 (Fla. 4th DCA 1991)*. In the present case the fact finder could have inferred from the concerted throwing of the tiles that the crime had been planned in advance, which, along with its being carried out, meets the above requirements and thus makes R.M. an aider and abettor. See e.g., *Staten v. State, 519 So.2d 622 (Fla. 1988)*.

Although we have not been cited any Florida cases involving similar facts, *Gillis v. United States, 586 A.2d 726 (D.C. App. 1991)* is on all fours. In *Gillis* the defendant was one of several people involved in a shooting, and the court held that he could have been convicted as an aider and abettor because of his participation, notwithstanding that there was no proof that he actually shot anyone. See, e.g., ***A.B.G. v. State***, *586 So.2d 445 (Fla. 1ˢᵗ DCA 1991).*

Unfortunately, we must reverse for a new trial because, although R.M. orally agreed to be represented by a certified legal intern, he did not do so in writing, and was not advised that he could refuse and be represented by a member of the bar. ***In Re A.R., 554 So.2d 640 (Fla. 4ᵗʰ DCA 1989).***

POLEN and PARIENTE, JJ., concur.

REVIEW

1. One may be convicted of aiding and abetting if _____.
    a. one assists
    b. one participates in advance planning of the crime
    c. both a and b
    d. neither a nor b

PRINCIPAL TO ROBBERY

Neither presence at the scene nor mere knowledge that an offense is being committed can be construed as participation in the robbery. Additionally, driving the perpetrator to and from the scene or a display of questionable behavior after the fact is not sufficient to establish participation. The State must provide some proof that the defendant somehow incited or encouraged the primary participant to commit the crime.

CASE

Taylor v. State, 747 So.2d 393 (Fla. 2d DCA 1996).

Defendant was convicted in the Circuit Court, Hardee County, J. Dale Durrance, J., of two counts of armed robbery. He appealed. The District Court of Appeal, Quince, J., held that evidence of defendant's participation was insufficient to support his convictions as aider and abettor.

Reversed.

QUINCE, Judge.

Warren Taylor appeals his convictions and sentences imposed for two counts of armed robbery. Because we conclude there was insufficient evidence of Taylor's participation as an aider and abettor to the robberies, we reverse.

Taylor and Kenneth Washington were charged with robbery of two ladies in the parking lot of a Circle K store shortly after midnight on February 3, 1994. Earlier that night Taylor had gone to a nearby Presto store where he was employed to request cleanup work. While he was in the store, another man was sitting in the driver's seat of Taylor's car trying to conceal himself from passing customers. Taylor left the store, entered the passenger side of the car, and he and the other person drove off. They crossed the highway and stopped on a side street adjacent to the Circle K. The car stopped, moved forward another fifty feet, stopped, then moved another fifty feet, and parked in a dark area with its lights on.

Ms. Christy Browning, one of the robbery victims, was in her friend's car parked at the Circle K store. Ms. Dorothy Straker, the other robbery victim, had gone inside the store. Ms. Browning observed the movements of Taylor's vehicle while she was waiting for Ms. Straker to return to the car. Ms. Browning's view of the car, however, was partially obstructed by some bushes along a chainlink fence and by the absence of street lights. Ms. Browning heard a car door open, saw a light from the front passenger door, and saw the passenger walk around the front of the car to the driver's side. She heard two people talking but could not hear the conversation. She heard another door open, heard two doors close and saw that the passenger door had been closed. The car remained in the same position with the headlights on.

Shortly thereafter, Ms. Straker came out of the Circle K. As Ms. Straker approached the front driver's side of her car, Ms. Browning heard running footsteps. She saw someone from about the middle of the legs to the shoulder standing near Ms. Straker, and that person had a gun. Ms. Browning heard the person say something to Ms. Straker, and Ms. Straker said she did not have anything. The person said "Give me your pocketbook." Ms. Straker took the pocketbook and threw it into the person's chest. After getting the pocketbook, the gunman walked around to the passenger side of the car. He opened the door, pointed the gun and demanded Ms. Browning's purse.

During this exchange, Ms. Browning was able to see more of the gunman. He was wearing a dark, hooded sweatshirt type jacket. He had on a mask that was either black or navy blue, made of shiny, stretchy material, like spandex, with bright neon green stitching going through it. The only parts of the face exposed were the eyes, lips and nose. Ms. Browning could tell that the gunman was black. He was approximately six feet tall with a skinny build. When the gunman turned away after getting the purse, Ms. Browning began to exit the car. As the gunman was running, he yelled to the victims to get down on the ground. Ms. Browning did not watch the gunman; therefore, she could not say that he got into the vehicle she had previously been watching. Ms. Browning did not get on the ground. She turned and ran into the store. Ms. Browning asked the clerk to dial 911. The clerk asked what number, and Ms. Browning turned and ran out of the store. The persons inside locked the door behind her.

Ms. Browning ran across Highway 17 to the Presto store and asked the person behind the counter to call the cops. The lady asked what happened. When she was told of the robbery, she called the police. Ms. Browning told Mike Ford, a person who was in the Presto store when she asked for assistance, that the robber had been in the Presto store just before the robbery. Mr. Ford and his son got into his personal vehicle and started after the robber.

After leaving the store, Mike Ford stopped at his own place of business, but then spotted the station wagon going north on Highway 17 toward Fort Meade. He followed closely for about seventeen minutes. While following the car, Ford saw what appeared to be a white sack and another object thrown from the driver's window, as well as something thrown from the passenger's window. Ford's son was keeping the police informed of their location via cellular phone. The Fords lost the car in Fort Meade. When they saw it again, it was being followed by two police cars.

The police officers stopped the car and an officer approached each side. Taylor was the driver of the vehicle, and Kenneth Washington was the passenger. Taylor exited the vehicle as the officers approached. Both suspects were frisked, but no weapons were found. The police also searched the vehicle, but again no weapons were located. A wallet containing a woman's identification was found on the back seat. A roll of quarters was found on the driver's floor, and lottery tickets were found on the front floor. Two black and green spandex masks were found in the rear of the station wagon. The police found eighty dollars on Washington, and nine dollars and change on Taylor.

The police searched the route taken by the station wagon but found no weapon. One victim recovered everything, and the other victim recovered all but some jewelry.

On these facts, Taylor was convicted of two counts of armed robbery after a motion for judgment of acquittal was denied. Both the state and the defense agree that Taylor's convictions can only be sustained if there is sufficient proof of his participation as an aider and abettor of these robberies. To be convicted as an aider and abettor the state must show the defendant assisted the actual perpetrator by doing or saying something which caused, encouraged, assisted or incited the perpetrator to commit the crime and the defendant intended to participate in the crime. *Christie v. State, 652 So.2d 932 (Fla. 4th DCA 1995)*; *Evans v. State, 643 So.2d 1204 (Fla. 1st DCA), review denied, 652 So.2d 818 (Fla. 1994)*; *Valdez v. State, 504 So.2d 9 (Fla. 2d DCA 1986)*.

We agree with Taylor that the state failed to prove that he had the specific intent to participate in the robberies. Neither presence at the scene nor mere knowledge that an offense is being committed can be construed as participation in the crime. *Christie*. Additionally, driving the perpetrator to and from the scene or a display of questionable behavior after the fact is not sufficient to establish participation. *Pack v. State, 381 So.2d 1199 (Fla. 2d DCA 1980)*. The state in this instance demonstrated that Taylor was present at the scene, and he was the driver of the car when it left the scene and when it was stopped. None of these factors, either individually or collectively, conclusively demonstrate Taylor aided and abetted Washington in the commission of these offenses. See *R.H. v. State, 649 So.2d 299 (Fla. 2d DCA 1995)*; *M.M. v. State, 627 So.2d 1269 (Fla. 2d DCA 1993)*. The state's evidence simply does not exclude the reasonable inference that Taylor was waiting for Washington to return from the Circle K store.

We, therefore, reverse Taylor's convictions for armed robbery.

SCHOONOVER, A.C.J., and PATTERSON, J., concur.

REVIEW

1. To convict one of aiding and abetting, it is necessary to prove _____.
    a. intent to participate in the crime
    b. mere presence
    c. mere knowledge
    d. being present during the preparation to and from the scene

PRINCIPAL TO THEFT

A person who stands as a look-out and shields the activities of another who is committing a theft can be convicted of the crime of aiding and abetting theft.

CASE

A.M. v. State, 755 So.2d 759 (Fla. 4th DCA 2000).

Juvenile was adjudicated guilty in the Nineteenth Judicial Circuit Court, Martin County, Robert R. Makemson, J., of petit theft. Juvenile appealed. The District Court of Appeal, Shahood, J., held that evidence supported adjudication.

Affirmed; remanded for resentencing.

SHAHOOD, Judge.

We affirm the disposition order adjudicating appellant guilty of petit theft, but remand for re-sentencing.

The trial court did not err in denying appellant's motion for judgment of acquittal. The elements of petit theft are: knowingly obtaining or using, or endeavoring to obtain or use, the property of another with intent to either temporarily or permanently "(a) Deprive the other person of a right to the property [or] (b) Appropriate the property to his or her own use or to the use of any person not entitled to use of the property." § 812.014(1), Fla. Stat. (1999).

To prove the crime of aiding and abetting, the state must show that the defendant "(1) assisted the actual perpetrators by doing or saying something that caused, encouraged, assisted, or incited the perpetrators to actually commit the crime, and (2) intended to participate in the crime." See *A.B.G. v. State, 586 So.2d 445, 447 (Fla. 1st DCA 1991)*; see also *T.S. v. State, 675 So.2d 196 (Fla. 4th DCA 1996)*.

The facts in this case are similar to those in *A.B.G.* There, as here, only one witness testified on behalf of the state. *A.B.G., 586 So.2d at 446.* In *A.B.G.*, a security officer at the store testified that he saw four boys, including appellant, go to the condom section. *Id.* Three of the boys, including appellant, stood elbow-to-elbow in front of the condoms. *Id.* Two of the boys placed condoms in their jacket pockets while appellant and another boy looked continuously from the condoms to the front and back of the store. *Id.* Appellant also conversed with the other boys during the theft. *Id.* Afterwards, the boys walked together out of the store. *Id.*

The appellate court affirmed the order adjudicating A.B.G. delinquent for the offense of petit theft stating the following:

> In the instant case, the fact finder could reasonably infer from the evidence presented that appellant's hypothesis of innocence, that he didn't know the other boys were going to take the condoms and that he was just nervously looking around, was not reasonable.... [By his actions, t]he appellant demonstrated a deliberate pattern of conduct, both before and after the other boys had concealed the condoms.... A fact finder could reasonably infer that, as a result of appellant's consistent actions both before and after the actual taking of the property, the only reasonable hypothesis from the evidence presented was that appellant intended to be, and was, an active participant in the theft as a lookout.

Id. at 447.

Similarly, in *T.S.*, appellant and his companion were seen entering a condominium development parking lot at 2:00 o'clock in the morning and walking under the carports in a "zigzagging" manner. *T.S., 675 So.2d at 198-99.* He was also observed standing near a red car while his companion entered the car and, in fact, admitted to the police that he was standing near the vehicle "looking around," while his companion entered the car and took a radar detector. *Id.* This court held that appellant's actions went beyond merely being present at the crime scene. *Id. at 199.* The evidence showed that appellant was not only a lookout, but actively participated in combing the parking lot looking for a car to break into. *Id.* As a result, appellant's conviction for burglary of a conveyance was upheld. *Id.*

In this case, although the manager of the store from which the merchandise was taken testified that he could not say that appellant took anything and put it in his pocket, the manager did testify that appellant was among a group of four boys who were seen rummaging through the store's school supply section. According to the manager, he noticed the boys, as a group, picking things up, walking down the aisle, and stuffing items into their pockets. All four of the boys left together. As in *A.B.G.* and *T.S.*, it could be reasonably concluded from the evidence in this case that A.M. intended to participate in the crime and assisted the perpetrators in committing it. Denial of his motion for judgment of acquittal was, therefore, appropriate.

Although we affirm A.M.'s adjudication of guilt, we remand for re-sentencing. The state concedes, and we agree, that: (1) it was error for the court to pronounce a general sentence in all three of appellant's cases, see **D.A.D. v. State**, *697 So.2d 234 (Fla. 5th DCA 1997)* (a single order of disposition may not be used where multiple convictions constitute the basis for an adjudication of delinquency); (2) it was error for the court not to orally pronounce all of the terms of appellant's sentence, see **T.A.R. v. State**, *640 So.2d 222 (Fla. 5th DCA 1994)*; and (3) it was error for the court not to impose an exact term of commitment, see **M.S. v. State**, *675 So.2d 215 n. 1 (Fla. 4th DCA 1996)* (re-sentencing required to specify commitment for one year, which was maximum allowable sentence, instead of commitment for "indeterminate period of time," not longer than 19th birthday or maximum sentence allowable by law).

AFFIRMED; REMANDED FOR RESENTENCING.

WARNER, C.J., and GROSS, J., concur.

REVIEW

1. Aiding and abetting includes _____.
   a. acting as a lookout
   b. participating in the crime
   c. both a and b
   d. neither a nor b

PRINCIPLE IN THE FIRST DEGREE

Where a person acts as a principal to one crime, and the primary actor in the crime commits a separate crime in furtherance of the first, the principal can be convicted of the second crime even if he knew nothing of the second crime before its commission.

CASE

Cable, Jr. v. State, 436 So.2d 160 (Fla. 2d DCA 1983).

Defendant was convicted in the Circuit Court, Hillsborough County, Richard E. Leon, J., of aggravated assault, and he appealed. The District Court of Appeal, Grimes, J., held that evidence was sufficient to permit a trier of fact to find that defendant was a principal in commission of aggravated assault.

Affirmed.

GRIMES, Judge.

This is an appeal from a conviction of aggravated assault.

Detective Richard Swann, an undercover narcotics officer, met an informant at about 5:00 p.m. on June 16, 1981. The informant introduced Swann to appellant, and Swann told appellant that he wanted to buy some cocaine. Appellant's first efforts to acquire the cocaine were unsuccessful, so he told Swann to return later. At about 8:00 p.m., Swann picked appellant up, and they went to several places searching for drugs. Appellant then directed Swann to return to a gameroom that they had earlier visited to see if he could find someone with cocaine. Before arriving at the gameroom, appellant directed Swann to turn in to see several men who were in the parking lot of a convenience store. One of the men in the parking lot was appellant's brother, William. After talking awhile, they decided to return to the gameroom.

Once at the gameroom, Swann noticed several others present, including a man named H.P. Brock. While the men talked, appellant drove off in William's car. He returned shortly and then told Swann to come outside. He took Swann to the side of the building away from the parking lot and told him that he could not find any cocaine that night. Suddenly, Swann turned and found William Cable advancing toward him with a large pair of hedge clippers. William Cable placed the clippers at Swann's throat and threatened to kill him. Appellant remained behind Swann, and Brock stood by as well. William Cable demanded Swann's wallet. As Swann gave it to him, Brock held the clippers. After searching Swann's wallet, William Cable ordered the officer against a car and patted him down. They also made Swann remove his shoes to see if he was carrying a weapon. After satisfying themselves that Swann was not a police officer, the men told him that if he would return the following night, they would sell him narcotics. Swann left without further incident. Appellant, his brother, and Brock were eventually arrested. The state charged Appellant with aggravated assault.

Unquestionably, William Cable committed an aggravated assault on Officer Swann. See *Lindsey v. State, 67 Fla. 111, 64 So. 501 (1914); Gilbert v. State, 347 So.2d 1087 (Fla. 3d DCA 1977);* Section 784.021(1), Florida Statute (1981). We now must decide whether appellant's activities were sufficient to make him a principal in the first degree pursuant to section 777.011, Florida Statutes (1981). Section 777.011 provides in pertinent part:

> Principal in first degree. – Whoever commits any criminal offense against the state, whether felony or misdemeanor, or aids, abets, counsels, hires, or otherwise procures such offense is committed or is attempted to be committed, is a principal in the first degree and may be charged, convicted, and punished as such, whether he is or is not actually or constructively present at the commission of such offense.

Before one can be convicted as an aider or abettor, there must be proof of his intent to participate in the crime. *Shockey v. State, 338 So.2d 33 (Fla.3d DCA 1976); McClamrock v. State, 327 So.2d 780 (Fla.3d DCA 1975).* The State must also show that the accused has done or said something which causes, encourages, assists, or induces the other person to actually commit the crime. *G.C. v. State, 407 So.2d 639 (Fla. 3d DCA 1981).*

In most cases of this type, the crime perpetrated by others is an end in itself, and the state simply seeks to prove that the defendant aided in the commission of that crime. Here, appellant actively tried to commit a crime, and the question is whether he can be convicted as a principal for the commission of a second crime carried out in furtherance of a scheme to commit the first one. Obviously, appellant and his brother and Brock were attempting to consummate a drug sale. At some point, they became suspicious that Swann was an undercover agent. Appellant asked Swann to come outside ostensibly to talk with him about the sale of the cocaine. When Swann was sufficiently removed from the premises, appellant's brother accosted him with some hedge clippers. While appellant did not handle the clippers, he was present at all times. His brother's acts did not appear spontaneous, and they were entirely consistent with the preservation of the common drug scheme. The jury was entitled to conclude that appellant was a principal in the commission of the aggravated assault.

AFFIRMED.

HOBSON, A.C.J., and SCHOONOVER, J., concur.

REVIEW

1. In order to convict one as a principal, the state must prove the defendant _____.

        a. caused another to commit a crime
        b. assisted another in committing a crime
        c. induced another to commit a crime
        d. all of the above are correct

ACCESSORY AFTER THE FACT

In order to convict someone of being an accessory after the fact to a crime, the State must prove five elements. (1) Obviously, a felony must have been committed. (2) After the felony has been committed the defendant must have maintained, assisted or given aid to the person who committed the felony. (3) The defendant must have known at that time the person committed the felony. (4) The assistance must be given with the intent that it will help that person avoid or escape detention, arrest, trial or punishment. (5) And lastly, in order to be convicted of being an accessory, one must not be related by blood or marriage as a husband, wife, parent, grandparent, child, grandchild, brother, or sister. The intent may be proven by circumstantial evidence.

CASE

***Brown v. State,** 672 So.2d 861 (Fla. 3d DCA 1996).*

Defendant was convicted in the Circuit Court, Dade County, Bernard S. Shapiro and Frederick N. Barad, JJ., pursuant to his guilty plea, of being accessory after the fact to second-degree murder. Defendant appealed denial. The District Court of Appeal, Green, J., held that: (1) family immunity statute did not provide immunity to defendant, and (2) successful prosecution of principal for second-degree murder was not condition precedent to prosecution of defendant as accessory after the fact to second-degree murder.

Affirmed.

Before JORGENSON, COPE, and GREEN, JJ.

GREEN, Judge.

Darryl Lamont Brown was charged with being an accessory after the fact to second degree murder in violation of section 777.03, Florida Statutes (1993). [FN1] He entered a plea to the charge and reserved his right to appeal the trial court's denial of his sworn motion to dismiss. For reasons which follow, we affirm the lower court's denial of his motion.

On October 2, 1994, Brown accompanied his first cousin John Marshall to a grocery store. Prior to their entering the store, Marshall became embroiled in a physical altercation with the victim, another male. At some point during their dispute, Marshall hit the victim in the head with a wooden two-by-four board. Brown then drove Marshall away from the scene. The victim later died. Marshall was subsequently charged with second degree murder and Brown was charged with being an accessory after the fact by virtue of his act of driving Marshall away from the scene. Prior to their trial, Brown moved to dismiss the accessory charge and as grounds therefor asserted that the statute under which he was charged, section 777.03, granted him immunity from prosecution; further, he argued that he could not be prosecuted for accessory after the fact prior to his cousin's conviction for the underlying second degree murder charge. The trial court denied the motion and Brown entered a plea to the charge subject to his right to appeal the denial of his motion. [FN2] Marshall proceeded to trial and was ultimately acquitted of the second degree murder charge.

On this appeal, Brown first asserts that his motion to dismiss should have been granted because he is shielded from prosecution as an accessory to his cousin's charge by the immunity given to family members in section 777.03. We disagree. This section provides in pertinent part that:

> Whoever, *not standing in the relation of husband or wife, parent or grandparent, child or grandchild, brother or sister by consanguinity or affinity to the offender*, maintains or assists the principal or accessory before the fact, or gives the offender any other aid, knowing that he had committed a felony or been accessory therefore before the fact, with intent that he shall avoid or escape detection, arrest, trial or punishment, shall be deemed an accessory after the fact, and shall be guilty of a felony of the third degree. . . .
> (emphasis added)

§ 777.03, Fla.Stat. (1993). The immunity provision of the statute by its plain language makes no reference to cousins. It is a firmly established principle of statutory construction that the mention of one thing in a statute implies the exclusion of another or "expressio unius est exclusio alterius." ***Thayer v. State,*** *335 So.2d 815, 817 (Fla. 1976)*; ***Tillman v. Smith,*** *533 So.2d 928, 929 (Fla. 5ᵗʰ DCA 1988)*. The terms "consanguinity" and "affinity" have correctly been construed to mean by "blood" and "marriage" respectively. ***State v. C.H.,*** *421 So.2d 62, 63-64 (Fla. 4ᵗʰ DCA 1982)*. The modifying phrase "by consanguinity or affinity" expanded the statute's immunity provision only to include "in-laws" and "step-relatives." *Id. at 64.* While we acknowledge that it is certainly possible for a cousin to simultaneously be a step-relative [FN3] of the principal offender and thereby receive immunity under this statute, the legislature has declined to extend immunity to persons such as Brown whose sole familial relationship to the principal offender is that of cousin. Thus since the legislature has not seen fit for whatever reason to date to grant immunity in section 777.03 to cousins, we are not at liberty to do the same in this case:

> [O]ur duty [is] to give effect to legislative enactments despite any personal opinions as to their wisdom or efficacy. No principle is more firmly embedded in our constitutional system of separation of powers and checks and balances.

State v. C.H., *421 So.2d at 65-66* (alteration in original) (quoting ***Moore v. State,*** *343 So.2d 601, 603-04 (Fla. 1977)*).

We next consider Brown's remaining argument that he may not be prosecuted for the crime of accessory after the fact without his cousin's conviction for the underlying second degree murder charge. With such an argument, Brown is apparently arguing that the underlying felony and accessory charges are inextricably intertwined such that a conviction of the former is a condition precedent for a conviction of the latter. Put another way, Brown suggests that the State is collaterally estopped from prosecuting him as an accessory after the fact where the principal has been acquitted of the underlying felony. We again disagree.

In support of his argument, Brown cites ***Hysler v. State,*** *136 Fla. 563, 187 So. 261 (1939)* and ***State ex rel. Maudlin v. Hardie,*** *114 Fla. 374, 154 So. 183 (1934)*, both of which recite the rule at common law that the conviction and punishment of the principal must precede or at the very least, accompany the conviction of the accessory. Brown's reliance upon these cases is misplaced. First of all, neither of these cases factually involved an accessory after the fact. [FN4] But more importantly, the common law rule espoused in these decisions was rendered obsolete in 1957 with the enactment of section 776.011, Florida Statutes (1957), later renumbered section 777.011, [FN5] which eliminated any distinction between accessories before the fact and principals in the first and second degree. See ch. 57-310, Laws of Fla.; ***Potts v. State,*** *430 So.2d 900, 902 (Fla. 1982)*. As a result, "principals in the first and second degree and accessories before the fact were treated equally and all were made principals in the first degree." ***Potts,*** *430 So.2d at 902*; see also ***Blackburn v. State,*** *314 So.2d 634, 637 (Fla. 4ᵗʰ DCA 1975)*

170

("Thus the terms 'principal in the second degree' and 'accessory before the fact' appear to have passed into the judicial history of the State of Florida."), *cert. denied, 334 So.2d 603 (Fla.), cert. denied, 429 U.S. 864, 97 S.Ct. 170, 50 L.Ed.2d 142 (1976).*

The crime of accessory after the fact, on the other hand, has remained a separate offense in Florida. See *Staten v. State,* **519 So.2d 622 (Fla. 1988)** (holding a defendant cannot be convicted and sentenced both as a principal and an accessory after the fact to the same criminal offense). The *Staten* court further observed that the accessory after the fact is not a party to the underlying crime but is an actor in a separate and independent crime, obstruction of justice. *519 So.2d at 626.* As such, the accessory after the fact is guilty only of a third degree felony regardless of the gravity of the underlying substantive offense committed. *Id.*

Prior to a conviction for accessory after the fact, the State must, of course, prove beyond a reasonable doubt that the underlying felony was indeed committed. See *Staten v. State, 519 So.2d at 625* (quoting *People v. Prado, 67 Cal.App.3d 267, 273, 136 Cal.Rptr. 521, 524 (1977)).* Contrary to Brown's contention, the guilt or innocence of the accessory after the fact is not contingent upon whether the alleged principal to the underlying felony is convicted. Rather, the accessory's guilt or innocence rests upon whether the underlying felony was committed and whether the accessory thereafter rendered aid to protect the principal or facilitate the principal's escape. *Id. at 625-26. Cf. Potts v. State, 430 So.2d at 902* ("In order to convict the aider-abettor it is not necessary to show that the principal perpetrator was convicted of the same crime, nor is it even necessary to show that he was convicted at all."). Indeed, an acquittal of the principal establishes only the absence of the principal's legal liability for the underlying felony. [FN6] It does not negate the existence of the underlying felony itself. In obvious recognition of this fact as well as the fact that an acquittal may be the result of any number of factors, our supreme court in another factual context has squarely rejected the collateral estoppel argument advanced by Brown for criminal cases:

> This Court has recently held that a defendant tried separately from his co-conspirators is not entitled to raise the conviction of a co-conspirator for a lesser offense as a bar to his own conviction for a greater offense. *Potts v. State* [, *430 So.2d at 901-03.*] In so holding we recognized that different evidence may be admissible against different defendants and that "jury pardon" may result in conviction for a lesser offense though the facts proved at trial would support a conviction for a greater offense.

Eaton v. State, 438 So.2d 822, 823 (Fla. 1983). We accordingly conclude therefore that the successful prosecution of the principal to the underlying felony was not a condition precedent to the prosecution of the accessory after the fact nor did the principal's ultimate acquittal collaterally estop the State from prosecuting the accessory if the State could prove beyond a reasonable doubt (1) the commission of the underlying felony beyond a reasonable doubt and (2) that, with the requisite intent, the alleged accessory rendered assistance to protect the principal perpetrator or facilitated the principal's escape. Because Brown entered a plea to the charge, we carefully reviewed the record to determine whether the State's proffered factual basis for the plea was sufficient, if proven at trial, to make a prima facie showing of the accessory charge. We found that it was.

Affirmed.

FN1. Chapter 95-184, §§ 13, at 1702-03, Laws of Florida has since rewritten section 777.03 to create varying degrees of offense severity depending on the classification of the underlying offense. Subsection 777.03 (1), Florida Statutes (1995), however, retains substantially the same wording as the prior definition of accessory after the fact.

FN2. In exchange for his plea, Brown received a withhold of adjudication and one year of probation with the special condition that he would be eligible for early termination after six months.

FN3. For example, this would be the result of a woman with at least one child marrying her brother-in-law who also has at least one child.

FN4. In *Hysler*, the court found the common law rule inapplicable to a situation where the principal in the second degree was convicted prior to the apprehension of the principal. *187 So. at 262-63*. In *Hardie*, the court held that the defendant's conviction for accessory before the fact was improperly entered prior to the principal's conviction. *154 So. at 183-84*.

FN5. Section 777.011, Florida Statutes (1995) reads:
Whoever commits any criminal offense against the state, whether felony or misdemeanor, or aids, abets, counsels, hires, or otherwise procures such offense to be committed, and such offense is committed or is attempted to be committed, is a principal in the first degree and may be charged, convicted, and punished as such, whether he is or is not actually or constructively present at the commission of such offense.

FN6. Indeed, under our system of criminal justice which requires the State to prove its case beyond a reasonable doubt, an acquittal does not even establish the factual innocence of the accused to the offense.

REVIEW

1. To convict one of accessory after the fact, the state must prove _____.
   a. the defendant gave aid
   b. the defendant knew the person committed the act
   c. the assistance was given to help that person avoid arrest
   d. all of the above

2. It is not a defense to accessory after the fact if the relationship is that of a
_____.

    a. husband
    b. grandparent
    c. cousin
    d. sibling

THINKING CRITICALLY

1.   Jane plans to rob an acquaintance. She enlists the help of Stacy. Jane provides Stacy a gun and directs the commission of the robbery. Stacy shoots and kills the individual she robs. Is Jane a principal to the murder? Why or why not?

2.   Linda is a companion and housekeeper to an elderly invalid woman named Emma. Linda and Tony plan to commit a burglary and rob Emma. Tony is to bring Harry and make it appear that Linda and Emma are both robbery victims. Linda gets fired. Tony and Harry go through with robbery anyway. Emma is killed during the robbery. Can Linda be convicted as a principal? Why or why not?

3.   James is driving to work. His friend Peter is in the back seat of the car changing clothes to go to work also. Peter finds a BB gun in the back seat. Peter claims the gun went off by accident. Sally is playing in her parents' front yard and is struck in the eye with a BB and severely injured. Peter is charged with aggravated battery. Can James be charged as a principal? Why or why not? Is mere presence at the scene of a crime and knowledge of that crime enough to charge James?

4.   Do you agree with the court's holding in *Potts*? Why or why not?

5.   Would the result be different if Ramirez had been found not guilty of the burglary? Should it be different?

6.   Should Donald Cable have been convicted as a principal? Would the result have been different if Donald had remained in the gameroom during the incident with the hedge clippers?

7.   Carol drives to the convenience store in her sister's car. Andy goes with her. Carol enters the store, buys some pretzels and a drink while Andy waits outside. After Carol comes out, Andy then enters the store. Andy tells the clerk he will shoot him unless he hands over all the money in the register. The clerk hands over the money to Andy. Andy then tells the clerk to get down on the floor. The clerk hears a car leave. A description goes out over the police scanner. A short time later, Carol and Andy are pulled over. Andy is searched and a marked bill is found on him. No money is found on Carol. The clerk comes down and identifies Andy as the robber. Can Carol be prosecuted as a principal? What if a gun is found in the car? What if Carol had witnessed the robbery?

8.   Was R.M. merely present at the scene of the crime? Would the result have been different if R.M. had not previously been banned from the arcade? What if only 1 or 2 of the youths made a throwing gesture? What if the manager could not identify which of the youths made the gesture?

9.   Do you agree with the holding in *Taylor*? What additional facts would the state need to prove to convict Taylor? What if items belonging to one of the victims had been found on Taylor? Would it change the result? Should it?

10. Distinguish *Taylor* and *A.M.*. Do you think the court reached the correct result in *A.M.*? What additional facts might be important to know?

11. Marshall and his cousin Todd go to the mall together. Marshall gets in a fight with someone at the mall. He kicks the person in the head. The victim later dies. Todd drove Marshall away from the mall. Can Todd be charged as an accessory? Why or why not?

12. Betsy works at the grocery store as an assistant manager. It is her responsibility to make the bank deposits. Betsy told Charlie, who she lives with, that the bank procedures were foolish and it would be easy for someone to rob her. A few nights later, Betsy and another employee are robbed of the bank deposit by Charlie. Betsy at first does not pick Charlie out of the line up. In fact, she tells no one she knows him at all. Several weeks later, Betsy admits to her relationship with Charlie. Is Betsy guilty of being an accessory after the fact? If she is charged, how will you defend her?

13. A witness observes Frank near a house. Frank then gets in Brad's car and they drive away. Moments later the house burns up. Frank is charged with arson. Can Brad be charged as accessory after the fact? What additional information would you like to have?

CHAPTER 5 ANSWER KEY

REVIEW QUESTIONS

Potts v. State
1. d
2. d

R.M. v. State
1. c

Taylor v. State
1. a

A.M. v. State
1. c

Cable, Jr. v. State
1. d

Brown v. State
1. d
2. c

CHAPTER 6

UNCOMPLETED CRIMES: ATTEMPT, CONSPIRACY AND SOLICITATION

ATTEMPT

In order for the State to convict a defendant of an attempt to commit a crime, the defendant must do some act toward committing the crime without actually completing the crime. Failure to complete the crime can be the defendant's own fault or may result from someone else preventing the completion of the criminal act. Thus, just thinking or talking about committing a crime is not sufficient to prove attempt. Moreover, abandonment of a plan is a defense. Nonetheless, to constitute abandonment there must be a complete and voluntary renunciation of the defendant's criminal purpose. In order to be guilty of an attempt a person must have both the intent to commit a particular crime and must do some overt act toward the commission of that crime.

CASE

Green v. State, 655 So.2d 208 (Fla. 3d DCA 1995).

Defendant who had been taxicab passenger was convicted of attempted robbery of driver in the Circuit Court, Dade County, Fredricka G. Smith, J., and she appealed. The District Court of Appeal held that evidence was sufficient to support conviction.

Affirmed.

PER CURIAM.

The defendant appeals her conviction for attempted robbery claiming the evidence was insufficient to demonstrate the taking of anything of value from the victim.

In the present case, the defendant hailed a taxi cab and directed it to a specific address. Upon arriving, she told the cab to go on. Ultimately, she directed the cab over to the curb. At that time, she asked the victim-cab driver whether he had change for a "ten." As the victim retrieved the cash from his pocket, the defendant leaned over and turned the ignition to the vehicle off. Almost simultaneously, the defendant's head was hit by an assailant who approached him from the curb. The cab driver quickly recovered and drove the cab with the defendant still in it back to his dispatcher where the defendant was arrested.

The crime of attempted robbery requires only the formation of an intent to take money or property of another and an overt act capable of accomplishing the goal. §

812.13, Fla. Stat. (1993); § 777.04, Fla. Stat. (1993); *Mercer v. State, 347 So.2d 733 (Fla. 4th DCA 1977).*

Under the circumstances, the testimony was more than adequate to support a verdict of attempted robbery.

Affirmed.

REVIEW

1. In order to be convicted of attempt, the state must prove _____.
   a. the defendant did some act toward committing the crime
   b. the crime was not completed
   c. both a and b
   d. neither a nor b

2. The crime of attempted robbery requires _____.
   a. intent to take money or property of another
   b. an overt act capable of accomplishing that goal
   c. both a and b
   d. neither a nor b

ATTEMPTED FELONY-MURDER

The doctrine of felony-murder provides when a person is killed during the commission of certain felonies, the felon is said to have the intent to commit the death - even if the killing was unintended. It further imputes intent for deaths caused by co-felons and police during the perpetration of certain felonies. However, the crime of attempted felony murder is logically impossible because a conviction for the offense of attempt requires proof of the specific intent to commit the underlying crime. Since the crime of felony-murder does not require specific intent to murder, there can be no attempt to commit felony-murder.

CASE

State v. Gray, 654 So.2d 552 (Fla. 1995).

Defendant was convicted of armed robbery with firearm and of attempted first-degree felony murder by the Circuit Court, Dade County, and he appealed. The District Court of Appeal reversed and remanded certified question to Supreme Court as one of great public importance. The Supreme Court, Harding, J., held that there is no crime of attempted felony murder.

Decision of District Court of Appeal approved.

HARDING, Justice.

We have for review *Gray v. State, 654 So.2d 934 (Fla. 3d DCA 1994)*, in which the district court certified this question as one of great public importance:

> WHETHER THE "OVERT ACT" REFERRED TO IN *AMLOTTE v. STATE, 456 So.2d 448, 449 (Fla. 1984)*, INCLUDES ONE, SUCH AS FLEEING, WHICH IS INTENTIONALLY COMMITTED BUT IS NOT INTENDED TO KILL OR INJURE ANOTHER?

We have jurisdiction based on article V, section 3(b)(4) of the Florida Constitution.

Gray also argues that this Court should reexamine its decision in *Amlotte*. Because we have jurisdiction based on the certified question, we also have jurisdiction over this issue. *Feller v. State, 637 So.2d 911, 914 (Fla. 1994)*.

We find it unnecessary to answer the certified question because we recede from our holding in *Amlotte* that there is a criminal offense of attempted felony murder.

The relevant facts of this case are that Gray and two codefendants robbed a restaurant in Dade County and fled by car. After police spotted the car, the driver went through a red light and hit another car. The driver of the other car was ejected and rendered a quadriplegic. Gray was convicted of armed robbery with a firearm and attempted first-degree felony murder.

On appeal, the Third District Court of Appeal affirmed the robbery conviction, reversed the attempted first-degree felony murder conviction, and remanded the case for resentencing. *Gray, 654 So.2d at 935*.

The district court acknowledged that this Court recognized the offense of attempted felony murder in *Amlotte*. *Id.* Gray did not dispute that he perpetrated the enumerated felony of robbery. But the district court agreed with Gray that the information charging him did not allege and the State did not offer proof of a separate overt act which could, but did not, cause the death of another. *Id.*

The court found insufficient evidence to present a jury question of whether the overt act - running the red light, which resulted in the collision - could have caused the victim's death and reversed Gray's conviction for attempted first-degree felony murder. *Id. 654 So.2d at 935*. The court also certified the question to this Court. *Id. at 936*.

In *Amlotte*, we determined by a five-to-two vote that there is a criminal offense of attempted felony murder. *456 So.2d at 449*. The essential elements of the crime are (1) perpetrating, or attempting to perpetrate an enumerated felony and, (2) during the commission of the enumerated felony, committing an intentional overt act, or aiding and abetting the commission of an intentional overt act, which could, but does not, cause the death of another. *Id.* We held that because the attempt occurs during the commission of a felony, the law, as it does under the felony murder doctrine, presumes the existence of the specific intent required to prove attempt. *Id. at 449-50.*

Justice Overton maintained in a dissent that the crime of attempted felony murder is logically impossible. *Id. at 450* (Overton, J., dissenting). He pointed out that a conviction for the offense of attempt requires proof of the specific intent to commit the underlying crime. *Id.*; see also §§ 777.04 (1), Fla. Stat. (1991). [FN1] He recognized that the crime of felony murder is based on a legal fiction that implies malice aforethought from the actor's intent to commit the underlying felony. *Amlotte, 456 So.2d at 450* (Overton, J., dissenting). This means that when a person is killed during the commission of certain felonies, the felon is said to have the intent to commit the death - even if the killing was unintended. *Id.* The felony murder doctrine also imputes intent for deaths caused by co-felons and police during the perpetration of certain felonies. *Id. at 451.* But, Justice Overton maintained, "Further extension of the felony murder doctrine so as to make intent irrelevant for purposes of the attempt crime is illogical and without basis in law." *Id.*

We now believe that the application of the majority's holding in *Amlotte* has proven more troublesome than beneficial and that Justice Overton's view is the more logical and correct position.

Recently, the Committee on Standard Jury Instructions in Criminal Cases, which was charged with recommending amendments to various criminal instructions, reported difficulty in drafting an amendment that incorporated the language of *Amlotte*. In fact, a majority of the committee members believed that there could be no crime of attempted felony murder. *Standard Jury Instructions in Criminal Cases (93-1), 636 So.2d 502 n. 1 (Fla. 1994).* [FN2]

The Fifth District Court of Appeal has also voiced concerns. In *Grinage v. State, 641 So.2d 1362, 1366 (Fla. 5ᵗʰ DCA 1994), review granted, No. 84,318, 651 So.2d 1196 (Fla. Sept. 8, 1994),* the court maintained that the Legislature did not intend for some criminal offenses, including first-degree felony murder, to support a conviction for their attempted commission. The district court said that the offense of murder contemplates a completed act of homicide and suggested that the law should not presume intent to murder when there is no death simply because the assault occurs during the commission or attempted commission of a felony. *Id.* While recognizing that parts of its analysis were contrary to the *Amlotte* majority opinion, the court said it had the responsibility "to point out to the court new or additional arguments that should be considered by it in determining whether questioned law should remain in effect." *Id. at 1367.*

In addition, questioning at oral argument in the instant case indicated difficulties with determining what constitutes an "overt act" that could, but does not, cause the death of another.

181

Although receding from a decision is not something we undertake lightly, we find that twenty-twenty hindsight has shown difficulties with applying *Amlotte* that twenty-twenty foresight could not predict. Based on these difficulties, we are convinced that we must recede from *Amlotte*. The legal fictions required to support the intent for felony murder are simply too great.

In reaching this decision, we are mindful of the importance of the doctrine of *stare decisis*. *Stare decisis* provides stability to the law and to the society governed by that law. *State v. Schopp, 653 So.2d 1016 (Fla. 1995)* (Harding, J., dissenting). Yet *stare decisis* does not command blind allegiance to precedent. "Perpetrating an error in legal thinking under the guise of *stare decisis* serves no one well and only undermines the integrity and credibility of the court." *Smith v. Department of Ins., 507 So.2d 1080, 1096 (Fla. 1987)* (Ehrlich, J., concurring in part, dissenting in part).

Accordingly, we recede from the holding in *Amlotte* that there is a crime of attempted felony murder in Florida. This decision must be applied to all cases pending on direct review or not yet final. *Smith v. State, 598 So.2d 1063, 1066 (Fla. 1992)*. Having reached this decision, we do not need to answer the certified question in *Gray*.

We also approve the result in *Gray*, where the district court affirmed Gray's robbery conviction, reversed his attempted first-degree felony murder conviction, and remanded for resentencing.

It is so ordered.

GRIMES, C.J., and OVERTON, SHAW, KOGAN, WELLS and ANSTEAD, JJ., concur.

> FN1. This Court has interpreted section 777.04(1), Florida Statutes (1991) to mean that an attempt to commit a specific intent crime requires (1) a specific intent to commit a particular crime and (2) an overt act toward its commission. See, e.g., *Thomas v. State, 531 So.2d 708, 710 (Fla. 1988)*; but see *Gentry v. State, 437 So.2d 1097, 1098-99 (Fla. 1983)*.

> FN2. The committee did, however, propose an amendment that incorporated *Amlotte,* which this Court adopted. *Standard Jury Instructions in Criminal Cases (93-1), 636 So.2d 502, 504-05 (Fla. 1994)*.

REVIEW SECTION

1. Attempted felony murder _____.
   a. is not a crime
   b. is a crime
   c. may be a crime, depends on the circumstances
   d. both b and c

CONSPIRACY

Conspiracy is a separate and distinct crime from the offense that is the object of conspiracy. The crime of conspiracy consists of two elements. First, the defendant must intend an offense be committed. Second, in order to carry out the intent the defendant must have agreed, conspired, combined or confederated with the other person to cause the object of the conspiracy to be committed by them, one of them, or some other person. Putting it simply, the second element of a conspiracy is that there be an agreement. No specific words need to be uttered. The defendant need not do any act in furtherance of the offense conspired. However, mere presence at the scene of a crime is not enough. Moreover, it is a defense if the defendant at some point persuades the person not to commit the offense or otherwise prevents its commission.

Under Florida law when all but one of the co-conspirators is acquitted, the remaining co-conspirator may still be convicted. There need not be an unindicted co-conspirator for this to apply.

CASE

Doolin v. State, 650 So.2d 44 (Fla. 1st DCA 1995).

Defendant was convicted in the Circuit Court, Leon County, James R. Wolf, Acting, J., of two counts of conspiracy based on agreement to kidnap and then to commit battery on intended victim, and he appealed. The District Court of Appeal, Zehmer, C.J., held that evidence was insufficient to support conviction for two counts of conspiracy where there was no evidence that initial conspiracy to kidnap was terminated or that defendant then entered new conspiracy to commit battery.

Reversed and remanded.

Booth, J., concurred specially and filed opinion.

ZEHMER, Chief Judge.

Appellant appeals his conviction on two counts of conspiracy. One count charged conspiracy to kidnap to inflict bodily harm contrary to sections 777.04 and 787.01(2), Florida Statutes. The other count charged conspiracy to commit aggravated battery contrary to sections 777.04 and 784.045(1)(a), Florida Statutes. The evidence proved, as the state concedes in its answer brief, that:

> [A]ppellant and his co-conspirators plotted to kidnap the victim by following her and then putting her in the trunk of their car, and they further plotted to commit aggravated battery upon her by breaking her knees and ankles, and they acquired an ax, a baseball bat and a board to help them accomplish this goal. Hence, although appellant and his co-conspirators planned to kidnap

and then batter the victim during the course of a single criminal transaction, the conspiracy to commit kidnapping and the conspiracy to commit aggravated battery were proven by separate and distinct conduct. In other words, appellant committed two distinct acts of conspiracy. Appellant cannot seriously suggest that co-conspirators who discuss and plot the commission of more than one distinct offense have engaged in only one conspiratorial act.

(Answer Brief, p. 5.)

It is readily apparent that the state has completely misconceived the nature of the offense of criminal conspiracy. The essence of the offense is the agreement to commit a criminal act or acts, and if a single agreement exists, only one conspiracy exists even if the conspiracy has as its objectives the commission of multiple offenses; and the conspiracy continues to exist until consummated, abandoned, or otherwise terminated by some affirmative act. *Griffin v. State*, 611 So.2d 20 (Fla. 1st DCA 1992); *Cam v. State*, 433 So.2d 38 (Fla. 1st DCA 1983); *Epps v. State*, 354 So.2d 441 (Fla. 1st DCA), cert. denied, 360 So.2d 1250 (Fla. 1978). [Footnote 1 omitted] In this case, the state's proof established that only one agreement was made to commit multiple offenses against the victim. There was no evidence to establish that the alleged conspiracy to kidnap to inflict bodily harm was terminated and a separate conspiracy to commit aggravated battery was thereafter agreed to by the co-conspirators. Under the cited authorities, the dual convictions must be reversed and the cause remanded for entry of judgment of conviction on only one conspiracy charge. [FN2]

Appellant was sentenced to 364 days in jail followed by two years' community control, which would thereafter be followed by two years' and five years' probation on the respective counts. The state concedes, and we agree, that this sentence was erroneous under the sentencing guidelines.

The judgment is reversed and the cause is remanded for entry of conviction on only one count of conspiracy and for resentencing on that count.

REVERSED AND REMANDED.

DAVIS, J., concurs.

BOOTH, J., specially concurring with opinion.

BOOTH, Judge, specially concurring.

I concur in the result of the majority opinion but would point out that, as conceded in appellant's brief, on remand, the court may impose the same or any other sentence, departure or not, on the single remaining conspiracy count as long as the court makes the necessary findings. Section 921.0016, Florida Statutes, and Rule 3.701, Fla.R.Crim.P. Thus, the court, in its wisdom, may consider the heinous nature of the multiple felonies planned to be committed against the helpless victim in this case and the fact that the conspirators went beyond the "talking" stage and took definite steps toward carrying out the conspiracy.

> FN2. We would be remiss in not noting that neither the Appellant nor the state cited these cases but premised their arguments on cases dealing with the commission of substantive offenses in a single transaction. This lack of understanding of the law of criminal conspiracy by the prosecution and defense may well have led the trial judge into committing this error.

REVIEW

1. Conspiracy consists of _____.
   - a. intent to commit an offense
   - b. an agreement
   - c. both a and b
   - d. neither a nor b

2. Conspiracy continues to exist until _____.
   - a. consummated
   - b. abandoned
   - c. terminated
   - d. all of the above

CASE

Mickenberg v. State, 640 So.2d 1210 (Fla. 2d DCA 1994).

Defendant was convicted in the Circuit Court, Pinellas County, R. Grable Stoutamire, J., of conspiracy to traffic in cocaine, and he appealed. The District Court of Appeal, Ryder, Acting C.J., held that evidence was insufficient to support conviction.

Reversed and remanded.

RYDER, Acting Chief Judge.

Steven Mickenberg attacks his conviction for conspiracy to traffic in 400 grams or more of cocaine. Because we hold that the evidence was insufficient to warrant a conviction, we reverse and remand with directions that the circuit court discharge him.

Mickenberg and three other codefendants were charged with conspiring with each other and seven other individuals to traffic in 400 grams or more of cocaine in violation of section 893.135(1), Florida Statutes (1989). Five of the coconspirators testified at trial for the state. The following is the evidence against Mickenberg presented in the light most favorable to the state.

Thomas Martin testified that during 1986-1987, he made his living selling cocaine. He met Mickenberg through Alejandro Ruiz, his supplier and Mickenberg's roommate for eighteen months during the time in question. Mickenberg mainly delivered the cocaine to Martin for Ruiz, and Martin paid an additional $1,000.00 as a delivery charge. He contacted Ruiz to set up the deals and never discussed price or quantity with Mickenberg. Martin did not believe he had ever talked to Mickenberg about arranging for a delivery.

Michael Perry testified that he and Michael Spinger, another codefendant, made several trips to Miami to pick up cocaine from Ruiz. He became a "mule" for Martin and Spinger. On one occasion, he picked up a bag from Mickenberg, but he never actually saw any drugs. He did not recall on which trip he saw the drugs. In the summer of 1987, he met Mickenberg in Lakeland where he picked up two kilos of cocaine. He never talked with Mickenberg about setting up the Lakeland trip, and he knew that Mickenberg was not involved in setting up the exchanges.

Three other co-conspirators testified, but two did not know Mickenberg. The third testified to a cocaine transaction when he and another codefendant, Scott Soares, went to Ruiz's apartment. Soares went into a bedroom with Mickenberg. When they came out, Mickenberg put a large amount of cash in a wall unit. Mickenberg admitted taking the cash for Ruiz, but denied giving anything in exchange.

The trial court denied the appellant's motion for judgment of acquittal at the close of the state's case and at the close of all the evidence. The appellant argued that the state had failed to show an express or implied agreement between two or more persons to commit a criminal offense and that a conspiracy involved more than aiding and abetting.

The crime of conspiracy consists of an express or implied agreement between two or more persons to commit a criminal offense. *Ramirez v. State, 371 So.2d 1063, 1065 (Fla. 3d DCA 1979), cert. denied, 383 So.2d 1201 (Fla. 1980)*. To prove the crime of conspiracy, the state must prove an agreement and an intention to commit an offense. *Saint Louis v. State, 561 So.2d 628, 629 (Fla. 2d DCA 1990)*. Mere presence at the scene is insufficient to establish conspiracy. *Saint Louis*. Conspiracy is a separate and distinct crime from the offense that is the object of the conspiracy. *Ramirez, at 1065*. Evidence that a person aided and abetted another in the commission of an offense, although insufficient to convict the person as a principal in such offense is insufficient to convict either person of a conspiracy to commit the subject offense. *Ramirez, at 1065*. One danger that lurks in the criminal charge of conspiracy is the tendency to make the crime so elastic, sprawling and pervasive as to defy meaningful definition. *Ramirez, at 1066-67*.

A review of the record shows that the state did not prove beyond a reasonable doubt that Mickenberg entered into an agreement with Ruiz or the other co-conspirators to traffic cocaine. Clearly, Mickenberg was aiding and abetting Ruiz in trafficking in cocaine. His participation, however, does not reach the level of the separate crime of conspiracy. We conclude, therefore, that the evidence was insufficient to withstand the appellant's motion for judgment of acquittal. Accordingly, we reverse and direct that he be discharged.

Because we reverse on this point, we do not address the appellant's other issues on appeal.

Reversed and remanded.

CAMPBELL and PATTERSON, JJ., concur.

REVIEW

    1. The agreement part of a conspiracy consists of _____.
        a. an express agreement
        b. an implied agreement
        c. both a and b
        d. neither a nor b

SOLICITATION

The charge of criminal solicitation has two elements. First, a defendant must have solicited another to commit an offense. Second, during the solicitation the defendant must have commanded, encouraged, hired, or requested the person to engage in specific conduct. The conduct must be the commission of the offense or an attempt to commit the offense.

The defendant need not do any act in furtherance of the offense solicited. The definition of solicit is to ask earnestly or try to induce the person to do something.

Just like the crime of conspiracy, it is a defense to persuade the person solicited not to do so or to otherwise prevent the commission of the offense. Even so, the crime need not ever be completed.

CASE

Luzarraga v. State, 575 So.2d 731 (Fla. 3d DCA 1991).

Defendant was convicted on drug charges, including solicitation to sell cocaine, by the Circuit Court, Monroe County, J. Jefferson Overby, J. Defendant appealed. The District Court of Appeal held that fact that person defendant solicited to sell cocaine was undercover police officer engaged in "reverse sting" operation was no defense to charge of solicitation to sell cocaine.

Affirmed.

PER CURIAM.

This is an appeal by the defendant Javier Luzarraga a/k/a Louis Perez from judgments of conviction and sentences for (1) purchasing cocaine, (2) solicitation to sell cocaine, (3) willfully fleeing a police officer, and (4) resisting arrest without violence. We reject that defendant's contention on appeal attacking the sufficiency of the evidence to support the solicitation conviction and hold that it is no defense to a charge of solicitation to sell cocaine that the person the defendant solicited was an undercover police officer engaged in a "reverse sting" police operation; we think the defendant's culpability in soliciting the undercover officer herein to commit such a crime should be measured by the circumstances which the defendant believed them to be, not by the fact that he foolishly selected an undercover police officer to solicit who surreptitiously intended to arrest the defendant after the solicited sale was completed. § 777.04(2), Fla. Stat. (1989); W. LaFave and A. Scott, *Criminal Law* § 6.1, at 15 (1986). " 'For the crime of solicitation to be completed, it is only necessary that the [defendant], with intent that another person commit a crime, have enticed, advised, incited, ordered or otherwise encouraged that person to commit a crime.' " ***State v. Gaines,*** *431 So.2d 736, 737 (Fla. 4ᵗʰ DCA 1983)* (quoting from W. LaFave and A. Scott, *Criminal Law* § 58, at 414) (emphasis omitted). It is therefore of no moment as to who the person solicited was or what that person's motives or intent might have been at the time he was solicited to commit the subject crime. It is enough that the defendant, with requisite criminal intent, solicited another to commit a crime.

The defendant raises no other points on appeal. Accordingly, the judgments of conviction and sentences under review are hereby

Affirmed.

REVIEW

   1. Solicitation consists of _____.
       a. doing an act in furtherance of the offense
       b. asking a person to do something
       c. inducing a person to do something
       d. two of the above

THINKING CRITICALLY

1. Martin is offered a ride home by Alex and Jean. Martin held a gun to Alex's head and ordered Jean to remove her clothes. Martin then reached over and squeezed her breast. Has Martin committed the crime of attempted sexual battery? Why or why not?

2. Law enforcement is running an undercover sting operation. Jerome motions the undercover officer to pull over. The officer asks for a "20;" that is a twenty dollar piece of crack cocaine. Jerome pulls out a small baggie with a rock in it. The officer pulls out a twenty dollar bill. Jerome has his hand on the twenty dollar bill when the take down team moves in to arrest him. Is Jerome guilty of sale and delivery of cocaine? What if the lab tested the rock and it was not in fact cocaine? What if Jerome threw the money and the suspected drugs on the ground as the police moved in for the arrest?

3. Should the defendant have been convicted of attempted robbery in *Green*? What is the assailant who approached from the curb guilty of? What if the cab driver had no money?

4. Do you agree with the *Gray* case? Why or why not? What about cases where a gun is used to attempt to commit a felony? What if any weapon is used? Should the result be different?

5. Is there still a crime of attempted premeditated murder in the State of Florida? Should there be?

6. Virginia and Hector are charged with criminal conspiracy. At a joint trial, Hector is found not guilty and Virginia is convicted. Should the verdict be set aside? Why or why not?

7. Do you agree with the court's holding in *Doolin*? Would it be possible to be convicted of more than one count of conspiracy? If so, how?

8.	Clara wants her husband killed. Wayne is out with friends at a bar and starts bragging that he is to be paid money from the insurance proceeds. Wayne discusses different plans for carrying out the murder. Wayne later shoots and kills Clara's husband. Can Wayne's friends be convicted of conspiracy? Can Clara or Wayne be convicted? Why or why not?

9.	What is the difference between aiding and abetting and the charge of conspiracy? Do you agree with the court's findings in *Mickenberg*? Why or why not?

10.	Is it fair to convict someone of soliciting a law enforcement officer? Should it be a defense to solicit someone who has no intention of committing the offense? Why or why not?

11.	Can a person be charged with solicitation to deliver cocaine, if it is shown he or she intended to purchase cocaine, if the substance produced is not in fact cocaine? Why or why not?

12.   What if a person asks another to lie for him in a court proceeding? Has the crime of solicitation to commit perjury occurred? What additional facts would you want to know?

13.   Tom asks Dennis to burn and destroy his car so he can collect the insurance proceeds. Dennis reports this to the police. Tom then asks Dennis to postpone any action until he has taken out more insurance. Tom is charged with solicitation to commit arson. Tom defends the solicitation charge by arguing that he prevented the commission of the offense. What should the jury's verdict be? Why?

CHAPTER 6 ANSWER KEY

REVIEW QUESTIONS

Green v. State
1. c
2. c

State v. Gray
1. a

Doolin v. State
1. c
2. d

Mickenberg v. State
1. c

Luzarraga v. State
1. d

CHAPTER 7

DEFENSES TO CRIMINAL
LIABILITY: JUSTIFICATIONS

SELF DEFENSE

Self defense justifies an individual in using force. The force used may be deadly or non-deadly depending on the circumstances.

DEADLY FORCE

The use of deadly force is justified if the defendant reasonably believes the force is necessary to prevent imminent death or great bodily harm to himself or herself. This need may arise as a result of someone's attempt to murder the defendant, commit a felony upon the defendant, or commit a felony in or upon the defendant's home when he or she is there. Deadly force is also justified to save another person from imminent death or the commission of a felony against that other person.

Deadly force is not justified if the defendant was attempting to commit, committing or escaping from the commission of a felony. As a general rule (with some exceptions), the defendant cannot have provoked the use of force against himself. For instance, if the force is so great the defendant believes himself to be in danger and had exhausted all reasonable means of escape, deadly force is justifiable. Likewise, if the defendant withdraws from the commission of a felony and so indicates to the assailant, but the assailant continues to use force, the use of deadly force would be justified.

The circumstances surrounding the defendant at the time the force is used must be analyzed and considered. The danger need not be actual, but the defendant must have believed it was real. The standard applied is that of a reasonably cautious and prudent person under the same circumstances.

Before resorting to deadly force, the defendant must have used reasonable means to avoid the danger. And of course, there are exceptions to that general rule. For instance, there is no duty to retreat in your own home. Prior threats may come into play as well. If there were threats or prior difficulties, the defendant may have the right to arm himself. Additional factors to be considered are the reputation of the victim for being a violent and dangerous person, and the relative physical abilities and capacities of both the defendant and the victim.

NON-DEADLY FORCE

A defendant may also be justified in the use of non-deadly force. It is a defense to use non-deadly force if a defendant reasonably believes such conduct is necessary to defend against the victim's use of unlawful force against either the defendant or another person. However, the unlawful force by the victim must appear ready to occur.

A defendant may use non-deadly force if the victim is trespassing and the force was needed to terminate that wrongful behavior. In cases like this, the State must prove the defendant was in lawful possession of the property. To do so, the State can establish it is the defendant's own property, that of a member of the defendant's immediate family or household, or someone's whose property the defendant has a legal duty to protect.

Like the use of deadly force, the use of non-deadly force is not justified if the defendant was attempting to commit, committing or escaping after the commission of a felony. Non-deadly force is also not justified where the defendant provokes the use of force unless that defendant reasonably believed he or she was in imminent danger of death or great bodily harm and had exhausted every reasonable means to escape the danger. The other exception that applies when the defendant provokes the use of force is where the defendant withdraws from physical contact and clearly indicates this but the assailant continues.

Force cannot be used to resist a lawful arrest when it is known or reasonably appears the individual is a law enforcement officer. When, however, an officer uses excessive force, the person is justified in the use of reasonable force. The extent of the force that can be used depends on the reasonable belief such force is necessary.

Again, the surrounding circumstances must be looked at. The danger facing the defendant need not be actual but based upon appearances the defendant must have actually believed that the danger was real. If the victim has a reputation of being a violent and dangerous person and that reputation is known to the defendant, that fact may be considered. Also to be considered are the relative physical abilities and capacities of both the defendant and the victim.

Were a Defendant asserts that he acted in self-defense, the State must rebut this assertion and establish that the Defendant *did not* act in self-defense.

CASE

Hunter v. State, 687 So.2d 277 (Fla. 5th DCA 1997).

Defendant was convicted in the Circuit Court, Seminole County, Wallace H. Hall, J., of second-degree murder, and he appealed. The District Court of Appeal, Thompson, J., held that whether defendant shot his brother in self-defense was jury question.

Affirmed.

THOMPSON, Judge.

Dwayne F. Hunter appeals from a conviction and sentence for second degree murder in the shooting of his brother, Kerry. We affirm.

Dwayne F. Hunter argued with Kerry while they visited the home of a friend. During the altercation, Kerry threatened to kill Hunter. Hunter drove away, returned to the scene of the argument and emerged from his truck armed with a .22 rifle. Kerry also left the scene and returned with a .380 handgun. The brothers confronted and shot at each other. Kerry was killed. Autopsy results revealed that Kerry had been shot three times in the chest and four times in the back. Although witnesses saw Hunter and Kerry approach each other, none saw the shooting or who fired first. Hunter testified that his brother was the aggressor and that he acted in self-defense. Citing *Brown v. State, 454 So.2d 596 (Fla. 5th DCA), rev. denied, 461 So.2d 116 (Fla. 1984)* and *Pierce v. State, 376 So.2d 417 (Fla. 3d DCA 1979), cert. denied, 386 So.2d 640 (Fla. 1980)*, Hunter argues that the trial court erred in denying his motion for judgment of acquittal, because the state failed to disprove his hypothesis of innocence and failed to prove he acted with a depraved mind regardless of human life. We disagree and affirm.

The state had the burden of proving Hunter's guilt beyond and to the exclusion of every reasonable doubt, including proving that Hunter did not act in self-defense. *Brown at 598.* Before Hunter can avail himself of the defense of self-defense, he must establish that his life was in imminent danger and he could not safely retreat. As we stated in *Brown*:

> The law of justifiable homicide by self-defense has many times been set forth in decisions of this court. There must be reasonable grounds to apprehend a design to commit a felony, or to do some great personal injury, and there shall be imminent danger of such design being accomplished. "Imminent means near at hand, mediate rather than immediate, close rather than touching." The one interposing the defense must not have wrongfully occasioned the necessity; he must not have used all reasonable means in his power, consistent with his own safety, to avoid the danger and to avert the necessity of taking human life; the circumstances must be such as to induce a reasonably cautious and prudent man to believe that the danger was actual the necessity real, in order that the slayer may be justified in acting upon his own belief to that effect.

Id. at 599 (quoting *Linsley v. State, 88 Fla. 135, 101 So. 273 (Fla. 1924)).* To justify homicide in self-defense, one must demonstrate a real necessity for taking a life and a situation causing a reasonably prudent person to believe that danger is imminent. *Reimel v. State, 532 So.2d 16, 18 (Fla. 5th DCA 1988), rev. denied, 542 So.2d 989 (Fla. 1989); citing Pressley v. State, 396 So.2d 1175 (Fla. 3d DCA), rev. denied, 407 So.2d 1105 (Fla. 1981).* "Before taking a life, a combatant must 'retreat to the wall' using all means in his power to avoid that need." *Id.* at 18, citing *Baker v. State, 506 So.2d 1056 (Fla. 2d DCA), rev. denied, 515 So.2d 229 (Fla. 1987); Cannon v. State, 464 So.2d 149 (Fla. 5th DCA), rev. denied, 471 So.2d 44 (Fla. 1985).*

In the instant case, there was evidence from which the jury could have concluded that Hunter did not "retreat to the wall" and that a reasonably cautious and prudent person would not believe there was a necessity for taking a human life. Accepting the state's evidence as true, the jury could have concluded that Hunter and the victim had a verbal altercation during which the victim mentioned killing Hunter. The jury could have concluded that it was at this point that Hunter's duty to retreat arose, but that he instead returned to his parents' home, retrieved his rifle, returned to the scene, and, at a minimum, escalated the situation. Because there was evidence which would support a jury's conclusion that Hunter's acts did not comport with the law regarding self-defense, the court properly denied his motion for judgment of acquittal. See *State v . Tai Van Le, 553 So.2d 258 (Fla. 2d DCA 1989)* (second degree murder conviction upheld where nothing prevented defendant from retreating).

Accordingly we affirm Hunter's conviction for second degree murder. Hunter raises two other points on appeal, which have no merit.

AFFIRM.

DAUKSCH and GRIFFIN, JJ., concur.

REVIEW

1. The state has the burden of proving a defendant _____.
    a. did act in self defense
    b. did not act in self defense
    c. both a and b
    d. neither a nor b

Where a Defendant acts in self-defense against an assailant and in so doing commits battery upon another innocent person, he can still assert he was acting in self-defense. The law allows this defense to be "transferred" and applied even where innocent parties may be injured. In a case like this, the State must still prove the Defendant did not act in self-defense in order to prove its case against the Defendant.

CASE

V.M., a child v. State, 766 So.2d 280 (Fla. 4th DCA 2000).

Delinquency proceedings were brought. The Circuit Court, Palm Beach County, Ronald V. Alvarez, J., entered an order withholding adjudication of delinquency but finding the juvenile guilty of felony battery. Juvenile appealed. The District Court of Appeal, Stevenson, J., held that state's failure to rebut the juvenile's claim of self-defense required reversal.

Reversed.

STEVENSON, Judge.

Appellant V.M. challenges an order withholding adjudication of delinquency but finding him guilty of felony battery pursuant to *section 784.047, Florida Statutes (1999)*, for hitting his teacher during a fight with another student. We reverse because the State failed to introduce any evidence to rebut V.M.'s claim of self-defense.

V.M. and another male student were fighting when their teacher entered the classroom. The teacher testified at trial that she was unable to determine who had initiated the fight, but when she tried to intercede, "I guess [V.M.} went to hit [the other student], who was in front of him, and brought his arm back to get a good swing and then got me in the nose." The teacher suffered a broken nose as a result of the incident. V.M. testified that the boy attacked him because V.M. told him he was not afraid of him. No other witnesses testified at the juvenile proceeding.

[1] [2] V.M. was charged with felony battery under the theory that his intent to commit battery upon the student was transferred to the teacher. *See D.J. v. State*, 651 So.2d 1255, 1256 *(Fla. 1st DCA 1995)* (recognized that the doctrine of transferred intent is a legal fiction which operated to transfer a defendant's intent as to the intended victim tot an unintended victim). Although the State successfully proved the elements to convict V.M. of felony battery on the teacher, the State failed to present any evidence to rebut V.M.'s assertion of self-defense. **[FN1]** Where self-defense is a viable defense to the charge of battery on an intended victim, the defense also operates to excuse the battery on the unintended victim. *See Pinder v. State*, 27 Fla. 370, 8 So. 837 (1891); *Battles v. State*, 498 So.2d 1028, 1030 (Fla. 1st DCA 1986). Because the State failed to rebut V.M.'s claim of self-defense, the trial court erred in denying V.M.'s motion for judgment of acquittal.

Reversed.

FN1. *See Thompson v. State*, 552 So.2d 264, 266 (Fla. 2d DCA 1989) (holding that when a defendant has established a prima facie case of self-defense, the State must prove beyond a reasonable doubt that the defendant did not act in self defense).

REVIEW

1. One may argue self-defense with regard to _____.
    a. an intended victim
    b. an unintended victim
    c. both a and b
    d. neither a nor b

CASTLE DOCTRINE

The Castle Doctrine is an exception to the general duty to retreat. It provides that a person may use deadly force to protect himself or herself in his or her home or "castle." The general rule is that a person attacked is not justified in using deadly force if, without increasing the danger, he or she can avoid the difficulty by retreating.

CASE

Frazier v. State, 681 So.2d 824 (Fla. 2d DCA 1996).

Defendant was convicted in the Circuit Court, Polk County, Robert A. Young, J., on charge of stabbing co-worker with intent to kill. Defendant appealed. The District Court of Appeal, Fulmer, J., addressing issue of first impression in the state, held that castle doctrine, providing that person may use deadly force to protect himself or herself in his or her home or "castle," does not apply at workplace when aggressor is co-worker.

Affirmed.

FULMER, Judge.

The question we address in this appeal is whether the castle doctrine applies at the workplace when the aggressor is a co-worker. We hold that it does not and affirm the trial court's denial of a jury instruction to the contrary.

William Frazier was charged with stabbing a co-worker with the intent to kill that person. At trial, Frazier claimed that he was acting in self-defense and requested a special jury instruction that he was justified in using deadly force to protect himself at his place of work. The trial court denied the requested instruction.

The jury instruction requested by Frazier is a variation of the castle doctrine which provides that a person may use deadly force to protect himself or herself in his or her home or "castle." *Danford v. State, 53 Fla. 4, 13-15, 43 So. 593, 596-598 (1907).* The general rule is that a person attacked is not justified in using deadly force if, without increasing the danger, he can avoid the difficulty by retreating. *Id.* Thus, the castle doctrine is an exception to the general duty to retreat.

In this case, Frazier sought to apply the castle doctrine to the workplace when assaulted by a co-worker. We agree with the prevailing view that the doctrine extends to protect persons in their place of employment while they are lawfully engaged in their occupation. See *Redondo v. State, 380 So.2d 1107 (Fla. 3d DCA 1980); State v. Smith, 376 So.2d 261 (Fla. 3d DCA 1979);* Jeffrey F. Ghent, Annotation, *Homicide: Duty to Retreat as Condition of Self-Defense When One is Attacked at his Office or Place of Business or Employment, 41 A.L.R.3d 584, 587 (1972).* However, the question raised in this appeal is whether the castle doctrine applies at the place of employment when the aggressor is a co-worker. No Florida case has addressed this issue. Out-of-state cases that address this question are fairly evenly divided. *Ghent, supra at 588.*

In *State v. Bobbitt, 415 So.2d 724 (Fla. 1982)*, the supreme court addressed the question of whether the castle doctrine applies where the victim and assailant are occupants of the same home and held that it did not apply. This holding was premised on the fact that "both Bobbitt and her husband had equal rights to be in the 'castle' and neither had the legal right to eject the other." *Id. at 726.* We rely on the same reasoning to hold that the doctrine does not apply in the workplace where the victim and the assailant are co-workers. Because Frazier and the victim were co-workers who both had a lawful right to be at the worksite where the altercation occurred, the castle doctrine does not apply and the trial court properly denied Frazier's requested instruction.

Frazier raised several other issues in this appeal which we do not address other than to say that none of them require reversal.

Affirmed.

THREADGILL, C.J., and BLUE, J., concur.

REVIEW

1. The Castle Doctrine applies in the _____.
     a. home
     b. workplace
     c. both of the above
     d. neither of the above

CASE

Barkley v. State, 750 So.2d 755 (Fla. 2nd DCA 2000).

Defendant was convicted in the Circuit Court, Lee County, William J. nelson, J., of second degree murder, and he appealed. The District Court of Appeal, Blue, J., Held: (1) defendant, who was co-occupant of home, was entitled to jury instruction on the privilege of nonretreat; (2) defendant properly preserved such issue for appellate review; and 93) failure to properly instruct jury was not harmless error.

Reversed and remanded.

BLUE, Judge.

Clint Michael Barkley appeals his conviction fro second degree murder in the death of Edward Collesano. Barkley argues that the trial court erred in refusing to instruct the jury that he had no duty to retreat from the home before using deadly force in self-defense. Based on the recent supreme court decision in ***Weiland v. State***, *732 So.2d 1044 (Fla. 1999)*, we agree and reverse. As to the second issue on appeal, we find no merit and affirm without discussion.

Barkley argues that the trial court erred in denying his requested jury instruction on the privilege of nonretreat based on the evidence that he was a co-occupant of the home. While Florida previously recognized that someone, while I his or her home, had no duty to retreat when attacked by an invitee, *see* ***Hedges v. State***, *172 So.2d 824 (Fla. 1965)*, this privilege did not apply when the attack came from a co-occupant, *see* ***State v. Bobbitt***, *415 So.2d 724 (Fla. 1982)*. In ***Weiland***, the supreme court receded from ***Bobbitt*** and held that a defendant is not required to retreat from his or her own residence before justifiably resorting to deadly force in self-defense against a co-occupant if that force is necessary to prevent death or great bodily harm. *See 732 So.2d at 1049-50.* We note that the trial court did not have the benefit of ***Weiland*** at the time of trial. This decision, however, is applicable to all cases pending on direct review or not yet final. *See 732 So.2d at 1058.*

The State argues that Barkley failed to preserve this issue for review because he did not make a request for the specific instruction approved in ***Weiland***. Barkley did request an instruction to explain that he had no duty to retreat from his new residence in the face of an attack by a co-occupant. He renewed his objection to this omission after the trial court instructed the jury. Therefore, we conclude that the issue was properly preserved. The State further argues that any error was harmless. In closing argument, the prosecutor emphasized Barkley's duty to retreat. Thus, we cannot say the error was harmless. Accordingly, we reverse.

Reverse and remanded for a new trial.

THREADGILL, A.C.J., AND STRINGER, J., Concur.

REVIEW

1. The Castle Doctrine applies _____.
    a. in the home
    b. to co-occupants of the home
    c. both of the above
    d. neither of the above

ALIBI

In cases where there is an issue concerning whether or not the defendant was present at the scene of the crime the defendant may have an alibi defense. The State must prove beyond a reasonable doubt that the defendant was in fact present in order to obtain a conviction. When claiming the defense of alibi, the defendant is claiming he or she was at a different place from the crime scene and therefore could not have committed the crime.

RESISTING AN UNLAWFUL ARREST

Force may be used in certain circumstances to resist an **un**lawful arrest. An individual may defend himself or herself against unlawful or excessive force. Thus, if there is no valid basis for arrest, a defendant may actually be entitled to run away or otherwise resist without using force.

CASE

C.K. v. State, 487 So.2d 93 (Fla. 3d DCA 1986).

Juvenile was adjudicated delinquent in the Circuit Court, Dade County, Ralph B. Ferguson, J., for obstructing police officer in lawful execution of legal duty and he appealed. The District Court of Appeal held that when juvenile fled after being ordered to stay, police officer had no reasonable suspicion that laws were being violated and thus no lawful duty was being carried out by police officers which juvenile could have obstructed.

Reversed.

PER CURIAM.

A police officer, acting on a "suspicious persons" report, responded to a wooded area where four school-aged males, including appellant, were crouched, distributing what the officer believed to be coins. The officer ordered them to "stay where you are." They all fled. Appellant, discovered hiding under a trailer home not far away, was placed under arrest. He was adjudicated delinquent for obstructing a police officer in the lawful execution of a legal duty. Arguing the correctness of the adjudication, the State contends that the legal duty which the officer was executing was the detention and/or arrest for the crimes of loitering and prowling, theft, and/or unlawfully damaging a vending machine with intent to commit theft.

No evidence was presented by the State in support of any offense. Neither at the time when appellant was ordered to remain where he was nor when he was arrested was there an articulable suspicion that he had committed, was committing, or was about to commit a felony or misdemeanor.

R.L.L. v. State, 466 So.2d 1230 (Fla. 2d DCA 1985), relied upon by the State, is, as appellant argues, clearly distinguishable. In that case the juvenile was in a vehicle with a person who was in apparent violation of a municipal ordinance and drug statutes. [FN1] It was held there that "[a]lthough [appellant's] presence in itself might not have been probable cause sufficient to justify an arrest, the circumstances were such that the officers were entitled to briefly detain appellant while they pursued their investigation." *Id. at 1231.* In this case there was no justification for a detention or arrest because of the absence of a reasonable suspicion that laws were being violated. See *Lee v. State,* 368 So.2d 395 (Fla. 3d DCA) (Schwartz, J., specially concurring) (one can resist unlawful arrest without violence), *cert. denied*, *378 So.2d 349 (Fla. 1979)*; ***Lowery v. State***, *356 So.2d 1325 (Fla. 4ᵗʰ DCA 1978)* (same); ***Marshall v. State***, *354 So.2d 107 (Fla. 2d DCA)* (same), *cert. denied*, *436 U.S. 920, 98 S.Ct. 2270, 56 L.Ed.2d 762 (1978)*. There was, therefore, no lawful duty being carried out by police officers which appellant could have obstructed.

Reversed.

> FN1. In ***R.L.L.***, appellant and a woman were seated in a parked car. When police officers on patrol approached the vehicle, the woman attempted to hide an object which the officers could see was an open can of beer. Having the open beer can in the car was a violation of a municipal ordinance. When the woman was asked for identification she opened and searched her purse, revealing what one of the officers recognized as a marijuana bag. The officers asked both people to step out of the car and began to read them their ***Miranda*** rights. Appellant ran away shortly after the rights were read.

REVIEW

   1. One may resist _____.
      a. a lawful arrest
      b. an unlawful arrest
      c. neither a and b
      d. neither a nor b

CASE

Jay v. State, 731 So.2d 774 (Fla. 4ᵗʰ DCA 1999).

Defendant pleaded nolo contendere in the Circuit Court, Broward County, William P. Dimitrouleas, J., to resisting an officer without violence and possession of a weapon by a convicted felon. Defendant appealed. The District Court of Appeal, Gunther, J., held that: (1) police officer's "sting operation" was not the execution of a legal duty, and (2) evidence of knife was discovered during unjustified pursuit following an attempted illegal arrest.

Reversed and remanded.

GUNTHER, Judge.

Tyrone Jay appeals his convictions for resisting an officer without violence and possession of a weapon by a convicted felon. We reverse.

The arresting officer testified that while on a "sting operation" he was attempting to solicit two females, one known to him as a prostitute, when Jay told the females "don't get in the car, he's a cop." The two females walked away and were never arrested. The officer, having perceived Jay's comment as obstructing him in the execution of his legal duty, told Jay he was under arrest but Jay immediately fled. When the officer caught Jay, the officer discovered a knife in Jay's possession. Jay was subsequently arrested and charged with resisting an officer without violence and possession of a weapon by a convicted felon. The resisting charge was based upon Jay's flight from the officer's attempted arrest for the uncharged offense of obstruction. Following the denial of Jay's motion to suppress, Jay pled nolo contendere, was adjudicated guilty, declared a habitual offender, and sentenced to nineteen months in prison.

Jay asserts his comment did not obstruct the officer in executing his legal duty so the attempted arrest for obstruction was unlawful, and therefore, he was free to resist the arrest without violence. Moreover, he maintains the resulting weapon charge cannot stand because the arrest for resistance without violence was illegal. We agree.

An essential element of resisting an officer without violence is that the arrest is lawful. See *In re T.M.M., 560 So.2d 805, 807 (Fla. 4th DCA 1990)*(citing *Johnson v. State, 395 So.2d 594 (Fla. 2d DCA 1981)*). "If an arrest is not lawful, then a defendant cannot be guilty of resisting it." *In re T.M.M., 560 So.2d at 807 (Fla. 4th DCA 1990)*(citing *Dean v. State, 466 So.2d 1216, 1217 (Fla. 4th DCA 1985)*). "[T]he common law rule still remains that a person may lawfully resist an illegal arrest without using any force or violence." *K.Y.E. v. State, 557 So.2d 956, 957 (Fla. 1st DCA 1990)*(citing *Smith v. State, 399 So.2d 70 (Fla. 5th DCA 1981)*); see also *Lowery v. State, 356 So.2d 1325, 1325-26 (Fla. 4th DCA 1978)*.

Although Jay was not charged with obstructing the officer, the state maintains that the attempted arrest for obstructing created the basis for the resisting arrest charge. [FN1] The attempted arrest of Jay was based upon Florida Statutes section 843.02, resisting an officer without violence, which provides, "[w]hoever shall resist, obstruct, or oppose an officer ... in the lawful execution of a legal duty." § 843.02, Fla. Stat. (1997)(emphasis added). Because the law permits a person to resist an illegal arrest without violence, Jay committed the crime of resisting an officer without violence only if the underlying attempted arrest for obstruction was lawful.

"To support a conviction under section 843.02, the state must show: (1) the officer was engaged in the lawful execution of a legal duty; and (2) the action by the defendant constituted obstruction or resistance of that lawful duty." *S.G.K. v. State, 657 So.2d 1246, 1247 (Fla. 1st DCA 1995)*. Thus, for the initial arrest to be legal: (1) the officer's involvement in the "sting operation" must have been the performance of a legal duty; and (2) Jay's words, "don't get into the car, he's a cop," must have obstructed the officer in executing his legal duty.

On the question of whether the officer was performing a legal duty, "[i]t is important to distinguish between a police officer 'in the lawful execution of any legal duty' and a police officer who is merely on the job." *D.G. v. State, 661 So.2d 75, 76 (Fla. 2d DCA 1995)*(defendant's verbal protests and refusal to answer police questions during a search for robbery suspect held not an obstruction of justice). Further, the court provides three legal duties, when coupled with words alone, which will result in obstruction of justice, (1) serving process; (2) legally detaining a person; or (3) asking for assistance. See *id*. The facts of the present case, however, do not fall within any of these three categories, and as such, we must decide if the officer's "sting operation" was the execution of a legal duty or if he was merely on the job.

In **Porter v. State**, officers, while on surveillance, observed drug deals taking place, and began to approach the scene to take the dealers by surprise and arrest them. See **Porter v. State,** *582 So.2d 41 (Fla. 4th DCA 1991).* As the officers approached, Porter, the lookout, yelled "28 plain clothes," to alert the suspected drug dealers of the officers' presence, thereby allowing the dealers to escape apprehension. See **Porter,** *582 So.2d at 42.* We upheld the conviction of Porter for obstructing and interfering because we concluded his words interfered with the police in the execution of their legal duty of arresting suspects by preventing their apprehension. See *id. at 43.*

However, the present case is clearly distinguishable. In **Porter**, the police officers had observed drug dealings taking place and were preparing to arrest the suspected dealers. See **Porter,** *582 So.2d at 42.* As such, this court concluded that Porter's words were "intended to impede the officers in the execution of their duties," i.e., Porter's words warned the suspects, allowing them to escape apprehension. See *id. at 43.* Furthermore, the duty in **Porter**, attempting to legally detain the suspects, is a duty which falls within one of the three categories of **D.G. v. State**. See **D.G. v. State,** *661 So.2d at 76.* Whereas, here, there is no evidence that the two targeted women had committed any crime from which they escaped apprehension. The two women simply walked away and were never arrested.

In **State v. Dennis,** during a drug sale, two officers waited out of sight for the undercover officer's cue to move in and arrest the dealers. See **Dennis,** *684 So.2d 848, 849 (Fla. 3d DCA 1996).* The defendant saw the two officers waiting in an unmarked car and yelled "ninety nine," a street term meaning police were in the area. See **Dennis,** *684 So.2d at 849.* The court concluded that Dennis' words did not obstruct justice because he was not involved nor did he have any knowledge of the criminal activity, unlike Porter. *Id.* However, it can be inferred from **Dennis** that the court reached the preliminary conclusion that the officers were engaged in the execution of a legal duty because absent the execution of a legal duty by the officer, the court's discussion of the effect of Dennis' conduct and the conclusion that his words did not constitute obstruction was unnecessary. Although in **Dennis** the officers were not yet moving in to make an arrest, the cases are similar in that criminal activity was actually taking place, i.e., a drug sale was occurring. See **Dennis,** *684 So.2d at 849.*

In the present case, while the officer was attempting to solicit from the two females, there is no evidence that the two women agreed to anything illegal before walking away. Thus, unlike the situations in **Porter** and **Dennis**, there was no criminal activity occurring at the time Jay told the women, "don't get in the car, he's a cop." Further, there is no evidence that the officer was detaining the two women or even attempting to detain them for a crime they had committed as was the case in **Porter**. See also **D.G. v. State,** *661 So.2d at 76.*

As such, we conclude that the officer in this case was merely on the job and not engaged in the lawful execution of any legal duty. See **D.G. v. State,** *661 So.2d at 76.* Because we conclude the officer was not engaged in the lawful execution of a legal duty, we need not address the second element, whether Jay's conduct constituted obstruction of a lawful duty. See **S.G.K. v. State**, *657 So.2d at 1247*. Accordingly, the attempted arrest for obstruction was illegal and Jay was free to resist such an arrest without violence. See **K.Y.E. v. State**, *557 So.2d at 957*.

The remaining charge, possession of a weapon by a convicted felon was based upon the officer's discovery of a knife during the unjustified pursuit following the attempted illegal arrest of Jay. Because the arrest for resisting was illegal, the evidence of the knife, discovered during the attempted illegal arrest, should be suppressed under the "fruit of the poisonous tree doctrine." See **Wong Sun v. United States**, *371 U.S. 471, 487-488, 83 S.Ct. 407, 9 L.Ed.2d 441 (1963)*; **D'Agostino v. State**, *310 So.2d 12 (Fla. 1975)*.

In sum, we conclude Jay's words did not obstruct the officer while he was executing his legal duty, and thus, the officer's attempted arrest for obstruction was unlawful. Absent a lawful arrest for obstruction, Jay was free to resist such an arrest without violence. Moreover, the knife found as a result of the illegal arrest for resisting should have been excluded. Accordingly, we reverse Jay's convictions and remand to the trial court.

REVERSED AND REMANDED.

STEVENSON, J., and BAKER, MOSES, JR., Associate Judge, concurs.

FN1. It is not necessary that the underlying criminal activity providing the basis for the arrest result in a charge and conviction. It is only necessary that the officer has a founded suspicion of criminal activity to make the detention. See **State v. Dwyer**, *317 So.2d 149, 150 (Fla. 2d DCA 1975)*; **Smith v. State**, *292 So.2d 69, 70 (Fla. 3d DCA 1974)*.

REVIEW

1. To resist an officer without violence, it is necessary that there be _____.
    a. a lawful arrest
    b. an execution of a lawful duty
    c. either a or b
    d. neither a nor b

THINKING CRITICALLY

1. Do you agree with the holding in *Frazier*? Would the result be different if the victim were the owner of the business? Should it be?

2. What if an attack occurs in the home by a houseguest? Is there a duty to retreat?

3. Do you agree with the holding in *Hunter*? Why or why not? Should one be able to argue self-defense after leaving an altercation and returning to it? Should it matter how much time elapses? What if someone leaves and then returns with a weapon?

4. A crime is committed on the first floor of a three story home in the kitchen. The defendant claims to have been in his third floor bedroom. Has he asserted an alibi defense? Is it enough to merely be in a different room in the house? Should it be?

5.   Ralph is charged with stealing Jill's purse from her outside a video store. Ralph produces records showing he was at work that day at an address more than 30 minutes away. Has an alibi defense been presented? Should Ralph be required to produce a witness who saw him at work?

6.   A police officer is trying to investigate a fight between two suspects. A third individual, Jerry, interrupts the officer. Jerry is yelling obscenities and making demands of the officer. The officer attempts to calm Jerry down with no success. The officer then places Jerry under arrest with no probable cause. Can Jerry resist being arrested? What amount of force will Jerry be justified in using?

7.   What if Jerry gets into a physical altercation with the officer? Assume the officer places Jerry under arrest for battery on a law enforcement officer. Can Jerry resist? To what extent? Do you need to know what amount of force the officer used in making the arrest? Why or why not?

8.   Jerry and the police officer get in a scuffle. The officer attempts to arrest Jerry. Jerry resists. What should the result be if the officer was the initial aggressor? What if it's Jerry?

9.	Do you agree with the court's holding in *C.K.*? What would have happened if the State presented evidence of an offense about to be committed? Would it still have been permissible under the law for the juvenile to flee?

10.	Would the result in *Jay* have been different if the two females were arrested? Should it be? Did Jay's words stop the officer from making the arrest? What if Jay resisted with violence? How would that change the result?

11.	Brad is standing in a group of people when a police car drives up. He puts his hands in his pockets and starts to walk quickly away. The police yell for him to stop. Brad starts running. As he pulls his hands from his pockets something falls to the ground. One officer picks up the item, which was a crack pipe. The other officer detains and arrests Brad. Is Brad guilty of resisting an officer without violence? What if no crack pipe had been dropped? Would the result be different?

CHAPTER 7 ANSWER KEY

REVIEW QUESTIONS

Hunter v. State
1. b

V.M., a child v. State
1. c

Frazier v. State
1. a

Barkley v. State
1. c

C.K. v. State
1. b

Jay v. State
1. c

CHAPTER 8

DEFENSES TO CRIMINAL
LIABILITY: EXCUSES

INSANITY

Insanity is a defense to a crime. In Florida the *McNaughton* rule is applied to insanity cases. The issues to be determined are (1) whether a person knows right from wrong and (2) understands the wrongfulness of his or her acts. All persons are presumed to be sane. The burden is on the defense to prove an individual was insane. The defendant has to meet this burden by clear and convincing evidence.

Unlike other defenses, a successful sanity defense does not always result in a defendant's release. In insanity cases, further proceedings are held to determine whether a defendant should be committed to a mental hospital or perhaps be given out-patient treatment. Like entrapment, to plead insanity one must first admit to having committed the crime.

To be insane a person must have had a mental infirmity, disease or defect. As a result of this condition, one of three things must have occurred. The first possibility is that the person either must not have known what he or she was doing or its consequences. The second is that although he or she knew what they were doing and its consequences, he or she did not know the action was wrong. The third situation is where because of the condition the person had hallucinations or delusions. The hallucinations or delusions cause the individuals to honestly believe to be facts things which are not true or not real. As a result of these beliefs, the person then acts. The jury may consider testimony of experts as well as lay witnesses. The question to be answered is whether the defendant was insane at the time of the offense. Unrestrained passion or ungovernable temper is not insanity.

Irresistible impulse is not recognized in Florida. Loss of control due to emotional impulse or explosion is not a recognized defense. Diminished capacity is also not a defense in Florida. An abnormal mental condition that does not rise to the level of an insanity defense is not even admissible to negate intent.

CASE

Viovenel v. State, 581 So.2d 930 (Fla. 3d DCA 1991).

Following nonjury trial before the Circuit Court, Dade County, Arthur L. Rothenberg, J., defendant was convicted of three counts of attempted first-degree murder, and one count each of trespass in a structure and criminal mischief. Defendant appealed. The District Court of Appeal held that State introduced sufficient evidence to satisfy its burden of proving defendant's sanity beyond a reasonable doubt.

Affirmed.

PER CURIAM.

Pierre Viovenel appeals his convictions and sentences imposed after the trial court found him guilty of three counts of attempted first degree murder, and one count each of trespass in a structure and criminal mischief, following a nonjury trial. We affirm.

In November, 1987, Frans Boivier was about to exit his home when his roommate, Viovenel, came at Boivier swinging a pair of scissors and yelling "I'm going to damn kill you." Viovenel stabbed Boivier in the stomach, head and leg. Viovenel then ran out of the house where he encountered Boivier's aunt and stabbed her also. Viovenel then ran into a neighbor's yard and chased a young boy into the neighbor's house. Viovenel cut open a screen door, ran into the house, stabbed a young girl sitting on the floor and attempted to stab the girl's mother. However, the mother was able to fend off his attack with her walker, causing Viovenel to drop the scissors. Viovenel then ran out of the house, continued down the street and climbed over a fence in another neighbor's yard. He tried to get in the house by pulling on a door but was unable to open it. He eventually entered another home where he was arrested by police.

Viovenel filed a notice of intent to rely on an insanity defense. At trial, the state offered lay witness testimony to establish the elements of the crimes and to testify as to Viovenel's sanity. Viovenel called three psychologists who were qualified as experts. One doctor testified that he did not have enough information to come to a conclusion as to Viovenel's sanity at the time of the crimes. The other two doctors testified that, under Florida law, Viovenel was insane at the time of the crimes in that he did not know right from wrong. [FN] The state vigorously cross-examined the doctors. The trial court found Viovenel guilty on all counts. Viovenel argues that the state failed to meet its burden of proving beyond a reasonable doubt that he was sane at the time of the crime.

In Florida, a person is presumed sane. *See **Yohn v. State**, 476 So.2d 123, 126 (Fla. 1985)* (citations omitted). Where the defendant introduces evidence sufficient to present a reasonable doubt of sanity, the presumption of sanity vanishes and the burden then shifts to the state to prove the defendant's sanity beyond a reasonable doubt. *Id.*

In this case Viovenel raised a reasonable doubt as to his sanity. The state offered evidence in the form of lay testimony to prove Viovenel was sane and the state effectively impeached the testimony of Viovenel's experts. The trial judge, sitting as the trier of fact, resolved the conflict in the evidence in favor of Viovenel's sanity. The trial judge was permitted to reject the expert testimony and to give more weight to the lay testimony. *See **Byrd v. State**, 297 So.2d 22, 24 (Fla. 1974); **Davis v. State**, 319 So.2d 611, 612 (Fla. 3d DCA 1975), cert. denied, 334 So.2d 604 (Fla. 1976); **Williams v. State**,*

275 So.2d 284, 285 (Fla. 3d DCA 1973). We may not invade the province of the trier of fact and reweigh the evidence. **Byrd**, *297 So.2d at 25.* We affirm.

> FN. Florida adheres to a modified M'Naughten Rule. *See **Wheeler v. State,** 344 So.2d 244 (Fla. 1977).*

REVIEW

1. To negate the defense of insanity, the state _____.
   - a. must call expert witnesses
   - b. may only call lay witnesses
   - c. must call both experts and lay witnesses
   - d. none of the above

AGE

In many cases, ignorance of the victim's age is not a defense. Thus, if a Defendant commits a crime against a person under the age of 18, he usually cannot assert as a defense that he did not know the victim's age.

CASE

Grady v. State, *701 So.2d 1181 (Fla. 5ᵗʰ DCA 1997).*

Defendant was convicted by the Circuit Court for Orange County, Cynthia Z. MacKinnon, J., of procuring for prostitution a person under the age of 18, and he appealed on the grounds that he was unaware of the person's underage status. The District Court of Appeal, Peterson, J., held that ignorance of age of victim is not a defense.

Affirmed.

PETERSON, Judge.

Section 796.03, Florida Statutes (1995) classifies the procurement for prostitution of a person under the age of 18 years as a second degree felony. Appellant asserts that an essential element of the crime is that a defendant must know that the person he or she procures for prostitution is under 18, but the statute is silent as to this requirement. We affirm.

While the general rule is that every crime must include a specific intent, or a mens rea, our legislature and courts recognize an exception to the specific intent requirement where the state has a compelling interest in protecting underage persons from being sexually abused or exploited. Stated differently, crimes against children fall "within the category of crimes in which, on grounds of public policy, certain acts are made punishable without proof that the defendant understands the facts that give character to his act ... and proof of an intent is not indispensable to conviction." *See State v. Sorakrai, 543 So.2d 294, 295 (Fla. 2d DCA 1989)* (quoting *Simmons v. State, 151 Fla. 778, 10 So.2d 436, 438 (1942)*). Thus, ignorance of the age of the victim is not a defense nor either is misrepresentation of age, or a defendant's bona fide belief that such victim is over the specified ages. *Sorakrai* (neither ignorance, misrepresentation, nor belief that victim was 16 years or older is available as a defense to defendant charged with committing a lewd and lascivious act upon child under age of 16 years in violation of § 800.04, Fla. Stat.); *Green v. State, 580 So.2d 321 (Fla. 1ˢᵗ DCA 1991)* (same); *Hicks v. State, 561 So.2d 1284 (Fla. 2d DCA 1990)* (defendant's ignorance of the victim's age was not a viable defense to defendant charged with use of a child in a sexual performance in violation of § 827.071(2), Fla. Stat*.), rev. denied, 574 So.2d 141 (Fla. 1990); State v. Robinette, 651 So.2d 926 (Fla. 1ˢᵗ DCA 1995)* (violation of § 827.071 (2) falls within the category of crimes which furthers the state's compelling interest to protect persons under the age of 18 from being sexually exploited, and on grounds of public policy, certain acts are made punishable without proof that the defendant understands the facts that give character to his act). *See also, Hendricks v. State, 360 So.2d 1119 (Fla. 3d DCA 1978)* (where the act involves the sexual organ of the actor there can be no question that the act itself infers a criminal intent requiring no specific intent, of sexual gratification or otherwise, than that evidenced by the doing of the acts constituting the offense), *cert. denied, 441 U.S. 964, 99 S.Ct. 2411, 60 L.Ed.2d 1069 (1979)*.

We find the charged offense in the instant case, procuring a person under the age of 18 for prostitution in violation of section 796.03, Florida Statutes (1995), falls within this category of crimes where the state has a compelling interest in protecting underage persons from being sexually abused or exploited. Accordingly, appellant's ignorance of the age of the victim is not a defense.

AFFIRMED.

GRIFFIN, C.J., and THOMPSON, J., concur.

REVIEW

1. Ignorance of age where the statute is silent as to the requirement of knowledge
_____.

     a. is not a defense
     b. is a defense
     c. both a and b
     d. neither a nor b

DURESS OR NECESSITY

Duress or necessity is a defense in Florida. The defendant must reasonably believe a danger or emergency existed not caused by himself or herself. The danger or emergency must threaten significant harm to the defendant or a third person. If the charge is escape, the danger or emergency must threaten death or serious bodily harm. The threat must be real, imminent, and impending. If not an escape, the defendant must have no reasonable means to avoid the danger or emergency except by committing the crime. A threat of future harm will not qualify. Neither will it be a defense if the danger had passed. The danger need not be actual, but it must be perceived as real by the Defendant. Duress is not a defense to an intentional homicide.

CASE

Aljak v. State, 681 So.2d 896 (Fla. 4th DCA 1996).

Defendant was convicted in the Circuit Court for the Seventeenth Judicial Circuit, Broward County, M. Daniel Futch, Jr., J., of being an accessory after the fact to armed robbery. Appeal was taken. The District Court of Appeal, Klein, J., held that: (1) defendant's testimony supported requested instruction on defense of duress; (2) testimony of participant in robbery, as to what another participant told him, was inadmissible hearsay; and (3) parties were entitled to opportunity to participate in discussion of action to be taken after jury posed question during deliberations.

Reversed and remanded for new trial.

KLEIN, Judge.

Appellant was convicted of being an accessory after the fact to armed robbery. We reverse and remand for a new trial because the court erred in refusing to instruct the jury on duress.

Shortly after a robbery, appellant and his three passengers were stopped by the police, and the robbery victim, who was brought to the scene, identified the passengers as having committed the robbery. Appellant, who was at the wheel, was not identified as having participated in the robbery, and told one of the police officers at the scene that he had not been aware that a robbery had taken place.

Appellant's testimony at trial, which conflicted with that of the state's witnesses, was that appellant was giving one of his employees and two of his employee's friends a ride, when they asked appellant to stop so that they could go into a store. According to appellant, when his employee and the two others returned to the car, they ordered him at gunpoint to drive away in a hurry. The jury acquitted him of robbery, but found him guilty of being an accessory after the fact.

Defendant requested the following jury instruction regarding his defense which was denied:

> If you, the jury, find or have reasonable doubt, that under all of the circumstances shown in the evidence presented by both the Defendant and the State that the Defendant had reasonable grounds to believe that there was real, imminent, and impending danger to him of death or serious bodily harm if he did not leave the place from which he was located and that he left because of such danger, rather than with the intent to commit a crime, you should find him not guilty of the crime of armed robbery or accessory after the fact.

In *Corujo v. State, 424 So.2d 43, 44 (Fla. 2d DCA 1982), rev. denied, 434 So.2d 886 (Fla. 1983),* the court explained when this type of defense is applicable:

> Coercion is a recognized defense to a criminal charge except where an innocent life is taken. *21 Am.Jur.2d Criminal Law § 148 (1981).* In *Hall v. State, 136 Fla. 644, 187 So. 392 (1939),* our supreme court held that one may be excused from the commission of a crime if his acts were done under the compulsion or coercion of a real, imminent and impending danger or of what he had reasonable grounds to believe was a real, imminent and impending danger. If there is evidence to support a theory of coercion, the jury must be properly instructed on the defense. *Koontz. v. State, 204 So.2d 224 (Fla. 2d DCA 1967).*

* * *

One of the requirements of the defense is that the coercion must be continuous and that the defendant must have no reasonable opportunity to escape the compulsion without committing the crime. *Koontz v. State.* The threat of future harm does not suffice. *Cawthon v. State, 382 So.2d 796 (Fla. 1st DCA 1980).*

The state argues that the jury instruction submitted by appellant was incorrect because it did not contain the above quoted statement that the coercion or duress must have been continuous, with no opportunity for defendant to avoid the compulsion. Although we agree that a complete instruction should probably have included the language emphasized by the state, it was unnecessary here. According to the appellant's testimony which provided the basis for the requested instruction, the passengers returned to his car and pointed a gun at him. The passengers never left the vehicle until the car was stopped by police a short time later while fleeing north on I-95. As such, there was no evidence in the record upon which the jury, if it believed the appellant's testimony that the passengers threatened his life, could have found the threat to be anything but continuous with no opportunity for escape.

On retrial the testimony of Davis, a participant in the robbery, as to what another participant told him, should not be allowed because it is hearsay. In addition, although the chances are that it will not recur, the court erred in not giving the parties an opportunity to participate in discussing the action to be taken after the jury posed a question during deliberations. *Mills v. State, 620 So.2d 1006 (Fla. 1993).*

Reversed and remanded for a new trial.

STEVENSON and SHAHOOD, JJ., concur.

REVIEW

1. Duress is a defense where _____.
    a. acts are done under compulsion
    b. acts are done under coercion
    c. there is no opportunity to escape the compulsion without committing the crime
    d. all of the above

NECESSITY

Necessity is a defense in certain circumstances. The essential elements of the defense of necessity are (1) that the defendant reasonably believed that his action was necessary to avoid an imminent threat of death or serious bodily injury to himself or others, (2) that the defendant did not intentionally or recklessly place himself in a situation in which it would be probable that he would be forced to choose the criminal conduct, (3) that there existed no other adequate means to avoid the threatened harm except the criminal conduct, (4) that the harm sought to be avoided was more egregious than the criminal conduct perpetrated to avoid it, and (5) that the defendant ceased the criminal conduct as soon as the necessary or apparent necessity for it ended.

CASE

Bozeman v. State, 714 So.2d 570 (Fla. 1st DCA 1998).

Defendant was convicted in the Circuit Court, Bay County, Clinton Foster, J., of felony driving while license suspended, revoked, or cancelled. He appealed. The District Court of Appeals, Wolf, J., held that defendant was entitled to necessity defense.

Reverse and remanded.

Miner, J., specially concurred in separate opinion.

WOLF, Judge.

Apellant raises a number of issues in this appeal from his conviction and sentence for the offense of felony driving while license suspended, revoked, or cancelled in violation of section 322.34, Florida Statutes (DWLS). We find that we need only address appellant's contention that the trial court abused its discretion in declining to give a requested instruction on the defense necessity. As to that issue, we reverse and remand for a new trial.

Shortly after midnight on October 26, 1996, police officers initiated a routine traffic stop of a vehicle driven by appellant. After appellant identified himself, it was determined that his driver's license was at that time suspended and he was placed under arrest for DWLS. The vehicle's female passenger appeared intoxicated and several open containers of beer were visible in the interior of the car. The female passenger in the vehicle was appellant's ex-wife, Teresa Haskins. Appellant and Haskins are the parents of a teenage daughter who resides with Haskins. According to appellant, his ex-wife, on the afternoon before the arrest, came to his residence in her vehicle to obtain his assistance in locating their daughter who had apparently left home following a fight with Haskins. Appellant got in the passenger seat of Haskins' car and drove off with her. Although appellant concluded that Haskins had "been drinking a little bit," he did not believe when he got in Haskins' car that she was at that point intoxicated. Appellant decided, however, after the two stopped at a store and Haskins bought more beer, that he had to drive because Haskins had been driving unsafely (i.e. "running through stop signs, stuff like this") and was a danger to others on the road. Appellant explained that he felt he could not have simply taken Haskins' keys because he feared he might get in trouble for having done so. He also explained that he had been very worried about his daughter's welfare at the time. Appellant further testified that it had been his *572 intention at the time he assumed the wheel of Haskins' car to drive her home and then resume his search for his daughter. He did not specify in his testimony whether or not he would have resumed his search for his daughter using Haskins' vehicle. In response to cross-examination regarding possible alternative measures to having placed himself behind the wheel, appellant responded: "I don't know, you know. When you're trying to control somebody that's drunk you don't always get to think like you want to." Appellant also testified on cross-examination that he could not have gotten a taxicab that night because he had not had any money. Appellant conceded on cross-examination, however, that he could have called "somebody" to come get him rather that driving Haskins' vehicle and the he could also have taken Haskins' keys from her.

Based upon this evidence, the defense requested an instruction on the defense of necessity which was denied by the trial court. The jury found appellant guilty as charged.

A trial court's decision on the giving or withholding of a proposed jury instruction is reviewed under the abuse of discretion standard of review. *See Pozo v. State*, 682 So.2d 1124, 1126 (Fla. 1st DCA 1996), rev. denied, 691 So.2d 1081 (Fla. 1997); see also *Lewis v. State*, 693 So.2d 1055, 1058 (Fla. 4th DCA), rev. denied, 700 So.2d 686 (Fla. 1997). Yet, as both parties have pointed out in their briefs, a defendant is entitled to have his jury instructed on the law applicable to his theory of defense if there is any evidence presented supporting such a theory, even if the only evidence supporting the defense theory comes from the defendant's testimony. *See, e.g., Hooper v. State*, 476 So.2d 1253, 1256 (Fla. 1985), cert. denied, 475 U.S. 1098, S.Ct. 1501, 89 L.Ed.2d 901 (1986); *Carruthers v. State*, 636 So.2d 853, 856 (Fla. 1st DCA), rev. dismissed, 639 So.2d 981 (Fla. 1994); *Williams v. State*, 588 So.2d 44, 45 (Fla. 1st DCA 1991).

The essential elements of the defense of necessity are (1) that the defendant reasonably believed that his action was necessary to avoid an imminent threat of death or serious bodily injury to himself or others, (2) that the defendant did not intentionally or recklessly place himself in a situation in which it would be probable that he would be forced to choose the criminal conduct, (3) that there existed no other adequate means to avoid the threatened harm except the criminal conduct, (4) that the harm sought to be avoided was more egregious that the criminal conduct perpetrated to avoid it and (5) that the defendant ceased the criminal conduct as soon as the necessary or apparent necessity for it ended. *See Hill v. State*, 688 So.2d 901, 905 n. 4 (Fla. 1996), cert. denied, 522 U.S. 907, 118 S.Ct. 265, 139 L.Ed.2d 191 (1997); *Jenks v. State*, 582 So.2d 676, 679 (Fla. 1st DCA), rev. denied, 589 So.2d 292 (Fla. 1991); *Marrero v. State*, 516 So.2d 1052, 1054-55 (Fla. 3d DCA 1987). The state contends in its brief that appellant failed to establish the second and third elements of the necessity defense as set forth above. Appellant's trial testimony appears, however, to include evidence supporting both elements. First, although appellant explained that he knew Haskins had "been drinking a little bit" before she arrived at his residence, he also explained that at the time he got in her vehicle he did not believe she was intoxicated. This testimony appears to have been sufficient, given the facts of this case, to show that appellant did not intentionally or recklessly place himself in the position of having to later choose to drive when he agreed to go with Haskins in search of their daughter. Second, he could get in trouble if he took Haskins' keys away and since he had no money for a taxicab that night. While appellant conceded at one point during his cross-examination that he could have called "somebody" to come get him rather than drive Haskins' vehicle and that he could have taken Haskins' keys form her, this testimony merely created an evidentiary dispute on the question of viable alternative measures which should have been resolved by the jury rather than the trial court. Thus, it appears that on the facts as presented at trial in this case, the trial court committed reversible error by not giving appellant's proposed instruction on the defense necessity.

DAVIS, J., concurs.

MINER, J., specially concurs with written opinion.

MINER, Judge, concurring specially.

Only because of the particular facts contained in the record at bar, I concur in the result reached by my esteemed colleagues.

REVIEW

1. Necessity _____.
   a. is a defense in Florida
   b. is a defense which entitles the defendant to a a special jury instruction
   c. both of the above
   d. neither of the above

ENTRAPMENT

Entrapment is a defense. In order to argue entrapment as a defense, an individual must admit he or she did in fact commit the crime. In order to be entrapped, a defendant must have committed the crime as a result of being induced or encouraged to by a law enforcement officer or an agent of a law enforcement officer. The methods of persuasion or inducement employed need to have created a substantial risk the crime would be committed by someone not otherwise ready to commit the crime. The defendant must not be a person ready to commit the crime. A judge can find entrapment as a matter of law or the jury may find a defendant was entrapped.

It is not entrapment if a defendant was predisposed to commit the crime. Predisposition is a readiness or willingness if an opportunity presents itself. Predisposition focuses on the defendant; inducement focuses on the officer. When an officer makes a good faith attempt to detect crime and provides a defendant who already intended to commit a crime, the opportunity, means, and facilities to commit the offense, it is not entrapment. Officers can use tricks, decoys and subterfuge to expose a defendant's criminal acts. This is not entrapment. Neither is it entrapment when an officer is present and pretends to aid or assist in the commission of a crime. Entrapment need only be proven by a preponderance of the evidence.

Three questions must be answered in entrapment cases. The first question is whether the government induced the accused, the second is whether the defendant was predisposed to commit the offense, and third is whether the question of entrapment should be decided by the judge or submitted to the jury.

CASE

Robichaud v. State, *658 So.2d 166 (Fla. 2d DCA 1995).*

Defendant was convicted in the Circuit Court, Hillsborough County, Bob Anderson Mitcham, J., of possession of cocaine, and conspiracy to traffic in cocaine. Defendant appealed. The District Court of Appeal, Campbell, J., held that: (1) defendant was entrapped as matter of law into committing offenses, and (2) trial court erred in submitting issue of entrapment to jury.

Reversed and convictions vacated.

CAMPBELL, Judge.

Appellant, convicted of possession of cocaine, delivery of cocaine, trafficking in cocaine and conspiracy to traffic in cocaine, argues on appeal that he was entrapped and that his convictions should accordingly be reversed. We agree because we conclude that under the subjective test for entrapment announced in *Munoz v. State*, *629 So.2d 90 (Fla. 1993),* and set forth in Section 777.201, Florida Statutes (1993), appellant met his burden of proving by a preponderance of the evidence that he was induced by the officers to commit the offenses and that he was not predisposed to do so. We conclude that appellant was entrapped as a matter of law and that he court erred in submitting the issue to the jury.

The issue of entrapment was presented to the court via a motion to dismiss prior to trial. The court concluded that there had been no showing of inducement and allowed the issue to go to the jury. Although instructed on the issue, the jury was not persuaded that appellant had been entrapped and convicted appellant of the charged offenses.

Appellant was convicted of his drug offenses following three cocaine buys that he arranged. Detective Debord had received an anonymous telephone tip from a female who lived in the trailer park where appellant lived. She complained generally of drug activity in the park, but did not identify appellant. Debord contacted a confidential informant (CI) he knew in the park. The CI was an older man who had supplied reliable information in the past. The detectives rated him as a "10," in terms of reliability. The CI was not monitored or supervised in any way during his interactions with appellant. Appellant was not identified or targeted by either the CI or law enforcement until the CI met appellant at a Super Bowl party and asked appellant if he could get him some cocaine. Appellant said no, and the CI explained that he needed the drugs to alleviate pain he suffered from cancer and chemotherapy treatments. Appellant was living in Anthony Sansony's trailer at that point. Since it was a very small trailer, appellant was sleeping on the couch. Appellant was still working at that point, unloading furniture from trucks.

According to appellant, the CI kept coming over to Sansony's trailer, "bumming" cigarettes and beer. When the CI's female roommate moved out, the CI approached appellant and asked him to move in with him since his trailer was much larger and the CI needed the rent money. Appellant agreed to move in with the CI and agreed to pay $65 per week in rent. Shortly after moving in, appellant hurt his back lifting a piano and could not work. He fell behind on his rent payments to the CI. According to appellant, the CI told him that he had Mafia connections in Las Vegas where the CI had been a bail bondsman. The CI repeatedly referred to "his boys" as being "family" who would "take care of him." The CI explained that he received money from "his boys" for past services. Given the fact that the CI frequently placed bets over the telephone, appellant believed the Mafia story. The CI's "boys" were, in actuality, undercover detectives Debord and Kennedy.

After appellant had been out of work for several weeks, his former roommate, Sansony, told him that the CI had told Sansony that the CI was mad at appellant because of the back rent and that the CI had told Sansony that the CI's "boys" were going to come by and "take care of" appellant that afternoon. When appellant went to see the CI about this, the CI said he was tired of appellant laying around on his "duff" and that "his boys weren't going to put up with me mooching off of him, that they take care of their family and that they'd be coming by to talk to me that afternoon. And he said that he had already stopped them once from coming and I told him I knew somebody who could get him some cocaine. That's the only reason they didn't come before that." (R 386). Appellant then replied that he did not know anyone who sold cocaine. The CI responded

221

that he would take a week off the rent if appellant would get him some cocaine for medicinal purposes. Appellant then called his friend from a couple of years ago, Dowling, who appellant knew had used cocaine before and thought could probably get him some.

Appellant called Dowling and arranged for the first buy to occur at a bar on Dale Mabry in Tampa. Shortly after the first buy was consummated, the CI threw appellant out of his trailer on the grounds that appellant "could not do these like this." (R 401). Apparently, the "boys" wanted to do another drug buy, but appellant refused because the first deal had not occurred as planned. After the CI threw him out, appellant moved back in with Sansony. Soon afterwards, the "boys" called appellant from the CI's trailer offering him a job as a security guard and a place to live at a compound in Lakeland where they said they stored stolen construction equipment. Appellant agreed, but the "boys" added a stipulation: Appellant would have to arrange another cocaine deal for them. They explained that their regular supplier had been busted and they needed cocaine. Appellant told them he'd have to think about it. After talking to Sansony, appellant decided to do it, explaining that he wanted the job and the place to live. The second and third drug buys occurred at another bar in Tampa.

For each of the three drug buys, the undercover agents drove appellant to the location. For the last deal, which was for a trafficking amount, appellant had to talk Dowling into doing it by explaining that this was his chance to get a place to stay and a job. Appellant said that he did the first deal because of the threats of physical harm and to help his friend, the CI. He did the second and third deals to secure the job and place to live offered by the "boys."

We conclude that these facts support appellant's position that he was entrapped as a matter of law. Under *Munoz*, the test for entrapment is as follows: (1) "[W]hether an agent of the government induced the accused to commit the offense charged;" (2) "whether the accused was predisposed to commit the offense charged; that is, whether the accused was awaiting any propitious opportunity or was ready and willing, without persuasion, to commit the offense;" and (3) whether the entrapment evaluation should be submitted to a jury." *629 So.2d at 99-100.*

On the first question, appellant must establish by a preponderance of the evidence that the government agent induced him to commit the offenses. Since the CI was not available to testify and the CI was not monitored, we have no way of knowing what the CI really told appellant. The only evidence of what the CI told appellant is contained in appellant's testimony and in Sansony's testimony corroborating the CI's Mafia story.

Appellant's and Sansony's testimony indicated that the CI induced appellant to participate in the first drug buy by appealing to his sympathy for a sick friend and threatening him that "his boys" from the Mafia would "take care of him" if he didn't. Appellant took this to mean that "the boys" would break his legs or his arms or kill him. To induce appellant to participate in the second and third drug buys, the undercover agents told appellant that they could provide him a job and a place to live if he would get them some more cocaine. This offer was made only after the CI kicked appellant out of the CI's trailer and appellant had lost his job unloading furniture due to a back injury. The security guard position would require no manual labor.

In considering whether these ploys were sufficient inducement to conclude that appellant was entrapped, we can conceive of no greater inducements than these: First, a threat of severe bodily harm combined with an appeal to mercy, and, second, an offer, made to a man who just lost his place to live (because the government agent kicked him out) of not only a place to live, but a job as well, only if appellant would do more drug deals for them. To further sweeten the offer, the job was one that would not require appellant to use his injured back. Essentially then, government agents threatened appellant with bodily harm, took away his residence and then, when appellant was jobless and virtually homeless, offered him a job and a residence on the condition that he obtain cocaine for them. We, accordingly, answer the first question in the affirmative and find that there can be no question here that the government agents induced appellant to commit the offenses.

Turning to the second question, whether appellant was predisposed to commit the offenses, we conclude that the answer is no. Detective Debord received no information that appellant was involved in the drug dealing in the trailer park. The anonymous phone call did not target anyone. Debord did not receive any information about appellant until the CI mentioned him to Debord. Appellant had no prior felonies, the testimony at trial did not reveal any prior drug offenses. The only evidence involving appellant and drugs was appellant's admission that when he lived with Dowling several years before, he and Dowling had used cocaine together. This, however, was not known to Debord when appellant was targeted by the CI for investigation. This case is like *State v. Ramos, 632 So.2d 1078 (Fla. 3d DCA 1994)*, where the court quoted the *Munoz* court, finding that there was " 'no history, information, or intelligence known to law enforcement of any involvement by [Diaz] in any narcotics activities or drug 'rip-offs' before the confidential informant brought [Diaz] into the scheme.' " *632 So.2d at 1079*. (Diaz was a co-defendant in *Ramos*.) We conclude then that appellant established that he had no predisposition; the state was unable to rebut this evidence beyond a reasonable doubt. See *Herrera v. State, 594 So.2d 275 (Fla. 1992)*.

The third question is whether the entrapment evaluation should have been submitted to the jury. We conclude that the trial court here should have made the determination as a matter of law. Appellant has conclusively shown that government agents induced him to act and that he was not predisposed to commit the offenses. See *Munoz*. Under these circumstances, the issue of entrapment should not have been submitted to a jury.

Having found that appellant was entrapped as a matter of law, we reverse and vacate appellant's convictions. Given our determination on the entrapment issue, we decline to discuss appellant's second point since, in light of our reversal, that point would be moot.

FRANK, A.C.J., and WHATLEY, J., concur.

REVIEW

1. Entrapment may be a defense _____.
    a. if the defendant does not admit to committing the crime
    b. if the defendant is predisposed to commit the crime
    c. if the government induced the defendant to commit the crime
    d. none of the above

ABANDONMENT

Abandonment is also a defense in Florida. However, to assert abandonment as a defense, the Defendant must exercise a voluntary (as opposed to involuntary) abandonment. Involuntary abandonment occurs where the defendant fails in his commission of a crime because of unanticipated difficulties in carrying out the criminal plan at the precise time and place intended and then decides not to pursue the victim under these less advantageous circumstances, [or] . . . when the defendant withdraws because of a belief that the intended victim has become aware of his plans, or because he thinks that his scheme has been discovered or would be thwarted by police observed in the area of the intended crime.

Therefore, if the Defendant abandons his criminal scheme for some reason other than because he is afraid he will be caught, or circumstances no longer make its commission advantageous, he may be able to establish the defense of abandonment.

CASE

Carroll v. State, 680 So.2d 1065 (Fla. 3d DCA 1996).

Defendant was convicted before the Circuit Court, Dade County, Maxine Cohen Lando, J., of petit theft, and he appealed. The District Court of Appeal, Cope, J., held that: (1) defense of abandonment is not limited to statutorily enumerated crimes of criminal attempt, criminal solicitation, or criminal conspiracy, but is available in a proper case as a defense against a substantive criminal charge, and (2) defendant's request for jury instruction on abandonment was properly refused, as evidence showed involuntary abandonment, not voluntary abandonment.

Affirmed.

Before BARKDULL, NESBITT and COPE, JJ.

COPE, Judge.

Aloysious Vereen Carroll appeals his conviction for petit theft. We affirm. [FN1]

Defendant challenges the legal sufficiency of the evidence. We affirm on authority of **Haslem v. State**, *391 So.2d 389 (Fla. 2d DCA 1980)*.

Defendant next argues that the trial court should have granted his requested jury instruction on abandonment. Defendant contends that the evidence showed he had abandoned the theft prior to completing it. He requested an instruction on abandonment, which was refused. We conclude that the trial court was correct.

Florida recognizes the common-law defense of abandonment, also referred to as withdrawal or renunciation. **Smith v. State**, *424 So.2d 726, 732 (Fla. 1982)* [FN2]; **Laythe v. State**, *330 So.2d 113, 114 (Fla. 3d DCA 1976)*.

The law distinguishes between a "voluntary abandonment" and an "involuntary abandonment." According to Professor LaFave, "The cases are in agreement that what is usually referred to as involuntary abandonment is no defense." 2 Wayne R. LaFave and Austin W. Scott, Jr., Substantive Criminal Law §§ 6.3 (b), at 53-54 (1986). An involuntary abandonment occurs when

> the defendant fails because of unanticipated difficulties in carrying out the criminal plan at the precise time and place intended and then decides not to pursue the victim under these less advantageous circumstances, [or] . . . when the defendant withdraws because of a belief that the intended victim has become aware of his plans, or because he thinks that his scheme has been discovered or would be thwarted by police observed in the area of the intended crime.

Id. (footnotes omitted). In order to constitute a defense, the abandonment must be complete and voluntary. See id. at 56; cf. §§ 777.04 (5) Fla. Stat. (1995). [FN3]

In the present case the evidence showed involuntary abandonment, not voluntary abandonment. After an encounter with a uniformed police officer in the K-Mart store, defendant waited until the officer walked away and then commenced to unload from his duffle bag two power drills, still in the original boxes, which he had taken from store inventory kept in an "employees only" storage closet. The requested jury instruction was properly refused.

Affirmed.

FN1. Defendant was also convicted of trespass. He does not challenge that conviction on this appeal.

FN2. The **Smith** decision refers to the defense interchangeably as withdrawal, abandonment, or renunciation. *424 So.2d at 732*.

FN3. The First District Court of Appeal has taken the position that abandonment can only be a defense in Florida where the defendant is charged with criminal attempt, criminal solicitation, or criminal conspiracy under section 777.04, Florida Statutes. ***Dixon v. State***, *559 So.2d 354, 356 (Fla. 1ˢᵗ DCA 1990)*. The court reasoned that since the defense of abandonment has been codified by statute only for the crimes of attempt, solicitation, or conspiracy, §§ 777.04 (5), Fla. Stat., it follows that the legislature did not intend to allow the defense of attempt for any other crime. Under the reasoning of the ***Dixon*** opinion, abandonment could not be a defense to the crime of theft. See *559 So.2d at 356*. We respectfully disagree.

We suggest that the ***Dixon*** case misconstrues the legislative intent in enacting subsection 777.04 (5), Florida Statutes. According to Professor LaFave, "The traditional view as expressed by most commentators is that abandonment is *never* a defense to a charge of attempt if the defendant has gone so far as to engage in the requisite acts with criminal intent." 2 LaFave and Scott, *Substantive Criminal Law* §§ 6.3 (b), at 54 (footnote omitted; emphasis in original). The Model Penal Code took the position that renunciation of criminal purpose should be recognized as a defense to an attempt. Model Penal Code and Commentaries §§ 5.01, at 296-98, 356-62 (1985). It appears reasonably clear that the Florida legislature enacted subsection 777.04 (5), Florida Statutes, in order to change the common law rule and allow renunciation to be a defense to the charge of criminal attempt. *See Model Penal Code and Commentaries §§ 5.01, at 360 n. 279.*

As we view the matter, the Florida Supreme Court has expressly recognized that the defense, whether termed withdrawal, abandonment, or renunciation, is available in a proper case as a defense against a substantive criminal charge. ***Smith v. State***, *424 So.2d at 732*. The effect of subsection 777.04 (5), Florida Statutes, is to expand the availability of the defense to the charge of attempt, where at common law the defense would not otherwise have been available.

REVIEW

1. Abandonment _____.
   a. is a defense in Florida
   b. is not a defense in Florida
   c. neither a nor b
   d. both a and b

GOOD FAITH

Where a Defendant acts "in good faith," that can be a complete defense to certain crimes charged. If he defendant establishes that he or she acted in good faith, he or she cannot be found guilty of the crime charged.

CASE

Philippoussi v. State, 691 So.2d 511 (Fla. 4th DCA 1997).

Defendant was convicted in the Seventeenth Judicial Circuit Court, Broward County, Joel T. Lazarus, J., of grand theft. She appealed. The District Court of Appeal, Klein, J., held that defendant was entitled to jury instruction that good faith was an absolute defense.

Reversed.

KLEIN, Judge.

Appellant was convicted of grand theft as a result of a transaction with an elderly woman. The charges were based on the opening of a joint bank account under circumstances in which the woman may not have realized what was happening, and the removal of funds from that account by the appellant. We reverse because the trial court failed to give a proper jury instruction on a good faith defense.

Appellant's theory of defense was based on her close relationship with the woman, who had previously made appellant the co-owner of two substantial bank accounts with rights of survivorship. The woman had, according to some witnesses, considered appellant the daughter she never had, and had made statements to the effect that she was going to leave appellant and appellant's son everything she had.

Appellant requested the following jury instruction:

> If the Defendant had a good faith belief that Frances Duhm consented to her having the money, she cannot be guilty of grand theft.

The trial court refused to give that instruction, but instead gave the following one:

> If Jacqueline Philippoussi had a good faith belief that Frances Duhm consented to the defendant's having the money, you may consider that as you would any other item of circumstantial evidence in determining whether the defendant is guilty of grand theft.

Appellant argues that the instruction given was insufficient because it did not inform the jury that good faith was a complete defense.

In *Rodriguez v. State, 396 So.2d 798 (Fla. 3d DCA 1981)*, the managers of a motel had failed to remit to the owner some funds received from room rental and were convicted of grand theft. They had admitted they had retained the funds, but claimed they were entitled to do so under their financial arrangement with the owner. The trial court refused to give a good faith instruction similar to that requested in the present case, and the third district reversed for a new trial, citing numerous cases to the effect that good faith can be a complete defense to a crime of theft.

Recently, in **United States v. Cavin**, *39 F.3d 1299 (5ᵗʰ Cir. 1994)*, the fifth circuit reversed a fraud conviction because the instruction which was given did not inform the jury that if the defendant was acting in good faith a conviction was precluded, explaining:

> The district court charged the jury that it "may" acquit the defendants if it found they acted in good faith. A good faith defense is the "affirmative converse of the government's burden of proving...intent to commit a crime." Acquittal is not optional upon a finding of good faith, as the court erroneously charged; it is mandatory because a finding of good faith precludes a finding of fraudulent intent. The implication of the charge as given was that the jury could convict without finding fraudulent intent.

39 F.3d at 1310. (footnote omitted).

We find that the instruction which the court gave in the present case suffers from a similar deficiency and reverse for a new trial. We have considered appellant's other points and find them to be without merit.

FARMER and SHAHOOD, JJ., concur.

REVIEW

1. Good faith is _____.
   a. an absolute defense
   b. not a defense
   c. both a and b
   d. neither a nor b

CASE

Bartlett v. State, *765 So.2d 799 (Fla. 1ˢᵗ DCA 2000).*

Defendant was convicted in the Circuit Court, Holmes County, Allen L. Register, J., of grand theft of a truck, petit theft of its contents, and trespass. Defendant appealed. The District Court of Appeal, Benton, J., held that evidence supported defense theory that defendant took the truck in a good faith belief that he had a legitimate right to do so.

Affirmed in part and reversed in part.

Browning, J., filed a concurring opinion.

Miner, J., concurred and dissented and filed an opinion.

BENTON, Judge.

William C. Bartlett appeals his convictions for grand theft of a truck, petit theft of its contents, and (in order to get the truck) trespass on property Russell Jones leased. The evidence was insufficient to establish the requisite intent to steal the truck. Uncontroverted evidence showed that Mr. Bartlett held title to the truck when he took the truck under an apparent claim of right. We affirm the convictions for petit theft and trespass but we reverse the grand theft conviction.

A person who takes possession in the good faith belief that he or she has a right to the property lacks the requisite intent to commit theft. *See J.L. v. State, 556 So.2d 1383, 1384 (Fla. 1st DCA 1990)* ("If J.L. took the property under the honest but mistaken belief that Dumas had given her permission, she cannot be found guilty of theft."); *Thomas v. State, 526 So.2d 183, 184 (Fla. 3d DCA 1988)* ("It is well settled that a well-founded belief in one's right to the allegedly stolen property constitutes a complete defense to a charge of theft."); *Mitchell v. State, 516 So.2d 22, 23 (Fla. 3d DCA 1987)* (finding that the record contained no evidence establishing criminal intent in part because the defendant "believed in good faith that she had a right to the [property]); *see also Board of Regents v. Videon, 313 So.2d 433, 435 (Fla. 1st DCA 1975)*. At the conclusion of the state's case here, the defense moved for judgment of acquittal on grounds the state had failed to prove "a prima facie case that [Mr. Bartlett] at the time of the taking of the vehicle had the intent to steal the vehicle."

Under Florida law, a theft requires proof of a taking animo furandi, i.e., with the intent to steal. As was explained in *Sassnett v. State, 156 Fla. 490, 23 So.2d 618, 619 (Fla. 1945)*,

> [a]n essential element of this crime, which must be established by testimony beyond a reasonable doubt, is that the taking was animo furandi, or with the intent to steal, and 'where it clearly appears that the taking was perfectly consistent with honest conduct, although the party charged with the crime may have been mistaken, he cannot be convicted of larceny.' *Cooper v. State, 82 Fla. 365, 90 So. 375 [(Fla. 1921)]*.

See also Kilbee v. State, 53 So.2d 533, 536 (Fla. 1951) ("It is essential in order to sustain a conviction of larceny that the evidence adduced by the State establishes beyond a reasonable doubt that the property was taken animo furandi. Likewise, it is well established law that where one takes the property of another, honestly believing that he has a right to it, or, in other words, under a bona fide claim of right, there can be no larceny." (citations omitted)); *Maddox v. State, 38 So.2d 58, 59 (Fla. 1948)*.

After agreeing to purchase an " '88 Dodge Dakota pick-up" from Mr. Bartlett, a long-time friend ("[b]een knowing him all my life"), Mr. Jones took possession of the truck and began making monthly installment payments. But before the full purchase price of two thousand dollars had been paid, Mr. Bartlett then lent Mr. Jones another sum of money. Eventually, because that sum had not been repaid, Mr. Bartlett took the truck, asserting in effect a security interest in the truck and a right to repossess it, even though the originally agreed-upon installment payments had by then been made.

Mr. Jones suspected what had happened and why, he testified, and did not report the truck as stolen for seventeen days. He thought that Mr. Bartlett had repossessed the truck because of the outstanding debt. Deputy Sheriff Aubrey Carroll testified:

> I said, "Mr. Bartlett, I understand that you went out to Russell Jones' house and took a truck out of his yard." And he said, "Yes, I did." ... And I said, "It's also my understanding that Mr. Jones and you had an agreement and he purchased the truck and has been in possession of the truck and has paid you for the truck." And he said, "That's right but he owes me some other money." And I said, "Well, I don't think you can go out there and take the truck under those circumstances." He said, "Well, I am not giving the truck back until he pays me the money that he owes me."

At issue is Mr. Bartlett's intent at the time he took the truck. See *Iglesias v. State*, *676 So.2d 75, 76 (Fla. 3d DCA 1996)*; *Stramaglia v. State*, *603 So.2d 536, 538 (Fla. 4th DCA 1992)*; *Szilagyi v. State*, *564 So.2d 644, 645 (Fla. 4th DCA 1990)*. At all pertinent times, the truck was registered in Mr. Bartlett's name. Mr. Jones acknowledged that, initially, he too thought Mr. Bartlett had a right to take the truck.

> In order to prove specific felonious intent, the state can rely on circumstantial evidence. Since intent necessarily involves the state of mind of the perpetrator, very often circumstantial evidence is the only evidence available to prove intent. However, such circumstantial evidence must exclude every reasonable hypothesis but that of guilt.

Szilagyi v. State, *564 So.2d at 646*; see also *McGough v. State*, *302 So.2d 751, 755 (Fla. 1974)*("Where an attempt is made by the State to prove [knowledge and intent] through circumstantial evidence, such proof must not only be consistent with guilt but also inconsistent with any other reasonable hypothesis of innocence.").

The requirement of animus furandi survived codification of what was formerly the common law crime of theft. Although a claim of a good faith taking may no longer be raised as a defense in robbery cases, see *Daniels v. State*, *587 So.2d 460, 462 (Fla. 1991)*; *Thomas v. State*, *584 So.2d 1022, 1023 (Fla. 1st DCA 1991)*, the defense remains available in theft cases. See *Jackson v. State*, *468 So.2d 346, 348 (Fla. 1st DCA 1985)*; *Adams v. State*, *443 So.2d 1003, 1006 (Fla. 2d DCA 1983)*. See generally *State v. Dunmann*, *427 So.2d 166, 169 (Fla. 1983)*; *State v. Allen*, *362 So.2d 10, 11 (Fla. 1978)*.

The state had the burden to establish "specific intent to commit theft, which is an essential element of the crime." *Redding v. State*, *666 So.2d 921, 922 (Fla. 1st DCA 1995)*. The state had the burden therefore to exclude Mr. Bartlett's hypothesis of innocence by virtue of a good faith claim to the right to possession. See *McGough*, *302 So.2d at 755*. Considerable evidence supported the defense theory that Mr. Bartlett took the truck in a good faith belief that he had a legitimate right to do so. When Mr. Bartlett took (repossessed) the truck, legal title was still in his name. The state failed to meet its burden.

The convictions for trespass and for petit theft are affirmed. The conviction for grand theft is reversed.

BROWNING, J., CONCURS WITH OPINION; MINER, J., CONCURS AND DISSENTS WITH OPINION.

BROWNING, J. concurring.

I concur with Judge Benton's majority opinion. I write only to amplify the factual basis that impels my joining in the majority opinion.

Appellant and victim were merely friends who "fell out" over a business transaction, and their differences concerning entitlement to possession of the truck constitute a civil matter, rather than a criminal one. This conclusion is based upon the facts that Appellant and victim, as stated, were friends; victim had often borrowed money from Appellant; Appellant had retained the title certificate to the truck, and Appellant was named as owner of the truck in the title certificate, which implies a right of repossession by Appellant; victim believed Appellant had the legal right to repossess the truck; victim owed Appellant money at the time Appellant claimed possession of the truck, albeit such funds were loaned after the sale of the truck, but before the agreed purchase price for the truck was paid by victim, which implies a future advancement by the conduct of the parties; the first hint of Appellant's not having the right to repossess the truck came from a deputy sheriff some 19 days after Appellant repossessed the truck from victim; and much of the state's evidence is based upon a conversation between Appellant and a deputy sheriff who was acting similar to a mediator between Appellant and victim by attempting to have Appellant return the truck to victim without initiating a prosecution. Appellant's conduct as exhibited to a deputy sheriff some 19 days after Appellant's repossession of the truck was less than commendable, but Appellant's offensive conduct does not make him the perpetrator of grand theft of the truck beyond a reasonable doubt.

MINER, J., concurring and dissenting.

Like my colleagues in the majority, I would affirm appellant's convictions for trespass and petit theft. Unlike the majority, I would also affirm Bartlett's conviction for grand theft of the pickup truck involved here.

While I agree that uncontroverted evidence supports the fact that Mr. Bartlett "held" title to the truck in question in the sense that it was titled in his name, there is no credible evidence of any kind that he took the truck "under an apparent claim of right." That contention was made in his behalf by defense counsel. Appellant himself never offered evidence of any kind, testimonial or otherwise, from which a jury could conclude that his intent was anything other than felonious at the time he went on Jones' property and took the truck Jones had completed paying for. To be sure, appellant "held" title to the truck at the time he wrongfully refused to deliver the certificate of title to Jones a day or so before trespassing on Jones' property and taking the truck.

In *Uber v. State, 382 So.2d 1321 (Fla. 1ˢᵗ DCA 1980)*, this court reiterated the proposition that in prosecutions of the type involved here, proof by the state of felonious intent is essential to a conviction. In reversing Uber's conviction, the court reminded us that the question of intent is normally a jury determination. Of particular interest in *Uber* is the repetition of an observation made previously in *Board of Regents v. Videon, 313 So.2d 433, 435 (Fla. 1ˢᵗ DCA 1975)*:

> The intent with which an act is done is an operation of the mind and, therefore, is not always capable of direct and positive proof. The intent may be presumed from the facts and circumstances surrounding the act of taking. It is then incumbent upon the taker to go forward with the evidence and show a lack of criminal intent on his part. Such can be done by presenting evidence that it was an honest mistake; that he believed he had a right to apply the property to his own use. When a taking or appropriation to one's own use is with an honest belief that the taker has the right to take the property (to apply it to his own use), there is no larceny, even though the taker may have been mistaken.

Uber, 382 So.2d at 1322 (Emphasis added). [FN1]

In the case at bar, appellant, the "taker" did not go forward with the evidence much less show a lack of criminal intent on his part. The sum total of his showing of a lack of criminal intent was his counsel's questioning of the only two state witnesses, Jones (the victim) and Deputy Carroll, regarding what they thought was in Bartlett's mind when he went on to Jones' property less than 24 hours after he had been told by Jones not to do so. At best, counsel's characterization of the taking of the truck Jones had paid for as a "repossession" seems to me to be but a generous play on words, certainly not "evidence" that Bartlett was possessed of an honest belief that he had the right to take the truck and apply it to his own use as he did. [FN2]

There is no evidentiary dispute regarding the facts and circumstances surrounding the act of taking of Jones' truck which demonstrate, at least in my view, an inconsistency with the defense theory (which is unsupported by any competent evidence) that Bartlett in good faith believed that he had a legitimate right to take the truck.

> 1. On the day prior to the taking, Bartlett advised Jones that he was going to withhold title to the truck until Jones repaid other money he had borrowed or as one of the attorney's described it, Bartlett was going to hold the truck, its title, and Jones' personal property "hostage" until Jones' collateral debt to him was repaid.

2. On the day Bartlett told Jones he was not going to deliver title to the truck, the two exchanged "words" and Jones invited Bartlett to leave the property and not to return.

3. Bartlett returned to Jones' property the following day during Jones' absence and took the truck which contained a number of items of personal property belonging to Jones (tires and rims, tools, groceries, etc.).

4. Bartlett does not take issue with the fact that Jones paid the agreed upon sum of $2000 for the truck in question.

5. After Bartlett took the truck Jones fully paid for, he held it for some two and a half weeks and made no attempt to contact Jones regarding the whereabouts of the truck or its contents.

6. Jones testified initially that he thought his brother, who was also his guardian and who had a key to the truck, had borrowed it. When he found out otherwise, he located the truck in the possession of Bartlett's son.

7. When Deputy Carroll received Jones' complaint about the missing truck, he contacted Bartlett and was told by Bartlett that he (Bartlett) did not care what the law was and that he would not return the truck or Jones' personal property until all money owed him by Jones was paid. He invited Deputy Carroll to arrest him with the words that he could "afford" to make bail. Deputy Carroll then took him up on his invitation. [FN3]

8. There was no evidence of any type of security agreement between Bartlett and Jones related to the other money Jones owed Bartlett. [FN4] The above stated facts and circumstances seem at odds with what his counsel describes as Bartlett's good faith belief that he had a right to do what he did.

To conclude, at most there is nothing whatsoever in the record from which it can be reasonably concluded that appellant, the "taker," went forward with any evidence to show a lack of criminal intent on his part when he went upon Jones' homesite and "repossessed" the truck Jones had purchased and paid for. At the very least, Bartlett's subjective intent when he took the truck was a jury question and there was more than sufficient evidence to sustain the jury's verdict of guilt as to all three charged offenses which came after less than a half-hour of deliberations. Accordingly, I would affirm Bartlett's convictions as to all charges.

FN1. In each of the cases cited in support of the majority opinion regarding good faith belief, the accused either testified before the jury regarding his intent or produced other evidence showing a lack of criminal intent. See *J.L. v. State, 566 So.2d 1383, 1384 (Fla. 1st DCA 1990)*; ***Thomas v. State, 526 So.2d 183, 184 (Fla. 3d DCA 1988)***; ***Mitchell v. State, 516 So.2d 22 (Fla. 3d DCA 1987)***; ***Board of Regents v. Videon, 313 So.2d 433 (Fla. 1st DCA 1975)***.

FN2. It hardly need be repeated that what attorneys say is not evidence.

FN3. The deputy testified, as follows: [A]ppellant said ..., "I am not giving him the truck until he pays me all the money he owes me. But he (Bartlett) stated to me that the money that he (Jones) owed him was for other reasons and the truck wasn't mentioned."

FN4. Jones testified under oath that after he finished paying for the truck, appellant told him that "he would not give me the title to [the truck] because I owed him some money." Jones further testified that when Bartlett had lent him money a couple of months earlier he said nothing about holding the truck title, there was no security agreement, and the loan had nothing to do with the truck.

> Q: So you had paid for the truck at that time?
> A: Right.
> Q: And it was your truck?
> A: I thought it was.
> Q: And he informed you that he was going to hold that title until you paid the rest of your [other] loan off?
> A: Right.
> Q: And that was the first time you heard of it?
> A: That's the first time I ever heard of it.
> Q: When you paid the truck off?
> A: Right.

REVIEW

1. A person who takes possession in good faith _____.
   a. has the intent to commit theft
   b. does not have the intent to commit theft
   c. has a good faith defense
   d. both b and c

VOLUNTARY INTOXICATION

Voluntary intoxication is no longer a defense in Florida. The voluntary consumption of alcohol or drugs will not excuse someone from criminal liability. This change occurred as a result of a bill passed by the legislature. The legislature passed a law abrogating intoxication as a defense for crimes occurring after October 1st, 1999.

However, there are limited circumstances under which evidence of voluntary intoxication may still be admissible. For instance, it may be used as evidence to negate specific intent in certain cases. Nonetheless, as a general rule voluntary intoxication is no longer a viable defense in Florida.

THINKING CRITICALLY

1. Errol goes to the convenience store and steals some food. The manager throws him out. Errol believes the manager has put a hex on him. Errol believes the hex will kill him if he does not kill the manager. Errol gets a gun, comes back, and shoots and kills the manager. You are defending Errol. Was he insane at the time of the offense?

2. The voices in Jesse's head tell him to kill his mother. He listens to them and does so. Was he insane at the time of the offense? What other information would you like to have?

3. Might the result have been different if Viovenel was not charged with such serious offenses? Why do you think this was a nonjury trial? What do you think a jury would have decided?

4. Do you agree with the opinion in *Grady*? What if the individual looks a lot older? What if the person has false identification showing they are over the age of 18? Should there be an exception for defendants who have a good faith basis for believing an individual is older than they are?

5. The owner of a video store rents an X-rated movie to a minor in the following situation. Law enforcement obtained a false video membership card. They then instructed a juvenile to lie about both her age and her relationship with the member named on the card. There was no evidence the owner had previously rented X-rated videos to minors. Has the owner been entrapped? Why or why not? What if the owner refused to rent to the girl the first ten times but did so the eleventh time?

6. Give an example of a situation where an individual commits a crime as a result of being under duress.

7. Should coercion excuse someone from responsibility for a crime? Why or why not?

8. What factors should be considered in determining whether someone was in fact acting under duress?

9. Law enforcement places an officer who appears intoxicated in a high crime area. Money can be seen hanging from his pocket. Gus walks by and steals the money. Gus has no criminal history and the officers have had no previous contact with him. Has Gus been entrapped? Should law enforcement be targeting specific ongoing criminal activity? Why or why not?

10. What do you think of the *Robichaud* case? Which of the inducements did you find the most egregious? What do you think should happen to the officers? What should happen to the confidential informant?

11. Jack is brought into a drug transaction by his codefendant Elaine. A confidential informant introduced Elaine to an undercover agent with whom the drug deal was negotiated. The confidential informant was paid a flat fee, not contingent on his trial testimony. He was not working off any charges. Can Jack assert the defense of entrapment? Can Elaine? Was the confidential informant an agent of the State? Can you be entrapped by a codefendant?

12. Should abandonment be a defense to any charge? Why or why not?

13. At what point in *Carroll* could the defendant have unloaded the items from his duffle bag and been able to claim abandonment? What if Carroll got up to the checkout counter and merely saw a police officer? What if Carroll got past the checkout counter but had not yet exited the store?

14. What crimes should there be a good faith defense to? Is good faith just another way of saying the defendant didn't intend to commit a crime? What's the difference?

15. Why do you think voluntary intoxication is no longer a defense? Do you think it should be? If so, in what cases? Under what circumstances should intoxication excuse someone from criminal liability?

CHAPTER 8 ANSWER KEY

REVIEW QUESTIONS

Viovenel v. State
    1. b

Grady v. State
    1. a

Aljak v. State
    1. d

Bozeman v. State
    1. c

Robichaud v. State
    1. d

Carroll v. State
    1. a

Philippoussi v. State
    1. a

Bartlett v. State
    1. d

CHAPTER 9

CRIMES AGAINST PERSONS I:
CRIMINAL HOMICIDE

MURDER IN THE FIRST DEGREE

The circumstances surrounding a killing will determine whether a homicide is classified as murder in the First Degree, Murder in the Second Degree, Murder in the Third Degree, or manslaughter. A killing that is excusable or was committed by the use of justifiable deadly force is lawful. The "year and a day" rule has been abrogated in the State of Florida.

The first element the State must prove in a homicide is that a victim is dead, and it is not necessary for the State to have found the victim's body.

There are two ways an individual may be convicted of first degree murder: (1) premeditated murder; or (2) felony murder. In a premeditated murder, the death must be caused by the criminal act of the defendant where the defendant makes the conscious decision to kill. Premeditation is more than mere intent to kill. It is the fully formed and conscious purpose to take human life. It is formed after reflection and deliberation. There need not have been an elaborate plan, and there is not a set period of time to premeditate. Whatever period of time allows reflection by the defendant is sufficient. The defendant need only be conscious of the nature of the act and the probable result. The State may prove premeditation through circumstantial evidence.

Moreover, premeditation may be inferred from the nature of the weapon used, the number of wounds, the nature and manner of wounds inflicted, the presence or absence of provocation, previous problems between the parties, the manner in which the murder is committed, and the accused's actions before and after the homicide. The premeditated intent may be transferred. Thus, if there is a premeditated design to kill one person and in the attempt to do so another person is killed, that killing is premeditated.

A defendant who does not actually kill the victim may be convicted of first degree murder under certain circumstances. If any of the principals commits one of the enumerated felonies listed below, each and every principal can be convicted of first degree murder. The enumerated felonies are trafficking, arson, sexual battery, robbery, burglary, kidnapping, escape, aggravated child abuse, aggravated abuse of an elderly person or disabled adult, aircraft piracy, unlawful throwing, placing, or discharging of a destructive device or bomb, carjacking, home invasion robbery, aggravated stalking, or the unlawful distribution of certain controlled substances when the drug is proven to be the proximate cause of the death of the user. The murder may occur as a consequence of the felony or an attempt to commit the felony or while escaping from the crime scene.

CASE

Kirkland v. State, 684 So.2d 732 (Fla. 1996).

Defendant was convicted in the Circuit Court, Calhoun County, John E. Roberts, J., of first-degree murder and was sentenced to death, and he appealed. The Supreme Court held that: (1) state's evidence was insufficient to support a finding of premeditation so as to sustain first-degree murder conviction, and (2) record supported conviction for second-degree murder.

So ordered.

Grimes and Wells, JJ., concurred in result only.

PER CURIAM.

We have on appeal the judgment and sentence of the trial court imposing the death penalty upon Dwayne Kirkland. We have jurisdiction. Art. V, §§ 3 (b)(1), Fla. Const. While we find that there is insufficient evidence in the record to support the finding of premeditation necessary to sustain Kirkland's first-degree murder conviction and sentence of death, we do find that the record supports a conviction of second-degree murder.

The record reflects the following. At some time on April 13 or 14, 1993, Coretta Martin was murdered in Blountstown, Florida. Her murder was accomplished by "a very deep, complex, irregular wound of the neck." That wound cut off Coretta Martin's ability to breathe and caused extensive bleeding. At the time of Coretta Martin's murder, Kirkland was living with her mother, Teresa Martin. Coretta Martin and her brother, Gregory, were living in the same dwelling with Kirkland and Teresa Martin.

When the murder occurred, Teresa Martin and Gregory Martin were in Tallahassee. When they returned home on the night of April 14, Teresa Martin discovered Coretta Martin's dead body in a bedroom of their dwelling.

On April 14, Kirkland left Blountstown, went to Quincy, and then to Atlanta, Georgia. The following day, Kirkland traveled from Atlanta to Fort Myers, Florida. Kirkland was arrested in Fort Myers on April 19, 1993. A grand jury handed down an indictment for first-degree murder against Kirkland on May 17, 1993.

On July 1, 1994, the jury convicted Kirkland of first-degree murder. Then, on July 5, 1994, the jury recommended that the sentence of death be imposed

On August 29, 1994, the trial judge entered a judgment and sentence that found Kirkland guilty of first-degree murder and announced that death was the appropriate penalty.

We find that this appeal, as to the conviction for first-degree murder and the sentence of death, is resolved through addressing only the first issue. We find that the evidence of premeditation is insufficient to support a conviction for first-degree murder.

The State's case was based upon circumstantial evidence. Kirkland moved for a judgment of acquittal at the conclusion of the State's case. The trial court denied Kirkland's motion. We have stated that such a motion should be granted unless the State can "present evidence from which the jury can exclude every reasonable hypothesis except that of guilt." *State v. Law,* 559 So.2d 187, 188 (Fla. 1989). We find that the circumstantial evidence in this case "is not inconsistent with any reasonable exculpatory hypothesis as to the existence of premeditation." *Hall v. State,* 403 So.2d 1319, 1321 (Fla. 1981). Indeed, a review of the record forces us to conclude, as a matter of law, that the State failed to prove premeditation to the exclusion of all other reasonable conclusions. "Where the State's proof fails to exclude a reasonable hypotheses [sic] that the homicide occurred other than by premeditated design, a verdict of first-degree murder cannot be sustained." *Hoefert v. State,* 617 So.2d 1046, 1048 *(Fla. 1993).*

Premeditation is defined as follows:

> Premeditation is a fully formed conscious purpose to kill that may be formed in a moment and need only exist for such time as will allow the accused to be conscious of the nature of the act he is about to commit and the probable result of that act.

Asay v. State, 580 So.2d 610, 612 (Fla. 1991). The State asserted that the following evidence suggested premeditation. The victim suffered a severe neck wound that caused her to bleed to death, or sanguinate, or suffocate. The wound was caused by many slashes. In addition to the major neck wound, the victim suffered other injuries that appeared to be the result of blunt trauma. There was evidence indicating that both a knife and a walking cane were used in the attack. Further, the State pointed to evidence indicating that friction existed between Kirkland and the victim insofar as Kirkland was sexually tempted by the victim.

We find, however, that the State's evidence was insufficient in light of the strong evidence militating against a finding of premeditation. First and foremost, there was no suggestion that Kirkland exhibited, mentioned, or even possessed an intent to kill the victim at any time prior to the actual homicide. Second, there were no witnesses to the events immediately preceding the homicide. Third, there was no evidence suggesting that Kirkland made special arrangements to obtain a murder weapon in advance of the homicide. Indeed, the victim's mother testified that Kirkland owned a knife the entire time she was associated with him. Fourth, the State presented scant, if any, evidence to indicate that Kirkland committed the homicide according to a preconceived plan. Finally, while not controlling, we note that it is unrefuted that Kirkland had an IQ that measured in the sixties.

In *Hoefert,* we were unable to find evidence sufficient to support premeditation in a situation in which Hoefert had established a pattern of strangling women while raping or assaulting them. Evidence was presented in that case indicating that the homicide victim, found

243

dead in Hoefert's dwelling, was likewise asphyxiated. Despite the pattern of strangulation, the discovery of the victim in Hoefert's dwelling, and efforts by Hoefert to conceal the crime, this Court found that premeditation was not established. *Hoefert, 617 So.2d at 1049.* In this case, there is no evidence that Kirkland had established a pattern of extreme violence as had Hoefert. A comparison of the facts in *Hoefert* and the instant case requires us to find, if the law of circumstantial evidence is to be consistently and equally applied, that the record in this case is insufficient to support a finding of premeditation.

The record leads us to conclude that, while the evidence does support a finding that Kirkland committed an unlawful killing, there is insufficient evidence to establish premeditation. Accordingly, we must reverse Kirkland's conviction for first-degree murder and vacate his sentence of death. In so holding, we note that Kirkland was tried for first-degree premeditated murder. There was no attempt to establish first-degree felony murder or to instruct the jury as to that alternative. Further, the record does not support a conviction of felony murder. This does not mean that Kirkland is not guilty of an unlawful killing. Second-degree murder is defined as "[t]he unlawful killing of a human being, when perpetrated by any act imminently dangerous to another and evincing a depraved mind regardless of human life, although without any premeditated design to effect the death of any particular individual." §§ 782.04 (2), Fla. Stat. (1991). We find that the record in this case does support a conviction for second-degree murder.

In accordance with our determination that the record supports a conviction for second-degree murder, section 924.34 of the Florida Statutes (1991) [FN2] authorizes us to remand this case to the trial court with instructions to enter judgment against Kirkland for second-degree murder and sentence him accordingly.

It is so ordered.

KOGAN, C.J., and OVERTON, SHAW, HARDING and ANSTEAD, JJ., concur.

GRIMES and WELLS, JJ., concur in result only.

(FN1 omitted).

FN2. This section reads:

When an appellate court determines that the evidence does not prove the offense for which the defendant was found guilty but does establish his guilt of a lesser statutory degree of the offense or a lesser offense not necessarily included in the offense charged, the appellate court shall reverse the judgment and direct the trial court to enter judgment for the lesser degree of the offense or for the lesser included offense. § 924.34, Fla. Stat. (1991).

REVIEW

1. The State must prove premeditation in order to convict one of _____.
   a. first degree murder
   b. second degree murder
   c. third degree murder
   d. manslaughter

2. Premeditation may be inferred from _____.
   a. the nature of the weapon
   b. the number of wounds
   c. the accused's actions before the homicide
   d. all of the above

3. Lack of premeditation may be found based upon _____.
   a. lack of intent to kill prior to the homicide
   b. lack of eyewitness to the homicide
   c. not obtaining a weapon in advance
   d. all of the above

CASE

Rodriguez v. State, 571 So.2d 1356 (Fla. 2d DCA 1990).

Defendant was convicted of first-degree felony murder. Judgment was entered in the Circuit Court. Hillsborough County, Barbara C. Fleischer, Acting J.. Defendant appealed. The Court of Appeal, Campbell, Acting C.J., held that defendant was entitled to instruction on independent action, as there was evidence that passenger in defendant's automobile, who was in convenience store alone, had spontaneously decided to kill store clerk.

Reversed and remanded.

CAMPBELL, Acting Chief Judge.

Appellant, Heriberto Rodriguez, appeals his conviction and sentence for first degree felony murder. We must reverse and remand for a new trial because the trial judge committed reversible error when she failed to give appellant's requested independent act jury instruction. The instruction would have informed the jury that if it found that appellant's co-defendant committed the murder as an independent act, not during the course of or in furtherance of the attempted robbery, it would have to find appellant not guilty of first degree felony murder.

The evidence presented during appellant's trial showed that on March 14, 1988, at approximately 9:00 p.m., appellant parked his car in the vicinity of a Shell service station and store. His passenger, Victor Ballester, exited appellant's vehicle, went into the Shell station, confronted the attendant on duty and demanded money. The attendant refused to give Ballester

245

the money and Ballester walked to the door of the station as if he were leaving. After a lapse of approximately four seconds, Ballester returned to the counter, placed a revolver to the head of the attendant and executed him on the spot. After the shooting, Ballester, without making any effort to take money or other property from the station or the body of the attendant, exited the station, apparently rejoined appellant in his vehicle and left the scene.

On March 19, 1988, appellant told his father that he had participated in an attempt to rob a store, but did not know about the killing until long after appellant and Ballester left the scene. Appellant expressed fear of Ballester and went to Puerto Rico to seek safety from him. On March 20, 1988, appellant's father drove to the Hillsborough County Sheriff Office in appellant's car and repeated appellant's story to the sheriff's personnel. Appellant was contacted in Puerto Rico and told his brother-in-law, a Tampa Police Department officer, that he did not know that a person had been shot until some time after the attempted robbery. Appellant stated that he was only the driver of his vehicle at the time of the attempted robbery, had not gotten out of his car and had seen nothing of the attempted robbery or the shooting. Arrangements were made for appellant's voluntary surrender to authorities. Appellant has continued to repeat the same version of the events that he told his father and brother-in-law.

The Shell station had a number of non-audio video tape cameras as part of a surveillance security system. The cameras were operational and recorded the attempted robbery and the shooting of the attendant in sequential pictures that indicated the date and timing of the events in seconds.

The video tape sequence of the attempted robbery and shooting was shown to the jury at trial. Twice during its deliberations, the jury requested and was allowed to view again the video tape sequences. As depicted in the video, only Ballester was seen when he first arrived at the store on March 14, 1988, at 20:55:06 (six seconds after 8:55 p.m.). The tape shows Ballester entering the store at 20:55:18, and no longer present in the store at 20:55:44.

During the course of the events shown on the tape, Ballester is seen to approach the attendant, turn as if to leave the scene after apparently being stymied in the attempt at robbery, return to the attendant holding a weapon and then shoot the attendant. It was undisputed at trial that appellant never knew Ballester intended to shoot anyone. It was also undisputed that nothing was taken from the store and that appellant never witnessed any of the events that took place as he was parked in his car some distance away from the store and out of the line of vision.

Appellant's entire defense to the felony murder charge was that the murder was an independent act on the part of Ballester and not committed in the course of or in furtherance of the attempted robbery.

In closing arguments, appellant's counsel focused on the murder as an independent act because it was committed after the attempted robbery had failed and, since the entire scene had been filmed by the three visible surveillance cameras, it was arguably not done as an attempt to eliminate the witness. Appellant's counsel argued that the video tape showed that the murder was a spiteful act in the nature of an execution committed by Ballester as an afterthought to the attempted robbery.

The jury here had for its consideration a video tape of the entire sequence of events from which it could determine as a matter of fact whether in its opinion the attempted robbery had terminated before the murder, thus rendering the murder of the attendant a separate, independent act. Where there is any evidence introduced at trial which supports the theory of the defense, the defendant is entitled to have the jury instructed on the law applicable to his theory of defense. *Gardner v. State, 480 So.2d 91 (Fla. 1985); Motley v. State, 155 Fla. 545, 20 So.2d 798 (Fla. 1945)*.

It is settled law in this state that the felony murder rule and the law relating to principals combine to make a felon liable for the acts of murder committed by his co-felons in the furtherance of their joint felony. However, where there is evidence from which a jury could determine that the acts of the co-felons resulting in murder were independent of the joint felony, a defendant is entitled to an instruction that if the murder was such an independent act, not committed in furtherance of or in the course of the joint felony, the jury should find the defendant not guilty of felony murder. *Bryant v. State, 412 So.2d 347 (Fla. 1982)*. There was such evidence in this case from which the jury could have determined that the murder of the attendant was an independent act of Ballester, unrelated to the attempted robbery. The jury should have been so instructed.

We therefore reverse and remand for a new trial.

THREADGILL and PATTERSON, JJ., concur.

REVIEW

    1. If the murder is an independent act committed by another, _____.
        a. the defendant is not guilty
        b. a special jury instruction must be given
        c. both a and b
        d. neither a nor b

MURDER IN THE SECOND DEGREE

Second degree murder is an unlawful killing by an act imminently dangerous to another and demonstrating a depraved mind without regard for human life. The first two elements are the same as for premeditated first degree murder, the victim must be dead and the death must be caused by the criminal act of the defendant. However, the state need not prove the defendant intended to cause death.

An act is imminently dangerous and demonstrates a depraved mind if three conditions are met. First, a person of ordinary judgment would know it is reasonably certain to kill or do serious bodily injury to another. Second, if it is done from ill will, hatred, spite, or an evil intent. Third, if it is of such a nature that the act itself indicates an indifference to human life.

Second degree felony murder again, requires that the victim must be dead. The death must be as a consequence of and while the crime is being committed or attempted or while there is an escape. The difference between first and second degree felony murder is who actually kills the victim. In second degree felony murder, the defendant does not actually kill the victim. One of two things occurs. The defendant may have knowingly aided, abetted, hired, counseled, or otherwise procured the commission of the felony. Or the person who actually killed the victim was not involved in the commission or the attempt to commit the crime at all. The person may be a victim of the felony, a police officer who comes upon the crime scene, or someone else who happens to be at the incident.

CASE

Parker v. State, 570 So.2d 1048 (Fla. 1st DCA 1990).

Defendant was convicted in the Circuit Court, Escambia County, Nickolas Geeker, J., of second degree felony murder, armed robbery, and kidnapping, and defendant appealed. The District Court of Appeal, Wolf, J., held that: (1) robbery was not complete until after death of police officer during chase of robbers; (2) alleged negligence of police officer did not constitute legally recognizable defense to second-degree felony murder; and (3) confinement in trunk of automobile was sufficient to constitute kidnapping.

Affirmed.

WOLF, Judge.

James Robert Parker appeals from his conviction and sentence for second degree felony murder armed robbery, and kidnapping. The issues raised are as follows: 1) Whether there was sufficient evidence to support the conviction for second degree felony murder; 2) whether the trial court erred in excluding evidence of police negligence as an intervening cause in the death of the victim; 3) whether there was sufficient evidence that the appellant was the perpetrator of the robbery and kidnapping; 4) whether the trial court erred in denying the motion for a judgment of acquittal on the charge of kidnapping because the crime was never completed; 5) whether the trial court erred in imposing a three-year mandatory minimum sentence for possession of a firearm during the commission of a robbery; and 6) whether the split sentence imposed on the appellant violates the constitutional prohibition against double jeopardy. We find issue 3 to be without merit and affirm without discussion. As to the other issues, we affirm for the reasons addressed herein.

On December 3, 1988, at about 7:00 o'clock in the evening, Ralph Stewart was driving along Interstate 10 in Santa Rosa County when he experienced engine trouble. Mr. Stewart pulled into a rest area to determine the source of the problem. Two men approached him and asked him if he needed any help. Stewart refused the offer. The appellant's codefendant (the appellant's brother) then pulled out a pistol and held it to the side of the victim's head. The appellant took a number of items from the victim's pockets, including some cash and a change purse. While the robbery was going on, the appellant then jammed an object into the victim's back, but the victim was unable to determine what it was. The robbers then shoved the victim into the trunk of his car. They attempted to close and lock the trunk lid; however, Stewart was able to block the latching mechanism with his coat, thus, preventing the trunk from locking.

Stewart stayed in his trunk, holding the latch down until he heard the men leave. He then got out of the trunk and spent approximately five minutes searching for his glasses and his extra set of car keys.

Mr. Stewart got into his car and went to a nearby convenience store. At the store, Mr. Stewart saw one of the men who robbed him filling his car with gas. Mr. Stewart went inside and saw the other man who robbed him. The man was holding Stewart's change purse which had been taken during the course of the robbery. Stewart approached the man and grabbed the purse out of his hand and told him that it was his. At that point, the man ran outside and told his partner that they had to leave quickly. The other perpetrator threw the gas hose on the ground and got in the trunk without putting the gas cap on the tank. They drove out of the gas station at a high rate of speed, almost hitting a pickup truck.

A bystander observed the robbers leave the gas station and followed them. The robbers traveled up and down several streets. The bystander stopped at another convenience store and called the police. While he was talking on the phone, one of the robbers came into the store and asked directions to the interstate highway going toward Pensacola. [FN1] The bystander gave the police the license tag number. Sheriff deputies from Santa Rose County began to follow the suspects in the westbound lane of I-10. When the deputies turned on their blue light, the suspects fled at a high rate of speed. During the chase, the vehicles were going as fast as 100 to 110 m.p.h. The deputies chased the suspects into Escambia County. During the chase, the suspects swerved at least twice in an attempt to run two of the Santa Rosa County deputies off the road. A one-car roadblock was set up in Escambia County by Deputy Sheriff Don Cook. Deputy Matroni of the Santa Rosa County Sheriff's Office saw the roadblock and attempted to cut off the suspects' avenue of escape by driving into the median. Deputy Matroni's vehicle struck Deputy Cook, who had left his vehicle and walked onto the median. Deputy Cook was killed by the impact from Deputy Matroni's vehicle. The chase continued on the interstate, and ultimately ended when the robbers collided with a police vehicle. The driver, appellant's brother, stuck his left arm out and tossed an automatic pistol onto the roof the car. The appellant, who was the passenger, attempted to flee. He had a revolver in his right hand as he ran away. He turned and attempted to fire at a deputy sheriff. The deputy fired his weapon three times, hitting appellant. When apprehended, appellant was in possession of 30 rounds of ammunition as well as the revolver. The entire incident from robbery to apprehension took no more than an hour.

The appellant and his brother, Johnny Walter Park, were tried on one count of armed robbery, one count of kidnapping, two counts of aggravated assault, and one count of second degree felony murder as a result of the death of Deputy Don Cook. The underlying felony which supported the second degree murder and kidnapping charge was the robbery of Ralph Stewart. The trial court granted a motion in limine filed by the state which prohibited the defense from introducing evidence, commenting on or arguing the negligence, if any, of Officer Larry Matroni, and the contributory negligence of Deputy Don Cook in the manner in which he set up the roadblock. The counts of aggravated assault against the appellant were dismissed. The appellant was found guilty of all other charges.

I. Whether the trial court erred in denying
appellant's motion for judgment of acquittal
on the second degree felony murder charge.

The appellant argues that the robbery of Ralph Stewart was completed prior to the time of the death of Deputy Don Cook and, thus, the robbery could not be utilized to support his conviction for second degree felony murder. The second degree felony murder statute in pertinent part reads: "When a person is killed *in the perpetration* of . . . [any] robbery . . . by a person other than the person engaged in the perpetration of . . . such felony, the person perpetrating . . . such felony is guilty of murder in the second degree." Sec. 782.04(3), F.S. (1989) (emphasis added).

The term "in the perpetration of" includes the period of time when a robber is attempting to escape from the scene of the crime. ***Hornbeck v. State***, *77 So.2d 876 (Fla. 1955).* In determining when flight has terminated, it is useful to consider the purpose of the felony murder statute. That purpose is to protect the public from inherently dangerous situations caused by the commission of the felony. ***State v. Hacker***, *510 So.2d 304, 306 (Fla. 4th DCA 1986).* Therefore, "[i]n the absence of some definitive break in the chain of circumstances beginning with the felony and ending with the killing, the felony, although technically complete, is said to continue to the time of the killing," ***Mills v. State***, *407 So.2d 218, 221 (Fla. 3d DCA 1981).*

Factors to be considered in determining whether there has been a break in the chain of circumstances include the relationship between the underlying felony and the homicide in point of time, place and causal relationship. One commentator suggests that in the case of flight, a most important consideration is whether the fleeing felon has reached a "place of temporary safety." LaFave, *Substantive Criminal Law*, Sec. 7.5 (1986).

In the instant case, the application of these factors demonstrates that the robbery was not completed at the time of the death of Deputy Sheriff Cook. The time from the robbery to the killing was no longer than an hour, the killing occurred no more than several miles from the robbery, and the only stops that the robbers made were to get gas and ask directions - all to accomplish their goal of fleeing from the scene of the crime to a place of safety, their motel room.

Further, it is apparent that there is a clear causal relationship between the robbery and the death of Deputy Sheriff Cook. The death was a result of the high-speed chase necessitated by the robbers' attempt to flee the scene of the crime. This was sufficient evidence to support the conviction of second degree felony murder. ***State v. Hacker***, *supra.*

II. Whether the trial court erred in
excluding proffered evidence of police negligence
as an intervening cause of Deputy Cook's death.

The appellant asserts that the trial court erred in not permitting him to introduce evidence that the negligence of the police in conducting the chase and setting up the road block was an intervening cause which would constitute a break in circumstances and a defense to second degree felony murder.

The trial court is not required to admit evidence unless it is relevant to a legally recognizable defense. *Chestnut v. State, 538 So.2d 820 (Fla. 1989)*. The alleged negligence of the police did not constitute a legally recognizable defense to second degree felony murder.

Second degree felony murder contemplates that the death will result from the actions of a person who is not involved in the commission of the felony. *State v. Dene, 533 So.2d 265 (Fla. 1988)*. *Dene* says, "[A]ll principals . . . are culpable for any killings which are committed during the felony by innocent bystanders, police officers, victims, or other persons not committing the felony." *Id at 269*. If a defendant was permitted to rely on the negligent conduct of the victim and third parties as intervening acts, it would defeat the obvious purpose of the statute as expressed in *Dene*, which is to hold felons accountable for unintended deaths caused by their dangerous conduct.

Where there is a clear causal relationship between the felony and the death or the inherently dangerous circumstances created by the felony, negligent acts of innocent parties will not act as a defense to second degree felony murder. The nexus between the robbery and death in the instant case is clear: the robbery created the circumstance which led to the high-speed chase which caused Deputy Cook's death.

*****

We affirm as to all issues.

WENTWORTH and MINER, JJ., concur.

FN1. Evidence later revealed the robbers were from South Carolina and were staying in a motel in Pensacola.

(FN2. and FN3 omitted)

251

REVIEW

1. To be convicted of second degree felony murder, _____.
    a. the defendant is not the one who kills the victim
    b. the one who kills is the victim of the felony
    c. the one who kills is a law enforcement officer
    d. all of the above

2. The term in the perpetration of the felony _____.
    a. includes the felony
    b. includes the period of time the defendant is escaping from the scene of the crime
    c. does not include a break in the chain of circumstances
    d. all of the above

CASE

Duckett v. State, 686 So.2d 662 (Fla. 2d DCA 1996).

Driver was convicted in the Circuit Court, Hillsborough County, Barbara Fleisher, J., of second-degree murder, and driving under the influence of alcohol (DUI) with serious bodily injury, personal injury, and property damage. Driver appealed. The District Court of Appeal, Parker, J., held that: (1) driver committed manslaughter, not second-degree murder, and (2) multiple convictions and sentences for DUI did not violate double jeopardy clause.

Reversed in part and affirmed in part.

PARKER, Judge.

Thomas Pearson Duckett, Jr., appeals his convictions and sentences for five counts of second-degree murder and his sentences for driving while under influence (DUI) with serious bodily injury, personal injury, and property damage. We conclude that the five convictions for second-degree murder must be reduced to convictions for manslaughter and Duckett must be resentenced for these five crimes. Otherwise, we affirm.

The offenses for which Duckett was convicted arose from an accident which Duckett caused. On the night of the accident Duckett was highly intoxicated. He had been speeding and weaving in and out of traffic for several miles and almost caused two other accidents. At one point Duckett had stopped on the side of the road and leaned against his vehicle. He then got back in his vehicle and continued his reckless driving. He eventually ran off the interstate into the grass and hit a tow truck and then a disabled church bus, both of which were clearly visible to other drivers. Duckett killed five people who were standing near the bus and injured several others. The state charged Duckett with five counts of second-degree murder, five counts of manslaughter, five counts of DUI manslaughter, two counts of DUI with serious bodily injury, eight counts of DUI with property damage or injury, driving with a suspended driver's license, unauthorized possession of a driver's license, and possession of marijuana.

The elements for second-degree murder set out in the Florida Standard Jury Instructions in Criminal Cases, are as follows:

> 1. (Victim) is dead.
> 2. The death was caused by the criminal act or agency of (defendant).
> 3. There was an unlawful killing of (victim) by an act imminently dangerous to another and evincing a depraved mind regardless of human life.

Fla.Std. Jury Inst. (Crim.) 66. The standard jury instructions define the term "imminently dangerous to another and evincing a depraved mind regardless of human life" as follows:

> An act is one "imminently dangerous to another and evincing a depraved mind regardless of human life" if it is an act or series of acts that:
>
> 1. a person of ordinary judgment would know is reasonably certain to kill or do serious bodily injury to another, and
> 2. is done from ill will, hatred, spite or an evil intent, and
> 3. is of such a nature that the act itself indicates an indifference to human life.

Fla.Std. Jury Instr. (Crim.) 66.

The facts in this case do not constitute second-degree murder because there was no evidence offered at trial to support the fact that Duckett's act was done from ill will, hatred, spite, or an evil intent toward the victims. We recognize this court's decision in *Manis v. State, 528 So.2d 1342 (Fla. 2d DCA), review denied, 534 So.2d 400 (Fla. 1988)*, holding that a driver impaired by alcohol causing death to another may be convicted of second-degree murder. The *Manis* court did not address the facts it found sufficient to prove the act which killed the victim was imminently dangerous to another evincing a depraved mind regardless of human life. Instead, this court focused on the facts it found supported a departure sentence. We agree with *Manis* that, under some circumstances, a person may be convicted of second-degree murder for vehicular homicide. In the instant case, however, the state failed to prove all of the elements of second-degree murder.

This case is similar to *Ellison v. State, 547 So.2d 1003 (Fla. 1ˢᵗ DCA 1989), approved in part, quashed in part, 561 So.2d 576 (Fla. 1990)*. Ellison was involved in a high speed police chase. He was weaving in and out of traffic until his vehicle jumped the median and he lost control of the car and struck another vehicle head on, killing a baby who was a passenger in that vehicle. The First District Court concluded that these facts did not support a second-degree murder conviction and reduced the conviction to manslaughter. The supreme court approved of the First District Court's conclusion that the facts did not support a finding that Ellison acted out of ill will, hatred, spite, or an evil intent toward his victim. See *State v. Ellison, 561 So.2d 576, 577 (Fla. 1990)*.

Pursuant to section 924.34, Florida Statutes (1991), we reverse Duckett's judgments on the five counts of second-degree murder (Counts 1, 4, 7, 10, and 13), and direct the trial court to enter judgments on these five counts for manslaughter, a second-degree felony, which is an offense necessarily included in the offense of second-degree murder. See *Gould v. State, 577 So.2d 1302 (Fla. 1991); Ellison*.

Duckett also challenges his multiple convictions and sentences for two counts of DUI with serious bodily injury (Counts 16 and 18), for the six counts of DUI with personal injury (Counts 17 and 19 through 23), and for the two counts of DUI with property damage (Counts 24 and 25). Duckett alleges that the trial court's imposition of multiple convictions and sentences for a single offense violates double jeopardy principles. The supreme court has decided the issue contrary to Duckett's position and held that multiple convictions for driving under the influence with serious bodily injury are permissible for injuries to multiple victims arising from a single driving episode. See *Melbourne v. State, 679 So.2d 759 (Fla. 1996)*. We affirm pursuant to *Melbourne*.

We reverse the convictions and sentences for the five counts of second-degree murder and direct the trial court to enter judgments of manslaughter and to impose sentences for these crimes. Otherwise, we affirm the judgments and sentences.

Reversed in part; affirmed in part.

THREADGILL, C.J., and PATTERSON, J., concur.

REVIEW

1. To be convicted of second degree murder, the act must be done from _____.
   a. ill will
   b. hatred
   c. spite
   d. all of the above are correct

MURDER IN THE THIRD DEGREE

One can only be convicted of third degree murder by a theory of felony murder. Again, the victim must be dead. The death must occur as a consequence of and while the defendant is committing, attempting to commit, or escaping from a felony other than the felonies which apply to first degree felony murder. The victim may be killed by the defendant or another principal in the commission of the felony. The state need not prove the killing was perpetrated with a design to effect death.

MANSLAUGHTER

To be convicted of manslaughter, the victim must be dead. Is this starting to sound familiar? Additionally, the state must prove one of three things. The defendant must either have intentionally caused the death of the victim, intentionally procured the death of the victim or the death of the victim must be caused by the culpable negligence of the defendant.

To procure is to persuade, induce, prevail upon, or cause a person to do something.

Culpable negligence is more than a failure to use ordinary care. It is gross and flagrant. It shows reckless disregard of human life or the safety of persons exposed to its dangerous effects. Culpable negligence is an entire want of care. The act must be committed with an utter disregard for the safety of others. The defendant knows or reasonably should know his or her actions are likely to cause death or great bodily injury.

CASE

State v. Ashley, 701 So.2d 338 (Fla. 1997).

State charged woman with manslaughter and third-degree felony murder, with underlying felony of criminal abortion, after mother shot herself in abdomen during third trimester of pregnancy, causing death of fetus born alive. The Circuit Court, Pinellas County, Brandt C. Downey, III, J., granted mother's motion to dismiss felony murder charge, but denied motion to dismiss manslaughter charge. The District Court of Appeal, 670 So.2d 1087, affirmed and certified questions. The Supreme Court held that common law immunity of pregnant woman for causing injury or death to fetus was not abrogated by felony murder, manslaughter, and termination of pregnancy issues.

Quashed in part; certified question answered.

Harding, J., specially concurred and filed an opinion in which Overton, J., concurred.

Anstead, J., concurred in the result only.

PER CURIAM.

We have for review *State v. Ashley*, 670 So.2d 1087 (Fla. App. 2d DCA 1996), wherein the district court certified the following questions:

> 1. May an expectant mother be criminally charged with the death of her born alive child resulting from self-inflicted injuries during the third trimester of pregnancy?

2.   If so, may she be charged with manslaughter or third-degree murder, the underlying predicate felony being abortion or attempted abortion?

Ashley, 670 So.2d at 1093. We have jurisdiction. Art. V, §3(b)(4), Fla. Const. We answer the first question in the negative as explained below, and this renders the second question moot. We quash *Ashley* in part.

Although Kawana Ashley, an unwed teenager, was in the third trimester of pregnancy (she was twenty-five or twenty-six weeks pregnant), she had told no one. Her three year old son was being raised by her grandmother, Rosa, with whom Ashley lived and Rosa had told Ashley that she would not care for another child if Ashley were to become pregnant again. On March 27, 1994, Ashley obtained a gun and shot herself. She was rushed to the hospital, underwent surgery, and survived. The fetus, which had been struck on the wrist by the bullet, was removed during surgery and died fifteen days later due to immaturity. [FN1]

As a result of the death of the fetus, the State Attorney charged the teenager with alternative counts of murder [FN2] and manslaughter, [FN3] with the underlying felony for the murder charge being criminal abortion. The trial court dismissed the murder charge but allowed the manslaughter charge to stand. The State appealed and Ashley cross-appealed. The district court affirmed, certifying the above questions.

The State argues that Ashley was properly charged with both murder and manslaughter, reasoning thusly: Ashley violated the criminal abortion statute, section 390.001, Florida Statutes (1993), by performing a third-trimester abortion on herself with a .22 caliber firearm without certification of necessity by two physicians; because the fetus died as a result of the uncertified procedure, the teenager committed third-degree murder under section 782.04, Florida Statutes (1993); and further, because the fetus was born alive, Ashley committed manslaughter under section 782.07, Florida Statutes (1993). We disagree.

At common law, while a third party could be held criminally liable for causing injury or death to a fetus, the pregnant woman could not be:

> At common law an operation on the body of a woman quick with child, with intent thereby to cause her miscarriage, was an indictable offense, but it was not an offense in her to so treat her own body, or to assent to such treatment from another; and the aid she might give to the offender in the physical performance of the operation did not make her an accomplice in this crime. The practical assistance she might thus give to the perpetration of his crime. It was in truth a crime which, in the nature of things, she could not commit.

State v. Carey, 76 Conn. 342, 56 A. 632, 636 (1904). Courts differentiated between those actions taken upon oneself and those taken by a third party.

> Ordinarily, a man may injure his own body by his own hand or the hand of an agent, without himself violating the criminal law. And the person who injures his body with

such assent may commit a crime of which the injured party is not guilty. A murderer cannot justify himself by proving the assent of his victim. Noninterference with a man's control of his person is not extended to the disposition of his life; but taking his own life is a thing distinct from the crime of murder. If a man in a moment of weakness should assent to the opening of a vein by another for the purpose of taking his life, and, when in the immediate expectation of death, make a statement of the facts attending the assault, it would hardly be claimed, upon trial of his assailant for felonious killing, that the dying declaration must be received with all the infirmities attending the testimony of an accomplice in the crime. The distinction between a man's injuring his own body himself, or through assent to such injury from another, and the crime that may be committed by another in inflicting such injury, has been strongly drawn in crimes akin to the one under discussion.

Carey, 56 A. at 635-36.

Ultimately, immunity from prosecution for the pregnant woman was grounded in the "wisdom of experience":

> While it may seem illogical to hold that a pregnant woman who solicits the commission of an abortion and willingly submits to its commission upon her own person is not an accomplice in the commission of the crime, yet many courts in the United States have adopted this rule, asserting that public policy demands its application and that its exception from the general rule is justified by the wisdom of experience.

Basoff v. State, 208 Md. 643, 119 A.2d 917, 923 (1956). The woman was viewed as the victim of the crime. See *Richmond v. Commonwealth, 370 S.W.2d 399, 400 (Ky. 1963)* ("[S]he is a victim rather than an offender."). [FN5] The criminal laws were intended to protect, not punish her. See *Gaines v. Wolcott, 119 Ga.App. 313, 167 S.E.2d 366, 370 (1969)* (noting that the criminal laws were designed for "the protection of . . . pregnant females"). [FN6]

The common law that was in effect on July 4, 1776, continues to be the law of Florida to the extent that it is consistent with the constitutions and statutory laws of the United States and Florida:

> 2.01 Common law and certain statutes declared in force. – The common and statute laws of England which are of a general and not a local nature, with the exception hereinafter mentioned, down to the 4th day of July, 1776, are declared to be of force in this state; provided, the said statutes and common law be not inconsistent with the Constitution and laws of the United States and the acts of the Legislature of this state.

§ 2.01, Fla. Stat. (1993). Even where the legislature acts in a particular area, the common law remains in effect in that area unless the statute specifically says otherwise:

The presumption is that no change in the common law is intended unless the statute is explicit and clear in that regard. *Unless a statute unequivocally states that it changes the common law, or is so repugnant to the common law and the two cannot coexist, the statute will not be held to have changed the common law.*

Thornber v. City of Fort Walton Beach, 568 So.2d 914, 918 (Fla. 1990) (emphasis added) (citations omitted).

In the present case, none of the statutes under which Ashley was charged "unequivocally" state that they alter the common law doctrine conferring immunity on the pregnant woman. See §§ 390.001, 782.04, 782.07, Fla. Stat. (1993). In fact, none even hint at such a change. Id. Nor are any of the statutes so repugnant to the common law that the two cannot coexist. [FN7] Accordingly, we conclude that the legislature did not abrogate the common law doctrine of immunity for the pregnant woman.

The State's reading of the present statutes has other flaws. First, the concept of a self-induced abortion via .22 caliber bullet is dubious in itself and is highly questionable as a procedure intended to be regulated by section 390.001. [FN8] Second, prosecution for third-degree murder based on the unenumerated felony of criminal abortion is an oxymoron - i.e., the third-degree murder statute requires an *accidental* killing, [FN9] while the criminal abortion statute requires an *intentional* termination of pregnancy. [FN10] [FN11] Under the State Attorney's scenario, a woman could be charged with, and face imprisonment for, an "accidental intentional" crime - whatever that phrase might mean. And third, to allow prosecution for manslaughter would require that this Court extend the "born alive" doctrine [FN12] in a manner that has been rejected by every other court to consider it. [FN13]

Based on the foregoing, we answer the first certified question in the negative as explained herein, and this renders the second question moot. Under the current statutory scheme, the State Attorney for Pinellas County cannot prosecute the teenager in the present case, Kawana Ashley, for either murder or manslaughter. Sections 782.04 and 782.07 contain no indication whatsoever that the legislature intended to modify the common law principles adopted in section 2.01 by eliminating the immunity of the pregnant woman.

We reached a similar result in *Johnson v. State, 602 So.2d 1288 (Fla.1992)*, wherein we held that a pregnant woman cannot be held criminally liable for passing cocaine *in utero* to her fetus. The relevant statutory section, we concluded, contained no indication of legislative intent to prosecute the woman. [FN14] Medical science prescribes rehabilitation, not imprisonment, for the offender:

> [Various] considerations have led the American Medical Association Board of Trustees to oppose criminal sanctions for harmful behavior by a pregnant woman toward her fetus and to advocate that pregnant [offenders] be provided with rehabilitative treatment appropriate to their specific psychological and physiological needs.

258

Id. at 1296. This prescription for rehabilitation applies to not just the mature woman, but the wayward teenager as well.

Under Florida's constitutional form of government, no branch of state government can arrogate to itself powers that properly inhere in a separate branch. [FN15] Accordingly, we must decline the State Attorney's invitation to join in this fray. This Court cannot abrogate willy-nilly a centuries-old principle of the common law - which is grounded in the wisdom of experience and has been adopted by the legislature – and install in its place a contrary rule bristling with red flags and followed by no other court in the nation. As we have said time and again, the making of social policy is a matter within the purview of the legislature - not this Court:

> [O]f the three branches of government, the judiciary is the least capable of receiving public input and resolving broad public policy questions based on a societal consensus.

Shands Teaching Hospital & Clinics, Inc. v. Smith, 497 So.2d 644, 646 (Fla. 1986). Our review of the present record reveals no novel legislative intent to trump the common law and pit woman against fetus in criminal court.

We quash *Ashley* in part as explained herein.

It is so ordered.

OVERTON, SHAW, GRIMES and WELLS, JJ., concur.

HARDING, J., specially concurs with an opinion in which OVERTON, J., concurs.

ANSTEAD, J., concurs in result only.

HARDING, Justice, specially concurring.

I concur with the majority opinion and write only to emphasize a point made in Ashley's brief. In her brief, Ashley acknowledges that the legislature could criminalize her conduct, but it has not done so. As the majority opinion points out, in order to overturn a long standing common law principle, the legislature must enact a statute which would clearly overturn the common law either by specific language or by language so repugnant to the common law that both principles could not consistently stand. Majority op. at 341. The majority further notes that the states which have altered the common law to criminalize conduct like Ashley's "have done so explicitly." *Id. at 341 n. 7.* Florida has not done so.

I believe that the circumstances of this case are tragic. However, I believe that it would be more tragic if this Court were so offended by Ashley's actions that we interpreted the statute in such a way as to abrogate the common law doctrine conferring immunity on the pregnant woman when the legislature has not acted to specifically change the common law.

In my judgment, such action by this Court would result in two wrongs. First, to interpret the statutes in order to criminalize Ashley's conduct would violate the constitutional guarantee against ex post facto laws. See U.S. Cons., art. I, § 9; art. I, § 10, Fla. Const. Second, it is properly the function of the legislature, and not the court to alter the common law in this respect.

The constitutional prohibition against ex post facto laws ensures that no person is prosecuted for conduct that occurred before a law prohibiting such conduct was enacted. This prohibition was incorporated in the United States Constitution as a remedy to one of the many abuses that American colonists had endured under the tyrannical English government. This prohibition satisfies a basic tenet of American due process: one must be given adequate notice as to the specific conduct prohibited by the law. This principle has endured for over two hundred years, and it is the continued adherence to such principles of law that has safeguarded our individual freedoms. In the instant case, the common law has conferred immunity on the pregnant woman from prosecution and Florida's statutory law has not *explicitly* changed that immunity. If a Florida statute had specifically proscribed Ashley's conduct before she acted, then due process would be satisfied. However, under the circumstances presented here, if we permit her prosecution for conduct that has historically been afforded immunity both due process and the prohibition on ex post facto laws would be violated.

As suggested in the briefs, criminalizing such actions by a pregnant woman raises a number of policy, social, moral, and legal implications. However, under our form of government, the appropriate place for those issues to be resolved is in the legislature. Accordingly, I concur with the majority opinion and defer to the legislature for consideration of this issue.

OVERTON, J., concurs.

FN1. Ashley gave conflicting reasons for her actions. She initially told officers that she had been the victim of a drive-by shooting, but later said she had shot herself "in order to hurt the baby." She told another officer, however, that she had not tried to kill the baby and wanted the baby, and told a friend that the gun had discharged accidently.

FN2. Ashley was charged under section 782.04, Florida Statutes (1993), which proscribes murder in the third degree and states in relevant part:

(4) The unlawful killing of a human being, when perpetrated without any design to effect death, by a person engaged in the perpetration of, or in the attempt to perpetrate, any felony other than any:

    (a) Trafficking...
    (b) Arson,
    (c) Sexual battery,
    (d) Robbery,
    (e) Burglary,

(f) Kidnapping,

(g) Escape,

h) Aggravated child abuse,

(i) Aircraft piracy, ...

is murder in the third degree and constitutes a felony of the second degree...

§ 782.04, Fla. Stat. (1993).

FN3. Ashley was charged under section 782.07, Florida Statutes (1993), which proscribes manslaughter and provides in relevant part:

782.07 Manslaughter. – The killing of a human being by the act, procurement, or culpable negligence of another, without lawful justification according to the provisions of chapter 776 and in cases in which such killing shall not be excusable homicide or murder, according to the provisions of this chapter, shall be deemed manslaughter and shall constitute a felony of the second degree . . .

§ 782.07, Fla. Stat. (1993).

FN4. Section 390.001, Florida Statutes (1993), governs the termination of pregnancy and provides in relevant part:

2.   TERMINATION IN LAST TRIMESTER; WHEN ALLOWED. – No termination of pregnancy shall be performed on any human being in the last trimester of pregnancy unless;

(a)   Two physicians certify in writing to the fact that, to a reasonable degree of medical probability, the termination of pregnancy is necessary to save the life or preserve the health of the pregnant woman; or

(b)   The physician certifies in writing to the medical necessity for legitimate emergency medical procedures for termination of pregnancy in the last trimester, and another physician is not available for consultation.

3.   PERFORMANCE BY PHYSICIAN REQUIRED. – No termination of pregnancy shall be performed at any time except by a physician as defined in this section....

****

(10)   PENALTIES FOR VIOLATION. –

(a)   Any person who willfully performs, or participates in, a termination of a pregnancy in violation of the requirements of this section is guilty of a felony of the third degree...

(b)   Any person who performs, or participates in, a termination of a pregnancy in violation of the provisions of this section which results in the death of the woman is guilty of a felony of the second degree ...

§ 390.001, Fla. Stat. (1993).

FN5. See also ***State v. Burlingame,*** *47 S.D. 332, 198 N.W. 824, 826 (1924)* ("She should be regarded as the victim of the crime, rather than a participant in it."); ***Meno v. State,*** *117 Md. 435, 83 A. 759, 760 (1912)* ("A woman on whom an abortion has been performed is regarded as a victim rather than an accomplice ..."); ***Peoples v. Commonwealth,*** *87 Ky. 487, 9 S.W. 509, 510 (1888),* ("She is looked upon rather as the victim than as a co-offender.").

FN6. The perilous conditions prompting the laws are well known. See ***Heath v. State,*** *249 Ark. 217, 459 S.W.2d 420, 421 (1970)* (noting that the practitioner used "a crochet needle and a catheter"); ***Commonwealth v. Hersey,*** *324 Mass. 196, 85 N.E. 2d 447, 450 (1949)* (noting that the practitioner used "a tampon with a medication which had a dark color and a foul odor").

FN7. Other states that have attempted to alter the common law in its regard have done so explicitly. Compare ***Cahill v. State,*** *84 Okla.Crim. 1, 178 P.2d 657, 658 (1947)* (quoting a pre-***Roe v. Wade,*** *410 U.S. 113, 93 S.Ct. 705, 35 L.Ed.2d 147 (1973),* Oklahoma statute: "Every woman who solicits of any person any medicine, drug, or substance whatever, and takes the same, or who submits to any operation, or to the use of any means whatever, with intent thereby to procure a miscarriage, unless the same is necessary to preserve her life, is punishable by imprisonment..."), with ***Guam Society of Obstetricians & Gynecologists v. Ada,*** *776 F.Supp. 1422, 1424 (D. Guam 1990)* (quoting a post-***Roe*** statute: "Every woman who solicits of any and takes the same, or who submits to any operation, or to the use of any means whatever with intent thereby to cause an abortion ... is guilty [of criminal abortion].").

FN8. See generally § 390.001, Fla. Stat. (1993).

FN9. See § 782.04, Fla. Stat. (1993) (proscribing "[t]he unlawful killing of a human being, when prepared without any design to effect death.").

FN10. See § 390.001 (10)(1), Fla. Stat. (1993) (providing punishment for "[a]ny person who willfully performs, or participates in, a termination of a pregnancy").

FN11. *Cf.* ***Hieke v. State,*** *605 So.2d 983, 983 (Fla. 4ᵗʰ DCA 1992)* ("In other words, under third degree, the death is *accidental* and while one can solicit the commission of a felony or solicit to kill anyone, there cannot be a solicitation to kill someone without any design to effect death because one cannot solicit an unintentional death. That is an oxymoron.").

FN12. Under the "born alive" doctrine, a fetus that suffers a prenatal injury at the hands of a third party and is born alive is capable of supporting certain civil or criminal charges against the third party. See ***Knighton v. State, 603 So.2d 71 (Fla. 4th DCA 1992)*** (applying the born alive rule to sustain a third-degree murder conviction against a defendant who shot a pregnant woman is the abdomen and the bullet lodged in head of the fetus which later died); ***Day v. Nationwide Mut. Ins. Co.,*** *328 So.2d 560 (Fla. 2d DCA 1976)* (applying the born alive rule to sustain a tort claim against a third party tortfeasor in an automobile accident wherein the fetus sustained cerebral injury.).

FN13. Ashley states in her brief: "Every court to address the issue has rejected the use of the born alive doctrine to hold a pregnant woman criminally liable for her prenatal conduct whether the woman is charged under homicide statutes or other criminal statutes." Ashley cites thirty-six cases in twenty-one states to support her point. The State Attorney, on the other hand, makes no substantive argument in opposition and cites no case in counterpoint.

FN14. See § 893.13 (1)(c)1, Fla. Stat. (1989).

FN15. See art II, § 3, Fla. Const. ("No [entity] belonging to one branch [of government] shall exercise any powers appertaining to either of the other branches unless expressly provided herein.").

REVIEW

1. Common law _____.
    a. always applies in Florida
    b. never applies in Florida
    c. applies unless a statute says otherwise
    d. none of the above

CASE

W.L.H. v. State, *702 So.2d 1347 (Fla. 5th DCA 1997).*

Juvenile appealed from order of the Circuit Court, Marion County, T. Michael Johnson, J., adjudicating him a delinquent based on determination that he had committed crime of manslaughter. The District Court of Appeal, Cobb, J., held that juvenile's act of intentionally pointing automatic pistol at victim and pulling trigger, resulting in victim's death, was manslaughter.

Affirmed.

COBB, Judge.

The issue in this case is whether the act of intentionally pointing an automatic pistol at another person and pulling the trigger, resulting in the victim's death, constitutes the crime of manslaughter, even though the perpetrator believed the pistol to be unloaded and did not intend to inflict physical harm. We believe the answer is *yes* based upon precedent from this and other courts. See ***Berry v. State,*** *547 So.2d 969 (Fla. 3d DCA 1989);* ***Dellinger v. State,*** *495 So.2d 197 (Fla. 5th DCA 1986);* ***Navarro v. State,*** *433 So.2d 1011 (Fla. 3d DCA 1983), rev. denied, 447 So.2d 887 (Fla. 1984);* ***Marasa v. State,*** *394 So.2d 544 (Fla. 5th DCA), rev. denied, 402 So.2d 613 (Fla. 1981).*

On August 19, 1996, the appellant, W.L.H., III, a 12-year old, was playing with two cousins and a friend. W.L.H. obtained a .380 semi-automatic pistol and a clip from his parents' bedroom. He previously had played with, and fired, the pistol without his parents' knowledge. He put the clip in the pistol, pulled the slide back, and then removed the clip. He pointed it at the other children, causing them to flee the room. W.L.H. called to them that he had taken the clip out of the pistol. When his 12-year old cousin, Kimberly, came out of a closet, where she had been hiding, he pointed the pistol in her direction, pulled the trigger, and the bullet struck her between the eyes. Later, W.L.H. told investigating officers that he did not know the pistol would fire after the clip was removed, and expressed remorse.

We agree with the state that the established facts show that W.L.H. acted with gross disregard for his cousin's safety and is criminally responsible for his deliberate actions. Indeed, there is authority for a finding, under the instant facts, of second degree murder had W.L.H. been an adult. See ***Dellinger,*** *supra.* We affirm the trial court's adjudication of delinquency.

AFFIRMED.

W. SHARP and ANTOON, JJ., concur.

REVIEW

1. To be convicted of manslaughter, one must _____.
   a. believe the gun to be loaded
   b. intend to commit harm
   c. both a and b
   d. neither a nor b

THINKING CRITICALLY

1.   Give an example of an underlying felony that would lead to a third degree murder conviction.

2.   Ben is seen leaving a store hurriedly carrying a paper bag. The clerk is found inside with a gunshot wound to her head. The police are unable to determine if anything is missing from the store. There are signs of a struggle. Several days later, Ben is arrested for an unrelated shooting. A gun is found on him at the time. The bullet recovered from the clerk's body was fired from that gun. What should Ben be charged with? Is this a premeditated killing?

3.   Jim and Bob decide to commit an armed robbery at the 7-11. They are both carrying 9 millimeter semiautomatic weapons. There is a silent alarm button which the clerk hits to summon the police. When the police arrive, there is a shootout. Officer Jones attempts to shoot Bob, who is attempting to shoot the clerk. The bullet ricochets and the clerk dies instead. Can Jim and Bob be charged with murder? Under what theory? What degree of homicide do you think they should be charged with? What if Bob had been shot and died? Could Jim be charged with murder? What degree?

4.   Mike is a drug dealer selling heroin out of his apartment. Mike sells to Kevin and Joe. Kevin and Joe leave Mike's apartment with the heroin and return to their car where they both shoot up. Joe dies of an overdose. Can Mike be charged with a homicide? Under what theory? What degree of homicide would apply to these facts? Can Kevin be charged with a crime?

5.   George and Debbie decide to burglarize a house. They've been watching the neighborhood and have picked the home of an elderly woman. The woman appears to live alone and goes out most mornings for several hours. Debbie goes to the front door and rings the doorbell to confirm the woman is in fact out of the house. George goes around the back to break in. If the woman should return, Debbie is to alert George. Unbeknownst to George and Debbie, the woman is home. She is in a back bedroom and does not hear the doorbell. She does hear George breaking in. She immediately picks up the phone and dials 911. She has a heart condition and the stress and fear cause her to have a heart attack and die. Are George and Debbie guilty of homicide? If so, what degree of murder?

6.   Mary is last seen screaming for help being dragged into the woods by Arthur. It is out of character for her to not come home. Nothing is missing from her apartment. If her body is never found, can Arthur be charged with her murder?

7.   Do you agree with the court's holding in ***Rodriguez***? Why or why not? What if Ballester testified that they had discussed the possibility of someone getting killed?

8.   Do you agree with the court's holding in ***Ashley***? Why or why not? Did Ashley intend to kill her child? Was she attempting to perform an abortion?

9.   Was the ***Parker*** case decided fairly based on the facts? Can you think of a scenario where a second degree felony murder conviction would be unjust?

10.   What crime would you have convicted Duckett of committing? Why?

11. Do you agree with the court's holding in **W.L.H.**? What if the defendant thought the pistol was loaded?

12. A homicide victim dies from a single stab wound. Can the defendant be charged with first-degree premeditated murder? Why or why not? What additional information do you need?

CHAPTER 9 ANSWER KEY

REVIEW QUESTIONS

Kirkland v. State, *684 So.2d 732 (Fla. 1996)*
1. a
2. d
3. d

Rodriguez v. State, *571 So.2d 1356 (Fla. 2d DCA 1990)*
1. c

Parker v. State, *570 So.2d 1048 (Fla. 1ˢᵗ DCA 1990).*
1. d
2. d

Duckett v. State, *686 So.2d 662 (Fla. 2d DCA 1996)*
1. d

State v. Ashley, *701 So.2d 338 (Fla. 1997)*
1. c

W.L.H. v. State, *702 So.2d 1347 (Fla. 5ᵗʰ DCA 1997)*
1. d

CHAPTER 10

CRIMES AGAINST PERSONS II:
CRIMINAL SEXUAL CONDUCT
AND OTHERS

SEXUAL BATTERY

Florida law provides for the prosecution of many different sex offenses, the most serious being capital sexual battery and the least serious being misdemeanors. Many different factors are taken into account in the charging of sex offenses. For example, the age of the defendant, the age of the victim, the amount of force used, whether there is penetration or just union, whether there is injury, the relationship of the parties, whether a weapon is used, the mental status of the victim, and the physical state of the victim are all issues addressed by different statutes. An act done for bona fide medical purposes is not a sexual battery.

A capital sexual battery is one where the defendant is over the age of 18 and the victim is less than 12 years of age. The state need not prove penetration; union is sufficient to sustain a conviction for capital sexual battery. Moreover, proof of penetration of the victim by an object is enough to prove the case. Whether an injury exists is not a factor to be considered, and consent is not a defense to the crime of capital sexual battery.

The penalty for sexual battery on a person 12 years of age or older is greater if the defendant uses a deadly weapon or great force. Penetration or union is sufficient to prove the charge; however, unlike capital sexual battery, consent is a defense. Nonetheless, coerced submission is not consent. A mentally incapacitated person cannot consent under the law. Incapacitation may result from use of a narcotic, anesthetic; or intoxicating substance administered without consent or due to an act committed without that person's consent. Furthermore, a mentally defective person may be unable to consent. A mental disease or defect may render a person temporarily or permanently incapable of appreciating the nature of his or her conduct.

Some sexual batteries are committed under what are known as specified circumstances. Specified circumstances may include instances where a victim may be physically helpless to resist. For instance, the defendant may have coerced the victim to submit by threatening the use of force or retaliation against someone. Additionally, the defendant may have administered a drug to the victim, or the victim may be mentally defective or physically incapacitated.

The law makes a distinction between "physically helpless" and "physically incapacitated." The term "physically helpless" means unconscious, asleep, or physically unable to communicate unwillingness to act. "Physically incapacitated" means bodily impaired or handicapped and substantially limited in his or her ability to resist or flee.

In cases where the defendant is in familial or custodial authority over the victim, the relationship in and of itself increases the punishment the court may impose.

In addition to sexual batteries, lewd and lascivious assaults or acts, exposure of sexual organs, and incest are all sex offenses under Florida law.

CASE

Bullington v. State, 616 So.2d 1036 (Fla. 3d DCA 1993).

Defendant was convicted of sexual battery on person physically helpless to resist, of conspiracy to commit anal sexual battery, and of conspiracy to commit oral sexual battery by the Circuit Court, Monroe County, Richard Fowler, J., and he appealed. The District Court of Appeal, Ferguson, J., held that state failed to establish, beyond reasonable doubt, that alleged victim did not consent to sex acts.

Affirmed in part and reversed in part.

Gersten, J., dissented.

Before HUBBART, FERGUSON and GERSTEN, JJ.

FERGUSON, Judge.

Harry Bullington appeals his convictions for the following offenses: count I: sexual battery upon a person twelve years of age or older while helpless to resist; count II: conspiracy to commit anal sexual battery; and count III: conspiracy to commit oral sexual battery on S.E.M. He contends that insufficient evidence was presented to support the convictions and that the fifty-year departure sentence imposed by the judge was illegal. We reverse.

S.E.M. was a fifteen-year-old runaway when she met Steve Lackey, the defendant's stepson. S.E.M. had been smoking crack cocaine before she first met Lackey at an entertainment center in Tampa, Florida. She went home with Lackey, drank beer, smoked marijuana, and had sexual intercourse. Days later, she met the defendant and accepted his invitation to accompany him, Lackey, and several other men and women to Key West. S.E.M. led everyone to believe she was nineteen. Upon arrival in Key West, S.E.M. asked Lackey to buy restraints for use during sexual intercourse, explaining that she liked to be tied down as it was the only way she could "get off." It is undisputed that S.E.M. then engaged in sex with Lackey on several occasions where she was restrained and that S.E.M. also engaged in consensual group sex with another couple where restraints were used on S.E.M.

On the day of the incident for which Bullington was convicted, S.E.M. and the others in Bullington's party consumed a large quantity of cocaine. S.E.M. told one of the women at the party that she wanted to try sex with another woman. The women removed their clothes, restraints were put on S.E.M.'s hands, and what can be described as an orgy ensued. At no time did S.E.M. indicate that she did not want to participate. The next morning, the defendant learned that S.E.M. was only fifteen. Over S.E.M.'s protest, Bullington ordered S.E.M. to leave and had Lackey deliver her money to buy a plane ticket to Orlando.

Count I charged Defendant with committing sexual battery upon a person 12 years of age or older, without that person's consent, while the victim was physically helpless to resist, in violation of section 794.011(4)(a), Florida Statutes (1989). We agree with the appellant that the evidence presented was insufficient to support a conviction under that section because the State failed to prove lack of consent.

Consent may be actual or implied. *Ralston v. State, 350 So.2d 791 (Fla. 3d DCA 1977), cert. denied, 364 So.2d 890 (Fla.1978).* The evidence in this case was generally uncontroverted that S.E.M. initially agreed to participate in a group sex act, and that if she ever withdrew her consent to participate in specific sexual acts, she never communicated a withdrawal of that consent. At trial, Lackey, a State witness who was not involved in the sexual episode but was a witness to it, testified that everything was done with S.E.M.'s consent. Another State witness, Teresa Smith, concurred that S.E.M. did not object to what was going on. S.E.M. admitted that Harry Bullington never forced her to do anything, and none of the evidence presented suggested that she was an unwilling participant.

Under the statute specified in the information, the State was required to prove that S.E.M. was "physically helpless to resist." Section 794.011(4)(3) defines a "physically helpless" person as one who is "unconscious, asleep, or for any other reason physically unable to communicate unwillingness to an act." Aside from the fact that S.E.M.'s hands were tied for sex acts by agreement, she was able to communicate orally and had full use of her legs. She was, therefore, free to articulate an objection or to use her legs to indicate any lack of desire to continue the sexual acts. The restraints on her hands did not render her physically helpless to resist. See *Davis v. State, 538 So.2d 515 (Fla. 2d DCA)* (crime of sexual battery of physically helpless victim requires proof that victim is physically unable to communicate unwillingness to act), *rev. denied, 544 So.2d 201 (Fla.1989).*

The State argues that the statutory requirement for physically helpless was satisfied with S.E.M.'s testimony at trial that she "passed out" for a period of time during the sexual episode. She was, however, unable to remember how long she was unconscious during the extended sexual encounter. Nor did the State present evidence that anyone violated S.E.M., as charged in the information, during a period of unconsciousness. On the facts of this case, which showed that S.E.M. was initially a willing participant in the carnal revelry, her testimony that she subsequently passed out for an indeterminate period is an insufficient basis to support a finding that the victim was physically helpless to resist. See *Norman v. State, 555 So.2d 1316 (Fla. 5ᵗʰ DCA 1990)* (where victim was able to communicate unwillingness prior to and during sexual battery, she was not physically helpless to resist).

In response to the State's argument that S.E.M. was rendered physically helpless by a voluntary consumption of cocaine, a review of the record reveals that the State offered no evidence to show that the use of cocaine caused the loss of an ability to communicate a disapproval of any of the sexual acts.

The conspiracy convictions must also be reversed. A conspiracy charge focuses primarily on the intent of the defendant. It must be shown not only that the defendant intended to combine with another, but that they combined to achieve a particular act which is criminal. W. LaFave, A. Scott, *Substantive Criminal Law*, Sec. 6.4, at 76 (1986). *Lavette v. State, 442 So.2d 265 (Fla. 1ˢᵗ DCA 1983), rev. denied, 449 So.2d 265 (Fla.1984)*. No evidence was presented showing that the defendant intended to perform a sexual battery on S.E.M. without her consent. Although the law of conspiracy contemplates that there may be a conspiracy to commit a sexual battery on an unconsenting person, notwithstanding the fact that the crime was impossible to commit because the person consented, see *United States v. Thomas, 13 U.S.C.M.A. 278, 32 C.M.R. 278 (1962)*, Jeffrey G. Ghent, Annotation, *Impossibility of Consummation of Substantive Crime as Defense in Criminal Prosecution for Conspiracy or Attempt to Commit Crime*, 37 A.L.R.3d 375 (1971), here the evidence did not suggest the presence of the requisite mental state to achieve an illegal objective. See, e.g., *State v. Burkett, 344 So.2d 868 (Fla. 2d DCA 1977)* (gravamen of criminal conspiracy is criminal intent to commit substantive offense).

This prosecution was doomed by the faulty charging document. According to the information the State had the burden to prove beyond a reasonable doubt that the victim did not consent and was physically helpless to resist. It failed in that burden. On the facts of this case, the State should have charged the Defendant with a violation of section 800.04, Florida Statutes (1989), entitled "lewd, lascivious, or indecent assault or act upon or in presence of child; sexual battery." Under section 800.04, neither the victim's consent nor the defendant's belief that the victim is sixteen or older is a defense to the crime charged. See *Green v. State, 580 So.2d 321 (Fla. 1ˢᵗ DCA 1991); Hicks v. State, 561 So.2d 1284 (Fla. 2d DCA), rev. denied, 574 So.2d 141 (Fla.1990); State v. Sorakrai, 543 So.2d 294 (Fla. 2d DCA 1989)*. On agreement of counsel, the trial court instructed the jury that section 800.04 is a lesser included offense of section 794.011(4). But the lesser offense was not necessarily included.

Under *Gould v. State, 577 So.2d 1302 (Fla. 1991)*, we are precluded from remanding with directions to convict under a lesser charge unless the lesser charge is a necessarily included lesser offense. See *West v. State, 585 So.2d 439 (Fla. 4ᵗʰ DCA 1991)*. Section 800.04 is not a necessarily included lesser offense of sexual battery because section 800.04, unlike section 794.011, requires that the victim be under the age of sixteen. Neither is the lesser included charge of simple battery, as defined in section

784.03, Florida Statutes (1991), applicable to this case because it requires that the touching be against the will of the victim.

For the sound legal reasons expressed above, the convictions on counts I, II and III must be reversed. Appellant does not challenge his convictions under counts IV and V, charging conspiracy to deliver cocaine and delivery of cocaine. Those convictions, therefore, are affirmed.

Affirmed in part; reversed in part.

HUBBART, J. concurs.

GERSTEN, J., dissents in opinion accompanying case no. 90-2182, *616 So.2d 1017*.

REVIEW

1. Consent may be _____.
   a. actual
   b. implied
   c. both a and b
   d. neither a nor b

2. It is a defense to a sexual offense on a person under the age of sixteen that
   _____.
   a. the victim consented
   b. the defendant believed the victim was over the age of sixteen
   c. both a and b
   d. neither a nor b

CASE

Soukup v. State, 760 So.2d 1072 (Fla. 5th DCA 2000).

Defendant, a male stripper, was adjudicated guilty in the Circuit Court, Brevard County, J. Preston Silvernail, J., of sexual battery of a physically incapacitated person and other offenses arising from incident at birthday celebration involving teenage young women. Defendant appealed. The District Court of Appeal held that evidence was insufficient to support sexual battery conviction.

Judgment and sentence reversed.

PER CURIAM.

Stephen J. Soukup timely appeals the trial court's order adjudicating him guilty of one count of sexual battery of a physically incapacitated person, [Footnote omitted] two counts of lewd, lascivious or indecent acts in the presence of a child [Footnote omitted], one count of a lewd, lascivious or indecent act upon a child [Footnote omitted], and four counts of permitting an alcoholic beverage to be served to a minor. [Footnote omitted] We have jurisdiction. [Footnote omitted] We affirm in part and reverse in part.

Soukup raises several points on appeal, only one of which merits comment. He contends that the evidence adduced below was insufficient to sustain a conviction as to sexual battery on a physically incapacitated person, as proscribed by section 794.011(4)(f), Florida Statutes, and as such his motion for judgment of acquittal on that count was improperly denied. That section states:

> (4) A person who commits sexual battery upon a person 12 years of age or older, without that person's consent, under any of the following circumstances, commits a felony of the first degree, punishable as provided in §§ 775.082, 775.083, or 775.08:

> * * * * *

> (f) When the victim is physically incapacitated.

§794.011(4)(f), Fla. Stat. (1995). Soukup suggests that the victim of this alleged crime consented to the alleged sexual battery and that the alleged victim was not physically incapacitated within the meaning of the statute when the alleged sexual battery took place. We agree with both arguments.

The sixteen year-old victim and three friends had obtained the business card of a stripper–who turned out to be Soukup–and one of the friends, another victim in this case, spoke with Soukup several times on the phone before the events which led to this appeal occurred. On the night in question, wanting a stripper to help them celebrate a birthday, the friend called Soukup and asked if they could get together with him. The four young women and Soukup drove to a home of an acquaintance of Soukup's for whom he was house sitting.

The testimony varied as to the amount each individual had to drink at the home, but the evidence showed that Soukup had provided the young women with various types of alcohol. The victim of the alleged sexual battery on a physically incapacitated person testified that she drank four or five shots of a strong liquor prepared by Soukup, along with some champagne. She then danced with Soukup and another girl, implored him to strip for them, and then proceeded to take her own clothes off and help Soukup remove his.

The victim and the other girl dancing with Soukup then ended up on the floor with Soukup, and some of the convictions on appeal arose from the lewd conduct which took place on the floor. The victim and Soukup then moved over to a couch in the home, where the victim began performing oral sex on Soukup. None of the witnesses to the victim's conduct described her conduct as anything other than consensual. *Cf. Bullington v. State, 616 So.2d 1036, 1038 (Fla. 3d DCA 1993) (holding that consent may* be actual or implied). For her part, the victim said she was numb at the time and not thinking straight.

The elements of this crime pursuant to this statute under the facts of this case are: i) the victim was twelve or older; ii) Soukup's sexual organ had union with the mouth and/or tongue of the victim; iii) without the victim's consent; and iv) the victim was physically incapacitated. *Cf. Fla. Std. Jury Ins. 171.* The statute defines "physically incapacitated" as meaning "that a person is bodily impaired or handicapped and substantially limited in his or her ability to resist or flee an act." § 794.011(1)(j), Fla. Stat. (1995).

The first two elements are clearly met. As to the third element of consent, it is defined as meaning "intelligent, knowing, and voluntary consent and shall not be construed to include coerced submission. 'Consent' shall not be deemed or construed to mean the failure by the alleged victim to offer physical resistance to the offender." §794.011(1)(a), Fla. Stat. (1995). As the state points out, evidence of the victim's resistance is no longer needed in order to prove lack of consent. See *Hufham v. State, 400 So.2d 133 (Fla. 5th DCA 1981).* The problem for the state, however, is that the alleged victim here did not just "not resist"–the evidence, including the testimony of the other young women, indicates that she was a willing participant in the alleged criminal conduct. The state has the burden of proving lack of consent beyond a reasonable doubt. See *Bullington, 616 So.2d at 1039.* "In order to reverse under the correct standard of review, this court must find that after viewing any conflicting evidence in the light most favorable to the jury's verdict, there is no substantial, competent evidence to support the verdict in this case." *Coley v. State, 616 So.2d 1017, 1028 (Fla. 3d DCA 1993)*(Gersten, J., concurring in part and dissenting in part)(citing *Heiney v. State, 447 So.2d 210, 212 (Fla.), cert. denied, 469 U.S. 920, 105 S.Ct. 303, 83 L.Ed.2d 237 (1984); Perez v. State, 479 So.2d 266 (Fla. 5th DCA 1985)).* Because there is a dearth of evidence of the victim's non-consent, there is no substantial, competent evidence to support the verdict. *Cf. Bullington, 616 So.2d at 1038.* Because the state failed to prove that the victim did not consent, we must refuse the state's invitation to order the entry of judgment of sexual battery without serious injury, per section 794.011(5), Florida Statutes (1995).

The fourth element which the state had the burden of proving is the physical incapacitation of the victim. Section 794.011(4)(f), Florida Statutes, was specifically drafted to protect those who are physically handicapped, see *Davis v. State, 567 So.2d 25 n. 1 (Fla. 2d DCA 1990), quashed on other grounds, 581 So.2d 586 (Fla. 1991),* and as such this element has not been proven because there was no evidence indicating she was physically handicapped. The young woman's drunken state does not rise to the level of incapacitation contemplated by section 794.011(4)(f).

Accordingly, the judgment of conviction and sentence for sexual battery of an incapacitated person are reversed.

JUDGMENT and SENTENCE REVERSED.

THOMPSON, C.J., HARRIS and PETERSON, JJ., concur.

REVIEW

1. Physically incapacitated is a defined as _____.
    a. bodily impaired
    b. handicapped
    c. limited ability to resist
    d. all of the above

2. Consent must be _____.
    a. knowing
    b. intelligent
    c. voluntary
    d. all of the above

3. To prove lack of consent, the State must show _____.
    a. resistance by acts
    b. resistance by words
    c. both a and b
    d. neither a nor b

4. Lack of consent must be proved _____.
    a. beyond a reasonable doubt
    b. by a preponderance of the evidence
    c. both a and b
    d. neither a nor b

BATTERY

The commission of a battery involves a defendant intentionally touching or striking a victim against his or her will, or a defendant intentionally causing bodily harm to a victim. A simple battery is classified as a misdemeanor, and sometimes may be an act of domestic violence depending on the relationship between the parties.

AGGRAVATED BATTERY

An aggravated battery is a felony. The State must prove all the elements of a misdemeanor battery plus an additional element of either great bodily harm, permanent disability or disfigurement to the victim. A misdemeanor battery can be reclassified as a felony where a deadly weapon is used or in cases where the victim is pregnant and the defendant knew she was pregnant or should have known it.

A weapon is a deadly weapon if it is used or threatened to be used in a way likely to produce death or great bodily harm. It may be used in an ordinary manner contemplated by its design and construction or the way it was used during the crime may cause it to be deadly.

CASE

Malczewski v. State, 444 So.2d 1096 (Fla. 2d DCA 1984)

Defendant was convicted in the Circuit Court, Pinellas County, William L. Walker, J., of aggravated battery, and he appealed. The District Court of Appeal, Boardman, Acting C.J., held that money bag, which victim clutched to his chest to protect himself from serious injury or death when defendant actually stabbed bag with a knife during his attack, was part of victim's "person," as contemplated by battery statute, and thus, defendant was guilty of aggravated battery.

Affirmed.

BOARDMAN, Acting Chief Judge.

Albert Malczewski appeals a conviction and sentence for aggravated battery imposed upon him after the denial of his motion to dismiss a count of an amended information which charged him with aggravated battery. We affirm.

The amended aggravated battery count which Malczewski sought to dismiss pursuant to Florida Rule of Criminal Procedure 3.190(c)(4) alleged that on March 16, 1983, Malczewski, "by use of a deadly weapon, to-wit [sic]: a knife, did knowingly and intentionally touch or strike Dwain Reeder against his will by stabbing the money bag Dwain Reeder was clutching to his chest, thereby placing Dwain Reeder in fear."

As grounds for dismissal of this amended count, which he labeled as "confusing and contradictory," Malczewski outlined the following material, undisputed facts:

    a.   That on March 16, 1983, Dwain Reeder, an employee of Publix Supermarkets was walking to a bank accompanied by one Tony Gregoris for the purpose of making a deposit in said bank.

    b.   Mr. Reeder was carrying a money bag which contained bundles of checks and currency in it.

    c.   While walking to the bank, Mr. Reeder was accosted by an armed individual who demanded Mr. Reeder relinquish possession of the money bag.

    d.   Mr. Reeder held said money bag next to his chest and at first did not drop it or relinquish possession of it.

    e.   The armed individual thereupon struck [sic] an object, believed by Mr. Reeder to be a knife, into said money bag, but not coming into contact with Mr. Reeder himself.

f.   Mr. Reeder's body never came into direct contact with the object he believed to be a knife, nor did he suffer any physical injury from said object.

The State filed a traverse under Florida Rule of Criminal Procedure 3.190(d) which admitted the allegations contained in paragraphs 1 through 6 of Malczewski's motion to dismiss. However, the traverse added the following facts which the state believed necessary for a fair determination of the issue:

a. The victim was carrying the night money bag from the Publix Store to a nearby bank for deposit.
b. In the bag was $4,650.00 in cash and over $6,000.00 in checks.
c. The Defendant approached from the rear, pulled out a pistol and pointed it at both victim Reeder and victim's assistant... The Defendant pointed the pistol at both of them and clicked it twice. Both victims believed the gun was real and deadly and were in great fear for their lives.
d. The Defendant ordered the victim to "drop the bag". Instead, the victim clutched the bag to his chest. The Defendant then pulled out a knife and lunged at the victim Reeder. The Defendant stabbed the bag, which was held against Reeder's chest. The knife blade went through the bag, puncturing several of the checks and deposit slips which were inside. The victim used the bag for protection and only the bag prevented the knife from entering victim's chest.

The applicable 1981 Florida Statutes provide in relevant part as follows: "784.03 Battery. – (1) A person commits battery if he: (a) Actually and intentionally touches or strikes another person against the will of the other; .... 784.045 Aggravated battery. – (1) A person commits aggravated battery who, in committing battery: ... (b) Uses a deadly weapon."

The trial court entered an order denying Malczewski's motion to dismiss the amended aggravated battery count. Malczewski thereafter pled nolo contendere as to the amended count, expressly reserving his right to appeal the denial of his motion to dismiss. The court subsequently rendered an order adjudicating him guilty of aggravated battery and sentencing him thereon to a ten-year term of imprisonment.

Malczewski contends that the stabbing of the money bag carried by Dwain Reeder did not constitute an aggravated battery because there was never any actual contact between the knife which he wielded and Reeder. He contends further than in order for a battery to occur the victim or plaintiff must suffer an actual harmful or unconsented contact which is caused by the criminal defendant or tort-feasor. *Goswick v. State, 143 So.2d 817 (Fla.1962); Chorak v. Naughton, 409 So.2d 35 (Fla. 2d DCA 1981); Rodriguez v. State, 263 So.2d 267 (Fla.3d DCA 1972)*. The state responds that the accusatory pleading establishes a harmful or offensive contact, stressing that it is a general proposition of criminal law that a battery may be against something carried by the victim. See 6A C.J.S. *Assault & Battery* Sec. 70; *Respublica v. DeLongchamps, 1 U.S.*

(Dall.) 111, 1 L.Ed. 59 (1784). The state contends and we agree that under the facts of this case the victim was subjected against his will to an intentional touching by Malczewski. See ***Grant v. State, 363 So.2d 1063 (Fla.1978)***.

The issue before us is whether the language of Florida's battery statute, section 784.03(1)(a), particularly the words, "[a]ctually ...touches or strikes another person," encompasses the conduct engaged in by Malczewski. None of the Florida cases cited by either party is directly on point.

Turning to hornbook law, Dean William Prosser wrote:

> The protection [afforded a plaintiff by an action for the tort of battery] extends to any part of the body, or to anything which is attached to it and practically identified with it. Thus contact with the plaintiff's clothing, or with a can, a paper, or any other object held in his hand, will be sufficient.... His interest in the integrity of his person includes all those things which are in contact or connected with it.

W. Prosser, *Laws of Torts*, Sec. 9 at 34 (4th ed. 1971). (Emphasis added.)

Commentators have stated that the above common law rule with respected to the tort of battery applies as well to the crime of battery. In 6 Am.Jur.2d *Assault and Battery* Sec. 37 at 38, it is stated:

> The rules that to be held liable for a battery the offender need not directly effect the unlawful contact with the person of the victim, and that a battery need not be committed directly against the person of the victim, but may be committed against anything so intimately connected with the person of the victim as in law to be regarded as a part of that person, are applicable in criminal prosecutions for battery, as are the principles that there may be a battery in the legal sense of the term even though no physical harm resulted therefrom....

(Footnotes omitted and emphasis added.) Similarly, in 6A C.J.S. *Assault and Battery*, Sec. 70 at 440-441, cited by the state, it is said: "It is essential to the [criminal] offense of battery ... that there be a touching of the person of the prosecutor, or something so intimately associated with, or attached to, his person as to be regarded as a part thereof.... The contact may have been ... with something carried by him." (Footnotes omitted and emphasis added.)

The eighteenth century criminal case cited by the state, ***Respublica v. DeLongchamps***, lends support to the logical and reasonable proposition of criminal law that there need not be an actual touching of the victim's person in order for a battery to occur, but only a touching of something intimately connected with the victim's body. See also ***Stokes v. State, 233 Ind. 10, 115 N.E.2d 442 (1953)***.

In ***Respublica v. DeLongchamps***, which is almost directly on point, the defendant struck the victim's cane. In affirming his conviction for assault and battery, the Supreme Court of Pennsylvania said that the assault and battery

> is, perhaps, one of that kind, in which the insult is more to be considered, than the actual damage; for, though no great bodily pain is suffered by a blow on the palm of the hand, or the skirt of the coat, yet these are clearly within the legal definition of assault and battery ... [T]herefore, anything attached to the person, partakes of its inviolability ...

1 U.S. (Dall. At 114, 1 L.Ed. At 61 (Emphasis added.)

In ***Stokes,*** the defendant fired a gun at the victim. The bullet perforated the victim's necktie and creased his shirt. In upholding the battery conviction, the Indiana Supreme Court held, quoting from one of its earlier cases, ***Kirland v. State, 43 Ind. 146 (1873),*** that " '[o]ne's wearing apparel is so intimately connected with the person, as in law to be regarded, in case of a battery, as a part of the person.' " *115 N.E.2d at 443.*

Several out-of-state cases have suggested the same result as ***DeLongchamps*** and ***Stokes*** by way of dicta. See ***Huffman v. State, 200 Tenn. 487, 292 S.W.2d 738 (1956); State v. Sudderth, 184 N.C. 753, 114 S.E. 828 (1922); Reese v. State, 3 Tenn.Cr.App. 97, 457 S.W. 2d 877 (1970).***

Considering the above-quoted authorities and case law on the subject of the crime of battery, we hold that the word "person" in our state's battery statute, section 784.03(1)(a), means person or anything intimately connected with the person. Applying this definition of "person" to the facts of this case, we submit that it would be an overly restrictive construction of section 784.03(1)(a) to decide that the money bag which Reeder clutched to his chest to protect himself from a serious injury or death, when Malczewski "actually" stabbed it with a knife during his attack, was not a part of Reeder's "person" as contemplated by the statute.

Accordingly, we affirm Malczewski's conviction and sentence for aggravated battery.

AFFIRMED.

GRIMES and LEHAN, JJ., concur.

REVIEW

1. To be convicted of aggravated battery, there must be _____.
    a. actual contact between the weapon and the victim
    b. actual harmful contact
    c. contact with an item the victim is holding
    d. none of the above

2. The definition of "person" includes _____.
   a. the person
   b. anything intimately connected with the person
   c. both a and b
   d. neither a nor b

ASSAULT

The crime of assault requires three elements be proven: (1) the defendant must intentionally and unlawfully threaten, either by word or act, to do violence to the victim; (2) at the time the defendant has to appear to have the ability to carry out the threat; and (3) the defendant's actions must create, in the mind of the victim, a well founded fear that the violence is about to take place. A conditional threat to do harm contingent on the occurrence or non-occurrence of some event does not constitute an assault.

An aggravated assault adds a fourth element. The assault must be made with a deadly weapon or be made with a fully formed conscious intent to commit a specific crime upon the victim.

An assault or battery may be enhanced depending on who the victim is. For instance, it is a more serious offense if the victim is a law enforcement officer, a fire fighter, or a person 65 years of age or older.

CASE

O.D. v. State, 614 So.2d 23 (Fla. 2d DCA 1993).

Juvenile was convicted in the Circuit Court, Hendry County, Kirby Sullivan, Acting J., of assault, and he appealed. The District Court of Appeal, Patterson, J., held that defendant's unarmed threat from across the street to one day kill victim was insufficient to constitute crime of assault.

Reversed.

PATTERSON, Judge.

This appeal arises from the state charging the appellant by juvenile petition with the assault of Patrick Dawson. Mr. Dawson and his wife testified that the appellant stated to Mr. Dawson: "Before I'm twenty-one, you will be dead." At the time the appellant made the statement, he did not have a weapon; Mr. Dawson was in his own yard behind a fence and the appellant was across the road. At the close of the state's case, the appellant made a motion for judgment of acquittal, which the trial court denied.

The state failed to prove the essential elements of assault. See § 784.011, Fla. Stat. (1991). The state's evidence failed to show that the appellant directed an overt act at Mr. Dawson to place him in fear. See *Lifka v. State, 530 So.2d 371, 375 (Fla. 1st DCA 1988); Battles v. State, 288 So.2d 573 (Fla. 2d DCA)*, <u>cert. denied</u>, *295 So.2d 302 (Fla. 1974)*. The state's evidence also failed to show a well-founded fear that violence was <u>imminent</u>. See *Johnson v. Brooks, 567 So.2d 34 (Fla. 1st DCA 1990)*. Thus, the trial court should have granted the appellant's motion for judgment of acquittal at the conclusion of the state's case.

Reversed.

FRANK, A.C.J., and BLUE, J., concur.

REVIEW

   1. To convict one of assault, the State must prove _____.
      a. an overt act
      b. a well founded fear
      c. both a and b
      d. neither a nor b

CASE

Butler v. State, 632 So.2d 684 (Fla. 5th DCA 1994).

Defendant was convicted in the Circuit Court, Volusia County, Gayle S. Graziano, J., of resisting an officer without violence, and he appealed. The District Court of Appeal, Cobb, J., held that sworn statement from defendant's ex-girlfriend that he had threatened to physically harm her "if she was around any other male" did not establish probable cause to believe defendant had committed assault.

Reversed.

COBB, Judge.

Steven Butler, charged with resisting an officer with violence, was convicted of the permissive lesser included offense of resisting an officer without violence. On appeal he correctly contends that the state's evidence at trial failed to show that the officer had probable cause to believe he was effectuating a legal arrest, which is an essential element of the offense. *Robinson v. State, 550 So.2d 1186 (Fla. 5th DCA 1989).*

The arresting officer's proffered testimony in regard to the legality of the arrest, which was improperly excluded by the trial judge, clearly revealed that the arrest was based on a sworn statement from the complainant, Butler's ex-girlfriend, that he had threatened to physically harm her "if she was around any other male." The statement does not indicate any overt act threatening violence. It sets out a conditional threat to do injury at some unspecified future time based upon a possible eventuality, and this does not constitute an assault. An assault is "an intentional, unlawful threat by word or act to do violence to the person of another, coupled with an apparent ability to do so, and doing some act which creates a well-founded fear in such other person that such violence is imminent." Sec. 784.011(1), Fla.Stat. (1991); *see also,* ***Johnson v. Brooks,*** *567 So.2d 34 (Fla. 1ˢᵗ DCA 1990);* ***Bell v. Anderson,*** *414 So.2d 550 (Fla. 1ˢᵗ DCA), rev. denied, 424 So.2d 760 (Fla. 1982).* Therefore, the attempt to arrest Butler was unlawful, and the trial court should have granted his motion for judgment of acquittal on the charge of resisting without violence at the conclusion of the state's case.

Accordingly, Butler's conviction and sentence are reversed.

REVERSED.

DAUKSCH and GRIFFIN, JJ., concur.

REVIEW

1. It is not an assault to _____.
   a. merely make a threat
   b. not have the apparent ability to carry out a threat made
   c. not commit an overt act
   d. all of the above

KIDNAPPING

The crime of kidnapping also requires proof of three elements. First, the defendant forcibly, secretly, or by threat confined, abducted, or imprisoned the victim against his or her will. The second element is that the defendant had no authority to do so. The third element addresses the intent of the defendant. The intent must be either: (1) to hold for ransom or reward or as a shield or hostage, to commit or facilitate the commission of a felony; (2) to inflict bodily harm upon or terrorize the victim or another person; (3) or to interfere with the performance of any governmental or political functions.

Additional issues arise in a kidnapping case. The confinement, abduction or imprisonment must not be slight, inconsequential, or merely incidental to the felony being committed, and it must not be inherent in the nature of the felony. The confinement, abduction, or imprisonment must have some significant independence of the felony in that it makes the felony easier to commit or lessens the risk of detection.

If the victim of the kidnapping is under the age of thirteen, the confinement will be found to be against his or her will if it is without the consent of the parent or legal guardian.

CASE

Wilcher v. State, 647 So.2d 1013 (Fla. 4th DCA 1994).

Defendant was convicted in the Circuit Court, Broward County, Jeffrey Streitfeld, J., of armed robbery and four counts of armed kidnapping. Defendant appealed. The District Court of Appeal, Stone, J., held that ushering employees to back of store was incidental to robbery and therefore could not constitute kidnapping.

Affirmed in part, reversed in part, and remanded.

STONE, Judge.

Appellant was convicted of armed robbery and four counts of armed kidnapping. We reverse the judgment of the four kidnapping counts and affirm as to the armed robbery.

Appellant, with two others, entered a store with the purpose of committing a robbery and, at gunpoint, ushered several employees into a back room approximately 50 to 60 feet from the front of the store. The victims were forced to lay on the floor and were told not to look at the perpetrators. The manager was then taken to the front to open the safe and was later returned to the floor with the others.

It was error to deny Appellant's motion for judgment of acquittal on the kidnapping charges. *Walker v. State, 604 So.2d 475 (Fla.1992).* In *Walker,* under similar circumstances, the supreme court determined that moving several victims 30 to 40 feet to the rear of a store in the course of a robbery is a slight and inconsequential act that is merely incidental to a robbery. In reaching this conclusion, the court applied the test adopted in *Faison v. State, 426 So.2d 963, 965-66 (Fla.1983),* used to determine whether evidence is sufficient to constitute kidnapping under section 787.01, Florida Statutes. Under this test, the movement or confinement: (a) must not be slight, inconsequential and merely incidental to the other crimes; (b) must not be the kind inherent in the nature of the other crimes; and (c) must have some significance independent of the other crimes in that it makes the other crimes substantially easier to commit or substantially lessens the risk of detection. See also, *Kirtsey v. State, 511 So.2d 744 (Fla. 5th DCA 1987).*

In *Walker,* the court distinguished related cases in which kidnapping convictions have been upheld:

> Unlike in *Faison,* the victims were not dragged from room to room. They were not bound and blindfolded for half an hour as in *Marsh v. State, , 546 So.2d 33 (Fla. 3d DCA 1989).* They were not barricaded inside the bathroom like in *Johnson v. State, 509 So.2d 1237 (Fla. 4th DCA 1987),* nor were they taken out of the store and put in the restroom located in the rear as in *Ferguson. [Ferguson v. State, 533 So.2d 763 (Fla.1988)]* . . .

Walker at 477.

The facts of this case are certainly more closely analogous to those in **Walker** than to the facts in the above cases distinguished in **Walker**. We recognize that the events in **Walker** occurred within a somewhat shorter time frame, and that apparently the victims in **Walker** did not obey the command to lie on the floor as they did here. Nevertheless, we cannot justify a failure to apply the **Walker** reasoning here simply because Appellant moved the victims 20 feet further, and across a threshold, and committed the crime within minutes rather than seconds.

Therefore, the judgments on the four kidnapping counts are reversed and we remand for resentencing on the robbery conviction. With respect to the other issue on appeal, we find no abuse of discretion.

FARMER and STEVENSON, JJ., concur.

REVIEW

1. The elements of kidnapping are _____.
   a. forcibly confining or abducting the victim
   b. no authority on the part of the defendant
   c. with the intent to hold as hostage
   d. all of the above

2. The confinement, abduction or imprisonment must not be _____.
   a. slight
   b. inconsequential
   c. merely incidental to the felony
   d. all of the above

3. To constitute kidnapping, the movement or confinement must _____.
   a. not be slight
   b. not inherent in the nature of other crimes
   c. make the other crime easier to commit or lessen detection
   d. all of the above

CASE

Patak v. State, 764 So.2d 689 (Fla. 1st DCA 2000).

Movant sought postconviction relief from his convictions, pursuant to guilty plea, for armed robbery and kidnapping. The Circuit Court, Suwannee County, Thomas J. Kennon, Jr., J., denied motion. Movant appealed. The District Court of Appeals, Davis, J., held that movant's actions during bank robbery, in ordering bank employees into the vault at gunpoint then spraying them with pepper spray or mace, provided a sufficient factual basis for separate kidnapping convictions.

Affirmed.

Benton, J., filed opinion concurring in part and dissenting in part.

DAVIS, Judge.

Appellant, Douglas John Patak, who pled guilty to and was convicted of one count of armed robbery and five counts of kidnapping, appeals the trial court's order denying his Florida Rule of Criminal Procedure 3.850 motion. Patak asserts in the motion that the trial court erred by failing to conduct a sufficiently detailed factual inquiry before accepting Patak's guilty plea and that his trial counsel was ineffective because he failed to investigate the circumstances underlying the kidnapping charges, which Patak claims did not constitute kidnapping, and because he advised Patak to plead guilty to five counts of kidnapping. We find no merit to any of the arguments and therefore affirm the order.

The record provided to this court indicates that Patak placed two bank employees inside the vault at gunpoint, ordered them to fill his bag with money, and after they had complied, ordered them to lie on the floor of the vault. The record also indicates that Patak ordered three other employees at gunpoint to lie on the bank floor, and then sprayed them with pepper spray or mace. Patak admitted that he sprayed the pepper spray or mace to aid his escape. See § 787.01(1)(a), Fla. Stat. (1997); *Berry v. State, 668 So.2d 967 (Fla. 1996)*; *Carter v. State, 468 So.2d 370 (Fla. 1ˢᵗ DCA 1985)*. There was no need for Patak to spray the victims because they had complied with his demands and were lying prone on the floor at the time he sprayed them. The actions of ordering the bank employees into the vault at gunpoint, further ordering them to lie on the vault floor, and ordering the others at gunpoint to lie prone on the bank floor, and then spraying them with pepper spray or mace, were not slight, inconsequential, and merely incidental to armed robbery. See *Berry, 668 So.2d at 969*; *Carter, 468 So.2d at 371*. The confinement that occurred as a result of these actions was not inherent in the nature of an armed robbery. See *id.* These actions were significantly independent of the armed robbery because they made the completion of the armed robbery substantially easier and substantially lessened the risk of detection. See *Berry, 668 So.2d at 969*; *Carter, 468 So.2d at 371*. Therefore, the record provided to this court conclusively demonstrates that a sufficient factual basis supported the kidnapping convictions. It is also clear that Patak's counsel was not ineffective in allowing him to plead guilty to kidnapping. See *Strickland v. Washington, 466 U.S. 668, 104 S.Ct. 2052, 80 L.Ed.2d 674 (1984)*(requiring that an appellant show the specific acts or omissions of counsel which fell below a standard of reasonableness under prevailing norms; and that the outcome of the case would have likely been different but for the acts or omissions).

We therefore affirm the trial court's order.

PADOVANO, J., CONCURS; BENTON, J., CONCURS IN PART AND DISSENTS IN PART WITH WRITTEN OPINION.

BENTON, J., concurring in part and dissenting in part.

On pleas of guilty, Douglas John Patak was convicted of one count of robbery and five counts of kidnapping. We now review the order denying the motion he filed under Florida Rule of Criminal Procedure 3.850 alleging that, while he was guilty of robbery, he did not commit kidnapping; and that his trial counsel was ineffective for advising him that what he did constituted kidnapping and for advising him to accept the state's plea offer, despite his actual innocence of those charges. The motion alleges that he would not have entered guilty pleas to the kidnapping charges if counsel had not erroneously advised him that none of the kidnapping charges was defensible.

In my judgment, as to the "kidnapping by pepper spray" counts only, the motion sets a facially sufficient claim of ineffective assistance of counsel that was not conclusively refuted by attachments to the order under review. See *Hill v. State, 642 So.2d 796, 797 (Fla. 3d DCA 1994)* ("If [the defendant's] contention is true that the movement or confinement of the victim's was slight, inconsequential and merely incidental to the robbery, there may have existed no factual basis for the plea entered on the armed kidnapping charges."); *Gust v. State, 558 So.2d 450, 453 (Fla. 1st DCA 1990)*. While I concur in affirming the denial of the motion otherwise, I would reverse and remand for further proceedings on the claim of ineffective assistance of counsel as to the "kidnapping by pepper spray" counts.

REVIEW

1. Which of the following are not slight, inconsequential, or incidental?
   a. ordering individuals into a back room
   b. ordering individuals to on the floor
   c. spraying individuals with mace
   d. all of the above

CASE

Muniz v. State, 764 So.2d 729 (Fla. 2d DCA 2000).

Defendant was convicted in the Circuit Court, Hillsborough County, Ralph Steinberg, J., of domestic violence battery and kidnapping, and he appealed. The District Court of Appeal, Altenbernd, Acting C.J., held that defendant could not be convicted of kidnapping his own five-week-old child.

Reversed in part and remanded.

ALTENBERND, Acting Chief Judge.

Anthony Muniz appeals his convictions for domestic violence battery [FN1] and kidnapping. [FN2] The kidnapping charge involved Mr. Muniz's five-week-old son. We affirm the conviction for domestic violence battery, but reverse the conviction for kidnapping. The kidnapping statute does not criminalize the confinement of a child under the age of thirteen by "a parent or legal guardian." See §787.01(1)(b), Fla. Stat. (1997). Although Mr. Muniz was not married to the child's mother at the time of this offense, he was the child's legal father and, thus, a "parent" of the alleged victim. At least in the absence of a court order depriving him of authority over the child, Mr. Muniz could not be convicted of kidnapping his own child. See *Johnson v. State, 637 So.2d 3, 4 (Fla. 3d DCA 1994). Cf. State v. Badalich, 479 So.2d 197, 199 (Fla. 5th DCA 1985)* (holding father of nonmarital child cannot be criminally liable for false imprisonment of child); *Lafleur v. State, 661 So.2d 346, 348 (Fla. 3d DCA 1995)* (holding father who takes child contrary to court order can be convicted of kidnapping his own child).

Mr. Muniz is the father of a nonmarital child born on September 28, 1998. The child bears Mr. Muniz's last name, and Mr. Muniz appears on the child's birth certificate as the father. See § 382.013(2)(c), Fla. Stat. (Supp. 1998) (prohibiting name of father from appearing on birth certificate for child born out-of-wedlock unless both parents sign consenting affidavit). When the child was born, and at least until the incident in this case occurred, Mr. Muniz either lived with the child's mother and child, or spent considerable time at their home.

On October 26, 1998, Mr. Muniz and the child's mother were drinking at her home and got into an argument. Sometime between 2 and 3 a.m. on October 27, 1998, the argument escalated and Mr. Muniz battered the mother. She fled the home, leaving the baby behind. About thirty minutes later, the mother called 911 from a nearby pay phone. She told the operator about the fight and asked the police to help her remove Mr. Muniz from her house and retrieve her baby. It is not clear whether she explained to the police that Mr. Muniz was the child's father.

When two police officers arrived, they escorted the mother back to the home and knocked on the door. At this point, the baby was sleeping and Mr. Muniz had begun to doze off. Mr. Muniz was startled and became scared. He did not respond to the officers' knock. Eventually, the child's mother opened the door and the officers went inside. They confronted Mr. Muniz with flashlights in the darkened home as he held the baby in his arms. The two officers, who were concerned for the child's safety, immediately demanded Mr. Muniz hand over the child. When Mr. Muniz refused, one officer approached him. At this point, Mr. Muniz saw a razor he had previously left on the floor and picked it up. He warded off the officers by threatening himself and the baby with the razor.

The situation deteriorated quickly. More officers arrived, and Mr. Muniz, still holding the baby, retreated backwards to a bathroom. Over a period of three hours, six officers attempted to convince Mr. Muniz to release the child to them. They called a tactical response team that arrived and lined up outside the residence. Finally, a group of officers seized Mr. Muniz and safely removed the baby. As a result of this incident, the State charged Mr. Muniz with armed kidnapping and domestic violence battery.

At trial, Mr. Muniz did not dispute the domestic violence charge and expressed remorse for the battery. With respect to the kidnapping charge, however, he testified that he never intended to harm the baby, but was concerned the officers would harm the baby. At the conclusion of the trial, Mr. Muniz moved for a judgment of acquittal, arguing that he could not be convicted of kidnapping his own child. The trial court denied this motion, reasoning that the mother was the sole natural guardian of this nonmarital child pursuant to section 774.301(1), Florida Statutes (1997). The jury returned a verdict of guilty of battery and of the lesser included offense of kidnapping. The trial court sentenced Mr. Muniz to time served for the battery, and 51.45 months' imprisonment for kidnapping.

Section 744.301(1) provides, "the mother of a child born out of wedlock is the natural guardian of the child and is entitled to primary residential care and custody of the child unless a court of competent jurisdiction enters an order stating otherwise." Despite the statute, because it appears that Mr. Muniz voluntarily acknowledged his paternity of this child, we question whether he may have some claim to be a legal guardian of the child. See § 742.10(1), Fla. Stat. (1997) (providing voluntary acknowledgment of paternity creates rebuttable presumption of paternity).

We need not resolve the question of whether Mr. Muniz was a legal guardian of the child. Even if the mother was the guardian of this child, Mr. Muniz clearly was a "parent" of the child. See §787.01(1)(b); *Johnson, 637 So.2d 3*. The kidnapping statute does not establish a special definition of "parent." Assuming that "parent" is not a plain and unambiguous concept, any interpretation of this statute must favor the defendant. See § 775.021(1), Fla. Stat. (1997). We must therefore interpret the statute to include as a "parent" of a child a man whose name appears as father upon the child's birth certificate and who has acknowledged paternity pursuant to the "Determination of Parentage" statute. [FN3]

The State argues that *Lafleur, 661 So.2d 346*, controls this case. In *Lafleur*, the Third District affirmed a father's conviction for kidnapping his child when a court order gave custody to the mother and when the father held the child at gunpoint resulting in an eight-hour crisis. See *Lafleur, 661 So.2d 346*. We recognize that the *Lafleur* court emphasized the father's ulterior and unlawful purpose in taking the child. Nonetheless, *Lafleur* is distinguishable on the ground that the father's conduct in that case violated an existing court order. Thus, we do not expressly conflict with *Lafleur*, although we question whether the court order in that case was sufficient to deprive Mr. Lafleur of his status as "parent" under section 787.01(1)(b).

There is no question that Mr. Muniz's behavior was inappropriate. We are inclined to believe that the State could have charged Mr. Muniz with assault on the child, see § 784.011, Fla. Stat. (1997); child abuse, see § 827.03(1)(b), Fla. Stat. (1997); contributing to the dependency of a minor, see § 827.04(1)(a), Fla. Stat. (1997); or resisting an officer, see § 843.02, Fla. Stat. (1997). Nevertheless, section 787.01(1)(b) prevents prosecution of Mr. Muniz for the first-degree felony offense of kidnapping his own child.

The legislature first created this exception to the crimes of false imprisonment and kidnapping in 1974. See ch. 74-383, Laws of Fla. Neither the holding in **Badalich** nor in **Johnson** prompted the legislature to amend these statutes to permit the state to charge a parent with kidnapping or false imprisonment of his or her child under certain circumstances. Given the complexity of modern family structure, it may be difficult for the legislature to improve upon the existing statute and to address the problems presented when a "parent" is not entitled to the custody of his or her child or when a parent confines a child for an unlawful purpose. Nevertheless, the legislature may want to consider whether the crime of kidnapping should include circumstances similar to those presented here.

We reverse the conviction for kidnapping and remand to the trial court for discharge on that count only.

NORTHCUTT and CASANUEVA, JJ., Concur.

FN1. See § 784.03(1)(a), Fla. Stat. (1997).

FN2. See § 787.01(1), Fla. Stat. (1997).

FN3. See ch. 75-166, Laws of Fla.; ch. 742 Fla. Stat. (1997) (entitled "Determination of Parentage"). See also § 382.013(2), Fla. Stat. (1997) (subsection of vital statistics statute entitled "Paternity" and prescribing who may be listed as father on newborn child's birth certificate).

REVIEW

1. One can be convicted of kidnapping one's own child if _____.
   a. the parent is not married to the other parent
   b. the child is under the age of five
   c. the individual is only the legal guardian of the child
   d. none of the above

FALSE IMPRISONMENT

False imprisonment, like kidnapping, also has three elements. The first two are the same as in a kidnapping. The third element, which goes to intent, is different. In a false imprisonment case, the defendant acts for a purpose other than the four categories that create the intent for a kidnapping. Again, if the victim is under 13, confinement is against the will of the victim unless the parent or legal guardian has consented.

CASE

State v. Smith, 840 So.2d 987 (Fla. 2003).

Defendant was convicted in a jury trial in the Circuit Court for Osceola County, Frank N. Kaney, J., of burglary of a dwelling, robbery with a weapon, and false imprisonment. Defendant appealed. The District Court of Appeal, Thompson, C.J., 785 So.2d 623, reversed in part, affirmed in part, and remanded. On review, the Supreme Court, Wells, J., held that: (1) defendant was properly convicted of both robbery and false imprisonment, and (2) Faison test for determining when a charge of kidnapping could stand in addition to charges of other forcible felonies was inapplicable to offense of false imprisonment; abrogating Taylor v. State, 771 So.2d 1233; Rohan v. State, 696 So.2d 901; Keller v. State, 586 So.2d 1258; Perez v. State, 566 So.2d 881.

So ordered.

Pariente, J., dissented and filed separate opinion in which Anstead, C.J., and Shaw, Senior Justice, concurred.

WELLS, J.

We have for review ***Smith v. State,*** 785 So.2d 623, 625-26 (Fla. 5th DCA 2001), which expressly and directly conflicts with the decision in ***Chaeld v. State,*** 599 So.2d 1362, 1364 (Fla. 1st DCA 1992). We have jurisdiction. *See* art. V, § 3(b)(3), Fla. *Const.* For the reasons that follow, we quash the decision below in part and direct that respondent's false imprisonment conviction be affirmed.

The respondent was convicted by a jury of burglary of a dwelling, robbery with a weapon, and false imprisonment. The facts are more fully set forth in the district court's opinion. *See **Smith,** 785 So.2d at 624-25.* The district court agreed with the respondent's argument that the false imprisonment was incidental to and inherent in the robbery, reversed the conviction for false imprisonment, but otherwise affirmed. *See id. at 625-26.* Regarding the reversal of the false imprisonment conviction, the district court compared ***Formor v. State,*** 676 So.2d 1013, 1015 (Fla. 5th DCA 1996), which reversed a kidnapping conviction based on the test announced in ***Faison v. State,*** 426 So.2d 963 (Fla.1983). [FN1] *See **Smith,** 785 So.2d at 625-26.* The district court held:

FN1. Under the ***Faison*** test,

[I]f a taking or confinement is alleged to have been done to facilitate the commission of another crime, to be kidnapping the resulting movement or confinement:

(a) Must not be slight, inconsequential and merely incidental to the other crime;

292

(b) Must not be of the kind inherent in the nature of the other crime; and

(c) Must have some significance independent of the other crime in that it makes the other crime substantially easier of commission or substantially lessens the risk of detection.

Faison, 426 So.2d at 965 (quoting *State v. Buggs,* 219 Kan. 203, 547 P.2d 720, 731 (1976)) (alteration in original).

Although the state argues that *Faison,* which involved a kidnapping charge, should not be applied to cases involving false imprisonment charges, this court has previously done so. *See Keller v. State,* 586 So.2d 1258, 1261-62 (Fla. 5th DCA 1991) (reversing convictions for false imprisonment where false imprisonment was incidental to sexual battery); *but see Chaeld v. State,* 599 So.2d 1362 (Fla. 1st DCA 1992) (refusing to apply *Faison* to false imprisonment charge). Therefore, there is no real legal difference between the convictions in *Formor,* robbery and kidnapping, and the convictions in the instant case, robbery and false imprisonment. Although Smith did not object below to this error, the error is fundamental.

Smith, 785 So.2d at 626 (citation omitted).

The respondent was convicted of false imprisonment under *section 787.02(1)(a), Florida Statutes (1997),* and robbery under section *812.13, Florida Statutes (1997). Section 787.02(1)(a)* defines false imprisonment as [:]

[F]orcibly, by threat, or secretly confining, abducting, imprisoning, or restraining another person without lawful authority and against her or his will.

Section 812.13 defines robbery as [:]

[T]he taking of money or other property which may be the subject of larceny from the person or custody of another, with the intent to either permanently or temporarily deprive the person or the owner of the money or other property, when in the course of the taking there is the use of force, violence, assault, or putting in fear.

Section 775.021(4)(b), Florida Statutes (1997), entitled "Rules of construction," expressly states:

The intent of the Legislature is to convict and sentence for each criminal offense committed in the course of one criminal episode or transaction and not to allow the principle of lenity as set forth in subsection (1) to determine legislative intent. Exceptions to this rule of construction are:

1.   Offenses which require identical elements of proof.
2.   Offenses which are degrees of the same offense as provided by statute.
3.   Offenses which are lesser offenses the statutory elements of which are subsumed by the greater offense.

Because the respondent's convictions for false imprisonment and robbery do not meet the exceptions listed in *section 775.021(4)(b)*, the convictions are separate criminal offenses committed in the course of one criminal episode. Thus, the respondent was properly convicted of both robbery and false imprisonment, and the district court erred in reversing the respondent's false imprisonment conviction. [FN2]

The *Faison* test is not applicable to false imprisonment convictions because the test was established for a particular element of the kidnapping statute that is not included in the false imprisonment statute. Kidnapping is defined in *section 787.01(1)(a), Florida Statutes (1997)*, as follows:

The term kidnapping means forcibly, secretly, or by threat confining, abducting, or imprisoning another person against her or his will and without lawful authority, with intent to:

1.   Hold for ransom or reward or as a shield or hostage.
2.   Commit or facilitate commission of any felony.
3.   Inflict bodily harm upon or to terrorize the victim or another person.
4.   Interfere with the performance of any governmental or political function.

As this Court stated in *Berry v. State, 668 So.2d 967, 969 (Fla.1996)*, the *Faison* test was established because this Court recognized that a literal interpretation *of subsection 787.01(1)(a)2* would result in a kidnapping conviction for "any criminal transaction which inherently involves the unlawful confinement of another person, such as robbery or sexual battery." Thus, in an effort to limit the circumstances under which a confinement, abduction, or imprisonment will constitute kidnapping *under subsection 787.01(1)(a)2*, this Court in *Faison* adopted the test of the Supreme Court of Kansas. *Berry, 668 So.2d at 969* (emphasis added). False imprisonment does not contain a provision requiring proof of the intent to commit or facilitate commission of any felony and therefore *Faison* is not applicable. [FN3]

A comparison of *sections 787.01(1)(a)* and *787.02(1)(a)* reveals they are identical except for the question of intent. We find the general intent of *section 787.02(1)(a)* (false imprisonment) is included in the specific intent of *section 787.01(1)(a)* (kidnapping), consequently false imprisonment is a necessarily lesser included offense.

In *State v. Lindsey, 446 So.2d 1074, 1076 (Fla.1984)*, this Court cited to *Faison* as support for upholding a false imprisonment conviction. This Court stated:

The district court ... rejected [the respondents'] other point on appeal in which they argued that their convictions for false imprisonment were reversible error because the acts of confinement were incidental to the commission of the offense of robbery or to the assault element of the aggravated burglary offense. The respondents now argue that this latter ruling by the district court of appeal was error. We disagree. The offense of false imprisonment was proved by evidence that the intruders confined the victim by tying her up with rope. It was entirely separate from the element of force exerted in committing the robbery and from the element of assault relied upon to aggravate or enhance the offense of burglary. *See Faison v. State, 426 So.2d 963 (Fla.1983).* Moreover, even if there were elements of factual proof common to two or more of the crimes, it is not clear that this would entitle respondents to the relief they seek since the matter of what statutory crimes were committed by the respondents' acts is purely one of legislative intent. *See 775.021(4), Fla. Stat. (1979); Borges v. State, 415 So.2d 1265 (Fla.1982).* We therefore approve the decision of the district court of appeal on this second issue.

Lindsey, 446 So.2d at 1076 (citation omitted). This passing reference to *Faison* has understandably caused some confusion.

After *Lindsey,* several district courts applied the *Faison* test to false imprisonment. *See, e.g., Taylor v. State, 771 So.2d 1233, 1234 (Fla. 2d DCA 2000); Rohan v. State, 696 So.2d 901, 903 (Fla. 4th DCA 1997); Keller v. State, 586 So.2d 1258, 1261-62 (Fla. 5th DCA 1991); Perez v. State, 566 So.2d 881, 884 (Fla. 3d DCA 1990).* However, in *Chaeld v. State, 599 So.2d 1362, 1364 (Fla. 1st DCA 1992),* the court held that a jury instruction based on *Faison* was not applicable when a charge alleges false imprisonment. The *Chaeld* court held:

This so-call *Faison* instruction must be given upon the defendant's request whenever the state charges kidnapping with the intent to commit or facilitate the commission of a felony under § 787.01(1)(a)2. It has no application when the charge alleges that the defendant kidnapped the victim with any of the other specific intentions identified in § 787(1)(a)1, 3 or 4. *See Bedford v. State, 589 So.2d 245, 251 (Fla.1991)* (holding that a defendant charged with kidnapping with the intent to inflict bodily harm upon or terrorize the victim is not entitled to a *Faison* instruction).

Because the *Faison* instruction is implicated only when the state is attempting to prove a kidnapping with the intent to commit or facilitate the commission of a felony, and the crime of false imprisonment by definition and as interpreted by the supreme court in *Sanborn* does not require proof of such intent, we conclude that the judge properly denied the appellant's request for a

Faison instruction. *Id. at 1364* (citations omitted). The ***Chaeld*** court noted that its holding possibly conflicted with other district court decisions. *See id.* [FN4]

The ***Chaeld*** court cited this Court's decision in ***Bedford v. State, 589 So.2d 245 (Fla.1991),*** in which this Court stated:

> Bedford was charged with confining, abducting, or imprisoning [the victim] with the intent to "[i]nflict bodily harm upon or to terrorize" [the victim] under *section 787.01(1)(a), (3),* rather than with the intent to "[c]ommit or facilitate commission of any felony," under subsection 787.01(1)(a), (2). Our decision in ***Faison v. State, 426 So.2d 963 (Fla.1983),*** which held that the latter subsection does not apply to unlawful confinements or movements that were merely incidental to or inherent in the nature of the underlying felony, has no application here.

> ***Bedford,*** *589 So.2d at 251* (second and fourth alterations in original).

This Court's decision in ***Bedford*** clearly supports the conclusion that the ***Faison*** test does not apply to the offense of false imprisonment. False imprisonment does not include an element requiring the intent to commit or facilitate commission of a felony, and therefore ***Faison*** is not applicable to the offense of false imprisonment. If a criminal defendant can be charged with kidnapping based on intent to terrorize and also be convicted of robbery based on confinement that is inherent to both crimes, it is illogical to find that a person could not be convicted of false imprisonment and robbery when false imprisonment only requires general intent. [FN5] Requiring ***Faison*** to be applied to false imprisonment would effectively be writing an intent element into the false imprisonment statute in derogation of the clear statutory language. *Cf.* ***McLaughlin v. State,*** *721 So.2d 1170, 1172 (Fla.1998)* ("[W]hen the language of the statute is clear and unambiguous and conveys a clear and definite meaning, there is no occasion for resorting to the rules of statutory interpretation and construction; the statute must be given its plain and obvious meaning.").

Accordingly, we quash the decision below in part, approve the decision of the First District Court of Appeal in ***Chaeld,*** *599 So.2d at 1364,* and hold that the ***Faison*** test is not applicable to the offense of false imprisonment. On remand, the respondent's false imprisonment conviction should therefore be affirmed.

It is so ordered.

LEWIS and QUINCE, JJ., and HARDING, Senior Justice, concur.

PARIENTE, J., dissents with an opinion, in which ANSTEAD, C.J., and SHAW, Senior Justice, concur.

PARIENTE, J., dissenting (omitted).

FN2. Convicting the respondent of both robbery and false imprisonment does not violate the Double Jeopardy Clause. *See U.S. Const. amend. V; art. I, § 9, Fla. Const.* "The Double Jeopardy Clause in both the state and federal constitutions protects criminal defendants from multiple convictions and punishments for the same offense." ***Gordon v. State***, *780 So.2d 17, 19 (Fla.2001).* Application of the test announced in ***Blockburger v. United States***, *284 U.S. 299, 52 S.Ct. 180, 76 L.Ed. 306 (1932),* codified in *section 775.021*, reveals that the Double Jeopardy Clause is not violated because the statutory elements of false imprisonment are different from the elements of robbery. *Compare § 787.02, Fla. Stat. (1997), with § 812.13, Fla. Stat. (1997).* False imprisonment is a separate offense from robbery.

FN3. This Court recognized the difference between the crimes of kidnapping and false imprisonment in *State v. Sanborn,* 533 So.2d 1169, 1170 (Fla.1988).

FN4. The parties in ***Chaeld*** did not seek review of the district court's decision.

FN5. Examination of the standard jury instructions for kidnapping and false imprisonment also supports the conclusion that ***Faison*** is only applicable to the offense of kidnapping. While the instruction for kidnapping requires a ***Faison*** instruction when intent to commit or facilitate the commission of a felony is alleged, the instruction for false imprisonment has no comparable language. *Compare* Fla. Std. Jury Instr.

(Crim.) 9.1 *with* Fla. Std. Jury Instr. (Crim.) 9.2; *see also* ***Chaeld****, 599 So.2d at 1364.*

REVIEW

1. False imprisonment requires _____.
    a. proof of the intent to commit a felony
    b. proof of the intent to facilitate a felony
    c. no proof of the intent to commit or facilitate a felony
    d. none of the above

THINKING CRITICALLY

1.　Do you agree with the court's rulings in the ***Bullington*** case? If a thirteen-year-old was the victim, would the result have been different? What about an eleven year old?

2.　Give an example of a victim who is physically helpless.

3.　Compare ***Bullington*** and ***Soukup***. Are the holdings consistent? If not, how are they inconsistent? Can alcohol ever render one physically incapacitated under the statute? What if the victim is under the influence of drugs? What if the defendant gives drugs to the victim without her consent?

4.　Can a spouse be prosecuted for sexual battery upon the other spouse?

5.　Is sexual gratification an element of sexual battery? Should it be?

6. Can a prostitute be a victim of a sexual battery?

7. Should child victims be allowed to testify via closed circuit television? Why or why not?

8. Do you agree with the court's ruling in *Malczewski*? Why not charge Malczewski with attempted robbery? If the item "stabbed" was something else, would the result change? Why or why not?

9. Gary and Ted stop their vehicle in front of a house owned by Rick. Rick comes out and yells at them to move their car. Gary and Ted tell him to leave and that they aren't moving their car. Rick continues to yell and states he's going in his house to get his gun and shoot them. Rick turns around and heads back towards his house. Ted goes after him. As Rick reaches for the door, Ted grabs him and Rick turns around and punches him. Has Rick committed a crime? If so, what? Was there a deadly weapon involved? If Ted needed stitches, would that then constitute serious bodily injury?

10. Do you agree with the holding in the **O.D.** case? Why or why not? What if the defendant had a weapon on him at the time he made the statement? Would the result have been different? What if the defendant had fired a gun at Patrick in the past? Would your answers change if it was a knife? What if he brought out a toy gun? Is it a deadly weapon? Why or why not?

11. Emma is babysitting for five-month-old Chelsea. Chelsea will not stop crying. Emma threatens to whip her with a belt that is hanging in a closet. Has Emma committed a crime? How can you prove the perceptions or feelings of a child so young?

12. Do you agree with the **Butler** case? What if Butler had beaten his girlfriend in the past when he found her speaking with another man?

13. Henry commits a robbery at the local fast food restaurant. He confines his victims by holding them at gunpoint. Henry then moves them to a back room and orders them not to come out. Have the victims been kidnapped? Why or why not? Have they been falsely imprisoned? Why or why not? What if he tied them up? What if he untied one of them before leaving?

14. Albert pulls a gun on Martin and orders him to drive downtown. Has Martin been kidnapped? Why or why not? Has Martin been falsely imprisoned? Why or why not?

15. Jordan commits a robbery at a local clothing store. After getting all the money out of the cash register, Jordan walks the employees to a shed out back and tells them not to move. Has there been a kidnapping? What if Jordan did it before he got the money?

16. Do you agree with *Wilcher*? What if the victims had been locked in the room?

17. In the *Patak* case, had the victims not been sprayed with mace would the kidnapping conviction have stood? Give an example of what would have been only slight or inconsequential.

18. Gabe accosts an employee in the parking lot just after closing. She is forced back into the business where Gabe empties the safe. Has the employee been kidnapped? Why or why not? What additional facts would be important to know?

19. Would the *Muniz* decision have been different if the defendant's name was not on the child's birth certificate? What if Muniz was in the house in violation of a restraining order the child's mother had taken out against him? Would the result be different if the court order addressed Mr. Muniz's access to his child? Why or why not?

CHAPTER 10 ANSWER KEY

REVIEW QUESTIONS

Bullington v. State
1. c
2. d

Soukup v. State
1. d
2. d
3. d
4. a

O.D. v. State
1. c

Butler v. State
1. d

Malczewski v. State
1. c
2. c

Wilcher v. State
1. d
2. d
3. d

Patak v. State
1. d

Muniz v. State
1. d

State v. Smith
1. c

CHAPTER 11

CRIMES AGAINST PROPERTY

THEFT

The crime of theft consists of two elements: (1) the defendant must knowingly and unlawfully obtain, use, endeavor to obtain or endeavor to use the property of the victim; and (2) he or she must do so with the intent to permanently or temporarily deprive the victim of his or her right to it. The second element is met by either using the property or letting another person who is not entitled to it, use the property.

The jury must determine the value of the property taken. The more valuable the property, the more serious the offense. If the value of the property is less than $300.00, the offense is only misdemeanor petit theft.

Grand theft in the third degree requires the value to be more than $300.00 and less than $20,000.00. Second degree grand theft is more than $20,000.00 but less than $100,000.00. Grand theft in the first degree applies to property valued at $100,000.00 or more. Certain items by their nature are grand theft in the third degree. The theft of a will, a codicil, a motor vehicle, a firearm, a commercially farmed animal, a fire extinguisher, two thousand or more pieces of fruit, an aquaculture species raised at a permitted aquaculture center, or property taken from a construction site are all grand theft in the third degree due to nature of the item taken.

Certain inferences may arise in a theft case. If someone presents false identification when leasing personal property or fails to return the property within seventy-two hours of the termination of the lease it can be inferred the property was obtained or is used with the unlawful intent to commit theft. The inference will not arise if a satisfactory explanation is given. If an individual is found in possession of recently stolen property, unless satisfactorily explained, it will give rise to an inference that the person knew or should have known the property was stolen.

The theft statute covers stealing, larceny, purloining, abstracting, embezzlement, misapplication, misappropriation, conversion, or obtaining money or property by false pretenses, fraud or deception. Within the statute, property means anything of value, including real property, tangible or intangible personal property or services. Moreover, value is defined as the market value of the property at the time and place of the offense. If the exact value cannot be determined, an attempt should be made to determine a minimum value. If unable to do so, the value will be found to be less than $300.00.

If separate properties are stolen pursuant to one scheme or course of conduct, the values may be totaled. The thefts may be from one or more than one person.

CASE

T.L.M. v. State, 755 So.2d 749 (Fla. 4th DCA 2000).

Juvenile was convicted in the Circuit Court, Palm Beach County, Ronald V. Alvarez and Karen L. Martin, JJ., of grand theft of a fire extinguisher. Juvenile appealed. The District Court of Appeal, Shahood, J., held that juvenile did not have the specific intent to appropriate or deprive school board of its property when he took fire extinguisher off the wall and threw it in a fit of anger.

Reversed and discharge.

SHAHOOD, Judge.

We reverse appellant's conviction for grand theft of a fire extinguisher on the grounds that there was insufficient evidence to sustain his conviction.

Appellant was charged by petition with grand theft of a fire extinguisher when he removed a fire extinguisher off the wall in the "time out room" at his school and threw it in the direction of the Assistant Discipline Coordinator's desk. Appellant's reaction was in response to a conflict between himself and the Discipline Coordinator just prior to the incident in question. In a fit of anger, appellant grabbed the fire extinguisher and threw it in the direction of the desk. At the time, the Discipline Coordinator was sitting approximately ten feet away from the desk. At most, appellant had the fire extinguisher in his possession for "a second or so."

We hold that the trial court erred in denying appellant's motion for judgment of acquittal and in sustaining his conviction where the state failed to prove that appellant had the requisite intent to commit the crime.

Courts should not grant a motion for judgment of acquittal unless, when viewed in a light most favorable to the state, the evidence does not establish the prima facie case of guilt. See *Proko v. State, 566 So.2d 918, 919 (Fla. 5th DCA 1990).* A party moving for judgment of acquittal admits the facts and evidence adduced, as well as every conclusion favorable to the adverse party that the jury might fairly and reasonably infer from the evidence. See *Lynch v. State, 293 So.2d 44 (Fla. 1974).*

Although the state is not required to conclusively rebut every variation of events which may be inferred from the evidence, it is required to present competent, substantial evidence which is inconsistent with the defendant's theory of events. See *State v. Law, 559 So.2d 187, 189 (Fla. 1989).* It is the trial judge's proper task to review the evidence to determine the presence or absence of competent proof from which the jury could infer guilt to the exclusion of all other inferences. See *id. at 189.* Once competent substantial evidence has been submitted on each element of the crime, it is for the jury to evaluate the evidence and credibility of the witnesses. See *Taylor v. State, 583 So.2d 323 (Fla. 1991).*

In determining whether the state presented sufficient evidence to overcome appellant's reasonable hypothesis of innocence, the state must prove each element of a crime charged beyond a reasonable doubt. See *M.P.W. v. State, 702 So.2d 591, 592 (Fla. 2d DCA 1997)*. If the State cannot do so, then a judgment of acquittal should be granted. See *id.*

Section 812.014(1), Florida Statutes (1997), defines "theft" as follows:

> (1) A person commits theft if he or she knowingly obtains or uses, or endeavors to obtain or use, the property of another with intent to, either temporarily or permanently:
>
> > (a) Deprive the other person of a right to the property or a benefit from the property.
> > (b) Appropriate the property to his or her own use or to the use of any person not entitled to the use of the property.

It is a third degree felony if the stolen property is a fire extinguisher. §812.014(2)(c)8, Fla. Stat. (1997).

The intent to steal or deprive the victim of the victim's property is a necessary element of grand theft. It is a well-established principle of law that the issue of felonious intent or state of mind of the defendant is generally a jury question that, in most instances, cannot be ascertained by direct proof, but must be inferred from the surrounding circumstances. See *Mosher v. State, 750 So.2d 120 (Fla. 3d DCA 2000); State v. West, 262 So.2d 457, 458 (Fla. 4th DCA 1972)*. This well-established principle, however, is subject to the legal requirement that there must be some substantial competent evidence from which the jury may reasonably infer the intent. See *id.*

Section 812.014 requires a finding of specific criminal intent to either (a) "deprive" the other person of a right to the property or a benefit therefrom or (b) "appropriate" the property to his own use or to the use of any person not entitled thereto. See *State v. G.C., 572 So.2d 1380, 1381 (Fla. 1991), receded from on other grounds, I.T. v. State, 694 So.2d 720 (Fla. 1997)*. The terms "deprive" and "appropriate" both connote a taking of another's property without authorization. See *id.* In *Daniels v. State, 587 So.2d 460 (Fla. 1991)*, the Florida Supreme Court explained that the specific intent to commit robbery, under section 812.014(1), is the intent to steal, i.e., to deprive an owner of property either permanently or temporarily. *587 So.2d at 462.*

In this case, appellant did not have the specific intent to appropriate or deprive the School Board of its property. Clearly, appellant's use of the fire extinguisher was incidental to another act since he took the fire extinguisher off the wall in a fit of anger over his pending discipline. We do not agree with the state, that a momentary taking, for only a second or two, constitutes the specific intent necessary to temporarily appropriate the School Board's property as defined under section 812.014(1).

Accordingly, we reverse appellant's conviction for grand theft of a fire extinguisher and direct that appellant be discharged.

REVERSE AND DISCHARGE.

WARNER, C.J., and GROSS, J., concur.

REVIEW

1. Theft is _____.
   a. a general intent crime
   b. a specific intent crime
   c. both a and b
   d. neither a nor b

CASE

State v. Iglesias, 676 So.2d 75 (Fla. 3d DCA 1996).

Defendant was convicted in the Circuit Court, Dade County, Stanford Blake, J., of second-degree grand theft and contracting without license. Defendant appealed. The District Court of Appeal, Gersten, J., held that evidence was sufficient to support conviction.

Affirmed.

Before SCHWARTZ, C.J., and GERSTEN and FLETCHER, JJ.

GERSTEN, Judge.

Appellant, Miguel Jose Iglesias (the "defendant"), appeals his conviction for second degree grand theft and contracting without a license. We affirm the defendant's conviction because the evidence was sufficient to establish felonious intent.

Charles and Irene Brooks (the "victims") suffered extensive damage to their home and sought a contractor to make the necessary repairs. Based upon a recommendation, the victims contacted the defendant.

The defendant told the victims that he was a licensed and insured contractor. He also showed them a certificate from the State of Florida purporting his authorization to work on homes. The defendant then presented the victims with a contract for $45,000 which had the words "State licensed and insured" printed on it followed by the handwritten designation "HC-00002623." The victims signed the contract believing the defendant was a licensed contractor.

Although he had not obtained the necessary permits, the defendant began working on the home a few weeks later. The defendant never explained to the victims that he had an occupational license from Broward County as opposed to a standard contractor's license issued by the State. Interestingly, the defendant did attempt to secure a contractor's license subsequent to his agreement with the victims.

After the victims had paid the defendant $35,000, they learned he was not licensed and threw him off the job. The defendant was found guilty of second degree grand theft and contracting without a license. He was sentenced to three years probation and $10,500 in restitution costs.

On appeal, the defendant argues that the trial court erred in denying his motion for a judgment of acquittal, alleging the evidence was insufficient to show the requisite felonious intent. According to the defendant, he lacked the specific intent necessary to sustain a conviction for grand theft because he believed his home improvement license allowed him to supervise home construction and because he partially performed under the contract. We disagree.

Felonious intent is an essential element of the crime of grand theft. § 812.014(1), Fla. Stat. (1992); *State v. Dunmann, 427 So.2d 166 (Fla. 1983); Bertoglio v. American Sav. And Loan Ass'n of Florida, 491 So.2d 1216 (Fla. 3d DCA 1986); Webb v. State, 441 So.2d 700 (Fla. 2d DCA 1983).* In order to sustain a conviction for grand theft, the State must show that the defendant had the specific intent to commit the theft at the time of or prior to the commission of the act of taking. *Rosen v. Marlin, 486 So.2d 623 (Fla. 3d DCA), rev. denied, 494 So.2d 1151 (Fla. 1986).* Because intent to commit the theft usually cannot be proven by direct evidence, such intent may be inferred from the circumstances surrounding the illegal act. *Coester v. State, 573 So.2d 391 (Fla. 4th DCA 1991).*

Turning to the circumstances here, the defendant's failure to disclose that he was not a licensed contractor coupled with his subsequent attempt to secure a contractor's license clearly evidences an intentional felonious misrepresentation. But for the defendant's successful use of *blatnaya muzika* [FN1] in affirmatively and intentionally misrepresenting that he was a licensed and insured contractor, the victims would not have paid him $35,000 to make the repairs.

Sufficient circumstantial evidence of felonious intent exists and we find the State met its burden of producing evidence inconsistent with the defendant's theory of innocence. See *McArthur v. State, 351 So.2d 972 (Fla. 1977); Jones v. State, 192 So.2d 285 (Fla. 3d DCA 1966).* Accordingly, because the record reveals legally sufficient evidence to support the conviction for grand theft, the conviction is affirmed.

Affirmed.

FN1. Russian, meaning "thieves' lingo."

REVIEW

1. Intent may be proven _____.
   a. by direct evidence
   b. by circumstantial evidence
   c. both a and b
   d. neither a nor b

CASE

State v. Wright, 626 So.2d 299 (Fla. 5ᵗʰ DCA 1993).

Defendant was convicted in the Circuit Court, Citrus County, John P. Thurman, J., of robbery with a firearm and grand theft, and he appealed. The District Court of Appeal, Cobb, J., held that state failed to prove that value of stolen items exceeded $300.

Reversed and remanded.

COBB, Judge.

The appellant, Elester Wright, was convicted of robbery with a firearm and grand theft. He challenges the grand theft conviction on two bases:

1) The state failed to prove the value of the stolen items was $300.00 or more.

2) If the theft underlying the robbery was petit theft instead of grand theft, as agreed above, then the theft is a necessarily lesser included offense of the robbery pursuant to *State v. Rodriguez, 500 So.2d 20 (Fla. 1986)*. The defendant also requests, in the event we determine that the evidence was sufficient to support a conviction for grand theft, that we certify the question as to whether grand theft and robbery are the same offense when predicated on a single act as we did in the recent case of *Sirmons v. State, 603 So.2d 82 (Fla. 5ᵗʰ DCA 1992), rev. accepted, 613 So.2d 9 (Fla. 1992)*.

In regard to the first argument, Wright points out that the state conceded in its closing argument to the jury that the value of the victim's stolen wallet and its contents did not amount of $300.00 unless the jury could consider two automatic teller machine cards (ATM cards) in the wallet as "written instruments" as defined by section 812.012(9), Florida Statutes (1991), which provides the following definition of "value" in regard to the crime of theft:

(9) "Value" means value determined according to any of the following:

(a) 1. Value means the market value of the property at the time and place of the offense or, if such cannot be satisfactorily ascertained, the cost of replacement of the property within a reasonable time after the offense.

2. The value of a written instrument that does not have a readily ascertainable market value, in the case of an instrument such as a check, draft, or promissory note, is the amount due or collectible or is, in the case of any other instrument which creates, releases, discharges, or otherwise affects any valuable legal right, privilege, or obligation, the greatest amount of economic loss that the owner of the instrument might reasonably suffer by virtue of the loss of the instrument.

3. The value of a trade secret that does not have a readily ascertainable market value is any reasonable value representing the damage to the owner, suffered by reason of losing an advantage over those who do not know of or use the trade secret.

(b) If the value of property cannot be ascertained, the trier of fact may find the value to be not less than a certain amount; if no such minimum value can be ascertained, the value is an amount less than $100.

(c) Amounts of value of separate properties involved in thefts committed pursuant to one scheme or course of conduct, whether the thefts are from the same person or from several persons, may be aggregated in determining the grade of the offense.

It was clearly established at trial that the victim's bank accounts for the ATM cards, together with the cash in the stolen wallet, exceeded $300.00. Wright argues, however, that ATM cards are governed by Part II of Chapter 817 of the Florida Statutes, which makes it only a misdemeanor to steal an ATM or a credit card. In other words, the value of an account corresponding to a card is relevant only at such time as the card is actually *used* to wrongfully withdraw or attempt to withdraw money from that account, which is not at issue in this case. The state has failed to effectively respond to this argument on appeal.

Based upon our reading of the provisions of sections 817.60(1) and 817.67(1), we agree with the argument of Wright. The mere theft of an ATM card is a misdemeanor irrespective of the bank account it represents. Its inherent value, for purposes of the theft statute, is an indeterminate one, which cannot support the state's argument in the instant case. Therefore, we reverse Wright's theft conviction as the petit theft is subsumed as a necessarily lesser included offense of the robbery. As a result, we do not reach the issue here which was certified in Sirmons.

Wright's conviction for grand theft is reversed and this cause is remanded for resentencing.

REVERSED AND REMANDED.

DAUKSCH and DIAMANTIS, JJ., concur.

REVIEW

1. To convict a person of grand theft, the State must prove the value of the item stolen   is _____.
     a. less than $300.00
     b. more than $300.00
     c. both a and b
     d. neither a nor b

DEALING IN STOLEN PROPERTY

The crime of dealing in stolen property is a separate crime than theft, and there are two ways to deal in stolen property. One is known as fencing, the other as organizing. A person who traffics or endeavors to traffic in property he or she knows or should have known was stolen is guilty of dealing in stolen property or fencing.

Stolen property is defined as property that has been the subject of any criminally wrongful taking or if the property has not been stolen property offered for sale as stolen.

To be guilty of organizing, a defendant must initiate, organize, plan, finance, direct, manage, or supervise the theft of the property.

A defendant may be charged with both theft and dealing in stolen property in connection with one scheme or course of conduct but can only be convicted of one or the other, not both.

CASE

State v. Camp, 596 So.2d 1055 (Fla. 1992).

In prosecution on various charges associated with defendant's alleged attempts to negotiate forged checks, the Circuit Court, Seminole County, C. Vernon Mize, Jr., J., dismissed counts alleging that defendant was dealing in stolen property, and state appealed. The District Court of Appeal, 579 So.2d 763, affirmed, and state petitioned for review. The Supreme Court, Barkett, J., held that attempting to negotiate stolen checks for personal use did not constitute crime of dealing in stolen property.

Affirmed.

BARKETT, Justice.

We review *State v. Camp, 579 So.2d 763 (5ᵗʰ DCA 1991),* based on direct and express conflict with *Dixon v. State, 541 So.2d 637 (Fla. 1ˢᵗ DCA), review dismissed, 547 So.2d 1209 (Fla. 1989).* [FN1]   The issue is whether attempting to negotiate forged checks constitutes dealing in stolen property under section 812.019, Florida Statutes (1989).

Jo Ann Camp obtained company checks from her employer and either forged her employer's signature or used blank checks pre-signed by him to satisfy her personal credit card debt at Citibank of South Dakota. The State charged her with 36 counts of forgery, 36 counts of uttering a forgery, and 42 counts of dealing in stolen property. [FN2] The trial court dismissed the 42 counts alleging that Camp was dealing in stolen property. The State appealed, and the district court affirmed, holding that one who "steals for his own account" does not violate section 812.019. *Camp, 579 So.2d at 764.*

Section 812.019(1) provides:

812.019 Dealing in stolen property --

(1) Any person who traffics in, or endeavors to traffic in, property that he knows or should know was stolen shall be guilty of a felony of the second degree, punishable as provided in ss. 775.082, 775.083, and 775.084.

"Traffic" is defined under section 812.012(7), Florida Statutes (1989), as:

(a) To sell, transfer, distribute, dispense, or otherwise dispose of property.

(b) To buy, receive, possess, obtain control of, or use property with the intent to sell, transfer, distribute, dispense, or otherwise dispose of such property.

The State argues that under this provision Camp "trafficked" in stolen property when she "transferred" the checks to the bank. The State asks this Court to define the term "trafficking" to include any form of transfer of property and relies on *Dixon v. State* for the proposition that the thief who puts a stolen check to its normal and intended personal use, thereby placing it into "the stream of commerce," is guilty of dealing or trafficking in stolen property. See *Dixon, 541 So.2d at 638.* We cannot interpret the pertinent statutes in this manner.

First, it is a well-established canon of construction that words in a penal statute must be strictly construed. See *Perkins v. State, 576 So.2d 1310 (Fla. 1991).* Where words are susceptible of more than one meaning, they must be construed most favorably to the accused. *Id;* § 775.021(1), Fla. Stat. (1989). Moreover, section 812.037, Florida Statutes (1989) expressly requires that section 812.019 "be construed in light of [its] purpose[ ] to achieve [its] remedial goals."

As noted by the court below, section 812.019, which is part of the Florida Anti-Fencing Act, Chapter 77-342, Laws of Florida, is intended to punish those who knowingly deal in property stolen by others. *Camp, 579 So.2d at 764.* The basic scenario envisions a person who steals and then sells the stolen property to a middleman (the "fence") who in turn resells the property to a third person. *See generally* G. Robert Blakely & Michael Goldsmith, *Criminal Redistribution of Stolen Property: The Need for*

Law Reform, 74 Mich.L.Rev. 1512 (1976). The statute punishes both the initial thief and the fence. See Sec. 812.012(7), Fla.Stat. (1989). According to its legislative history, this law is

> an adaptation of the Model Theft and Fencing Act, consistent with the organization of Florida law, as proposed by G. Robert Blakely and Michael Goldsmith in their exhaustive study on stolen property law. Blakely and Goldsmith, *Criminal Redistribution of Stolen Property: The Need for Law Reform*, 74 Mich.L.Rev. 1512 (1976). That article focuses on the receivers of stolen property as the central figures in theft activities, and that the law should be focused on the criminal system that redistributes stolen goods.

Staff of Fla. H.R. Select Comm. on Organized Crime, CS for SB 1431 (1977) Memorandum (April 7, 1977) (emphasis added). Thus, this statute was not designed to punish persons who steal for personal use. [FN3] Rather, it was designed to dismantle the criminal network of thieves and fences who knowingly redistribute stolen property.

We therefore agree with the court below that negotiating stolen checks for personal use, or otherwise deriving personal benefit from stolen merchandise, does not constitute the crime of "dealing in stolen property" as envisioned by the legislature in enacting section 812.019. Otherwise every theft of money in which the money is ultimately transferred to a third person in exchange for goods would constitute a violation of the anti-fencing statute. We agree with the First District that

> [e]vidence of theft only, with the intent personally to put the stolen item or items to normal use, constitutes only the crime of theft and not the crime of trafficking or dealing in stolen property within the meaning of chapter 812, Florida Statutes, even if the normal use is achieved by some form of transfer, distribution, dispensation, or disposition of the item.

Grimes v. State, 477 So.2d 649 (Fla. 1st DCA 1985) (tendering stolen food stamps in exchange for food does not constitute dealing in stolen property); *accord Williams v. State*, 590 So.2d 515 (Fla. 2d DCA 1991) (purchasing stolen alcohol and cigarettes for personal consumption does not constitute dealing in stolen property); *Townsley v. State*, 443 So.2d 1072 (Fla. 1st DCA 1984) (purchasing stolen Mercedes for personal use does not constitute dealing in stolen property); *Lancaster v. State*, 369 So.2d 687 (Fla. 1st DCA 1979) (finding a defendant who installed a stolen engine into his own vehicle did not deal in stolen property); *cf. Bailey v. State*, 559 So.2d 742 (Fla. 1st DCA 1990) (attempting to sell stolen typewriter was neither a personal use nor a necessary incident of personal use and thus constituted dealing in stolen property).

Accordingly, we approve the decision below and disapprove *Dixon*.

It is so ordered.

SHAW, C.J., and OVERTON, McDONALD, GRIMES, KOGAN, and HARDING, JJ., concur.

FN1. We have jurisdiction pursuant to article V, section 3(b)(3) of the Florida Constitution.

FN2. The State did not charge Camp with theft under section 812.014, Florida Statutes (1989).

FN3. In this case, Camp herself negotiated the checks. Our analysis would not apply had she stolen and sold blank checks for others to negotiate.

REVIEW

1. Dealing in stolen property includes _____.
    a. negotiating checks for personal use
    b. deriving a personal benefit from stolen merchandise
    c. both a and b
    d. neither a nor b

FORGERY AND UTTERING A FORGERY

The crime of forgery involves two elements. First, the defendant falsely makes, alters, forges, or counterfeits a specific document. Second, the defendant must intend to injure or defraud a person or a firm. The defendant need not use the document himself or profit from its use. It is sufficient that he or she intended someone use it to injure or defraud. Importantly, it is not necessary to prove what person the defendant intended to injure or defraud.

The crime of uttering, on the other hand, has three elements.   The defendant passes or offers to pass as true a particular document.   The defendant knows the document to be false, altered, forged or counterfeited, and the defendant intends to injure or defraud some person or firm.

CASE

State v. Friedman, *533 So.2d 309 (Fla. 1ˢᵗ DCA 1988).*

Defendant was charged with uttering altered private academic transcript. The Circuit Court, Alachua County, Stan R. Morris, J., dismissed information for failure to charge offense. State appealed. The District Court of Appeal, Wentworth, J., held that submitting allegedly private academic transcript to public university did not violate prohibition against uttering altered record.

Affirmed.

WENTWORTH, Judge.

The state seeks review of an order dismissing an information for failure to charge an offense. We conclude that the act charged, uttering an altered private academic transcript, does not violate section 831.02, Florida Statutes, and we affirm the order appealed.

In an amended information the state charged appellee with violating section 831.02, Florida Statutes, by knowingly submitting to the University of Florida an altered "record, to wit: a school transcript..." The court dismissed this information upon appellee's motion, determining that section 831.02 proscribes uttering only those records delineated in section 831.01, Florida Statutes, and that appellant's academic transcript is not such a record.

Section 831.02 prohibits uttering:

> ... a false, forged, or altered record, deed, instrument or other writing mentioned in s. 831.01

Section 831.01 addresses the forgery of a "public record" and various other specified documents. These two statutes embrace separate and distinct offenses. See **Bronstein v. State, 355 So.2d 817 (Fla. 3d DCA 1978).** But they involve a closely related subject and are thus properly construed in pari materia, upon comparison with each other considering the entire statutory scheme. See generally, **Ferguson v. State, 377 So.2d 709 (Fla. 1979).** Since section 831.02 is a penal statute, it must give clear notice of the acts it proscribes and should be strictly construed. See **Ferguson, supra.; State v. Winters, 346 So.2d 991 (Fla. 1977);** see also section 775.021(1), Florida Statutes.

We agree with the trial court that section 831.02 proscribes uttering only such records and documents as are mentioned in section 831.01, and that the state's information does not charge an offense under section 831.02. The allegation that appellee uttered an altered record relates to a private academic transcript, which is neither a public record nor other document identified in section 831.01. Uttering such a transcript is therefore not a violation of section 831.02, as strictly construed in pari materia with sections 831.01. The state's information was properly dismissed.

The order appealed is affirmed.

ERVIN and ZEHMER, JJ., concur.

REVIEW

1. One can be convicted of forgery with regard to _____.
    a. a private document
    b. a public record
    c. both a and b
    d. neither a nor b

ROBBERY

There are four elements to the crime of robbery. The first element is that the defendant takes money or property from a person. It is not necessary that the person who is robbed be the actual owner of the property. It is enough if the victim has custody of the property. The taking must be with force, violence, or an assault so as to overcome the resistance of the victim or put the victim in fear so he or she does not resist. The property taken must be of some value.

The fourth element is the same as a required element of grand theft. The taking must be with the intent to permanently or temporarily deprive the victim of his or her right to the property or any benefit from it. The robber may use the property himself or let another not entitled to it use it.

A victim is not required to resist if the victim fears death or great bodily harm might result. Unless prevented by fear, however, there needs to be some resistance to have the taking be by force or violence.

It is robbery to administer a substance to a victim to make them unconscious and then take their property.

As with most crimes, the punishment is greater if a firearm or a weapon is used.

There is also a crime known as home invasion robbery. There are three elements. A defendant must enter a dwelling with the intent to commit a robbery and in fact commit the robbery.

CASE

Bass v. State, 698 So.2d 885 (Fla. 4th DCA 1997).

Defendant was convicted in the Circuit Court, Nineteenth Judicial Circuit, Martin County, David Harper, Acting Circuit Judge, of attempted robbery with weapon and battery and was sentenced. Defendant appealed. The District Court of Appeal, Polen, J., held that: (1) fact that defendant hit victim only after she refused defendant's demand for money did not preclude finding of force, violence, assault, or putting in fear in course of attempted taking as required for attempted robbery with weapon, and (2) attempted robbery with firearm was second-degree, rather than first-degree, felony.

316

Affirmed in part, reversed in part, and remanded.

POLEN, Judge.

Thaddeus Bass appeals his conviction and sentence for attempted robbery with a weapon and battery, claiming there was no evidence of an attempt to take the victim's money by force, violence, assault or putting in fear. We affirm the conviction, but remand for correction of appellant's judgment and sentence.

In the early morning hours, while working as a street sweeper, Brenda Chapman was approached by a man who asked her to give him some money. When she told him she did not have any money he took out some type of wire and hit her in the arm twice. She then picked up a wrench and he ran away. She subsequently reported the incident to the police. Bass was eventually identified and charged with attempted robbery with a weapon and aggravated battery with a weapon.

In moving for a judgment of acquittal, Bass argued that since the only evidence of force (hitting Ms. Chapman with a wire) occurred after she refused his demand for money, there was no force, violence, assault or putting in fear "in the course of [attempted] taking." [FN1]

Under section 812.13(3)(b), Florida Statutes (1995), however, "in the course of the taking" is defined:

> (b) An act shall be deemed "in the course of the taking" if it occurs either prior to, contemporaneous with, or subsequent to the taking of the property and if it and the act of taking constitute a continuous series of acts or events.

Thus, it made no difference that Bass hit the victim after she refused his demand for money. See *Jones v. State, 652 So.2d 346, 349 (Fla.), cert. denied, 516 U.S. 875, 116 S.Ct. 202, 133 L.Ed.2d 136 (1995)* (stating that under section 812.13, the violence or intimidation may occur prior to, contemporaneous with, or subsequent to the taking of the property so long as both the act of violence or intimidation and the taking constitute a continuous series of acts or events); *Santilli v. State, 570 So.2d 400, 401-402 (Fla. 5th DCA 1990)* (stating submission of robbery offense to jury was justified even though defendant's forceful act of hitting officer with his car as he attempted to flee occurred after defendant completed act of shoplifting greeting card). We affirm Bass' conviction.

As to the written judgment, the state concedes and we agree that the final judgment should be corrected to reflect that attempted robbery with a firearm is a second degree, rather than a first degree, felony.

In accordance with section 777.04, Florida Statutes (1995), if the offense attempted is a life felony or a felony of the first degree, the offense of criminal attempt is a felony of the second degree. In accordance with section 812.13, robbery with a weapon is a felony of the first degree. Accordingly, we remand for the trial court to correct the judgment to reflect that attempted robbery with a weapon is a second degree felony.

AFFIRMED IN PART, REMANDED IN PART.

GUNTHER and FARMER, JJ., concur.

FN1. The robbery statute, section 812.13(1), Florida Statutes (1995) provides:

(1) "Robbery" means the taking of money or other property which may be the subject of larceny from the person or custody of another, with intent to either permanently or temporarily deprive the person or the owner of the money or other property, when *in the course of the taking* there is the use of force, violence, assault, or putting in fear.

(Emphasis supplied.)

REVIEW

1. To convict a person of robbery, the State must prove _____.
   a. an assault
   b. force
   c. putting the victim in fear
   d. any of the above

2. In the course of the taking includes _____.
   a. prior to
   b. contemporaneous with
   c. after
   d. all of the above

CASE

Schram v. State, *614 So.2d 646 (Fla. 2d DCA 1993).*

Defendant was convicted in the Circuit Court, Hillsborough County, M. William Graybill and Susan Sexton, JJ., of robbery with a deadly weapon. Defendant appealed. The District Court of Appeal, Frank, J., held that evidence was insufficient to sustain conviction.

Reversed and remanded.

FRANK, Judge.

Betty Schram was convicted of robbery with a deadly weapon after she walked into a convenience store and announced to the clerk that she intended to take two twelve-packs of beer. The clerk saw a bulge in Schram's back pocket, which he assumed was a knife, and he testified that Schram moved her hands toward her back before she took the beer from the counter and walked out.   At trial the clerk testified that he feared for his safety because he felt that Schram might remove a knife from her pocket and use it. Furthermore, her appearance made him anxious; she wore a black mesh shirt over a black bra; the left side of her head was shaved and tattooed; and her nose was pierced with a ring. On appeal, Schram contends that the evidence was insufficient to convict her of robbery with a deadly weapon and that the trial court should have granted her motion for directed verdict. We agree. The other points she raises we have considered and find without merit.

On cross examination the clerk admitted that Schram never drew a knife or any weapon. She expressed no threats, and he made no attempt to stop her from taking the beer. Much of his fear was generated by her unusual appearance. Schram testified that she took the beer after consulting with a friend because neither of them had money to pay for it.   Rather than a knife, her pockets contained a wallet, cigarettes, and a lighter. Although she had a knife in her pocket when she was later arrested at her apartment, she stated that she had not carried it with her to the store but had been using it at home to carve mannequins.

In a case such as this, where no force has been used, the defendant can be convicted of robbery only if the victim is placed in fear of death or great bodily harm. **Brown v. State,** *397 So.2d 1153 (Fla. 5th DCA 1981).* The controlling factor, however, is not the victim's mere statement that he had been placed in fear:

> [T]he question is not whether the victim here actually feared appellant, but whether a jury could conclude that a reasonable person under like circumstances would be sufficiently threatened to accede to the robbers demands. *397 So.2d at 1155.*

In a cogent analysis, the fourth district in **Butler v. State,** *602 So.2d 1303 (Fla. 1st DCA 1992),* examined precisely what it would take for a reasonable person to be "sufficiently threatened to accede to the robber's demands," and determined that the evidence must be sufficient for the jury to conclude that the perpetrator actually carried a deadly weapon during the offense. The facts in **Butler** bear a striking similarity to those in this case. The defendant walked into a dry cleaning establishment carrying a pair of pants over his arm and concealing what the victim assumed was a gun. Neither employee saw a gun or even the outline of a gun. The defendant pointed toward the object under the pants, but he never told them he had a gun or threatened to shoot or kill them. Although in **Butler** a gun was never recovered, the fact that a knife was later found in Schram's possession in this case is a distinction of no consequence; there was no evidence indicating that Schram actually carried the knife during the robbery. Thus, in this case, as was true in **Butler,** the state presented no more than the victim's subjective belief that the defendant was armed. This evidence is insufficient for an armed robbery conviction.

Although the armed robbery conviction must be reversed, the state did prove beyond a reasonable doubt that Schram stole beer valued at $16.52. Therefore, on remand, the trial court shall enter judgment against Schram for that offense and sentence her accordingly.

Reversed and remanded.

CAMPBELL, A.C.J., and PATTERSON, J., concur.

REVIEW

1. To convict a defendant of armed robbery, _____.
    a. the victim must see the weapon
    b. the State must produce the weapon at trial
    c. both a and b
    d. neither a nor b

EXTORTION

Florida law criminalizes extortion and requires a showing of a threat made maliciously and accompanied by a demand for money or other pecuniary advantage.
To prove extortion, the State must establish that the extortionist intended to damage the victim by coercing him to take some action, such as the payment of money, against his will. There is no requirement, however, that the extortionist intend (or even have the ability) to carry out his threat.

Extortion may occur verbally or in writing. It may be by letter or fax. It is a malicious threat to injure a person, property, or their reputation. It could be a malicious threat to expose one to disgrace or expose a secret of impute a deformity or lack of chastity. There must be an intent to extort money or a financial advantage or to compel the person to do an act or refrain from doing an act.

CASE

Alonso v. State, 447 So.2d 1029 (Fla. 4th DCA 1984).

Defendant was convicted in Circuit Court, Palm Beach County, Maurice J. Hall, J., of extortion, and he appealed. The District Court of Appeal, Hersey, J., held that: (1) evidence established that defendant intended to extort money, and (2) instruction on "malice" was correct.

Affirmed.

HERSEY, Judge.

Andres Alonso appeals his conviction for extortion. He contends that the trial court gave an incorrect instruction on "malice" and that the intention to extort money was not proved. The latter point is totally lacking in merit. The former issue, while more persuasive, is also lacking in merit.

Appellant was charged under Section 836.05, Florida Statutes (1981), which requires a showing of a threat made maliciously and accompanied by a demand for money or other pecuniary advantage. At trial it was argued by appellant that an instruction to the jury on malice should be based upon the standard jury instruction defining the crime of shooting or throwing missiles into a dwelling. That instruction includes the requirement that the state show the defendant acted "with the knowledge that injury or damage will or may be caused to another person or the property of another person." Such an instruction would have been inappropriate here because of its potential for confusing the jury. The extortionist must intend to damage the victim by coercing him to take some action, such as the payment of money, against his will. There is no requirement, however, that the extortionist intend (or even have the ability) to carry out his threat. Suppose the extortionist at one time possessed photographs showing a public figure in a compromising situation. He writes a letter threatening exposure unless an amount of money is paid. The photographs are lost in a fire. The injury actually caused the victim by the extortionist is the extraction of an amount of money. It is no longer possible for him to injure or damage the reputation of the victim by publishing the photographs. Under the requested instruction the jury might be led to suppose that since the threat was impossible of fulfillment there could realistically be no malicious intent to injure or damage the victim. That would be an appropriate exercise of reasoning under the instruction requested. It is an inappropriate interpretation of the law. Thus the proffered instruction was properly rejected by the trial court.

Further, the extortionist need not hate his victim. That kind of malice is not contemplated by the crime of extortion. The basic statutory ingredients are a threat made maliciously with the intent to require another to perform an act against his will. The malice requirement is satisfied if the threat is made "willfully and purposely to the prejudice and injury of another, ..." Black's Law Dictionary, 4th Ed.

> The extortion statute prohibits only those utterances or communications which constitute malicious threats to do injury to another's person, reputation, or property. Furthermore, the threats must be made with the intent to extort money or the intent to compel another to act or refrain from acting against his will.

Carricarte v. State, 384 So.2d 1261 (Fla. 1980). A threat is malicious if it is made intentionally and without any lawful justification. Coupled with the requisite intent it constitutes the crime of extortion. The trial court's instructions conveyed these requirements to the jury in appropriate instructions.

Finding no error, we affirm.

AFFIRMED.

ANSTEAD, C.J., and LETTS, J., concur.

REVIEW

1. To convict one of extortion, the State must prove _____.
   a. intent to damage the victim
   b. the ability to carry out the threat made
   c. both a and b
   d. neither a nor b

CRIMINAL MISCHIEF

The crime of criminal mischief requires proof that a defendant willfully and maliciously injures or damages by any means any real or personal property belonging to another, including, but not limited to, the placement of graffiti thereon or other acts of vandalism thereto.

Criminal mischief can be a felony or a misdemeanor. If the damage is more than $1,000.00 it is a felony. If the damage is greater than $200.00 but less than $1,000.00 it is a first degree misdemeanor. It is a second degree misdemeanor if the damage is $200 or less. The State must prove damage and that the damage was done both willfully and maliciously. The criminal mischief statute covers both graffiti and vandalism.

CASE

In the Interest of J.R.S., a child, v. State, 569 So.2d 1323 (Fla. 1st DCA 1990).

Juvenile was adjudicated delinquent in the Circuit Court, Clay County, Giles P. Lewis, J., for criminal mischief. Juvenile appealed. The District Court of Appeal, Joanos, J., held that juvenile was not shown to have acted with malice and did not commit criminal mischief when he gained entry into parents' locked home.

Reversed and remanded.

JOANOS, Judge.

J.R.S. appeals an adjudication of delinquency for criminal mischief. Appellant contends the trial court erred in denying his motion for judgment of acquittal. We agree, and reverse the finding that appellant committed the offense of criminal mischief.

The facts reveal that the fifteen year old appellant argued with his mother one morning and then left for school. Appellant did not return home that day, and was reported missing by his family. The next morning, appellant gained entry into his locked home by "jimmying" a sliding glass door at the rear of the house.

On the basis of his forced entry into the home in which appellant resided with his parents, a petition for delinquency was filed alleging that appellant "did willfully and maliciously injure or damage the real or personal property of another, to-wit: door, the property of [his father], by prying open said door, . . . contrary to the provisions of Section 806.13, Florida Statutes." A second count charged that appellant committed trespass.

Appellant's father and the investigating officer testified at the adjudicatory hearing. Appellant's father stated the door latch had markings of the entry, and the screws which formerly held the latch could not be retightened. According to appellant's father, he repaired the latch with an oversized screw at a cost of ten cents. The father further testified that a neighbor called to tell him that his son had returned home. Upon receipt of that call, appellant's father notified the sheriff's department that his son was no longer missing, and then went home. The testimony of appellant's father established that appellant was living in his parents' home at the time, that his father had not told him he could not return, nor had his father asked him to leave.

An officer of the Sheriff's Department went to appellant's home on February 15, 1990, after being notified that appellant had been found. The officer inspected the point of entry, and stated that in his opinion, there was no permanent damage. Consequently, he did not list any damage on his report.

Appellant was not sworn as a witness. However, under questioning from the trial court, appellant said he went into the house only because he was hungry. He explained that he did not call his father, because he thought if he did so he would get into trouble.

The defense moved for judgment of acquittal at the close of the state's case, and again after the officer testified on behalf of the defense. In addition, defense counsel advised the trial court that the parties were proceeding only on the charge of criminal mischief. The state argued that appellant's conduct constituted criminal mischief, even though no permanent damage had been done. The defense countered that the state failed to prove criminal intent, because appellant was just trying to get back into his house. Defense counsel analogized appellant's conduct to that of one who breaks a window to get into his own home, when he finds he has locked himself out. Observing that it would have been more prudent for appellant to call his father and ask for the key, the trial court found appellant committed the offense of criminal mischief. The subsequently entered order contained the finding that appellant "committed a delinquent act by violating Florida Statutes, Section(s) 806.13 and 810.08 which constitutes the offense of Criminal Mischief (60) days and Trespass (60 days), as evidenced by testimony and evidence adduced at the Adjudicatory Hearing on March 14, 1990."

The criminal mischief statute, section 806.13(1)(a), Florida Statutes (1989), provides:

> A person commits the offense of criminal mischief if he willfully and maliciously injures or damages by any means any real or personal property belonging to another, including, but not limited to, the placement of graffiti thereon or other acts of vandalism thereto.

The offense has its origin in the common law offense of malicious mischief. *Reed v. State,* 470 So.2d 1382, 1394 (Fla. 1985). *Black's* defines "malicious mischief" thusly:

> Willful destruction of personal property, from actual ill will or resentment towards its owner or possessor. Though only a trespass at the common law, it is now, by most statutes, made severely penal.

Black's Law Dictionary 863 (5th ed. 1979).

Damage to the property of another is an essential element of the offense of criminal mischief. **D.B. v. State,** *559 So.2d 305 (Fla. 3d DCA 1990)*; **Valdes v. State,** *510 So.2d 631, 632 (Fla. 3d DCA 1987), review denied,* **State v. J.C.B.,** *520 So.2d 586 (Fla. 1988)*; **Roberts v. State,** *461 So.2d 212, 214 (Fla. 1ˢᵗ DCA 1984)*; **N.R. v. State,** *452 So.2d 1052 (Fla. 3d DCA 1984).* However, the specific value of the property damage is relevant only to the severity of the crime. **Valdes,** *510 So.2d at 632.*

As the state concedes, the opinions dealing with the offense of criminal mischief do not state expressly that the element of malice required by the statute is presumed upon a finding of property damage. We reject the state's contention that pertinent case law can be read as standing for such a sweeping proposition. Rather, the cases affirming a finding of guilt of criminal mischief indicate that the circumstances surrounding the conduct which resulted in damage will determine whether the element of malice was present.

We conclude that the facts in this case do not constitute the offense of criminal mischief. The state failed to establish the element of malice, i.e., that appellant acted from actual ill will or resentment toward his parents as owners of the allegedly damaged property. In addition, the state agrees that appellant was found guilty of and adjudicated for the offense of criminal mischief only, and that the ambiguity in the order should be corrected to reflect that fact.

Accordingly, the order adjudicating appellant guilty of criminal mischief and trespass is reversed, and the cause is remanded with directions to enter a clarifying order reflecting that appellant was tried only for the offense of criminal mischief, and that this court has determined the evidence is insufficient for a finding of guilt of the charged offense.

SHIVERS, C.J., and ZEHMER, J., concur.

REVIEW

1. To convict one of criminal mischief, the State must prove _____.
   a. damage
   b. motive
   c. both a and b
   d. neither a nor b

BURGLARY

Florida law distinguishes between burglary and robbery: property is burglarized while people are robbed. A burglary occurs where a defendant enters and remains in a structure, conveyance, or dwelling with the intent to commit a crime therein. A defendant can commit a burglary by either entering the property without permission or by remaining in it after consent to be there has been withdrawn. The latter is limited to incidents where the remaining is done surreptitiously, and where no permission is given by the owner or anyone authorized to act on the owner's behalf. Additionally, the defendant at the time of the incident must have had a fully formed conscious intent to commit a particular offense.

For instance, if premises were open to the public but a defendant remains after closing, he or she may be guilty of burglary. Moreover, the defendant's entire body need not enter the premises. Enough of the defendant's body must enter in order to be able to commit the crime.

Unexplained possession of recently stolen property may justify a burglary conviction. The circumstances of the burglary and the possession of the stolen properly must be taken into consideration.

A structure is a building of any kind, temporary or permanent. However, the structure must have a roof. Structures also include the enclosed space of ground and outbuildings surrounding that structure.

A conveyance is any motor vehicle, ship, vessel, railroad car, trailer, aircraft, or sleeping car. Entering a conveyance includes taking apart any portion of the conveyance.

The punishment for burglary is greater if there are certain aggravating circumstances present. For example, if the defendant commits a battery or an assault, it is a more serious offense. The penalties are harsher if the defendant is armed. If there is no intention to commit a particular crime, a defendant will only be guilty of trespass.

CASE

Perkins v. State, 682 So.2d 1083 (Fla. 1996).

Defendant was convicted in the Circuit Court, Duval County, John D. Southwood, J., of burglary of dwelling, and defendant appealed. The District Court of Appeal, 630 So.2d 1180, affirmed. Accepting jurisdiction to review question certified to be of great public importance, the Supreme Court held that it is not necessary for structure or conveyance to be occupied in order for it to be "dwelling," for purposes of statute proscribing burglary of dwelling.

Ordered accordingly.

PER CURIAM.

We have for review *Perkins v. State, 630 So.2d 1180 (Fla.1st DCA 1994).* We accepted jurisdiction to answer the following question certified to be of great public importance: [FN1]

> DO THE 1982 AMENDMENTS TO CHAPTER 810, FLORIDA STATUTES, SUPERSEDE THE COMMON LAW DEFINITION OF A DWELLING, WHEREBY A STRUCTURE'S DESIGN OR SUITABILITY FOR HABITATION, RATHER THAN ACTUAL OCCUPANCY OR INTENT TO OCCUPY, IS CONTROLLING IN DETERMINING WHETHER A STRUCTURE CONSTITUTES A DWELLING?

Id. at 1182. For the reasons expressed below, we answer the certified question in the affirmative and approve the decision under review.

FACTS

Houston D. Perkins was charged with and convicted of the offense of burglary of a dwelling, a second degree felony, under section 810.011(2), Florida Statutes (1995). The burglarized house was built in 1953 by the present owner and was unoccupied at the time of the burglary. The owner lived in the house for many years, but moved out several months prior to the burglary. The owner had no intent to return to the house as an occupant; however, he periodically rented the home and hoped to rent or sell it in the future "for someone to live in." *Perkins, 630 So.2d at 1181.*

On the day of the burglary, the house contained various items of personalty, including a stove, refrigerator, washer, microwave, and assorted items in the closets and cabinets. The telephone had been disconnected and the water turned off, but the electricity was on and well water was available on the property. The owner last visited the house three to four weeks before the burglary when he moved the grass and picked up the trash.

Perkins appealed his conviction and sentence, contending that the house he burglarized did not constitute a "dwelling" under section 810.011(2) because it was unoccupied and, therefore, he should have been adjudicated and sentenced only for the offense of burglary of a structure, a third-degree felony under section 810.02, Florida Statutes (1995). In a split decision, the First District affirmed, holding the house Perkins burglarized was a "dwelling" within the meaning of section 810.011(2), but certified the above question for our review.

LAW AND ANALYSIS

Prior to 1982, the courts had to rely on the common law definition of "dwelling" as that word was used in the statutory crime of burglary of a dwelling. For example, in ***Smith v. State**, 80 Fla. 315, 85 So. 911 (1920),* we held that under the common law a house was not a "dwelling" where the owner, who had occupied the home with his family, had moved out nine months before the burglary. We focused on the requirement that the house be occupied or that the owner intend to return in explaining the common law:

> Temporary absence of the occupant does not take away from a dwelling house its character as such, but it must be made to appear that such occupant left the house animo revertendi [FN2] in order to constitute an unlawful breaking and entry of the house during such absence burglary.

80 Fla. at 318, 85 So. at 912 (citations omitted). Thus, we held that the common law definition of "dwelling" contemplated that a structure be occupied and not merely capable of or suitable for occupation. See also ***Tukes v. State**, 346 So.2d 1056 (Fla. 1st DCA 1977)* (holding a former residence unoccupied for one month and for sale was no longer a "dwelling"). However, section 810.011(2) was amended in 1982 and now provides in pertinent part:

> "Dwelling" means a building or conveyance of any kind, either temporary or permanent, mobile or immobile, which has a roof over it and is designed to be occupied by people lodging therein at night, together with the curtilage thereof.

This amendment constitutes a significant change in the meaning of the word "dwelling" as used in the burglary statute.

The First District concluded that the house Perkins burglarized constituted a "dwelling" under the plain meaning of section 810.011(2) as amended in 1982. ***Perkins**, 630 So.2d at 1181.* Judge Lawrence, writing for the court, explained the significance of the 1982 amendment compared to the prior common law definition of "dwelling":

> Occupancy is no longer a critical element under this [statutory] definition. Rather, it is the design of the structure or conveyance which becomes paramount. If a structure or conveyance initially qualifies under this

definition, and its character is not substantially changed or modified to the extent that it becomes unsuitable for lodging by people, it remains a dwelling irrespective of actual occupancy. It is, therefore, immaterial whether the owner of an unoccupied dwelling has any intent to return to it.

Id. at 1181-82. We agree with the approve of this reasoning and analysis.

In *Holly v. Auld, 450 So.2d 217 (Fla. 1984),* we explained that the legislature's use of clear and unambiguous language which impairs a definite meaning renders unnecessary a resort to rules of statutory construction and interpretation unless a literal interpretation would produce an "unreasonable or ridiculous conclusion." The court's task is clear: "the statute must be given its plain and obvious meaning." *Id. at 219* (quoting *A.R. Douglass, Inc. v. McRainey, 102 Fla. 1141, 1144, 137 So. 157 (1931)).*

We find that the legislative definition of "dwelling" under section 810.011(2) is both clear and unambiguous, and a literal interpretation thereof does not lead to an "unreasonable or ridiculous conclusion." [FN3] We have long recognized the legislature's prerogative in defining or, in this case, redefining crimes. See *State v. Hamilton, 660 So.2d 1038 (Fla.1995); Chapman v. Lake, 112 Fla. 746, 151 So. 399 (1933).* It is apparent here that the legislature has extended broad protection to buildings or conveyances of any kind that are designed for human habitation. Hence, an empty house in a neighborhood is extended the same protection as one presently occupied.

CONCLUSION

The house Perkins burglarized served as the owner's residence for many years before becoming a residential rental property. Although no one occupied the house at the time of the burglary, it was "designed to be occupied by people lodging therein at night," and the owner intended it be used for that purpose. Because the house falls within the plain meaning of the definition of "dwelling" under section 810.011(2), we conclude that Perkins was properly convicted and sentenced for the second-degree felony of burglary of a dwelling. See § 810.011(2), Fla.Stat. (1995).

Accordingly, we answer the certified question in the affirmative, approve the decision under review, and disapprove *L.C. v. State, 579 So.2 783 (Fla. 3d DCA 1991),* to the extent it is inconsistent herewith.

It is so ordered.

KOGAN, C.J. and OVERTON, SHAW, GRIMES, HARDING, WELLS and ANSTEAD, JJ., concur.

FN1. We have jurisdiction pursuant to article V, section 3(b)(4) of the Florida Constitution.

FN2. "With intention to return." *Black's Law Dictionary,* 80 (5th ed. 1979).

FN3. The dissent below relied on portions of legislative staff materials and dicta in *L.C. v. State,* *579 So.2d 783 (Fla. 3d DCA 1991).* The legislative staff materials noted that "The practical effect of this bill is that the burglary of an unoccupied recreational vehicle or travel trailer is a second-degree felony rather than a third-degree felony." Of course, if the amendment were limited to this effect, the penalty for burglary of an unoccupied travel trailer would be greater than the penalty for burglary of an unoccupied house, a result that would appear to be unreasonable on its face. Because we have found the statute clear and not unreasonable in its plain meaning, we express no opinion as to the meaning of the staff materials. In *L.C.,* the appellants were adjudicated guilty of burglary of a dwelling after they broke into and entered a house that had been unoccupied for several months after the former occupant died. *Id. at 783.* Although the Third District affirmed the appellants' delinquency adjudications for burglary of a dwelling because "under the common law definition, the house burglarized in this case would still meet the definition of a dwelling," *id. at 784,* the court "agree[d] with appellants' argument that, in amending section 810.011(2), the legislature did not intend to overrule the common-law definition of a dwelling for purposes of the burglary statute." *Id.* We disapprove of this language in *L.C.*

REVIEW

1. For a building to be a dwelling, _____.
   a. it need not be occupied
   b. the owner need not intend to live in the structure him or herself
   c. both a and b
   d. neither a nor b

CASE

Bean v. State, *728 So.2d 781 (Fla. 4th DCA 1999).*

Defendant was convicted in the Circuit Court, Palm Beach County, Mary E. Lupo, J., of burglary of occupied structure with assault or battery. Defendant appealed. The District Court of Appeal, Dell, J., held that attached garage constituted structure within burglary statute, despite absence of door.

Affirmed.

DELL, Judge.

Dan Edward Bean appeals his conviction and sentence for burglary of an occupied structure with assault or battery. We affirm.

At about four o'clock in the afternoon, appellant entered Bernard Osting's garage, where Osting's friend had previously placed his bicycle. Osting saw appellant in the garage on his friend's bicycle. When Osting confronted appellant, he was straddling the bicycle and had his tools on the handlebars. A scuffle ensued and appellant punched Osting in the chest. The trial court denied appellant's motion for a judgment of acquittal.

Appellant has failed to demonstrate reversible error in his arguments that the State failed to prove stealthy entry, that the State did not rebut his defense that he entered he garage to avoid the rain, and that the State relied on an improper theory of guilt. Appellant also argues that the State failed to prove that the garage was a structure as defined in section 810.02(1), Florida Statutes (1997). Appellant concedes that he failed to make this argument in trial court. We deny his request to consider this question as a fundamental error. We will, however, address its factual implication.

Appellant argues that the garage did not constitute a "structure," because it did not have a door. He misplaces his reliance on *Small v. State, 710 So.2d 591 (Fla. 4th DCA 1998)*, where we held that a carport was not a "structure" as the term is used in the burglary statute. *Small* did not create a bright line test to determine whether the element of a "structure" has been met under the burglary statute. Rather, the court must make that determination on a case-by-case basis.

In this case, the attached garage is located in one wing of the house, sharing a common roof and three walls. The garage does not have a door. However, the absence of the door does not alter the reality that the garage, as depicted in State's Exhibit 1, is an integral part of the house, and is a "structure" within the meaning of section 810.02(1), Florida Statutes (1997).

AFFIRMED.

KLEIN and GROSS, JJ., concur.

REVIEW

1. To be a structure, it is necessary to _____.
   a. have a door
   b. be attached
   c. both a and b
   d. neither a nor b

CASE

Cowart v State, 582 So.2d 90 (Fla. 2d DCA 1991).

Defendant was convicted in the Circuit Court, Hillsborough County, Donald F. Castor, Acting J., of burglary of conveyance and petty theft. Defendant appealed. The District Court of Appeal, Schoonover, C.J., held that State presented insufficient evidence as to burglary charge.

Affirmed in part and reversed in part.

SCHOONOVER, Chief Judge.

The appellant, Tyrone Cowart, challenges the judgments and sentences entered against him pursuant to jury verdicts finding him guilty of burglary of a conveyance and petit theft. We affirm in part and reverse in part.

We find no merit in the appellant's contention concerning the conduct of his trial or in his contention that the trial court erred by denying his motion for a judgment of acquittal on the petit theft charge. We, accordingly, affirm the conviction and sentence on that charge.

We agree, however, with appellant's position that the trial court erred by not granting his motion for judgment of acquittal on the burglary of a conveyance charge. In order to prove the offense of burglary of a conveyance, it is necessary to prove, among other things, that the defendant entered or remained in a conveyance. § 810.02, Florida Statutes (1987). This element of the offense was not proven in this case. There was no evidence that the appellant entered or remained in the vehicle. The evidence merely established that the appellant was in possession of the victim's purse. This circumstantial evidence was not sufficient to allow the jury to return a guilty verdict.

Where the only proof of guilt is circumstantial, a conviction may not be upheld no matter how strongly the evidence may suggest guilt, unless the evidence is inconsistent with any reasonable hypothesis of innocence. *Bradford v. State, 460 So.2d 926 (Fla. 2d DCA 1984), petition for review denied, 467 So.2d 999 (Fla. 1985).* The defendant's version of the events must be believed if circumstances do not show that his version is false. *Bradford.* In this case, the state did not present sufficient evidence to allow the jury to find that the appellant's testimony that the had found the victim's purse behind a pawn shop was unreasonable. See *J.A.L. v. State, 409 So.2d 70 (Fla. 3d DCA 1982).*

We, accordingly, reverse and remand with instructions to discharge the appellant on the burglary of a conveyance charge. We affirm the petit theft conviction and sentence.

Affirmed in part and reversed in part.

DANAHY and THREADGILL, JJ., concur.

REVIEW

1. To convict a person of burglary, it is necessary to prove _____.
   a. entering
   b. remaining
   c. either a or b
   d. neither a nor b

CASE

Johnson v. State, 786 So.2d 1162 (Fla. 2001).

Defendant was convicted in the Circuit Court, Duval County, of, inter alia, causing bodily injury during commission of felony, specifically burglary. Defendant appealed. The District Court of Appeal affirmed, 737 So.2d 555, but certified conflict. The Supreme Court, Harding, J., held that record supported finding that even though store was open to public, defendant committed burglary by entering area behind store's cash register counter, which was not open to public.

Decision approved.

HARDING, J.

We have for review *Johnson v. State, 737 So.2d 555 (Fla. 1st DCA 1999)*, which is in apparent conflict with the opinions in *State v. Laster, 735 So.2d 481 (Fla.1999); State v. Butler, 735 So.2d 481 (Fla.1999);* and *Miller v. State, 733 So.2d 955 (Fla.1999)*. We have jurisdiction pursuant to *article V, section 3(b)(3) of the Florida Constitution*. We approve the result reached by the First District Court of Appeal in *Johnson*. Following a trial by jury, Johnson was convicted of attempted armed robbery while wearing a mask, attempted second-degree murder, and causing bodily injury during the commission of a felony, specifically burglary. The facts of the case are as follows:

In need of bail money for his girlfriend, appellant and his co-defendant, with masked faces and guns drawn, entered a convenience store that was open for business. While holding a gun on Mr. Goswami, one of the store owners, appellant followed him behind the check-out counter where the cash register was located, heedless of the other store owner's command that appellant was not permitted in that area. After appellant entered the prohibited area, he turned and fired twice at Mrs. Goswami, wounding her hand. Mr. Goswami immediately began to struggle with appellant's co-felon, and when appellant began striking her husband, Mrs. Goswami fought with appellant. During the fray, Mrs. Goswami obtained the gun she and her husband kept in their shop. Having armed herself,

332

she held the gun on appellant, told the two perpetrators to leave her husband alone, and shot appellant's cohort.

Johnson, 737 So.2d at 556. Johnson argues that his conviction for causing bodily injury during the commission of a felony cannot stand because the State did not establish an essential element of this crime, i.e., burglary. Johnson asserts that because the convenience store was open to the public when he entered, his conduct in this case is excluded from the burglary statute.

Section 810.02(1), Florida Statutes (1995), defines burglary:

"Burglary" means entering or remaining in a dwelling, a structure, or a conveyance with the intent to commit an offense therein, unless the premises are at the time open to the public or the defendant is licensed or invited to enter or remain.

In *Miller v. State*, 733 So.2d 955 (Fla.1998), this Court addressed another case involving an alleged burglary of an "open to the public" structure. The State's argument in *Miller* was geared towards showing that Miller did not have consent to enter the grocery store to commit a crime, as evidenced by the prosecutor's closing arguments to the jury:

As to burglary, the state must show that the defendant entered or remained in a structure owned or in the possession of James Jung, the store. Did not have the permission or consent of James Jung or anyone else to authorized to allow him to come in there.

Now its an open store, yes, at first, but you heard Mr. Bledsoe ask Mr. Jung did you give them or anyone permission to come in your store, pull guns on you and your security guard, shoot you both and take your money and take his gun?

Well, no, of course not, so at the time they committed the crime Willie Miller was remaining in a structure and did not have the permission or consent of Mr. Jung and at the time of entering or remaining in the structure the defendant, Willie Miller, had a fully formed conscious intent to commit an offense therein.

(Record at 1094).

This Court rejected the State's theory and held that "if a defendant can establish that the premises were open to the public, then this is a *complete* defense" to a burglary charge. *733 So.2d at 957.* However, it was never argued in *Miller* that although the store was open to the public, the area behind the counter was not open to the public. Hence, the *Miller* opinion did not address the question of whether the area behind the counter could be "closed" to the public.

Shortly thereafter, this Court issued decisions in *State v. Butler*, 735 So.2d 481, 482 (Fla.1999), and *State v. Laster*, 735 So.2d 481, 481 (Fla.1999), wherein we stated, "We do not find any merit to the State's argument in this case that the area behind the counter was not open to the public." This Court treated *Butler* and *Laster* as being controlled by our decision in *Miller*. We determined that both cases were resolved by our holding in *Miller* that if a defendant can establish that the premises were open to the public, then this is a complete defense to the charge of burglary. But contrary to Johnson's argument, the opinions in *Butler* and *Laster* were not intended to foreclose the State from proving to a jury that an area behind a counter was not open to the public.

In *Dakes v. State, 545 So.2d 939 (Fla. 3d DCA 1989)*, the district court was faced with a similar question-whether entry into a storeroom of an open retail store amounted to burglary. The district court concluded that "although the store itself was open to the public, the closed storeroom to which access was clearly restricted was not part of the premises open to the public." *Id. at 940*. Subsequent to the *Dakes* decision, this Court adopted the following amendment to the burglary jury instruction:

> A person may be guilty of this offense if he or she entered into or remained in areas of the premises which he or she knew or should have known were not open to the public. *Standard Jury Instructions in Criminal Cases*, 697 So.2d 84, 90 (Fla.1997).

In a comment to the amendment, the Supreme Court Committee on Standard Jury Instructions (Criminal) cited to *Dakes* and stated the following:

> The committee believes that the additional language is necessary in certain factual situations. *See Dakes v. State, 545 So.2d 939 (Fla. 3d DCA 1989)*. *Id. at 90-91*.

We conclude that the question of whether the area behind the counter was open to the public is a question of fact for the jury to decide. The standard jury instruction properly instructs the jury on how to make this determination. Accordingly, we approve the result of the First District Court of Appeal in this case.

It is so ordered.

WELLS, C.J., and SHAW, ANSTEAD, PARIENTE and LEWIS, JJ., concur.

QUINCE, J., recused.

REVIEW

1. It is a defense to burglary if the premises are _____.
   a. open to the public
   b. the defendant had permission to be on the premises
   c. both a and b
   d. neither a nor b

CASE

Blanchard v. State, 767 So.2d 573 (Fla. 5th DCA 2000).

Defendant was convicted in the Circuit Court, Osceola County, Anthony H. Johnson, J., of burglary with a weapon and petit theft. Defendant appealed. The District Court of Appeal, Cobb, J., held that: (1) defendant who stole bicycle from enclosed front porch could be convicted of burglary, and (2) burglary conviction was properly scored as first-degree felony.

Affirmed.

COBB, Judge.

The appellant, Blanchard, was convicted of burglary with a weapon and petit theft. The facts indicate Blanchard entered the glass-enclosed front porch area of a duplex home through a screen door. Separate doors connected the two units to the shared porch. The doorbell on the front of the building was inoperative. Ms. Mejia, the occupant of one unit, heard the screen door, looked out a window, saw Blanchard, and called 911. She saw that he was taking her bicycle off the porch and when she protested Blanchard produced a knife and warned her to desist.

Blanchard argues that the evidence was insufficient to prove entry into a residence since he stole the bicycle from a "common area" of an apartment building that was open to the public. In support of his argument he relies on *Miller v. State,* 733 So.2d 955 (Fla. 1998). He also contends in the alternative that his conviction for burglary was wrongfully scored as a first degree felony under section 810.02(2), Florida Statutes, because the jury made a specific finding that he possessed a weapon, but not a dangerous weapon. [FN1]

In response to the first argument the state points to evidence that the porch was enclosed, had an outside bell (even though inoperative), that the victim kept plants and furniture on her part of the porch and treated it as part of the home, and testified repeatedly that she considered the porch "private." The state also points out that the statutory definition of "dwelling" expressly includes "any attached porch." See § 810.011(2), Fla. Stat. (1999). The state argues that Blanchard's claim that the porch was "open to the public" was an affirmative defense, and, as such, was properly left for jury determination. The state also relates that in *Miller* the supreme court expressly limited its decision to public structures, such as the grocery store involved in that case, while the instant case concerns a private home. As the state observes, there was no evidence adduced that Blanchard was either an invitee or licensee. We agree with the state and affirm the burglary conviction.

We find no merit in Blanchard's remaining issue. Given the wording of the amended information and the jury finding that the defendant possessed a weapon, the burglary conviction was properly reclassified and scored as a first degree felony pursuant to section 775.087(1), Florida Statutes.

AFFIRMED.

SAWAYA and PLEUS, JJ., concur.

FN1. The jury also specifically found that in the course of committing the offense no assault was committed.

REVIEW

1. A dwelling includes _____.
    a. the garage
    b. an attached porch
    c. both a and b
    d. neither a nor b

ARSON

There are three different arson offenses a person can be charged with. First degree arson is the more serious of these. To commit arson, a defendant damages a structure or its contents by fire or explosion. The damage must be done wilfully and unlawfully or caused while the defendant was committing a felony. The structure may be a dwelling, an institution, or a structure. In first degree cases, the defendant also knows or has reason to know people are inside. In second degree arson, the human being element is missing.

Structures include buildings, enclosed areas with roofs, any real property, tents, portable buildings, vehicles, vessels, watercraft or aircraft.

The third crime of arson involves a fire bomb. The defendant either manufactures, possesses, gives, offers, transfers, loans, or sells to another, or transports or disposes of a fire bomb. The defendant must intend the fire bomb be used wilfully and unlawfully to damage any structure or property. A fire bomb may be a container of flammable liquid, combustible liquid or any incendiary chemical mixture or compound. It needs a wick or means of ignition. No device commercially manufactured primarily for the purpose of illumination, heating or cooking will be found to be a fire bomb.

CASE

Knighten v. State, 568 So.2d 1001 (Fla. 2d DCA 1990).

Defendant was convicted of arson by the Circuit Court, Polk, J. Tim Strickland, J., based upon defendant's setting fire to his shirt while incarcerated in drunk tank of municipal jail. Defendant appealed. The District Court of Appeal held that: (1) minor damage to interior of jail cell from burning shirt was sufficient to support defendant's conviction; (2) all that State needed to show in order to convict defendant was that defendant intentionally started fire, not that he intended to damage structure; and (3) trial court erred in imposing court costs on defendant without adequate prior notice to defendant.

Convictions and sentences affirmed; court costs stricken and remanded.

PER CURIAM.

John Henry Knighten appeals his conviction and sentence for arson, a violation of section 806.01, Florida Statutes (1987). [Footnote 1 omitted] With the exception of that portion of the trial court's order which requires the payment of court costs, we affirm.

Knighten, while incarcerated in the "drunk tank" of the Lake Wales municipal jail, set fire to his shirt. It appears that Knighten may have become enraged when the police did not respond to his demand for a telephone call. The burning shirt, which Knighten hung on a wire descending from the ceiling, caused minor damage to the interior of the cell. We believe this structural damage is sufficient to support a conviction. *Granville v. State, 373 So.2d 716 (Fla. 1st DCA 1979).* The fact Knighten characterizes the damage as *"de minimis"* is more relevant, we believe, when considering the severity of the punishment merited by his actions than when determining the legal sufficiency of the evidence. [FN2]

Knighten also argues that the state failed to prove he intended to damage the structure. Arson, however, is a general intent crime. *Linehan v. State, 442 So.2d 244 (Fla. 2d DCA 1983), aff'd, 476 So.2d 1262 (Fla. 1985).* All that needed to be shown was that Knighten intentionally started the fire. Knighten admitted this in his own testimony, though claiming the fire was only an attention-getting device.

We do agree that the trial court erred in imposing court costs without adequate prior notice to Knighten. See *Wood v. State, 544 So.2d 1004 (Fla. 1989).* Accordingly, we strike this provision of the judgment and sentence without prejudice to the state to seek reimposition of these costs after proper notice.

Convictions and sentenced affirmed; court costs stricken; remanded for further proceedings consistent with this opinion.

SCHEB, A.C.J., and DANAHY and HALL, JJ., concur.

FN2. We note that the sentence in this case, which was not cross-appealed by the state, represents a substantial departure downward from the guideline recommendation.

REVIEW

1. Arson _____.
   a. is a general intent crime
   b. is a specific intent crime
   c. both a and b
   d. neither a nor b

2. To convict one of arson, the State must prove _____.
   a. intent to start a fire
   b. intent to do damage
   c. both a and b
   d. neither a nor b

THINKING CRITICALLY

1. What was the defendant's intent in the *T.L.M.* case? Did T.L.M. deprive anyone of a benefit? What if there had been a fire that day? Would the result in the case have been different?

2. Walter snatches a purse out of an open car. Both money and a firearm were in the purse. There is an eyewitness to the crime. There was $28.73 in the purse. What should Walter be charged with? Why?

3.   Ray accepts a ride from a friend driving a stolen car. The steering column is broken leading Ray to suspect the car was stolen. Can Ray be charged with grand theft of a motor vehicle? As a passenger, has Ray "used" the car? Did he deprive the owner of the car? Is grand theft a specific or general intent crime?

4.   Several kids are found sleeping in a van with no tags and a broken back window. Are they guilty of grand theft? What if the van is only worth $225.00?

5.   What was the "property" that was stolen in *Iglesias*? Do you agree with the court's reasoning? What if the work was done properly and for a reasonable price? Would it change the outcome?

6.   Was the incident in the *Wright* case a grand theft or a petit theft? What if the ATM card had been used to withdraw money?

7.   Do you agree with the court's holding in *Camp*? What if she was using the checks to satisfy the credit card debt of several family members? Is it still personal use? What about for friends?   What if JoAnn Camp had sold the checks to a third party?

8.   Natasha presents a forged prescription to the pharmacist. She had been asked by a friend to go to the drugstore and get the prescription filled. Has Natasha committed a crime? If so, what? What if she intended to receive some of the pills obtained? What additional information would you like to have about the incident?

9.   Do you agree with the court's ruling in *Friedman*? Should the statute be changed to include private records? Why or why not?

10. Carmen forges a fictitious court order and sends a copy to a client. The order looks authentic and contains a forged signature of the judge. The original was never actually filed with the court. Can Carmen be convicted of uttering a forgery? Is the order a public record?

11. Rod signs a friend's name to his traffic citation. Has he committed a criminal offense? If so, what?

12. Do you agree with the result in *Bass*? What if Brenda handed over $3.00 and then was struck because she didn't have enough money? Would it be "in the course of the taking?"

13. Chase pawned Susan's VCR within hours after she is found murdered in her home. His prints are found in her house. Can he be convicted of home invasion robbery? Why or why not? Does it matter whether she was killed first or the VCR was taken first? Why or why not? Can you rob a dead person?

14. Janice leaves her purse at the table in a bar and is out on the dance floor. Howard takes her money and her credit cards. Has he committed a robbery? Why or why not? What if she comes back the table as he is doing so and confronts him? What additional facts do you need to know?

15. Two co-defendants hold up a pizza place. One of them demands an employee give him his shirt to wear to prevent passers by from becoming suspicious. Has the employee been robbed of his shirt? Why or why not?

16. Should Betty have been convicted of robbery in the *Schram* case? Should one's appearance be found to be sufficient to place a victim in fear? Should one's size?

17. Did Alonso need to be paid money to be convicted of extortion? How does extortion differ from theft or robbery?

18.   Alex threatens to have Bruce arrested if Bruce does not give him money. Bruce has not committed any crimes for which Alex could have him arrested. Out of fear, Bruce pays anyway. Can Bruce have Alex charged with extortion? Why or why not?

19.   Would the result in *J.R.S.* be different if the father had told his son not to return to the home? Should it be? Is it relevant that J.R.S.' reason for entering the home was that he was hungry? Should it be? Would it pass constitutional muster if malice was presumed upon a finding of property damage? Should it be?

20.   How can the state prove ill will or malice in a criminal mischief case? What circumstances should the court look to?

21.   Do you agree with the court's holding in *Perkins*? What if the property has been abandoned and condemned? What if the house is waiting to be torn down?

22. What if someone lives in a back room of a business? Is it a dwelling then? What about a carton box that someone lives in? Is it a dwelling?

23. What if the garage was not attached to the house in **Bean**? Would the result have been different? Should a carport be considered a structure?

24. Hank enters Frank's yard to steal a motor attached to a boat parked on a trailer in the yard. The backyard is not fenced or enclosed in any way. Can Hank be charged with burglary? Why or why not?

25. Wilson enters the yard of a home. The property is a private residence hidden from the road by trees and shrubs and the back yard is surrounded by a 6 foot privacy fence on three sides. Wilson removes a screen from a rear window, breaks the glass and sets off an alarm. He flees. Has Wilson committed a burglary? Why or why not?

26. Gabe steals items from the open bed of a pickup truck. Has he committed a burglary? Why or why not?

27. Stella gets a restraining order against her husband Nicholas. Pursuant to a court order, Nicholas is not to enter the marital home that Stella and he own jointly. Nicholas goes to the house and batters Stella. Can Nicholas be charged with burglary of a dwelling he owns? Why or why not?

28. Do you agree with the Court's holding in *Cowart*? What other facts about the heft of the purse would be important to know? What if Tyrone had tried to return the purse but items were missing?

29. Should the defense bear the burden of proving consent in a burglary case? Why or why not?

30.   Should the prosecution be required to prove the "remaining in" element of burglary was done surreptitiously? Why or why not?

31.   Jay pulls into a drive thru of a fast food restaurant. While the employee's back is turned, Jay reaches in and grabs money from the register. Has a burglary been committed? What if Jay demanded the money but did not reach into the window himself? Is your answer the same? Why or why not?

32.   What if the porch in *Blanchard* could be reached only by a walkway? Is it still "attached" for purposes of the burglary statute? What if the porch had been empty? Would the conviction have been upheld?

33.   Did John Henry commit arson in your opinion? What if there had been no damage other than to his own shirt? What if John Henry had hurt himself?

34. A group of juveniles build a campfire in a garage to see what will happen. The garage burns down. Are they guilty of arson? Why or why not?

CHAPTER 11 ANSWER KEY

REVIEW QUESTIONS

T.L.M. v. State
1. b

State v. Iglesias
1. c

State v. Wright
1. b

State v. Camp
1. d

State v. Friedman
1. b

Bass v. State
1. d
2. d

Schram v. State
1. a

Alonso v. State
1. a

In the Interest of J.R.S., a child, v. State
1. c

Perkins v. State
1. b

Bean v. State
1. b

Cowart v State
1. c

Johnson v. State
1. c

Blanchard v. State

1. c

Knighten v. State
1. a
2. a

CHAPTER 12

CRIMES AGAINST PUBLIC
ORDER AND MORALS

PANHANDLING

In general, Florida law prohibits solicitation of money without a license in certain restricted areas. The constitutionality of laws prohibiting panhandling has been scrutinized as a violation of the First Amendment right to Freedom of Speech. Nonetheless, Florida maintains on the books certain narrowly tailored laws prohibiting panhandling without a license and in certain areas.

Many counties and cities in Florida have their own laws regarding panhandling. There may be designated areas outside of which panhandling is a violation. An individual may be required to have a permit to panhandle. Local law enforcement may issue picture I.D.'s after running a criminal history on the person. Some restrictions on panhandling are permissible, others may violate the Constitution.

CASE

Ledford v. State, *652 So.2d 1254 (Fla. 2d DCA 1995).*

Defendant pleaded no contest to charge under city ordinance prohibiting begging for money while about or upon any public way. The Circuit Court, Pinellas County, sitting in its appellate capacity, affirmed county court's order denying motion to dismiss, and defendant filed petition for writ of certiorari. The District Court of Appeal, Frank, C.J., held that: (1) ordinance was unconstitutionally overbroad, and infringed on defendant's free speech rights in manner which, under strict scrutiny, was more intrusive than necessary, and (2) ordinance was also unconstitutionally vague.

Petition granted, writ issued and cased remanded.

FRANK, Chief Judge.

Wayne Dean Ledford seeks review of a decision of the circuit court acting in its appellate capacity affirming the county court's determination that section 20-79, City of St. Petersburg Code, "Begging for Money," is constitutional. We conclude that the ordinance is unconstitutional, grant the petition, issue the writ, and remand for further proceedings.

Ledford was arrested and charged with begging for money in violation of section 20-79, which provides as follows:

(a) It shall be unlawful for any person to beg for money in the City while about or upon any public way, and it shall be unlawful for any persons to be in or upon any public way in the City for the purpose of begging money for themselves or any other person.

(b) This section shall not apply to any solicitation made by a person who holds a valid solicitor's certificate of registration as required by section 17-166; nor shall this section apply to a solicitation contemplated by section 25-8 [Doing Business on streets and sidewalks], if the person making the solicitation has a permit as required by section 25-8.

The county court found the ordinance constitutional. Thereafter, Ledford pleaded no contest, specifically reserving the right to appeal the issue of the constitutionality of the ordinance. The circuit court per curiam affirmed the county court's order denying a motion to dismiss.

Ledford now launches several attacks upon the constitutionality of the ordinance. "Begging" is entitled to some constitutional protection and it cannot be disputed that the ordinance regulates speech in a public forum. Hence, the ordinance is subject to strict constitutional scrutiny. First Amendment analysis subjects the regulation of speech occurring on property traditionally available for public expression to the highest scrutiny. Such property includes streets and parks, which are said to "have immemorially been held in trust for the use of the public and, time out of mind, have been used for purposes of assembly, communicating thoughts between citizens, and discussing public questions." *Loper v. New York City Police Dept.*, *999 F.2d 699, 703 (2d Cir. 1993)* (quoting *Hague v. Committee for Indust. Org.*, *307 U.S. 496, 59 S.Ct. 954, 83 L.Ed. 1423 (1939)*). We conclude that the ordinance challenged here is overbroad and vague.

Florida courts have assessed the constitutionality of various ordinances restricting begging. For example, in *CCB v. State*, *458 So.2d 47 (Fla. 1st DCA 1984)*, the court examined a Jacksonville municipal ordinance prohibiting all forms of begging or soliciting alms in the streets or public places. Jacksonville's interest was to control undue annoyance and to prevent blockage of vehicular and pedestrian traffic. The First District determined that such an interest must be measured and balanced against the "rights of those who seek welfare and sustenance for themselves, by their own hand and voice" rather than by means of a charitable group's efforts undertaken in the same forum. The ordinance was declared overbroad and unconstitutional because it abridged in a "more intrusive manner than necessary ... the [F]irst [A]mendment right of individuals to beg or solicit alms for themselves." *CCB*, *458 So.2d at 48*. In condemning the Jacksonville ordinance, the court noted that, although the beggar's right is subject to regulation, it may not be precluded. "Protecting citizens from mere annoyance is not a sufficient compelling reason to absolutely deprive one of a [F]irst [A]mendment right." *458 So.2d at 50*. While the City of Jacksonville could not foreclose begging, it was allowed to "regulate that right subject to strict guidelines and definite standards closely related to permissible municipal interests, such as could be imposed by a narrowly drawn permit system." *Id.*

Other jurisdictions have confined the determination of the constitutionality of begging ordinances to the level of restriction imposed upon protected speech. The New York courts have held unconstitutional a penal law that *broadly* prohibits loitering, see *Loper v. New York City Police Dept., 999 F.2d 699 (2d Cir. 1993)*, and upheld as constitutional a prohibition against begging and panhandling in the New York City subway system, see *Young v. New York City Transit Authority, 903 F.2d 146 (2d Cir.), cert. denied, 498 U.S. 984, 111 S.Ct. 516, 112 L.Ed.2d 528 (1990)*. The restrictions on speech in the subway were constitutional because they were no greater than necessary to further the government's interest in preventing disruption and startling of passengers. Ordinances from Washington and Texas have been upheld because they prohibit "aggressive begging." The narrowly drawn laws protect the public from beggars who intimidate and accost those who pass to obtain money. *See Roulette v. City of Seattle, 850 F.Supp. 1442 (W.D. Wash. 1994); Johnson v. City of Dallas, 860 F.Supp. 344 (N.D. Tex. 1994)*. Both of these ordinances had the aim of preventing the passerby from being coerced, threatened, or intimidated by aggressive beggars.

We hold that begging is communication entitled to some degree of First Amendment protection. In the present case, since the ordinance restricts speech on the "public ways," a traditional public forum, the regulation is subject to intense scrutiny. Such regulations survive only if: (1) they are narrowly drawn to achieve a compelling governmental interest; (2) the regulations are reasonable; and (3) the viewpoint is neutral.

In subjecting the ordinance to strict scrutiny, we hold that section 20-79 of the City of St. Petersburg Code is unconstitutionally overbroad and infringes on Ledford's free speech rights in a manner more intrusive than is necessary. We embrace the holding in *CCB* that the aim of protecting citizens from annoyance is not a "compelling" reason to restrict speech in a traditionally public forum. *See CCB, 458 So.2d at 50*. Although section 20-79 does not ban begging in all public places, the ordinance is overbroad; it does not distinguish between "aggressive" and "passive" begging. Furthermore, section 20-79 is vague. To withstand a challenge for vagueness, an ordinance must provide adequate notice to persons of common understanding concerning the behavior prohibited and the specific intent required: it must provide "citizens, police officers and courts alike with sufficient guidelines to prevent arbitrary enforcement." *City of Seattle v. Webster, 115 Wash.2d 635, 645, 802 P.2d 1333, 1339 (Wash.1990), cert. denied, 500 U.S. 908, 111 S.Ct. 1690, 114 L.Ed.2d 85 (1991)*. The ordinance under review does not define the terms "beg" or "begging," nor is its intent expressed. Consequently, the danger of arbitrary enforcement exists.

For these reasons, the decision of the circuit court must be reversed. Accordingly, we grant the petition, issue the writ, and remand for further proceedings consistent with this opinion.

BLUE and WHATLEY, JJ., concur.

REVIEW

1. An individual's right to beg may be _____.
   a. precluded
   b. regulated
   c. both a and b
   d. neither a nor b

2. The regulation will be upheld if _____.
   a. narrowly drawn to achieve compelling governmental interest.
   b. reasonable
   c. viewpoint is neutral
   d. all of the above

LOITERING AND PROWLING

The crime of loitering and prowling involves two elements: (1) a person must be loitering or prowling in a place, at a time or in a manner not usual for law-abiding individuals; and (2) under circumstances that warrant a justifiable and reasonable alarm or immediate concern for the safety of persons or property in the vicinity. To prove the second element, the State must prove that the defendant's conduct is alarming in nature, creating an imminent threat to public safety. Because this second element requires such a high standard of proof, the crime of loitering and prowling is very difficult to prove.

It is unlawful to loiter and prowl in a place, at a time or manner not usual for law abiding citizens. Additionally the circumstances must warrant justifiable and reasonable alarm or an immediate concern for the safety of persons or property. Mere suspicion of future conduct is not sufficient. There are a number of circumstances to be taken into account. They are whether the person takes flight or refuses to identify themselves. Another issue is whether the person tries to conceal himself or herself or an object. The individual is to be afforded the opportunity to dispel any alarm or concern. One cannot be convicted if the law enforcement officer does not follow this procedure or if it appears the explanation is true and if believed would have dispelled the alarm or concern. The exception to this is if flight or another circumstance makes it impracticable to provide the chance for an explanation.

CASE

R.M. v. State, 754 So.2d 849 (Fla. 2d DCA 2000).

Defendant was convicted in the Circuit Court, Sarasota County, Lynn Silvertooth and Becky Titus, JJ., of loitering and prowling. Defendant appealed. The District Court of Appeal, Casanueva, J., held that defendant's walking on a public street in the company of a female at 11:00 p.m. would not support conviction for loitering and prowling.

Reversed and remanded with instructions.

CASANUEVA, Judge.

R.M. appeals his conviction for loitering and prowling in violation of section 856.021, Florida Statutes (1997), and contends that the trial court erred in failing to grant his motion for judgment of acquittal. Because the evidence presented by the State was legally sufficient for a conviction, we reverse.

On the night of February 6, 1999, a gas station manager in Sarasota saw a young man and woman in the parking lot of the Cadillac dealership across the street. For approximately ten minutes, the manager observed the two pulling on the door handles of one car after another. Because of their conduct and the late hour–it was almost 11:00 p.m.– the manager called the police. While she was on the phone the manager told the dispatcher that the two had begun walking down an adjacent street, but she never saw them again after they were arrested, and at trial the manager was unable to identify R.M. as the young man she saw pulling on the door handles.

Having presented this background information at the outset of the trial, the State turned its attention to the circumstances surrounding R.M.'s apprehension. An officer stopped R.M. and a companion as they walked in a public street approximately 50 feet away from the Cadillac dealership. When asked what he was doing there, R.M. gave somewhat inconsistent and improbable answers. A second officer testified that he inspected the lot and found what appeared to be fingerprints and pry marks on the windows or doorjambs of several cars, but because the vehicles were covered with dew and precipitation he could not obtain any more evidence. The police investigation uncovered no tools, either in the lot or on R.M.'s person. The second officer speculated that R.M. was conducting a "probe"-surveying the premises in anticipation of possible future criminal conduct.

In *J.S.B. v. State, 729 So.2d 456, 457 (Fla. 2d DCA 1999)*, this court held that to obtain a conviction for loitering and prowling the State must prove the following two elements: first, the accused must be loitering and prowling in a manner not usual for law-abiding citizens; and second, the factual circumstances must warrant a justifiable and reasonable concern for the safety of persons or property in the vicinity. To satisfy the second prong the State must prove that the accused's conduct is alarming in nature, creating an imminent threat to public safety.

Here, the State demonstrated that a citizen's concerns were aroused by what she observed in the Cadillac dealership, but no evidence actually linked R.M. to the parking lot. The manager did not identify R.M. as the person she saw on the lot, nor did the State connect the fingerprints on the vehicles with R.M. Furthermore, when apprehended, R.M. was walking on a public street in the company of a female at 11:00 p.m., behavior that cannot be described as particularly unusual or alarming. Thus, any suspicion that R.M. might have aroused by giving inconsistent or puzzling answers to the officer's questions is irrelevant, because there was no need for R.M. to dispel any alarm. See *W.A.E. v. State, 654 So.2d 193 (Fla. 2d DCA 1995)*; *K.R.R. v. State, 629 So.2d 1068 (Fla. 2d DCA 1994)*.

The factual circumstances might have been, as the officer conjectured, consistent with a "probe." However, mere suspicions of future criminal conduct will not satisfy the statute, which

354

requires proof that the suspect's actions created an immediate concern for the safety of nearby property. These facts did not rise to that level as there was no evidence of an imminent threat.

Accordingly, we reverse the order finding R.M. guilty of loitering and prowling and remand with instructions that he be discharged.

GREEN, A.C.J., and SALCINES, J., Concur.

REVIEW

1. To convict one of loitering and prowling, the State must prove _____.
   a. the defendant was loitering and prowling in a manner not usual for a law abiding citizen
   b. concern for safety of persons or property must be warranted
   c. both a and b
   d. neither a nor b

PROSTITUTION

Prostitution is not legal in the state of Florida. One cannot force, compel, or coerce another to be a prostitute. It is also unlawful to live off the earnings of a prostitute. A landlord may not rent space knowing it will be used for acts of prostitution. Violating these laws may be a felony or a misdemeanor.

CASE

Register v. State, 715 So.2d 274 (Fla. 1ˢᵗ DCA 1998)

Defendant was convicted in the Circuit Court for Columbia County, Thomas J. Kennon, Jr., J., of unlawfully procuring for prostitution a person under the age of 18 and misdemeanor possession of marijuana. Defendant appealed. The District Court of Appeal, Mickle, J., held that mere offer of money to a person under 18 to have sex with offeror is solicitation, rather than procurement for prostitution, and concluded that State failed to make prima facie case of charge.

Reversed in part, affirmed in part.

MICKLE, Judge.

Johnny Register appeals a conviction for unlawfully procuring for prostitution a person under the age of 18, a felony of the second degree pursuant to *section 796.03, Florida Statutes (1995).* The appellant contends that the trial court should have granted his motion for judgment of acquittal on this charge because, viewed in a light most favorable to the State, the evidence established, at most, that Register offered money to a 12- year-old girl to have sex with him. She refused his offer and immediately reported the incident to her mother, who notified authorities.

Having determined that the mere offer of money to a person under 18 to have sex with the offeror is solicitation, rather than procurement for prostitution, we conclude that the State failed to make a prima facie case of the crime charged. Accordingly, we reverse Register's conviction of procurement for prostitution (Count One). We affirm his conviction and sentence for misdemeanor possession of marijuana (Count Two) pursuant to *section 893.13, Florida Statutes (1995)*. *Section 796.03* states:

> Procuring person under age 18 for prostitution. --- A person who procures for prostitution, or causes to be prostituted, any person who is under the age of 18 commits a felony of the second degree, punishable as provided in [Chapter 775, Florida Statutes].

Section 796.07, Florida Statutes (1995), defines "prostitution": Prohibiting prostitution, etc.; evidence; penalties; definitions. ---

> (1) As used in this section:

>> (a) "Prostitution" means the giving or receiving of the body for sexual activity for hire but excludes sexual activity between spouses.

The act of prostitution "involves a financial element." *Gonzales v. State, 107 Fla. 121, 144 So. 311 (1932)*. Another subsection of this statute outlaws certain related activities:

> (2) *It is unlawful:*
>
> ....
>
> (f) *To solicit,* induce, entice, or procure *another to commit prostitution,* lewdness, or assignation.
>
> ....
>
> (4) A person who violates any provision of this section commits:

>> (a) A misdemeanor of the second degree for a first violation, punishable as provided in [Chapter 775].

§ 796.07, Fla. Stat. (emphasis added). The pertinent statutes do not define either "procure" or "solicit." The appellant argued at trial and on appeal that "solicitation" and "procurement" constitute different acts. According to the appellant's reasoning, the two terms are related only insofar as an initial act of *solicitation, i.e.,* seeking "to obtain by persuasion, entreaty, or formal application," or approaching a person "with an offer of sexual services" according to *The American Heritage Dictionary of the English Language* at 1229 (1973), might lead to an act of procurement, *i.e.,* obtaining, acquiring, or bringing about a result such as "obtain[ing] (a woman) to serve as a prostitute" according to *The American Heritage Dictionary of the English Language* at 1044 (1973). *See Ford v. City of Caldwell, 79 Idaho 499, 321 P.2d 589, 593 (1958)* (" 'Procure' means to cause, acquire, gain, get, obtain, bring about, cause to be done; it connotes action. 'Procurement' is the act of obtaining, attainment, acquisition, bringing about, effecting."). To show solicitation in the context of sexual activity:

[I]t is only necessary that the actor, with intent that another person commit a crime, have enticed, advised, incited, ordered, or otherwise encouraged that person to commit a crime. The crime solicited need not be committed.

Black's Law Dictionary at 1249 (5th ed.1979). That is, solicitation is the attempt to induce one to have sex. On the other hand, procurement contemplates the attaining, bringing about, or effecting of the result sought by the initial solicitation, such as obtaining someone as a prostitute for a third party. *See id. at 1087.*

*****

In the case at bar, the young victim testified that while she was babysitting at a friend's house, the 65-year-old appellant visited the residence, offered the victim "a joint," and asked her to walk over to his camper, which was situated on the same property. When the victim walked inside Register's dwelling, Register asked her to "spend the night" with him. The victim understood this offer to refer to sex. When the victim refused the offer, Register offered her $50 and then $100 to sleep with him. She told him "No" and immediately left and reported the incident to her mother. The victim's 12-year-old friend testified that she had remained discreetly outside the appellant's camper and overheard Register offering the victim various amounts of money to "stay over" at his place. She agreed that the victim had answered "No" and that the two girls immediately had reported what happened. The victim's mother testified that after speaking to her daughter, she confronted Register, who initially denied making the offer but subsequently admitted propositioning the girl and offering her drugs.

*****

After the State rested its case, the defense moved for judgment of acquittal on the grounds that section 796.03 does not proscribe someone's soliciting another person for the solicitor's own sexual benefit (rather than for a third party), and that the State had not proved a prima facie case of guilt of the charged offense. In support of its position, the defense cited **Barber v. State**, *397 So.2d 741, 742 (Fla. 5th DCA 1981)*, for the proposition that "the underlying purpose of section 796.03 ... appears to be to protect children from sexual exploitation for commercial purposes. " *See Grady v. State, 701 So.2d 1181, 1182 (Fla. 5th DCA 1997)* (affirming conviction of procurement for prostitution, despite defense of lack of knowledge that victim was under age 18, because the state's "compelling interest in protecting underage persons from being sexually abused or exploited" renders certain acts upon children punishable under section 796.03 despite the offender's ignorance of the victim's age). Defense counsel asserted that the "procurement" statute is directed toward persons (such as pimps) who seek to profit financially from engaging minors in prostitution with third parties. The State offered no evidence to suggest that Register sought to exploit the victim sexually for his own financial gain or sought to involve a third party in sexual activity with the victim.

The State, on the other hand, construed section 796.03 so broadly that the mere request and attempt to have sexual activity with a minor, without any resulting sexual activity, would constitute the completed act of procurement. That is, the prosecutor argued that the mere offer of money for sex, even where the child refused to oblige, was sufficient to bring Register's act within the proscriptions of section 796.03. The trial court denied the motion for judgment of acquittal. The court subsequently gave the jury the following instruction governing prostitution and procurement:

> Prostitution means the giving or receiving of the body for sexual activity for hire, but excludes sexual activity between spouses. It is not necessary that such sexual activity take place for the crime to be completed. Procure means to cause, acquire, gain, get, obtain, bring about, cause to be done; to instigate, to contrive, bring about, effect or cause; to persuade, induce, prevail upon, or cause a person to do something.

The record clearly demonstrates that the jury was concerned and very much confused regarding the meaning of the procurement charge. Fifteen minutes after starting deliberations, the jury asked the court for a dictionary definition of "procure." The trial judge denied the request but repeated the jury instruction on procurement. Less than an hour later, the jury requested a written definition of "procure," which the court sent to them over a defense objection. A third time, the jury returned with additional questions and was reinstructed on procuring a person under age 18. Within thirty minutes, the jury found Register guilty as charged.

*****

The Florida Legislature has classified as a felony the act of procuring for prostitution anyone under age 18. This designation is consistent with the intent to proscribe the commercial exploitation of children induced to engage in sexual activity with others for the financial benefit of the procurer pimp. Given the absence of a third party in the present case, we need not decide whether successfully inducing a person under age 18 to have sexual activity with the offeror himself falls within section 796.03 or 796.07. Procuring for prostitution anyone 18 years of age or older is a misdemeanor under section 796.07. Soliciting anyone (irrespective of age) for prostitution likewise is a misdemeanor under section 796.07. The appellant tried to induce the minor victim to have sex with him, but she refused his offer. This was mere solicitation, not procurement. *See Stevens v. State, 380 So.2d 495 (Fla. 2d DCA 1980)* (reversing conviction of procurement for prostitution under section 796.03 and remanding for discharge, where evidence showed that a man known to be a pimp had merely offered 15-year-old victim money and clothes, which she refused to accept, and that victim had refused to work for him). We find nothing in either statute that would support the State's argument that offering money while soliciting someone to have sex with the offeror was intended to have the same criminal consequences as inducing a victim to engage in sexual activity with a third party to the financial benefit of the pimp. A person who offers money to a minor to have sex with him commits a crime. The Florida Legislature has designated such an act of solicitation as a less severe crime than exploiting a minor to engage in sexual activity with a third party, to the procurer's financial advantage. This distinction is a matter within the exclusive prerogative of the legislative branch. If it had intended to classify the act of solicitation of a minor as a felony, the Florida Legislature easily could have done so.

We REVERSE the conviction in Count One pursuant to section 796.03 and AFFIRM the conviction in Count Two pursuant to section 893.13.

KAHN and LAWRENCE, J.J., concur.

REVIEW

1. The mere offer of money in exchange for sex is _____.
   a. procurement
   b. solicitation
   c. both a and b
   d. neither a nor b

THINKING CRITICALLY

1.   Locate a copy of the Street Terrorism Enforcement and Prevention Act. Is it constitutional? Why or why not? What purpose do the enhanced penalties serve? Do you think the Act will be effective? Why or why not?

2.   Read Florida Statutes, Chapter 876. Do you know of any cases prosecuted in your county under this chapter? Where do you think some of these laws originated? Do we still need them? Why should it be a crime to wear a mask or a hood? Who is being targeted? Give an example of a subversive organization.

3.   Should "begging" be a protected communication? Why or why not?

4.   How could the statute be rewritten so as to make it constitutional?

5.   Compare *Ledford* and *Papachristou.* How are the cases similar? Different?

6.   Should panhandling be a crime? Can you be required to obtain a permit to panhandle? Should you be? Should it be a crime to beg for money for a specific purpose and then spend the funds on something else? Do the laws assist the homeless? Why or why not? Who do these laws aim to protect?

7.   Sleeping in the park is a crime in most cities. What if a businessman happens to take a nap on a blanket mid-day in a downtown park? Do you think he will be arrested? Has he committed a crime?

8.   What is the purpose of the loitering and prowling statute? Give an example of behavior that would constitute criminal behavior under the statute.

9.   Should we legalize prostitution? Why or why not?

CHAPTER 12 ANSWER KEY

REVIEW QUESTIONS

Ledford v. State
1. b
2. d

R.M. v. State
1. c

Register v. State
1. b

CHAPTER 13

CRIMES AGAINST THE STATE

STREET TERRORISM ENFORCEMENT AND PREVENTION

In 1996, the Florida legislature passed the Criminal Street Gang Prevention Act of 1996. The legislature found the State to be facing a mounting crisis caused by criminal street gangs. Because members of street gangs threaten and terrorize peaceful citizens and commit crimes, they present a clear and present danger. The State has a compelling interest to prevent such activity.

This statute was found unconstitutional as discussed in Chapter 2. Please refer to *State v. O.C., 748 So.2d 945 (Fla. 1999)*. Mere association as a crime violates substantive due process.

CRIMINAL ANARCHY

Criminal anarchy is concerned with advocating or teaching the overthrowing of the government by force or violence. It also includes the assassinating of government officials. It may be done by word of mouth or in writing. If one is a member of an organization that embodies a Communist, Nazi, or Fascist ideology, it is a crime to belong to, or give aide to that organization. These groups advocate overthrowing our existing form of government by force, violence or assassination.

Whenever two or more persons assemble for the purpose of promoting, advocating, or teaching the doctrine of criminal anarchy, criminal Communism, criminal Naziism or criminal Fascism, the assembly is unlawful, and every person voluntarily participating therein by his or her presence, aid, or instigation shall be guilty of a felony of the second degree. Those who participate in criminal anarhcy are defined as:

(1) By word of mouth or writing advocates, advises, or teaches the duty, necessity, or propriety of overthrowing or overturning existing forms of constitutional government by force or violence; of disobeying or sabotaging or hindering the carrying out of the laws, orders, or decrees of duly constituted civil, naval, or military authorities; or by the assassination of officials of the Government of the United States or of the state, or by any unlawful means or under the guidance of, or in collaboration with, officials, agents, or representatives of a foreign state or an international revolutionary party or group; or

(2) Prints, publishes, edits, issues, or knowingly circulates, sells, distributes, or publicly displays any book, paper, document, or written or printed matter in any form, containing or advocating, advising, or teaching the doctrine that constitutional government should be overthrown by force, violence, or any unlawful means; or

(3) Openly, willfully and deliberately urges, advocates, or justifies by word of mouth or writing the assassination or unlawful killing or assaulting of any official of the Government of the United States or of this state because of his or her official character, or any other crime, with intent to teach, spread, or advocate the propriety of the doctrines of criminal anarchy, criminal Communism, criminal Naziism, or criminal Fascism; or

(4) Organizes or helps to organize or becomes a member of any society, group, or assembly of persons formed to teach or advocate such doctrines; or

(5) Becomes a member of, associated with or promotes the interest of any criminal anarchistic, Communistic, Naziistic or Fascistic organization, or helps to organize or becomes a member of or affiliated with any subsidiary organization or associated group of persons who advocates, teaches, or advises the principles of criminal anarchy, criminal Communism, criminal Naziism or criminal Fascism.

If one is an employee of the government, one is required to take an oath to uphold both the United States and Florida Constitution. You can be fired for refusing to do so. Any governing authority or person, who continues to employ an individual failing to an oath, shall be guilty of a misdemeanor of the second degree.

No person or persons over sixteen years of age, while wearing a mask, hood, or device where a portion of the face is hidden, concealed, or covered as to conceal their identity can be on a public way or on public property. Of course there are exceptions such as holiday and theatrical costumes, emergency gear, and masks for occupational safety. It is also unlawful to be on the property of another and demand entrance or admission into the premises, enclosure, or house of any other person while wearing a mask or hood. A person may wear a mask or hood on the private property of another if they have first obtained consent form the property owner or occupant.

It is also a crime to burn a cross on any public property or on someone's lawn or property. The burning can be real or simulated for it to be a crime. If one wants to burn a cross on someone's property they must first obtain the written permission of the owner or occupier of the premises to so do. Any person who violates this section commits a misdemeanor of the first degree.

CASE

State v. T.B.D., a child, 656 So.2d 479 (Fla. 1995).

Delinquency petition was filed charging juvenile with placing burning or flaming cross on property of another without obtaining written permission. The Circuit Court dismissed petition, and state sought review. The District Court of Appeal, 638 So.2d 165, affirmed. State appealed. The Supreme Court, Shaw, J., held that Florida's anticross burning statute does not violate First Amendment.

Reversed.

SHAW, Justice.

We have on appeal *State v. T.B.D.*, 638 So.2d 165 (Fla. 1st DCA 1994), wherein the district court declared Florida's anti-cross burning statute, *section 876.18, Florida Statutes (1993)*, unconstitutional. We have jurisdiction. *Art. V, § 3(b)(1), Fla. Const.*

We reverse.

I. FACTS

T.B.D., a minor, was charged with erecting a flaming cross on the property of Atef Abdul-Nour in Jacksonville on August 2, 1993, in violation of *section 876.18, Florida Statutes (1993)*. The trial court held the statute unconstitutional under the First Amendment and the district court affirmed. The State appealed.

T.B.D. claims that the statute on its face violates the First Amendment because it is a content-based law prohibiting expressive conduct. He postulates that the statute violates *R.A.V. v. City of St. Paul, 505 U.S. 377, 112 S.Ct. 2538, 120 L.Ed.2d 305 (1992)*, is overbroad, and is unnecessary in light of other Florida laws covering related conduct.

Chapter 876, Florida Statutes (1993), entitled "Criminal Anarchy, Treason, and Other Crimes Against Public Order," protects Florida citizens against anarchy, treason, and terrorism. *Section 876.18* prohibits the placing of a flaming cross on the property of another without written permission:

876.18: Placing burning or flaming cross on property of another. -- It shall be unlawful for any person or persons to place or cause to be placed on the property of another in the state a burning or flaming cross or any manner of exhibit in which a burning or flaming cross, real or simulated, is a whole or part without first obtaining written permission of the owner or occupier of the premises to so do. Any person who violates this section commits a misdemeanor of the first degree, punishable as provided in s. 775.082 or s. 775.083.

§ 876.18, Fla.Stat. (1993). Because this statute restricts expressive activity, the First Amendment is implicated.

II. THREATS AND FIGHTING WORDS

The First Amendment promotes the free flow of ideas and information in our society by prohibiting government from restricting speech or expressive conduct because of the message expressed. *See, e.g., **Texas v. Johnson**, 491 U.S. 397, 109 S.Ct. 2533, 105 L.Ed.2d 342 (1989).* Content-based restrictions are presumptively invalid. *See, e.g., **Police Dept. of Chicago v. Mosley**, 408 U.S. 92, 92 S.Ct. 2286, 33 L.Ed.2d 212 (1972).*

Limited exceptions to this rule are allowed where the speech or expressive conduct constitutes "no essential part of any exposition of ideas, and [is] of such slight social value as a step to truth that any benefit that may be derived from [it] is clearly outweighed by the social interest in order and morality." ***Chaplinsky v. New Hampshire**, 315 U.S. 568, 572, 62 S.Ct. 766, 769, 86 L.Ed. 1031 (1942).* Such speech "can, consistently with the First Amendment, be regulated *because of [its] constitutionally proscribable content.*" ***R.A.V.**, 505 U.S. at 383, 112 S.Ct. at 2543.* Examples of proscribable speech include defamation and obscenity. *See id.*

"Threats of violence" against individual citizens is one such category. ***Cf. Watts v. United States**, 394 U.S. 705, 89 S.Ct. 1399, 22 L.Ed.2d 664 (1969)* (threats of violence against the President are outside the First Amendment). Threats of violence can be regulated because government has a valid interest in "protecting individuals from the fear of violence, from the disruption that fear engenders, and from the possibility that the threatened violence will occur." ***R.A.V.**, 505 U.S. at 388, 112 S.Ct. at 2546.* "Fighting words" is another such proscribable category. ***Chaplinsky.*** These words "by their very utterance inflict injury or tend to incite an immediate breach of the peace." ***Id.**, 315 U.S. at 572, 62 S.Ct. at 769.*

The present statute proscribes conduct that falls within the category of "threats of violence." "An unauthorized cross-burning by intruders in one's own yard constitutes a direct affront to one's privacy and security and has been inextricably linked in this state's history to sudden and precipitous violence -- lynchings, shootings, whippings, mutilations, and home- burnings. The connection between a flaming cross in the yard and forthcoming violence is clear and direct. A more terrifying symbolic threat for many Floridians would be difficult to imagine.

The banned conduct also constitutes "fighting words." A flaming cross erected by intruders on one's property "inflicts [real] injury" on the victim in the form of fear and intimidation and also "tends to incite an immediate breach of the peace" where the victim or intruder may be inclined to take further action. *See generally Chaplinsky.* In the lexicon of the United States Supreme Court, it is the extraordinarily threatening *mode* of expression, not the idea expressed, that is intolerable. *See R.A.V., 505 U.S. at 391-93, 112 S.Ct. at 2548-49.* Again, it is difficult to imagine a scenario more rife with potential for reflexive violence and peace-breaching.

III. *R.A.V. v. CITY OF ST. PAUL*

The United States Supreme Court addressed the issue of proscribable speech in *R.A.V. v. City of St. Paul, 505 U.S. 377, 112 S.Ct. 2538, 120 L.Ed.2d 305 (1992),* where a juvenile was charged with burning a cross in a neighbor's yard in violation of a city ordinance providing:

> Whoever places on public or private property a symbol, object, appellation, characterization or graffiti, including, but not limited to, a burning cross or Nazi swastika, which one knows or has reasonable grounds to know arouses anger, alarm or resentment in others on the basis of race color, creed, religion or gender commits disorderly conduct and shall be guilty of a misdemeanor. St. Paul, Minn.Legis.Code § 292.02 (1990).

The United States Supreme Court held the ordinance invalid because it played favorites: Rather than proscribing certain types of "fighting words" across the board, the ordinance prohibited such words only in special cases, i.e., only where the words may offend due to "race, color, creed, religion or gender." "Such a restriction would open the door to government favoritism and protectionism of certain topics and view-points and implicit censorship of disfavored ones...." *State v. Stalder, 630 So.2d 1072, 1075 (Fla.1994).*

The present statute comports with *R.A.V.* because the Florida prohibition is "not limited to [any] favored topics," but rather cuts across the board evenly. No mention is made of any special topic such as race, color, creed, religion or gender. The targeted activity is proscribed because it is one of the most virulent forms of "threats of violence" and "fighting words" and has a tremendous propensity to produce terror and violence. The statute is an even-handed and neutral ban on a manifestly damaging form of expressive activity.

IV. OVERBREADTH

A statute is overbroad "if in its reach it prohibits constitutionally protected conduct." *Grayned v. City of Rockford, 408 U.S. 104, 114, 92 S.Ct. 2294, 2302, 33 L.Ed.2d 222 (1972).* The overbreadth doctrine comes with a strong caveat, particularly where conduct, as opposed to pure speech, is concerned: "Application of the overbreadth doctrine ... is, manifestly, strong medicine. It has been employed by the Court sparingly and only as a last resort." *Broadrick v. Oklahoma, 413 U.S. 601, 613, 93 S.Ct. 2908, 2916, 37 L.Ed.2d 830 (1973).*

[T]he plain import of our cases is, at the very least, that facial overbreadth adjudication is an exception to our traditional rules of practice and that its function, a limited one at the outset, attenuates as the otherwise unprotected behavior that it forbids the State to sanction moves from "pure speech" toward conduct and that conduct--even if expressive--falls within the scope of otherwise valid criminal laws that reflect legitimate state interests in maintaining comprehensive controls over harmful, constitutionally unprotected conduct.... To put the matter another way, particularly where conduct and not merely speech is involved, we believe that the overbreadth of a statute must not only be real, but substantial as well, judged in relation to the statute's plainly legitimate sweep. *Id., 413 U.S. at 615, 93 S.Ct. at 2917-18.*

We conclude that T.B.D.'s overbreadth challenge to the statute must fail because the full range of conduct embraced by the statute's plain language--the unauthorized placing of a flaming cross on the property of another--is eminently proscribable under the First Amendment for the reasons explained above. Although one might be able to imagine a hypothetical situation wherein the statute could be impermissibly applied, the threat of overbreadth is speculative at best and is insufficiently substantial to invalidate this statute on its face:

> The concept of "substantial overbreadth" is not readily reduced to an exact definition. It is clear, however, that the mere fact that one can conceive of some impermissible applications of a statute is not sufficient to render it susceptible to an overbreadth challenge.... In short, there must be a realistic danger that the statute itself will significantly compromise recognized First Amendment protections of parties not before the Court for it to be facially challenged on overbreadth grounds.

City Council of Los Angeles v. Taxpayers for Vincent, 466 U.S. 789, 800- 01, 104 S.Ct. 2118, 2126, 80 L.Ed.2d 772, 783-84 (1984).

V. CONCLUSION

Florida has a compelling interest in protecting the right of each of its citizens to live at peace in the sanctity of his or her home, free from violence and the threat of violence. Given this state's history and its vast cultural and ethnic diversity, we find the present statute reasonably necessary to promote the state's goals. While other Florida statutes may address unauthorized cross-burnings indirectly, e.g., via trespassing or disorderly conduct bans, those restrictions fail to confront the issue head on and to affirmatively discourage the conduct.

The statute is a legitimate legislative attempt to protect Floridians of every stripe from a particularly reprehensible form of tyranny. The statute plays no favorites--it protects equally the Baptist, Catholic, Jew, Muslim; the Communist, Bircher, Democrat, Nazi, Republican, Socialist; the African- American, Caucasian, Haitian, Hispanic, native

American, Vietnamese; the heterosexual, the male homosexual, the lesbian; the established politician, the neophyte, the activist; the author, the editor, the publisher; the artist, the curator; the teacher, the school administrator; the union organizer, the plant owner.

The statute ensures that those who exercise freedom of association or who join in robust debate on controversial issues need not fear this particular threat of violence. Although the First Amendment confers on each citizen a powerful right of self-expression, it gives no citizen a boon to launch terrorist raids against his or her neighbor. Few things can chill free expression and association to the bone like night-riders outside the door and a fiery cross in the yard.

Based on the foregoing, we find section *876.18, Florida Statutes (1993),* constitutional. We reverse the district court decision in ***T.B.D.***

It is so ordered.

GRIMES, C.J., and KOGAN, HARDING, WELLS and ANSTEAD, JJ., concur.

OVERTON, J., dissents with an opinion.

OVERTON, Justice, dissenting.

While I would personally prefer to uphold the constitutionality of this statute and to prohibit through this statute the type of conduct at issue, I find that the United States Supreme Court's decision in ***R.A.V. v. City of St. Paul***, *505 U.S. 377, 112 S.Ct. 2538, 120 L.Ed.2d 305 (1992),* eliminates any choice that I have in this matter. ***R.A.V.*** not only mandates a holding that this statute is unconstitutional but even goes so far as to explain how to draft a law that constitutionally prohibits this type of conduct. In my view, rather than attempting to uphold this statute, we should declare the statute to be unconstitutional and strongly suggest to the legislature how it can immediately draft a statute that is enforceable.

The issue in this case is not whether the State can prohibit the contemptible act of cross-burning. Clearly, it can. As noted by the district court, T.B.D. could have been charged with any number of offenses other than the one at issue, including assault, breach of the peace or disorderly conduct, criminal mischief, criminal nuisance, failure to control or report a dangerous fire, or trespass. The issue here is whether the State has prohibited cross-burning under this statute in a manner consistent with the First Amendment as interpreted by the United States Supreme Court.

In ***R.A.V.***, the United States Supreme Court reviewed a law that was almost identical to the statute at issue here. The statute at issue in ***R.A.V.*** read as follows:

Whoever places on public or private property a symbol, object, appellation, characterization or graffiti, including, but not limited to, a burning cross or Nazi swastika, which one knows or has reasonable grounds to know arouses anger, alarm or resentment in others on the basis of race, color, creed, religion or gender commits disorderly conduct and shall be guilty of a misdemeanor.

R.A.V., 505 U.S. at ----, 112 S.Ct. at 2541.

As in the instant case, in **R.A.V.** the defendant had burned a cross on the private property of another. In analyzing that ordinance, the United States Supreme Court found it to be unconstitutional because it discriminated on the basis of content in that it prohibited otherwise permitted speech solely on the basis of the subject the speech addressed. Even though the statute in **R.A.V.** reached only those symbols or displays that aroused "anger, alarm or resentment in others," which were otherwise characterized as "fighting words," the Court found that the prohibition of such "fighting words" could not be limited in connection with other "bias-motivated hatred" such as cross-burning. Similarly, the statute at issue in our case prohibits the "bias-motivated hatred" of burning a cross. Contrary to the majority's conclusion, it is not just the subjects to which protection is afforded that must be neutral, it also is the expressive activity itself that must be prohibited in a neutral fashion. Under the principles established by the **R.A.V.** decision, if the legislature were to enact a statute that proscribed all burnings and fires that are set with the intent to threaten or intimidate the owner or occupant of the property, rather than proscribing the burning of a cross, the statute would be constitutional.

I strongly suggest that the legislature examine this matter and enact a statute in accordance with the principles directed by **R.A.V.** As the United States Supreme Court expressed in **R.A.V.**, although the act of "burning a cross in someone's front yard is reprehensible," the State has "sufficient means at its disposal to prevent such behavior without adding the First Amendment to the fire." *505 U.S. at ----, 112 S.Ct. at 2550.*

REVIEW

1. Erecting a flaming cross on someone else's front yard is _____.
   a. constitutional expressive conduct
   b. a threat of violence that is unlawful
   c. inflicts injury in the form of fear and intimidation
   d. both b and c

SUBVERSIVE ACTIVITIES

Belonging to a subversive organization is unlawful as well. A subversive activity is one that constitutes a clear and present danger to the security of the United States or Florida. A "subversive person" means any person who aids, attempts are participates in an act intended to overthrow, or destroy the constitutional form of the Government of the United States, or Florida. Any person who is convicted of committing a subversive act will be charged with a second degree felony. In addition, a person found guilty of a subversive act, is barred from holding any elective or appopintive office, and voting in any election held in Florida.

TREASON

Treason is a crime in the State of Florida. It consists of levying war against the State, adhering to enemies of the State, or giving the enemy aid and comfort. Misprision of treason is the failure to report an act of treason one has knowledge of. Acts of treason are to be made known to the governor, a Supreme Court Justice or a Circuit Court Judge.

THINKING CRITICALLY

1.   Should it be a crime to be a Nazi? Why or why not?

2.   Why is it a crime to wear a hood or mask? Should the Ku Klux Klan be allowed to have demonstrations? Why or why not?

3.   Should government employees be required to take an oath? Why or why not?

4.	Why is cross burning illegal? Are there any circumstances under which it is lawful? Should there be?

5.	Give an example of an act of treason.

CHAPTER 13 ANSWER KEY

REVIEW QUESTION

State v. T.B.D., a child,
1. d

APPENDIX A

FLORIDA CONSTITUTION - 1968 REVISION
ARTICLE I - DECLARATION OF RIGHTS

Section

§ 1.   Political power.

All political power is inherent in the people. The enunciation herein of certain rights shall not be construed to deny or impair others retained by the people.

§ 2.   Basic rights.

All natural persons, female and male alike, are equal before the law and have inalienable rights, among which are the right to enjoy and defend life and liberty, to pursue happiness, to be rewarded for industry, and to acquire, possess and protect property; except that the ownership, inheritance, disposition and possession of real property by aliens ineligible for citizenship may be regulated or prohibited by law. No person shall be deprived of any right because of race, religion, national origin, or physical disability. *Am. S.J.R. 917, 1974; adopted 1974; Am. proposed by Constitution Revision*

Commission, Revision No. 9, 1998, filed with the Secretary of State May 5, 1998; adopted 1998.

§ 3.   Religious Freedom

There shall be no law respecting the establishment of religion or prohibiting or penalizing the free exercise thereof. Religious freedom shall not justify practices inconsistent with public morals, peace or safety. No revenue of the state or any political subdivision or agency thereof shall ever be taken from the public treasury directly or indirectly in aid of any church, sect, or religious denomination or in aid of any sectarian institution.

§ 4.   Freedom of speech and press

Every person may speak, write and publish sentiments on all subjects but shall be responsible for the abuse of that right. No law shall be passed to restrain or abridge the liberty of speech or of the press. In all criminal prosecutions and civil actions for defamation the truth may be given in evidence. If the matter charged as defamatory is true and was published with good motives, the party shall be acquitted or exonerated. *Am. proposed by Constitution Revision Commission, Revision No. 13, 1998, filed with the Secretary of State May 5, 1998; adopted 1998.*

§ 5.   Right to assemble

The people shall have the right peaceably to assemble, to instruct their representatives, and to petition for redress of grievances.

§ 6.   Right to work.

The right of persons to work shall not be denied or abridged on account of membership or non-membership in any labor union or labor organization. The right of employees, by and through a labor organization, to bargain collectively shall not be denied or abridged. Public employees shall not have the right to strike.

§ 7.   Military power

The military power shall be subordinate to the civil.

§ 8.   Right to bear arms

(a) The right of the people to keep and bear arms in defense of themselves and of the lawful authority of the state shall not be infringed, except that the manner of bearing arms may be regulated by law.

(b) There shall be a mandatory period of three days, excluding weekends and legal holidays, between the purchase and delivery at retail of any handgun. For the purposes of this section, "purchase" means the transfer of money or other valuable consideration to the retailer, and "handgun" means a firearm capable of being carried and used by one hand, such as a pistol or revolver. Holders of a concealed weapon permit as prescribed in Florida law shall not be subject to the provisions of this paragraph.

(c) The legislature shall enact legislation implementing subsection (b) of this section, effective no later than December 31, 1991, which shall provide that anyone violating the provisions of subsection (b) shall be guilty of a felony.

(d) This restriction shall not apply to a trade in of another handgun. *Amended, general election, Nov. 6, 1990.*

§ 9.   Due process

No person shall be deprived of life, liberty or property without due process of law, or be twice put in jeopardy for the same offense, or be compelled in any criminal matter to be a witness against oneself. *Am. proposed by Constitution Revision Commission, Revision No. 13, 1998, filed with the Secretary of State May 5, 1998; adopted 1998.*

§ 10.   Prohibited Laws

No bill of attainder, ex post facto law or law impairing the obligation of contracts shall be passed.

§ 11.   Imprisonment for debt

No person shall be imprisoned for debt, except in cases of fraud.

§ 12.   Searches and seizures

The right of the people to be secure in their persons, houses, papers and effects against unreasonable searches and seizures, and against the unreasonable interception of private communications by any means, shall not be violated. No warrant shall be issued except upon probable cause, supported by affidavit, particularly describing the place or places to be searched, the person or persons, thing or things to be seized, the communication to be intercepted, and the nature of evidence to be obtained. This right shall be construed in conformity with the 4th Amendment to the United States Constitution, as interpreted by the United States Supreme Court. Articles or information obtained in violation of this right shall not be admissible in evidence if such articles or information would be inadmissible under decisions of the United States Supreme Court construing the 4th Amendment to the United States Constitution. *Amended, general election, Nov. 2, 1982.*

§ 13.   Habeas corpus

The writ of habeas corpus shall be grantable of right, freely and without cost. It shall be returnable without delay, and shall never be suspended unless, in case of rebellion or invasion, suspension is essential to the public safety.

§ 14.   Pretrial release and detention
Unless charged with a capital offense or an offense punishable by life imprisonment and the proof of guilt is evident or the presumption is great, every person charged with a crime or violation of municipal or county ordinance shall be entitled to pretrial release on reasonable conditions. If no conditions of release can reasonably protect the community from risk of physical harm to persons, assure the presence of the accused at trial, or assure the integrity of the judicial process, the accused may be detained. *Amended, general election, Nov. 2, 1982.*

§ 15.   Prosecution for crime; offenses committed by children

(a) No person shall be tried for capital crime without presentment or indictment by a grand jury, or for other felony without such presentment or indictment or an information under oath filed by the prosecuting officer of the court, except persons on active duty in the militia when tried by courts martial.

(b) When authorized by law, a child as therein defined may be charged with a violation of law as an act of delinquency instead of crime and tried without a jury or other requirements applicable to criminal cases. Any child so charged shall, upon demand made as provided by law before a trial in a juvenile proceeding, be tried in an appropriate court as an adult. A child found delinquent shall be disciplined as provided by law.

§ 16.   Rights of accused and of victims

(a) In all criminal prosecutions the accused shall, upon demand, be informed of the nature and cause of the accusation, and shall be furnished a copy of the charges, and shall have the right to have compulsory process for witnesses, to confront at trial adverse witnesses, to be heard in person, by counsel or both, and to have a speedy and public trial by impartial jury in the county where the crime was committed. If the county is not known, the indictment or information may charge venue in two or more counties conjunctively and proof that the crime was committed in that area shall be sufficient; but before pleading the accused may elect in which of those counties the trial will take place. Venue for prosecution of crimes committed beyond the boundaries of the state shall be fixed by law.
(b) Victims of crime or their lawful representatives, including the next of kin of homicide victims, are entitled to the right to be informed, to be present, and to be heard when

relevant, at all crucial stages of criminal proceedings, to the extent that these rights do not interfere with the constitutional rights of the accused. *Am. S.J.R. 135, 1987; adopted 1988; Am. proposed by Constitution Revision Commission, Revision No. 13, 1998, filed with the Secretary of State May 5, 1998; adopted 1998.*

§ 17. Excessive punishments

Excessive fines, cruel and unusual punishment, attainder, forfeiture of estate, indefinite imprisonment, and unreasonable detention of witnesses are forbidden. The death penalty is an authorized punishment for capital crimes designated by the Legislature. The prohibition against cruel or unusual punishment, and the prohibition against cruel and unusual punishment, shall be construed in conformity with decisions of the United States Supreme Court which interpret the prohibition against cruel and unusual punishment provided in the Eighth Amendment to the United States Constitution. Any method of execution shall be allowed, unless prohibited by the United States Constitution. Methods of execution may be designated by the Legislature, and a change in any method of execution may be applied retroactively. A sentence of death shall not be reduced on the basis that a method of execution is invalid. In any case in which an execution method is declared invalid, the death sentence shall remain in force until the sentence can be lawfully executed by any valid method. This section shall apply retroactively. *Am. H.J.R. 3505, 1998; adopted 1998.*

§ 18. Administrative penalties

No administrative agency, except the Department of Military Affairs in an appropriately convened court-martial action as provided by law, shall impose a sentence of imprisonment, nor shall it impose any other penalty except as provided by law. *Am. proposed by Constitution Revision Commission, Revision No. 13, 1998, filed with the Secretary of State May 5, 1998; adopted 1998.*

§ 19. Costs

No person charged with crime shall be compelled to pay costs before a judgment of conviction has become final.

§ 20. Treason

Treason against the state shall consist only in levying war against it, adhering to its enemies, or giving them aid and comfort, and no person shall be convicted of treason except on the testimony of two witnesses to the same overt act or on confession in open court.

§ 21. Access to courts

The courts shall be open to every person for redress of any injury, and justice shall be administered without sale, denial, or delay.

§ 22. Trial by jury

The right of trial by jury shall be secure to all and remain inviolate. The qualifications and the number of jurors, not fewer than six, shall be fixed by law.

§ 23. Right of privacy

Every natural person has the right to be let alone and free from governmental intrusion into the person's private life except as otherwise provided herein. This section shall not be construed to limit the public's right of access to public records and meetings as provided by law. *Added, C.S. for H.J.R. 387, 1980; adopted 1980; Am. proposed by Constitution Revision Commission, Revision No. 13, 1998, filed with the Secretary of State May 5, 1998; adopted 1998.*

§ 24. Access to public records and meetings

(a) Every person has the right to inspect or copy any public record made or received in connection with the official business of any public body, officer, or employee of the state, or persons acting on their behalf, except with respect to records exempted pursuant to this section or specifically made confidential by this Constitution. This section specifically includes the legislative, executive, and judicial branches of government and each agency or department created thereunder; counties, municipalities, and districts; and each constitutional officer, board, and commission, or entity created pursuant to law or this Constitution.

(b) All meetings of any collegial public body of the executive branch of state government or of any collegial public body of a county, municipality, school district, or special district, at which official acts are to be taken or at which public business of such body is to be transacted or discussed, shall be open and noticed to the public and meetings of the legislature shall be open and noticed as provided in Article III, Section 4(e), except with respect to meetings exempted pursuant to this section or specifically closed by this Constitution.

(c) This section shall be self-executing. The legislature, however, may provide by general law for the exemption of records from the requirements of subsection (a) and the exemption of meetings from the requirements of subsection (b), provided that such law shall state with specificity the public necessity justifying the exemption and shall be no broader than necessary to accomplish the stated purpose of the law. The legislature shall enact laws governing the enforcement of this section, including the maintenance, control, destruction, disposal, and disposition of records made public by this section, except that each house of the legislature may adopt rules governing the enforcement of this section in relation to records of the legislative branch. Laws enacted pursuant to this subsection shall contain only exemptions from the requirements of subsections (a) or (b) and provisions governing the enforcement of this section, and shall relate to one subject.

(d) All laws that are in effect on July 1, 1993 that limit public access to records or meetings shall remain in force, and such laws apply to records of the legislative and judicial branches, until they are repealed. Rules of court that are in effect on the date of adoption of this section that limit access to records shall remain in effect until they are repealed. *Added, general election, Nov. 3, 1992.*

Historical Notes
For effective date of Const.Art.1, § 24, see Const.Art. 12, §20.

§ 25.   Taxpayers' Bill of Rights.

By general law the legislature shall prescribe and adopt a Taxpayers' Bill of Rights that, in clear and concise language, sets forth taxpayers' rights and responsibilities and government's responsibilities to deal fairly with taxpayers under the laws of this state. This section shall be effective July 1, 1993. *Added, general election, Nov. 3, 1992.*

Note: This section, originally designated section 24 by Revision No. 2 of the Taxation and Budget Reform Commission, 1992, was redesignated section 25 by the editors in order to avoid confusion with section 24 as contained in H.J.R.'s 1727, 863, 2035, 1992.